Crime, Law and Popular Culture in Europe, 1500–1900

Crime, Law and Popular Culture in Europe, 1500–1900

Edited by
Richard Mc Mahon

Routledge
Taylor & Francis Group

LONDON AND NEW YORK

First published by Willan Publishing 2008
This edition published by Routledge 2013
2 Park Square, Milton Park, Abingdon, Oxon OX14 4RN
711 Third Avenue, New York, NY 10017 (8th Floor)

Routledge is an imprint of the Taylor & Francis Group, an informa business

First published 2008

ISBN   978-1-84392-118-9 paperback
ISBN   978-1-84392-119-6 hardback

British Library Cataloguing-in-Publication Data

A catalogue record for this book is available from the British Library

Project managed by Deer Park Productions, Tavistock, Devon
Typeset by GCS, Leighton Buzzard, Bedfordshire

Contents

Acknowledgements   *vii*
Notes on the contributors   *ix*

Introduction   1
Richard Mc Mahon

1   Popular violence and its prosecution in
    seventeenth- and eighteenth-century France   32
    Julius R. Ruff

2   The containment of violence in Central European
    cities, 1500–1800   52
    Joachim Eibach

3   Royal justice, popular culture and violence:
    homicide in sixteenth- and seventeenth-century Castile   74
    Rudy Chaulet

4   Prosecution and public participation – the case of
    early modern Sweden   96
    Maria Kaspersson

5   Towards a legal anthropology of the early modern
    Isle of Man   118
    James Sharpe

6   'For fear of the vengeance': the prosecution of
    homicide in pre-Famine and Famine Ireland   138
    Richard Mc Mahon

7   Violent crime and the public weal in England, 1700–1900   190
    Greg T. Smith

8   Atonement and domestic homicide in late Victorian
    Scotland   219
    Carolyn A. Conley

9   'A second Ireland'? Crime and popular culture in
    nineteenth-century Wales   239
    Richard W. Ireland

Index   262

Acknowledgements

This collection of essays has its origins in a conference entitled 'Crime, law and popular culture in Europe since 1500' which was hosted by the Moore Institute for Research in the Humanities and Social Studies at the National University of Ireland, Galway. I would like to take the opportunity to thank the Director of the Institute, Professor Nicholas Canny, the project leader, Dr William O'Reilly, and the Institute's manager, Martha Shaughnessy, for their help in organising the conference. I would also like to acknowledge the funding provided for the conference by the Higher Education Authority/An tÚdarás um Ard-Oideachas and the Department of Education and Science. Much of the final editorial work for this collection was conducted while I was employed as an Associate Lecturer with the Open University in Ireland and I am grateful for the support provided by that institution.

Thanks are also due to the individual contributors to this volume. All have been a pleasure to deal with and have shown considerable grace in dealing with my many queries. I am particularly grateful to Professor James Sharpe for his comments on the introduction. I would also like to thank Professor Xavier Rousseaux, Professor Robert Shoemaker, Professor W.N. Osborough, Mr Tom O'Malley and Professor Gearóid Ó Tuathaigh for their participation in the conference as either speakers or as chairs of the various sessions. I would also like to thank Brian Willan and all at Willan Publishing for their support and formidable patience. Thanks must also go to Dr John Cronin, Professor Clive Emsley (who also participated in the original conference) and Dr Chris A. Williams who kindly agreed to read over the introduction to this volume at very short notice and for whose comments and suggestions I am extremely grateful (I, of course, am responsible for all errors). Thanks are also due to Robert Fahy (Galway Media) for his assistance with the cover image. Thanks also to Cathal Coughlan and Sean O'Hagan. I would also like to take the opportunity to thank my parents for their support and encouragement during the preparation of this collection. Finally, special thanks must go to Dr Lesa Ní Mhunghaile whose encouragement and support went, as usual, far beyond what anyone could reasonably expect and for this, and for many other things, I thank her.

Richard Mc Mahon
Dundee

Notes on contributors

Rudy Chaulet is an Assistant Professor in the Université de Franche-Comté (Besançon, France). His primary research interests are crime and other social history questions in early modern Spain. He is the author of *Crimes, Rixes et bruits d'épée. Homicides pardonnés en Castille aux XVIe et XVIIe siècles* (forthcoming, 2008).

Carolyn A. Conley is a Professor of British and Irish History at the University of Alabama at Birmingham. Her most recent book is *Certain Other Countries: Homicide, Gender and National Identity in Late Nineteenth Century England, Ireland, Scotland and Wales* (Ohio State University Press, 2007). She is currently working on a history of female killers in London from the seventeenth to the twentieth century and on a survey of British encounters with non-European peoples both inside and outside the Empire.

Joachim Eibach is based at the Universität Bern in Switzerland. His major fields of research are the history of crime and criminal justice in early modern Europe, the history of the family, the history of intercultural communication and the history of administration as social practice. His latest publication (edited with Raingard Esser) is: 'Urban Governance and Petty Conflict in Early Modern Europe', *Urban History* (Special Issue), 34, 1 (2007).

Richard W. Ireland is a Senior Lecturer in the Department of Law and Criminology at Aberystwyth University where he teaches and researches in legal history. His latest book *'A Want of Order and Good Discipline': Rules, Discretion and the Victorian Prison* was published in 2007.

Maria Kaspersson is a Senior Lecturer in Criminology at the University of Greenwich. Her research interests are the history of violence, in particular domestic homicide and honour-related violence as well as comparative perspectives on crime. She has published work in English on the decline in homicide from the sixteenth century onwards as well as on homicide and infanticide in interwar Stockholm.

Richard Mc Mahon is a researcher on the AHRC-funded project 'From Peaceable Kingdom to Wild West: Violence and Crime on the Early American Frontier' and is based in the School of Humanities (History) at the University of Dundee in Scotland. He was the recipient of the first postgraduate studentship from the Irish Legal History Society under the auspices of which he completed a PhD on 'Homicide, the Courts and Popular Culture in pre-Famine and Famine Ireland' in the School of Law at University College Dublin in 2006. His current research interests lie in the history of violence and the legal and criminal justice history of Ireland and North America.

Julius R. Ruff is Professor of History at Marquette University in Milwaukee, Wisconsin. A student of the history of early modern France and a past President of the Society for French Historical Studies, he is the author of *Crime, Justice and Public Order in Old Regime France: The Sénéchaussées of Libourne and Bazas, 1696–1789* and *Violence in Early Modern Europe, 1500–1800*.

James Sharpe is a Professor in the History Department at the University of York. He has published extensively on crime in early modern England and, more recently, on the history of witchcraft. He is also the author of *Early Modern England: A Social History 1550–1760* (2nd edn, Edward Arnold, 1997). His main research interest is currently the history of violence in England since the late Middle Ages, although he also maintains an interest in the legal system of the early modern Isle of Man.

Greg T. Smith is Assistant Professor of History at the University of Manitoba. He is the co-editor of *Criminal Justice in the Old World and the New: Essays in Honour of J.M. Beattie* (Toronto, 1998) and *City Limits: Interdisciplinary Essays on the Historical European City* (forthcoming) and has published on domestic violence, child abuse as well as the hangman in Victorian England. His principal research interests lie in the social and cultural history of violence in eighteenth-century London, the administration of justice, capital and non-capital punishment, and the regulation of the poor.

Introduction

Richard Mc Mahon

This collection of essays explores the relationship between crime, law and popular culture in different areas of Europe between 1500 and 1900. The essays illuminate how experiences of, and attitudes to, crime and the law corresponded or differed in varying locations and contexts in early modern and modern Europe and they aid in the reconstruction and interpretation of the legal cultures of different jurisdictions through the particular perspective offered by the operation of the courts and the criminal law. This introduction provides an outline of the relevant historiography and explores some of the key themes which inform the essays that follow.

Context

Over the last thirty or so years, criminal justice history has been researched in a variety of different national and regional contexts.[1] This volume alone, although by no means comprehensive, contains essays on early modern France, early modern Germany and Switzerland, sixteenth- and seventeenth-century Castile, seventeenth- and eighteenth-century Sweden, the early modern Isle of Man and eighteenth- and nineteenth-century Britain and Ireland. Thirty years ago little research had been undertaken in crime and criminal justice history in many of these areas.

The study of criminal justice history is, of course, more firmly established in some regions rather than in others. The English historiography of crime and criminal justice has been, and continues to be, central to developments in criminal justice history since the emergence of crime history as a significant subdiscipline of social history in the 1970s. At that time, the ground-breaking work of, among others, E.P. Thompson and Douglas Hay on eighteenth-century England provided a framework through which criminal activity could be reconstructed and reinterpreted.[2] The study of early modern England has, indeed, produced perhaps the most thorough, impressive and influential body of work in the field of criminal justice history in Europe. Historians such J.M. Beattie, J.S. Cockburn, Douglas Hay, Cynthia Herrup, Peter King, Norma Landau, John Langbein, Peter Linebaugh, James Sharpe and Robert Shoemaker (among a host of others) have offered compelling (and at times conflicting) analyses of the role of crime and/or the law in the social and cultural life of seventeenth- and eighteenth-century England.[3]

Historians of nineteenth-century England have also contributed to the development of the field. The pioneering works of both David Philips and V.A.C. Gatrell, among others, provide considerable insight both into the nature of criminal activity and reactions to it in the Victorian era.[4] The last thirty years have also witnessed, with varying degrees of success, a notable expansion in the field of criminal justice history research in England to cover a diverse range of topics such as interpersonal violence,[5] juvenile delinquency,[6] prostitution,[7] domestic violence,[8] sexual abuse[9] and infanticide[10] as well as more technical areas such as the development of criminal statistics.[11] There is also a considerable body of work dealing with the development and role of policing (particularly for the nineteenth century) as well as a number of studies of different aspects of the criminal justice process.[12]

The work of English historians has overshadowed and, to some degree, serves to expose the relative neglect of crime and criminal justice history in its neighbouring countries. Yet, here too, some impressive work has been carried out over the last number of decades. Wales has produced some important studies. Sharon Howard has carried out valuable work on the prosecution of crime in early modern Wales.[13] The work of David J.V. Jones and Richard Ireland on the nineteenth century has also done much to illuminate our understanding of both crime and the criminal justice process in that country. Jones has provided a good overview of patterns of criminal activity and reactions to it, while Richard Ireland has focused on more discrete topics such as the prosecution of infanticide, the part played by the jury in criminal trials and, more recently, the place of the prison in nineteenth-century Wales.[14]

There have also been a number of studies which offer a general insight into crime and criminal justice in early modern and modern Scotland.[15] More specifically, a number of studies have investigated the relationship between gender and crime in early modern and modern Scottish history[16] with a particular emphasis on the incidence and prosecution of violent crime. Anne-Marie Kilday, for example, has looked at violent crimes involving women in Enlightenment Scotland.[17] Carolyn A. Conley, a flavour of whose work can be found in this volume, has also investigated reactions to homicide in that country in the late nineteenth century.[18]

In an Irish context, Neal Garnham's study of the eighteenth century remains the most comprehensive and sustained study of both patterns of criminality in the country and the workings of the Irish criminal justice system.[19] James Kelly has also explored different aspects of criminal activity and the administration of criminal justice in the eighteenth century.[20] Desmond McCabe has offered a general account of the operation of the criminal justice system in the early nineteenth century.[21] More recently, Terence Dooley has looked at the operation of the system in the context of a particular set of trials, namely those emerging from the infamous Wildgoose Lodge murders in Co. Louth in the 1810s.[22] The nature and role of violence within particular contexts has also been explored in some detail for pre-Famine and Famine Ireland.[23] The work of Mark Finnane and Carolyn A. Conley on the latter half of the nineteenth century has also contributed to our understanding of crime in that period.[24] There are also a number of useful studies focusing on the operation of particular aspects of the criminal justice apparatus in the nineteenth century.[25] Criminologists too have begun to display a keen interest in the criminal justice history of Ireland.[26]

With regard to Continental Europe, perhaps the most firmly established and long-standing tradition of research has been on early modern and modern France.[27] There is a range of work covering different aspects of the criminal justice system. For instance, there are studies on the role of the police and policing, and in particular the part played by the Maréchaussée and, later, the Gendarmerie in rural France.[28] The operation of the courts has also come in for some attention from historians. Nicole Castan, for instance, has charted the pressures on, and difficulties encountered by, the French courts in the eighteenth century.[29] More recently, Steven Reinhardt has examined the competing and, at times, complementary claims of popular, royal and seigneurial justice in the Sarladais in the late eighteenth century.[30] While Julius Ruff has looked at the records of the *Sénéchaussées* of Libourne and Bazas and, in doing so, has at least called into question some of the negative stereotypes surrounding the French monarchy's criminal justice system in the pre-Revolutionary period.[31] There has, of course, also been important work carried out on the role and changing nature of punishment, with the influence of Michel Foucault's *Discipline and Punish* still being felt both within and far beyond the field of criminal justice history.[32] Some studies dedicated to the examination of particular forms of criminal activity have also been undertaken. There is, for example, a growing body of work on violence in early modern France. A number of studies have dealt with issues such as domestic violence, the feud and the duel and, more generally, with quotidian public violence in rural France in the sixteenth, seventeenth and eighteenth centuries.[33] The role of violence in areas under French control has also been examined. Stephen Wilson, for instance, has explored the nature and impact of the feud in nineteenth-century Corsica.[34]

While less developed than the French historiography, the German-speaking countries of Central Europe have also witnessed a marked increase in crime and criminal justice history research over recent decades. Work on crime in nineteenth-century Germany has, for instance, contributed much to our understanding of the relationships between crime and broader socio-cultural changes, in particular the impact of industrialisation and urbanisation.[35] Historians have also delved over the last fifteen to twenty years, as Joachim Eibach makes clear in his contribution to this volume, into the court records of a variety of areas in Central Europe in an effort to understand both the nature of and reactions to criminal activity in the early modern period.[36] Studies of interpersonal violence, and reactions to it, have, moreover, played a major role in this process. The work of Gerd Schwerhoff has, in particular, highlighted the importance of violence as an agent of social control and, in turn, the significant role of honour in violent behaviour. Indeed, Schwerhoff's work has done much to highlight the complex relationship between violence and the law and how that relationship may have developed in Germany in the early modern period.[37]

Spain has perhaps not been as well served in the field of criminal justice history as some other Western European countries. Yet, here too considerable work has been undertaken over the last number of decades. Historians such as Tomás A. Mantecón, Rudy Chaulet and Fabio López-Lázaro, among others, have explored issues such the interplay between the courts and local communities in the administration of criminal justice, the nature of the criminal trial as well as the use of capital punishment and the exercise of the prerogative of mercy in the early modern period.[38]

Arguably one of the most impressive developments in crime and criminal justice history, certainly for the early modern period, is the work that has emerged from Sweden and the other Nordic countries. The studies of crime and criminal justice by Eva Österberg and others in Sweden as well as the analysis of long-term trends in violent crime in Finland offered by Heikki Ylikangas have added considerably to our understanding of crime and criminal justice in those countries as well as providing useful theoretical approaches through which such behaviour can be cogently analysed.[39] The production of the volume *People Meet the Law* also represents an excellent model which could and, perhaps, should be adopted in examinations of other jurisdictions.[40]

It should also be borne in mind that the areas included in this volume do not provide a complete list of those jurisdictions within Europe in which criminal justice history has or is being undertaken. Although not represented in this volume, the Low Countries have been well-served and have been at the forefront of much of the key developments in the field of criminal justice history. The work, for instance, of Pieter Spierenburg on crime and criminal justice in the Netherlands in the early modern period has done much to provoke debate concerning long-term trends in homicide as well as issues surrounding the changing nature of punishment in early modern Europe.[41] There has also been some important work undertaken on criminal justice history in early modern and modern Italy. Of particular note is John Davis's study of crime and the law in nineteenth-century Italy.[42] Countries in Eastern Europe have also seen some significant developments in the field. Stephen Frank, for instance, has drawn on techniques from subaltern studies to provide an account of crime and criminal justice in late imperial Russia.[43] There has also obviously been important and vital work carried out in the field of criminal justice history beyond the boundaries of Europe, particularly in North and, more recently, South America.[44]

The last three decades or so have also seen the establishment of specialist criminal justice history journals and the proliferation of conferences as well as a number of edited volumes dealing with areas relating to the broad field of criminal justice history. A range of studies have explored, among other themes, the relationship between crime and gender,[45] crime and youth,[46] crime and urbanisation,[47] crime and the media,[48] crime and empire[49] as well as one which has specifically explored the potential for and possibilities of comparative crime history.[50] There are, moreover, a number of studies dedicated to specific areas of the criminal justice system, for instance, on policing and on penal policy and practice in Europe.[51] Some studies, though by no means all, have also placed their findings in the context of wider theoretical explanations for social and cultural change – with the works of Michel Foucault and Norbert Elias proving particularly influential.[52]

Of course, while acknowledging the considerable amount of work carried out in the field, we must also concede, as others have done, that much of the history of crime and criminal justice remains unwritten.[53] This volume attempts to fill at least a few of the existing gaps in the literature. This will be done, not by seeking to encompass all the diverse strands alluded to above, but rather by focusing on a particular theme within the broad field of criminal justice history which deserves greater attention, namely the interaction of and relationship between ordinary people and the official legal systems of Europe between 1500 and 1900 – a period in which a number of key changes were initiated in the administration of criminal justice.

The relationship between the mass of the people, the courts and the law in early modern and modern Europe has, to a considerable degree, been overshadowed within the historiography by other, and arguably somewhat narrower, questions. Some important work has, however, been undertaken. There have been a number of national or, more commonly, regional studies of the interplay between the courts and the mass of the people. This is particularly so for territories such as France, England, Germany and the Nordic countries but, as will be seen in this volume, work has also begun in areas hitherto relatively under-explored by criminal justice historians such as Ireland, Scotland, Wales and the Isle of Man. Attempts have also been made to explore the nature of this relationship in a broad pan-European framework. Perhaps, the key work here is the ground-breaking article, 'The State, the Community and the Criminal Law in Early Modern Europe', written nearly thirty years ago by Bruce Lenman and Geoffrey Parker. In this article, the authors posited a fundamental shift or, indeed, a revolution in the relationship between the state, the law and local communities over the course of the early modern period whereby a relatively flexible form of community law, in which the courts played a peripheral role, was gradually displaced by a more rigid and punitive form of state law, in which the courts became the dominant player. Moreover, in their view, over the course of the early modern period, ordinary people were transformed, by a combination of church, state and commercial interests, from reluctant participants in the criminal justice process to willing supporters of the operation of the criminal law.[54] More recent studies have sought to look at the role of the law and courts less as serving the immediate needs of the state to impose control but rather as acting in response to, as Martin Dinges puts it, a 'popular demand for social control'. Such approaches have, moreover, sought to place more emphasis on the use made by 'ordinary people' of the criminal courts and what that might reveal about broader relations between the state and the mass of the people.[55] It is with this issue, of the interplay of ordinary people and the state in early modern and modern Europe as seen through the operation of the courts, that this volume is primarily concerned.

How was crime understood and dealt with by ordinary people, to what degree did they resort to the official law and criminal justice system as a means of dealing with different forms of criminal activity and how, in turn, did the courts and, more generally, the authorities respond to and interpret the cases which were brought before them? The issues addressed include the participation of ordinary people as prosecutors, witnesses and jurors in the courts, the dynamics of court sittings, the sentencing practices adopted by the courts, the exercise of the prerogative of mercy and, on a broader scale, how attitudes and ways of understanding crime and the law may have changed or evolved over time in different jurisdictions.

There is also a particular, although not exclusive, emphasis in this volume on the incidence and prosecution of violent crime. Violent crime is of particular significance to the concerns of this volume as violent acts constituted not simply a breach of the law but also, in some respects, an alternative to it. Violence, in this sense, provided another means of resolving disputes and of self-assertion on the part of those who resorted to it. Thus, a number of articles within this volume examine the nature of violent acts and the wider cultural significance which may have been attached to them as well as examining their prosecution through the courts.

Although the historiography of violence has undergone a period of sustained and even remarkable growth over the last twenty-five years or so,[56] the role of the courts in dealing with violent offences has not been a central concern. When dealt with, the courts are often portrayed as key engines of social change – reflecting a growing hostility on the part of the state towards interpersonal violence and as a key component in the attempts by the emerging nation states of Europe to acquire and sustain a monopoly on the use of violence.[57] Yet, there has been relatively limited exploration of how this played out in practice and, in particular, of the part played (if any) by the mass of the people in such changes.

Was there a growing opposition between the use of interpersonal or group violence and the use of the law and the courts as a means of resolving conflict and, if so, when did they become mutually exclusive rather than complementary strategies of social control in early modern and modern Europe? Also, to what extent did the participation of ordinary people aid or thwart the operation of the courts in this process and what might this reveal about wider attitudes within popular culture? Of course such broad questions cannot be comprehensively addressed within the confines of this volume but by exploring the nature of violent acts and how they were viewed and dealt with by the courts in different jurisdictions it is hoped that we can gain a particularly pertinent insight into the broader relationship between crime, the law and popular culture in early modern and modern Europe.

The courts are, admittedly, often seen as a somewhat dubious source for the study of the actions and attitudes of ordinary people or, in a wider sense, popular *mentalité* and culture.[58] It might be argued, for instance, that the actions of, and statements made by, people in court or when addressing those in authority did not reflect their real positions and views as they were acting under pressure and were in unusual circumstances. Such evidence might then be of little value in attempting to understand popular *mentalité* or culture as it fails to give an accurate impression of the private views of the subject.

This assumes, however, that what is said in the private sphere is somehow more 'real' or 'authentic' than what is declared in the public sphere – that there exists a kind of authentic voice of popular culture hidden from public view. In a sense, it imposes a hierarchy of authentic experience and somehow privileges what is said in the kitchen over what is said in the courthouse. There can be little doubt that what people say in private can be and often is different from their public utterances but to assume that one is inevitably more real or indicative of what a person really is or thinks is somewhat dubious. One could equally argue that someone can say what they like in private but it is ultimately what they do in the public sphere which reveals their priorities and interests and perhaps truly reflects their place, position and power in society. Moreover, public actions and utterances can have a considerable practical effect. The absence of public action and expression can also be telling. Thus, while the study of public action may not provide a complete or comprehensive picture of popular culture, it does constitute an indispensable and integral part of any wider understanding of that culture.

Another difficulty often raised with regard to the concept of popular culture, including by some contributors to this volume,[59] is that it implies an unwarranted degree of homogeneity in the actions and attitudes of the mass of the people by downplaying or, indeed, failing to grasp the complexity and diversity of actions rendered and attitudes held by ordinary people. Yet, I would contend that, rather than being a difficulty, this is, in some respects, the utility of the concept of popular culture – it allows us to look beyond the specific and to engage with wider trends and practices. Thus, we can examine participation in or, indeed, resistance to the courts as phenomena in their own right and explore which played a more dominant role without necessarily negating the fact that there were a variety of ways in which ordinary people either participated in or resisted the operation of the courts. In this sense, the general and the specific should not be mutually exclusive areas of inquiry but rather the examination of both should allow us to arrive at a clearer understanding of the dynamic nature of culture and, in particular, popular culture in a given period. One of the key aims of this volume then is to reveal popular culture, and in particular popular legal culture, in action – in the process of creating itself through the multiplicity of individual statements and actions in the public arena.

Content

The first essay in this volume by Julius Ruff emerges from one of the more long-established traditions of criminal justice history research, namely the study of the incidence and prosecution of violence in early modern France. Historians have long noted the pervasiveness and centrality of violent activity in early modern French society.[60] Ruff explores the nature of this 'popular' violence through a case study of a particular incident and locates it within what he categorises as the 'ostensibly violent society' that was seventeenth- and eighteenth-century France. He stresses both the centrality of violence in the maintenance of male honour and the functional aspects of such activity for those drawn both from the middle orders and from lower down the social scale. Violence, he suggests, permeated various forms of social interaction but was also very much controlled within such interactions by commonly-held understandings of what constituted appropriate action. Thus, violence tended to find expression through ritualised actions (generally carried out in public) in which the *dramatis personae* were aware of the rules of the game in which they were participating.[61] There is also little evidence of an intention to inflict fatal or indeed even serious injury on the body of an opponent – the aim was rather to humiliate than to kill. This is reflected in the relatively rare use of lethal weapons and the low annual murder rate that Ruff finds in samples from Libourne and Bazas – which, if nothing else, strongly suggests that this was a society in which violence, if pervasive, was also very carefully controlled, rarely extending to homicide or serious violence as a means of dealing with interpersonal conflict.

The role of the courts and the law in the control of violent activity was, however, somewhat ambiguous. The courts could often be bypassed as communities preferred to deal with matters without recourse to the official law. The decision to actually initiate a prosecution also could often be dictated by broader considerations such as the social position of the alleged aggressor. Ruff points out, for instance, that prosecutions were far more likely where the assailant was from outside or existed on the margins of the local community – such figures were far easier to prosecute successfully than locals of equal or higher social status who could muster support for their defence among the local community. The circumstances in which an assault arose could also have a bearing on the course of a prosecution – with mitigating factors such as the drunkenness of the parties involved being cited as reasons for not pursuing a charge. More importantly, perhaps, the courts themselves were often difficult to gain access to, either through expense, or distance, or a combination of both factors. Thus, while the courts could prove useful in restoring an individual's honour and in extracting compensation from one's opponent, for reasons of cost and, at times, also wider communal considerations, the courts were not regarded as the primary means of resolving conflicts.

Yet, while perhaps not dominant, the courts and legal officials were far from redundant and knowledge of the law and legal procedures among the mass of the people was quite high. Ruff, in fact, highlights the utility of legal officials and the courts in helping ordinary people to reach infrajudicial settlements which provided an alternative means of restoring the honour of the 'victim' while avoiding the costs of pursuing a full criminal prosecution – with the threat of court proceedings encouraging those accused of violent crime to settle the case. Ruff stresses also that we should avoid the temptation to see such settlements as simply an 'anachronism' rooted in essentially medieval practices and at odds with royal justice. On the contrary, such settlements complemented royal institutions, to a large degree, by helping to restore and maintain a definite level of social stability within local communities. The utility of such settlements was, in fact, acknowledged and considerably reinforced after the Revolution when the role of the arbitrator was given legal status and a professional magistracy was established to mediate minor disputes on a local level.

Similar themes of violence and its control run through Joachim Eibach's study of the cities of central Europe in the early modern period. Eibach offers a broad overview of developments in the study of the incidence and prosecution of violence in the German-speaking cities of central Europe between the sixteenth and eighteenth centuries. In doing so, through an analysis of the participants in violent activity, the forms that such violence took and the manner in which it was understood by plebeian and patrician alike within the urban world of early modern central Europe, he highlights elements of both continuity and change in the uses of and attitudes towards violence over the course of this period. For Eibach, there was a marked decline at this time in the participation of the elite members of urban society in acts of interpersonal violence while the courts gradually adopted a more punitive attitude towards violent activity. Such developments indicate an increased marginalisation of interpersonal violence as a legitimate response to personal disputes and conflicts as well as the increased and increasing willingness on the part of the courts and criminal justice systems generally to intervene and assert themselves in the resolution of interpersonal conflicts and the punishment of offenders. Yet, Eibach is also careful not to exaggerate the nature of the change in the prominence and role of violence and reactions to it. He stresses a degree of continuity in the resort to violence albeit with less and less likelihood that those drawn from the upper and increasingly the middle orders would be involved in public violent disputes. He also points out that, at both the beginning and the end of the period he is dealing with, it was the participation of ordinary citizens and, indeed, non-citizens in the criminal justice system which contributed most to the control of violent activity and, in turn, to the maintenance of order and stability. There is, in this sense, not so much a move from the disorder of the earlier period to the order of the later but rather the development of new strategies for maintaining order over the course of the period under review.

Themes of violence and attitudes towards it also permeate Rudy Chaulet's analysis of homicide cases in sixteenth- and seventeenth-century Castile. Chaulet argues that Castilian society maintained a high degree of tolerance towards violent activity in defence of male honour, as a means of recreation and as an expression of hostility towards those from outside the local community and the national polity. The emphasis here is less on the operation of the courts (due, it seems, primarily to the lack of sources) than on the operation of the prerogative of mercy. For Chaulet, the Castilian state afforded a good deal of leeway to violent offenders and, indeed, in some respects, contributed to a tolerant attitude towards violent activity through its encouragement of men to bear arms and in its hostility towards those who deviated from prevailing religious and social norms. Thus, violence perpetrated in order to defend or assert personal status or wider communal norms could be at least partially excused. The exercise of and tolerance shown towards violence was, moreover, a feature not alone of popular but also elite culture – a fact which serves to blur, or even call into question, any neat distinction between elite and popular attitudes towards violence.

Cohesion of perhaps a somewhat different hue is evident in Maria Kaspersson's contribution to this volume in which she explores the nature of popular participation in the courts of early modern Sweden and how it might be understood in the light of the dominant perspectives offered within the existing historiography. In doing so, she highlights both the importance of popular participation to the functioning of the courts and the changing nature of that participation over time. In particular, she notes the increasing role played by the state in the prosecution of criminal cases and the consequent bureaucratisation of that process. However, she stresses that this did not inhibit participation but rather encouraged it, even if the nature of such participation did not always cohere with the interests and priorities of the state.

Kaspersson also draws attention to the conflicting interpretations of participation in the courts offered by historians of the early modern period. Swedish historians have tended to posit a 'harmony model' to explain the use of and participation in the courts, whereas Finnish interpretations, at least as provided by Heikki Ylikangas, have tended to focus rather on the underlying conflicts which give rise to participation in the courts. She concludes, unsurprisingly perhaps, that it is the former model, with its emphasis on popular support for and use of the law, rather than the latter model, with its emphasis on conflict, which best fits the experiences of early modern Sweden.

A compelling level of popular participation in the courts is also evident in James Sharpe's contribution. Drawing on the work of some leading legal anthropologists and based primarily on a study of civil litigation, Sharpe draws attention to the centrality of the law and legal system in one of the less developed societies in early modern Europe, namely the Isle of Man. Similar, in many respects, to the aforementioned studies of the courts in Sweden, Sharpe highlights the extent of participation by ordinary men in the courts as officials, jurors and litigants and the degree to which the courts were seen as useful in resolving disputes and, more generally, in the maintenance of order and social stability. This, moreover, is in a context where there is little evidence to suggest that violence was resorted to, in any sustained or pervasive manner, in order to deal with interpersonal conflicts and disputes. Sharpe also reflects on the changing nature of participation in the courts over the course of the sixteenth and seventeenth centuries and the implications this may have for our understanding of wider European developments in the operation of the law. In particular, he explores the critiques offered by legal anthropologists of the notion of a 'judicial revolution'. Such critiques have, as Sharpe notes, tended to question notions of legal evolution which focus on a move from community to state law. Yet, Sharpe also points out that we need to be careful in dismissing such 'meta-narratives' of change.

Participation in the courts is also at the heart of Richard Mc Mahon's contribution on the prosecution of homicide in pre-Famine and Famine Ireland. Through a detailed study of the extent and nature of witness participation in the prosecution of homicide, Mc Mahon calls into question the dominant view, within the Irish historiography, that witnesses were reluctant to testify in open court for the prosecution. He also concludes that in most cases the courts were seen by the mass of the people as the most appropriate or at least the most practical forum to deal with acts of lethal violence and that when combined with the fact that there was also widespread participation in and use of the lower courts in this period, those who participated in the courts should not be easily dismissed as an isolated group who defied wider social norms and cultural expectations in order to participate in the trial process.

Greg T. Smith's contribution on eighteenth- and nineteenth-century England, reflecting the more advanced state of the English historiography, provides a somewhat broader and longer-term view of the incidence and prosecution of violent activity. For Smith, violent acts in early modern England should be located and understood within a broader culture of violence which pervaded both the public and private spheres and which was central to maintaining social discipline. Acts of interpersonal violence also reflected the utility of violence, particularly for men, as a means of asserting, maintaining or defending their identity and status within the wider community. Smith, however, also identifies, in similar terms to historians such as Robert Shoemaker and Martin Weiner,[62] a gradual reshaping of male behaviour and, indeed, of male identity emerging in the late eighteenth century, which both reflected and served to underpin a growing intolerance towards interpersonal violence both within and outside the domestic sphere. A sustained move away from violence as a means of resolving personal disputes might, for instance, be reflected in the declining rates of homicide to be found in England, and highlighted by Smith, in the two centuries preceding the First World War. It may also be found in an increasing unwillingness to tolerate defences of drunkenness and, more generally, of provocation in trials for violent offences – particularly when violence was directed against women and children. Smith also demonstrates how changes in sentencing policy from the late eighteenth century onwards might be seen as part of a broader cultural shift in attitudes towards violent activity. In particular, he highlights the increasing tendency, from the 1770s, among magistrates at quarter sessions to sentence those convicted of assault to terms of imprisonment rather than allowing for private settlements among the protagonists, which appears to have been the norm in the earlier part of that century. Such changes, for Smith, reflected a wider change in sensibilities whereby there was growing intolerance towards the perpetration of violent acts in the public sphere. Smith concludes that the reasons behind such changes (if such might be said to exist) remain elusive.

As with Smith's contribution, the role of the courts in reaching verdicts and passing sentence, along with wider questions of gender and identity, also play a central role in Carolyn A. Conley's contribution to this volume. Conley focuses on the prosecution of 'domestic homicides' in late Victorian Scotland and, in doing so, stresses the flexibility of the courts in reaching verdicts and imposing sentences in such cases. While the courts recognised the need for the accused to atone for their actions, they also displayed a readiness to acknowledge possible mitigating circumstances connected to individual cases. These might involve a consideration of the sanity (or otherwise) of the accused, drunkenness and any provocation on the part of the alleged victim. Wider consideration of the social position of the parties could also have an influence. For instance, in cases of child killing, the issue of whether the victim was or was not legitimate appears to have had a considerable bearing on the outcome of the case and the sentence. Similarly, in cases of spousal homicide, the social position of the parties involved could have, it seems, a clear influence on the verdicts reached and sentences imposed. Thus it was often, Conley points out, the wider cultural circumstances, in particular issues of gender and class, which informed the interpretations of particular cases before the courts.

Richard Ireland's contribution to this volume provides a provocative (in the best possible sense of the word) analysis of representations of crime and criminal justice in nineteenth-century Wales and how these might relate to actual experiences in Wales at the time with particular reference to the participation of the 'crowd' or 'audience' in the criminal justice process. Ireland draws attention to the often active part played by 'ordinary people' in the prosecution of criminal activity (before, during and after trial). In doing so, however, he also highlights significant points of disjuncture between 'popular' and 'official' notions of criminality which may often appear hidden beneath the apparent stability of Welsh society in the nineteenth century. Questions of religion and language, he points out, served, if not to alienate, certainly to render Welshmen and woman reluctant to contribute to the full enforcement of the criminal law on those brought forward for trial. Conversely, he also notes the ability and willingness of ordinary people to pass their own judgments on suspects where the criminal courts had failed to act. This, moreover, was within the context of a largely reformed criminal justice system where one might expect the degree of central control to have overridden local resistance to the full and 'objective' implementation of the criminal law. Ireland also offers a searching analysis of public participation in the rituals of punishment in nineteenth-century Wales, stressing the persistence of the crowd or audience in the criminal justice process long after the execution crowd was rendered obsolete by the ending of public executions in the 1860s.

Taken as a whole, the essays contained in this volume have some broader implications for the existing historiography.[63] To begin, a number of the essays serve to undermine the notion, put forward by Lenman and Parker, that the mass of the people were reluctant participants in the criminal justice process at the outset of the early modern period. Eibach clearly demonstrates that, throughout the early modern period, ordinary people were far from being 'reluctant prosecutors' but were, in fact, willing participants in the process. Sharpe's study of the operation of the courts in the early modern

Isle of Man also points to a clear readiness and desire to participate in the official legal system throughout the period. Indeed, this willingness to participate seems, if anything, to have been greater in the sixteenth century than it was by the end of the seventeenth century. This, moreover, was the case both in terms of civil litigation and criminal prosecutions. There is, admittedly, some support for Lenman and Parker's thesis in the evidence gleaned by Kaspersson from early modern Stockholm, which suggests a marked increase in participation between the seventeenth and eighteenth centuries. Yet, even here, as Kaspersson acknowledges, the evidence is based on a relatively limited sample and evidence from other sources suggests that, in fact, the pattern in Scandinavia was quite different to that suggested by Lenman and Parker.[64] On the whole, the evidence from early modern Sweden points to a high level of willingness to have recourse to the courts to deal with both criminal offences and civil disputes. Thus, there appears to have been a clear underestimation by Lenman and Parker of the extent of popular participation in and influence on the courts.

This points, I think, to a wider problem with Lenman and Parker's analysis, namely the lack of agency they accord to ordinary people – whose participation in the criminal courts (as they present it) is seen as an almost slavish response to the pressures exerted by the state, the churches and emerging commercial interests. The evidence presented in this collection provides a somewhat different picture. One of the striking features of many of the essays in this volume is that they reveal not only a high degree of willingness on the part of the general public to participate in the courts but also that such participation was integral to, and had a considerable influence on, the operation of the criminal justice process. Again, Eibach demonstrates that throughout the early modern period the authorities in the cities of Central Europe continued to depend on the participation of the inhabitants of these cities to maintain order and to ensure urban stability. In the early modern Isle of Man, it is also evident that the legal system was largely dependent on the efforts of local officers, prosecutors, witnesses and jurors to ensure its smooth operation. In Scandinavia too public participation was integral to the criminal justice process. Historians of the courts in England have also long noted the importance of popular participation in the courts for the effective operation of the criminal justice system in that country.[65]

Even where the legal system was not particularly conducive to the widespread participation of ordinary people, it is evident that recourse could be had to the courts as part of a wider game of dispute resolution. Thus, in France, where access to the courts, as Ruff demonstrates, was not always an attractive or even a viable proposition, use was still made of the courts and legal officials to deal with conflicts, even if (or maybe even because) the full force of the law was not imposed. Studies of early modern Spain have reached similar conclusions.[66] One of the striking aspects of all the contributions to this volume is also not only the willingness to participate and the importance of such participation but the relative absence of overt resistance to the operation of the criminal law. The clearest evidence of resistance comes from nineteenth-century Ireland. Even here, however, such resistance did not unduly inhibit the operation of the courts or the participation of ordinary people in the legal process, something which the courts depended on in order to function effectively.

Moreover, the fact that the legal system of the state had to depend to a considerable degree on lay participation undoubtedly helped to shape the operation of the courts. The recognition of and support for the norms of the communities on the part of court officials may also have encouraged participation in these institutions. In the case of violent crime, it certainly seems as if the decisions reached by the courts, and indeed the manner in which cases were handled generally, often corresponded with wider societal notions of what constituted legitimate activity. The practice of out-of-court settlement, prevalent in many jurisdictions, also seems to reflect a certain flexibility in dealing with violent activity on the part of the courts, which encouraged ordinary people to at least utilise the threat of a criminal prosecution to deal with interpersonal conflicts.

The courts in a number of jurisdictions, of course, did demonstrate a greater willingness to intervene and impose more punitive sanctions in criminal cases, particularly towards the close of the early modern period. Smith's essay on England, for instance, points to an increasing criminalisation of violent behaviour in the eighteenth century and greater and more coherent punitive strategies to deal with it, including a renewed emphasis on imprisonment as a means of punishing offenders as well as a greater intolerance of out-of-court settlements at quarter sessions. There is also clear evidence of the withdrawal of social elites from violent activity, under pressure in many jurisdictions from a centralising state apparatus keen to establish its authority. A number of historians of early modern France have, for instance, detected this trend in that country. Urban areas in the German-speaking countries of Central Europe also saw a decline in elite participation in violent activity and an increasingly punitive attitude towards violence. It is evident that over the course of the early modern period the resort to interpersonal violence in many jurisdictions became increasingly (although not wholly) inconsistent with the exercise of political power and, more generally, with membership of the upper and also, by the nineteenth century, the middle orders, and that the courts adopted a more consistent and punitive stance when it came to cases of even relatively minor violent crime. This would suggest an increasingly important role for the state and those in positions of authority in the control and limiting of interpersonal violent conflict and, moreover, that the control of interpersonal violence within communities was inextricably linked to and dependent upon a wider process of state formation in the early modern period.

Yet we should not simply see the control of violent activity within communities as being dependent on a strong, interventionist and 'modern' state. In a society such as the early modern Isle of Man, where the central state apparatus was relatively weak, rates of violence also appear relatively low which might suggest that a strong and interventionist state is not a necessary or sufficient condition for maintaining a relatively peaceable society. It is clear also, in the case of eighteenth-century France, that although there was a high rate of out-of-court settlement, there was also, as Ruff demonstrates, a very low annual rate of murder. Thus the extent and nature of violence, if common at the level of petty infraction, was also contained and controlled within communities without the need for overt and persistent intervention by the courts to enforce the full letter of the law. Furthermore, where a tolerant attitude towards violence was necessary and helpful to those in positions of authority – a degree of tolerance could be maintained on the part of the state. For instance, in Spain, Chaulet points to the degree to which the authorities were tolerant of violent behaviour at least until the end of the seventeenth century, as it cohered with the wider military interests of the Castilian state. In England, the increasingly punitive sentencing policies adopted at quarter sessions occurred largely independently of central direction and intervention and was very much driven by local initiative in the different localities. It is also worth noting that, even as the courts became more repressive in their prosecutions and more punitive in their judgments in certain jurisdictions, ordinary people continued, as Eibach clearly demonstrates, to be vital and, indeed, central to the prosecution of crime. This would suggest that the part played by ordinary people in the control and restriction of violent activity should not be underestimated and that we should be wary of engaging in a form of 'trickle-down' history. Overall then, the operation of the courts and popular participation in them seems to point to a good deal of cohesion and shared values between rulers and ruled, rather than simply reflecting the efforts of the authorities to impose their peculiar notion of order on an unwilling population.

We also need, however, to be careful. The courts were not simply an expression of state and/or elite power, nor were they a simple expression of a 'moral consensus' shared by ruler and ruled. Indeed, Richard Ireland's contribution on crime in nineteenth-century Wales serves to remind us that behind apparent social stability and cohesion may lie serious and, at times, compelling differences and disagreements between elite ideals and popular practices. While there may be agreement on the utility of the courts and the rule of law, clear differences may also arise which serve to question or even, in some cases, inhibit the operation of the legal system. Evidence from Ireland likewise suggests that while overt resistance did not inhibit the overall operation of the courts or popular participation in them, significant differences and difficulties could at times emerge, which serve to highlight that there was no blind allegiance to or all-encompassing acceptance of the courts and the law. Historians of eighteenth-century England have also long noted the extent to which the operation of the courts in that country did not simply reflect a broad consensus about the prosecution of crime but rather were an arena for negotiation between and within social classes.[67] Similar findings have also been gleaned from other countries, both within and, indeed, beyond the boundaries of Europe.[68] The courts, in this sense, were primarily forums for negotiation into which the participants in the process brought their own interests and ideas of law and justice and sought to assert them in the public arena.

We also need to recognise that those negotiations which did take place in court were largely determined by the ability of the participants to mobilise support for their cause, not only within the court but probably, more importantly, within their communities and by their ability to appeal to prevailing norms and assumptions within the legal framework provided by the courts. Indeed, there is considerable evidence throughout this volume that one's success in the courts was closely (although, of course, not inevitably) linked to the degree to which one could prove one's social and cultural integration within the local community. This was the case at the beginning of our period and was arguably still the case towards the end. This is certainly evident in the account of domestic homicide cases in late Victorian Scotland offered by Carolyn A. Conley.

This ability or, more accurately, power was not wholly or necessarily determined by economic and social position – thus, it was possible for those on the margins to successfully appeal to the courts if sufficient support could be won for their cause or to prosecute those who were similarly positioned. Yet there can also be little doubt that, in the main, it was those who were friendless and on the margins or, to a lesser degree, those whose actions placed them in that position who suffered most at the hands of the courts and those who enjoyed positions of authority and respectability within local areas who often enjoyed most success whether as defendants or prosecutors. In this sense, the courts were not an expression of the will of the whole community nor did they simply reflect the power of the state to exercise control over communities; they were, in the main, an arena for the expression and negotiation of relations of power within communities. They were, in fact, probably a necessary outlet for the expression of power in communities and their activities serve to remind us of the importance of the law in the regulation and, indeed, definition of daily existence in early modern and modern European society.

Possibilities

By way of conclusion, it may be useful to reflect on the scope for and possibilities of future research. There is a need to explore in greater detail the relationship of crime and the criminal justice process to other social and cultural phenomena. The importance of such relationships is, indeed, evident in a number of the essays contained in this volume. Conley's analysis of domestic homicide in late Victorian Scotland, for instance, sees the treatment of offenders as being rooted in the distinctive religious, educational and broader cultural outlook of Scotland at the time. Similarly, Rudy Chaulet notes the influence of the martial character and religious culture of early modern Castile on the attitudes towards criminal, or more specifically violent, activity. Richard Ireland too emphasises the impact that both religious and linguistic difference played in the administration of justice in Wales. Such differences have also often been seen as crucial factors (although at times overstated) in the operation of the criminal justice system in Ireland.

Evidence of disjuncture and resistance is also more likely to emerge, it seems, where there is a marked difference between the religious cultures of those who administer the law and the general populace – even if such resistance is less overt in some jurisdictions than others. Conversely, evidence of resistance at least appears more limited where there are greater links in religious belief and culture between the mass of the people and those responsible for the operation of the criminal justice system. Thus, the relationship between legal and religious cultures within jurisdictions seems evident but what the nature of that relationship was and ultimately what precise effect this had on both the operation of the law and, indeed, criminal activity undoubtedly requires further research. It is, at this stage, not sufficient to note the connection. We should also ask under what conditions this connection exists and examine in greater detail how it plays out in practice.

Other relationships also require greater attention. Having clearly established the relationship between violence and male honour in early modern Europe, historians need to reflect, to a greater degree, on the nature of that relationship and, in particular, whether violence was the dominant means or simply one strategy among many others for maintaining or upholding a sense of personal honour. To this end, greater links between historical and anthropological studies of violence may prove useful.

While much work of value has been carried out on the relationship between crime, criminal justice and gender, there is still considerable scope for examining the possibility of differing roles and treatment of men and women in the courts as witnesses, prosecutors and defendants and differences and similarities in patterns of criminal activity. The relationship between crime, law and the family, raised in a number of essays in this volume, also requires further research. The differing treatment of different forms of criminal activity by the courts also needs to be explored in greater detail and a more in-depth study of the lower courts (particularly of those with a summary jurisdiction) needs to be undertaken. It may also prove fruitful to examine in greater detail and on a broader scale the differences between the prosecution of crime in cities and in the countryside.

There can be little doubt also of the need for greater links between legal and criminal justice historians and a greater integration of existing criminal justice and legal approaches. There has been, as René Lévy has pointed out, an unfortunate lack of mutual understanding and cooperation between legal historians and historians of social and cultural history.[69] Yet, the potential for cross-fertilisation between legal and criminal justice historians is immense. To take but one example, the defence of provocation and how this was put forward and presented in different jurisdictions and over time would surely provide an insight not only into the development of the criminal law in Europe but also into wider attitudes towards violence and what constituted legitimate or, at the very least, partially excusable behaviour in different jurisdictions throughout Europe. There are also many other areas where a greater understanding of the law, of legal procedures and technicalities would contribute greatly to our understanding of the role of the criminal justice system in early modern and modern Europe. Representations of crime and criminal justice, which unfortunately do not form a significant element in this volume, also undoubtedly require greater, and more in-depth, research. Although not a theme covered in the current volume, the issue of migration and its impact on both patterns of crime and the operation of criminal justice systems both within and beyond Europe should also prove to be a very fruitful area of research in the future. To what extent, for instance, did practices and procedures, which seem deeply engrained within 'home' jurisdictions, translate and interact with developing practices and procedures in 'new' jurisdictions across the Atlantic and elsewhere?

Although perhaps something of a trite statement upon which to conclude, the essays contained in this volume and the possibilities for future research outlined above suggest, if nothing else, that there remains enormous scope for research in the broad field of criminal justice history and the history of legal cultures in early modern and modern Europe.

Notes

1 The following represents a broad overview of developments relevant to the concerns of this volume rather than any attempt to account for or detail the vast array and variety of work carried out in this area over the last thirty years or so. For those seeking bibliographies and bibliographical essays in the field of crime and criminal justice history, see Xavier Rousseaux, 'Criminality and Criminal Justice History in Europe, 1250–1850: A Select Bibliography', *Criminal Justice History*, 14 (1993), 159–81. See also Clive Emsley and L.A. Knafla, 'Bibliographical Essay', in idem (eds), *Crime History and Histories of Crime: Studies in the Historiography of Crime and Criminal Justice in Modern History* (Westport, CT: Greenwood Press, 1996), 291–4. Similar to the approach adopted by Emsley and Knafla in their bibliographical essay, the introduction to this volume focuses on works in English. Each essay in this volume also contains a section with recommendations for further reading, which should be of use to the general reader. For a broad overview of the historiography and some of the key

issues raised by it, see also Xavier Rousseaux, 'From Medieval Cities to National States, 1350–1850: The Historiography of Crime and Criminal Justice in Europe', in Emsley and Knafla (eds), *Crime History and Histories of Crime*, 3–32. See also L.A. Knafla, 'Structure, Conjuncture, and Event in the Historiography of Modern Criminal Justice History', in ibid., 33–44.

2 Douglas Hay, Peter Linebaugh and E.P. Thompson *et al.*, *Albion's Fatal Tree: Crime and Society in Eighteenth-Century England* (London: Allen Lane, 1975); E.P. Thompson, *Whigs and Hunters: The Origin of the Black Act* (London: Allen Lane, 1975).

3 Among the key works in the field are J.M. Beattie, *Crime and the Courts in England, 1660–1800* (Oxford: Clarendon Press, 1986); J.S. Cockburn, 'Patterns of Violence in English Society: Homicide in Kent, 1560–1985', *Past and Present*, 130 (1990), 70–106; Douglas Hay, 'War, Dearth and Theft in the Eighteenth Century: The Record of the English Courts', *Past and Present*, 95 (1982), 117–60; Cynthia Herrup, *The Common Peace: Participation and the Criminal Law in Seventeenth-Century England* (Cambridge: Cambridge University Press, 1987); Peter King, *Crime, Justice and Discretion in England, 1740–1820* (Oxford: Oxford University Press, 2003); Norma Landau, 'Indictment for Fun and Profit: A Prosecutor's Reward at Eighteenth-Century Quarter Sessions', *Law and History Review*, 17 (1999), 507–36; J.H. Langbein, *The Origins of Adversary Criminal Trial* (Oxford: Oxford University Press, 2003); Peter Linebaugh, *The London Hanged: Crime and Civil Society in the Eighteenth Century* (London: Allen Lane, 1991); Robert Shoemaker, *The London Mob: Violence and Disorder in Eighteenth-Century London* (London: Hambledon, 2004). There are also a number of important edited collections. See, for instance, J.S. Cockburn (ed.), *Crime in England, 1550–1800* (London: Methuen, 1977); John Brewer and John Styles, *An Ungovernable People: The English and Their Law in the Seventeenth and Eighteenth Centuries* (London: Hutchinson, 1980); Douglas Hay and Francis Snyder (eds), *Policing and Prosecution in Britain 1750–1850* (Oxford: Clarendon Press, 1989) and Norma Landau, *Law, Crime and English Society, 1660–1830* (Cambridge: Cambridge University Press, 2002). For surveys of crime in early modern and modern England, see J.A. Sharpe, *Crime in Early Modern England: 1550–1750*, 2nd edn (London: Longman, 1999); Clive Emsley, *Crime and Society in England 1750–1900*, 3rd edn (London: Longman, 2005) and David Taylor, *Crime, Policing and Punishment, 1750–1914* (Basingstoke: Macmillan, 1998).

4 David Philips, *Crime and Authority in Victorian England: The Black Country, 1835–60* (London: Croom Helm, 1977); V.A.C. Gatrell, 'The Decline of Theft and Violence in Victorian and Edwardian England', in V.A.C. Gatrell, Bruce Lenman and Geoffrey Parker (eds), *Crime and the Law: The Social History of Crime in Western Europe since 1500* (London: Europa Publications, 1980), 238–365.

5 Shani D'Cruze (ed.), *Everyday Violence in Britain, 1850–1950: Gender and Class* (Harlow: Pearson Education, 2000); J. Carter Wood, *Violence*

and Crime in Nineteenth-Century England: The Shadow of Our Refinement (London: Routledge, 2004); Clive Emsley, *Hard Men: Violence in England Since 1750* (London: Hambledon, 2005).

6 See, for instance, Heather Shore, *Artful Dodgers: Youth Crime in Early Nineteenth-Century London* (Woodbridge: Royal Historical Society/Boydell Press, 1999).

7 See, for instance, Judith R. Walkowitz, *Prostitution and Victorian Society: Women, Class, and the State* (Cambridge: Cambridge University Press, 1980) and Paula Bartley, *Prostitution: Prevention and Reform in England, 1860–1914* (London: Routledge, 1999).

8 Shani D'Cruze, *Crimes of Outrage: Sex, Violence and Victorian Working Women* (London: UCL Press, 1998); A. James Hammerton, *Cruelty and Companionship: Conflict in Nineteenth-Century Married Life* (London: Routledge, 1992); Maeve Doggett, *Marriage, Wife Beating and the Law in Victorian England* (Columbia, SC: University of South Carolina Press, 1993); Anna Clark, 'Domesticity and the Problem of Wife-Beating in Nineteenth-Century Britain: Working-Class Culture, Law, and Politics', in D'Cruze (ed.), *Everyday Violence in Britain*, 27–40; Martin Wiener, *Men of Blood: Violence, Manliness, and Criminal Justice in Victorian England* (Cambridge: Cambridge University Press, 2004); Elizabeth A. Foyster, *Marital Violence: An English Family History, 1660–1857* (Cambridge: Cambridge University Press, 2005).

9 Louise A. Jackson, *Child Sexual Abuse in Victorian England* (London: Routledge, 2000).

10 Mark Jackson (ed.), *Infanticide: Historical Perspectives on Child Murder and Its Concealment, 1500–2000* (Aldershot: Ashgate, 2001). See also Mark Jackson, *New-Born Child Murder: Women, Illegitimacy and the Courts in Eighteenth-Century England* (Manchester: Manchester University Press, 1996).

11 Howard Taylor, 'Rationing Crime: The Political Economy of Criminal Statistics since the 1850s', *Economic History Review*, 51, 3 (1998), 569–90; idem, 'The Politics of the Rising Crime Statistics of England and Wales, 1914–1960', *Crime, Histoire & Sociétés/Crime, History & Societies*, 2, 1 (1998), 5–28; R.M. Morris, 'Lies, Damned Lies and Criminal Statistics: Reinterpreting the Criminal Statistics in England and Wales', *Crime, Histoire & Sociétés/ Crime, History & Societies*, 5, 1 (2001), 111–27.

12 For an overview of the work carried out on the history of policing in England, see Clive Emsley, 'Crime and Punishment: 10 Years of Research. Filling In, Adding Up, Moving On: Criminal Justice History in Contemporary Britain', *Crime, Histoire & Sociétés/Crime, History & Societies*, 9, 1 (2005), 121–3. For an overview of the operation of the criminal justice process in the nineteenth century, see David Bentley, *English Criminal Justice in the Nineteenth Century* (London: Hambledon, 1998). On juries, see J.S. Cockburn and Thomas A. Green (eds), *Twelve Good Men and True: The Criminal Trial Jury in England, 1200–1800* (Princeton, NJ: Princeton University Press, 1988); Thomas A. Green, *Verdict According to Conscience: Perspectives on the English Criminal Trial Jury, 1200–1800* (Chicago: University

of Chicago Press, 1988). On lawyers, the law and criminal procedure, see Allyson N. May, *The Bar and the Old Bailey, 1750–1850* (Chapel Hill, NC: University of North Carolina Press, 2003); D.J.A. Cairns, *Advocacy and the Making of the Adversarial Criminal Trial, 1800–1865* (Oxford: Clarendon Press, 1998). On punishment, see, among others, Leon Radzinowicz, *A History of English Criminal Law and Its Administration from 1750, Vol. 1: The Movement for Reform* (London: Stevens & Sons, 1948); Michael Ignatieff, *A Just Measure of Pain: The Penitentiary in the Industrial Revolution 1750–1850* (London: Macmillan, 1978); V.A.C. Gatrell, *The Hanging Tree: Execution and the English People 1770–1868* (Oxford: Oxford University Press, 1994); David Garland, *Punishment and Welfare: A History of Penal Strategies* (Aldershot: Gower, 1985); idem, *Punishment and Modern Society: A Study in Social Theory* (Oxford: Clarendon, 1990); Randall McGowen, 'A Powerful Sympathy: Terror, the Prison and Humanitarian Reform in Early Nineteenth-Century Britain', *Journal of British Studies*, 25 (1986), 312–34; idem, 'Civilizing Punishment: The End of the Public Execution in England', *Journal of British Studies*, 33, 3 (1994), 257–82.

13   Sharon Howard, 'Investigating Responses to Theft in Early Modern Wales: Communities, Thieves and the Courts', *Continuity and Change*, 19, 3 (2004), 409–30.

14   See, in particular, David J.V. Jones, *Crime in Nineteenth-Century Wales* (Cardiff: University of Wales Press, 1992); R.W. Ireland, 'Putting Oneself on Whose Country? Carmarthenshire Juries and Crime in the Mid-Nineteenth Century', in T. G. Watkin (ed.), *Legal Wales: Its Past, Its Future* (Cardiff: Welsh Legal History Society, 2001), 63–87; R.W. Ireland, '"Perhaps My Mother Murdered Me": Child Death and the Law in Victorian Carmarthenshire', in Christopher Brooks and M.J. Lobban (eds), *Communities and Courts in Britain, 1150–1900* (London: Hambledon, 1997), 229–44; R.W. Ireland, '*A Want of Good Order and Discipline': Rules, Discretion and the Victorian Prison* (Cardiff: University of Wales Press, 2007).

15   See, for instance, Ian Donnachie, 'Profiling Criminal Offences: The Evidence of the Lord Advocate's Papers During the First Half of the Nineteenth Century in Scotland', *Scottish Archives: The Journal of the Scottish Records Association*, 1 (1995), 85–92 and idem, '"The Darker Side": A Speculative Survey of Scottish Crime During the First Half of the Nineteenth Century', *Scottish Economic and Social History*, 15 (1995), 5–24. See also M.A. Crowther, 'The Criminal Precognitions and Their Value for the Historian', *Scottish Archives*, 1 (1995), 75–84 and Lindsay Farmer, *Criminal Law, Tradition and Legal Order: Crime and the Genius of Scots Law 1747 to the Present* (Cambridge: Cambridge University Press, 1997).

16   See Yvonne Galloway Brown and Rona Ferguson, *Twisted Sisters: Women, Crime and Deviance in Scotland Since 1400* (East Linton: Tuckwell Press, 2004).

17   Anne-Marie Kilday, *Women and Violent Crime in Enlightenment Scotland* (London: Royal Historical Society, 2007).

18 Carolyn A. Conley, *Certain Other Countries: Homicide, Gender, and National Identity in Late Nineteenth-Century England, Ireland, Scotland, and Wales* (Columbus, OH: Ohio State University Press, 2007).

19 Neal Garnham, *The Courts, Crime and the Criminal Law in Ireland, 1692–1760* (Dublin: Irish Academic Press, 1996).

20 See, for instance, James Kelly, *Gallows Speeches from Eighteenth-Century Ireland* (Dublin: Four Courts Press, 2001); idem, *That Damn'd Thing Called Honour: Duelling in Irish History, 1570–1860* (Cork: Cork University Press, 1995); idem, 'Infanticide in Eighteenth-Century Ireland', *Irish Economic and Social History*, 19 (1992), 5–26; idem, '"A Most Inhuman and Barbarous Piece of Villainy": An Exploration of the Crime of Rape in Eighteenth-Century Ireland', *Eighteenth-Century Ireland/Iris an dá chultúr*, 10 (1995), 78–107.

21 D.J. McCabe, '"That Part that Laws or Kings Can Cause or Cure": Crown Prosecution and Jury Trial at Longford Assizes, 1830–45', in Raymond Gillespie and Gerard Moran (eds), *Longford: Essays in County History* (Dublin: Lilliput Press, 1991), 153–72. See also Richard Mc Mahon, 'Homicide, the Courts and Popular Culture in Pre-Famine and Famine Ireland' (PhD thesis, University College Dublin, 2006).

22 Terence Dooley, *The Murders at Wildgoose Lodge: Agrarian Crime and Punishment in Pre-Famine Ireland* (Dublin: Four Courts Press, 2007).

23 Richard Mc Mahon, '"Do You Want to Pick a Fight Out of Me, or What Do You Want?": Homicide and Personal Animosity in Pre-Famine and Famine Ireland', in Katherine D. Watson (ed.), *Assaulting the Past: Violence and Civilization in Historical Context* (Newcastle: Cambridge Scholars Publishing, 2007), 222–49 and idem, '"The Madness of Party": Sectarian Homicide in Ireland, 1801–1850', *Crime, Histoire & Sociétés/Crime, History & Societies*, 11, 1 (2007), 83–112. See also S.J. Connolly, 'Unnatural Death in Four Nations: Contrasts and Comparisons', in S.J. Connolly (ed.), *Kingdoms United? Great Britain and Ireland since 1500* (Dublin: Four Courts Press, 1999), 200–14. For longer-term trends in violent activity, see Ian O'Donnell, 'Lethal Violence in Ireland, 1841–2003: Famine, Celibacy and Parental Pacification', *British Journal of Criminology*, 45 (2005), 671–95 and idem, 'Unlawful Killing: Past and Present', *The Irish Jurist*, xxxvii, new series (2002), 56–90. There is also a considerable body of work on the specific issue of rural unrest in eighteenth- and nineteenth-century Ireland. See, for instance, Samuel Clark and J.S. Donnelly, Jr, (eds), *Irish Peasants: Violence and Political Unrest* (Manchester: Manchester University Press, 1983).

24 Mark Finnane, 'A Decline in Violence in Ireland? Crime, Policing and Social Relations, 1860–1914', *Crime, Histoire & Sociétés/Crime, History & Societies*, 1, 1 (1997), 51–70 and Carolyn A. Conley, *Melancholy Accidents: The Meaning of Violence in Post-Famine Ireland* (Lanham, MD: Lexington Books, 1999). See also Conley, *Certain Other Countries*.

25 Patrick Carroll-Burke, *Colonial Discipline: The Making of the Irish Convict System* (Dublin: Four Courts Press, 2000); S.H. Palmer, *Police and Protest in England and Ireland, 1780–1850* (Cambridge: Cambridge University Press,

1988); Brian Griffin, 'Prevention and Detection of Crime in Nineteenth-Century Ireland', in N.M. Dawson (ed.), *Reflections on Law and History: Irish Legal History Society Discourses and Other Papers, 2000–2005* (Dublin: Four Courts Press, 2006), 99–125; Elizabeth Malcolm, *The Irish Policeman, 1822–1922: A Life* (Dublin: Four Courts Press, 2005); D.S. Johnson, 'Trial by Jury in Ireland 1860–1914', *Journal of Legal History*, 17 (1996), 270–93; J.F. McEldowney, 'Crown Prosecutions in Nineteenth-Century Ireland', in Hay and Snyder (eds), *Policing and Prosecution in Britain*, 427–57. Unfortunately, some of the most impressive work on crime and criminal justice history in Ireland remains unpublished. See Andres Eiriksson, 'Crime and Popular Protest in Co. Clare 1815–52' (PhD thesis, Trinity College Dublin, 1992) and D.J. McCabe, 'Law, Conflict and Social Order: County Mayo, 1820–45' (PhD thesis, University College Dublin, 1991).

26 Shane Kilcommins, Ian O'Donnell, Eoin O'Sullivan and Barry Vaughan, *Crime, Punishment and the Search for Order in Ireland* (Dublin: Institute of Public Administration, 2004).

27 For a discussion of the French historiography, see Xavier Rousseaux, 'Historiographie du crime et de la justice criminelle dans l'espace Français (1990–2005). Partie I: du Moyen-Âge à la fin de l'Ancien Régime', *Crime, Histoire & Sociétés/Crime, History & Societies*, 10, 1 (2006), 123–58; idem, 'Historiographie du crime et de la justice criminelle dans l'espace Français (1990–2005). Partie II: de la Révolution au XXIᵉ siècle', *Crime, Histoire & Sociétés/Crime, History & Societies*, 10, 2 (2006), 123–61 and René Lévy, 'Crime, the Judicial System, and Punishment in Modern France', in Emsley and Knafla (eds), *Crime History and Histories of Crime*, 87–108.

28 Clive Emsley, *Gendarmes and the State in Nineteenth-Century Europe* (Oxford: Oxford University Press, 1999); Iain Cameron, *Crime and Repression in the Auvergne and the Guyenne, 1720–1790* (Cambridge: Cambridge University Press, 1982). See also Clive Emsley, 'Policing the Streets of Early Nineteenth-Century Paris', *French History*, 1, 2 (1987), 257–82 and J.M. Berlière, 'The Professionalization of the Police under the Third Republic in France, 1875–1914', in Clive Emsley and Barbara Weinberger (eds), *Policing Western Europe: Politics, Professionalism, and Public Order, 1850–1940* (Westport, CT: Greenwood Press, 1991).

29 Nicole Castan, 'Crime and Justice in Languedoc: The Critical Years (1750–1790)', *Criminal Justice History*, 1 (1980), 175–84 and *Justice et répression en Languedoc à l'époque des lumières* (Paris: Flammarion, 1980).

30 Steven G. Reinhardt, *Justice in the Sarladais, 1770–1790* (Baton Rouge, LA: Louisiana State University Press, 1991). See also Benoît Garnot, *Justice et société en France aux XVIᵉ, XVIIᵉ et XVIIIᵉ siècles* (Gap: Editions Orphrys, 2000); Jeremy Hayhoe, 'Neighbours Before the Court: Crime, Village Communities and Seigneurial Justice in Northern Burgundy, 1750–1790,' *French History*, 17 (2003), 127–48; Anthony Crubaugh, *Balancing the Scales of Justice: Local Courts and Rural Society in Southwest France, 1750–1800* (University Park, PA: Pennsylvania State University Press, 2001).

31 Julius R. Ruff, *Crime, Justice and Public Order in Old Regime France: The Sénéchaussées of Libourne and Bazas, 1696–1789* (London: Croom Helm, 1984).

32 Michel Foucault, *Discipline and Punish: The Birth of the Prison* (New York, 1977).

33 Julie Hardwick, 'Early Modern Perspectives on the Long History of Domestic Violence: The Case of Seventeenth- and Eighteenth-Century France', *Journal of Modern History*, 78 (2006), 1–36; Malcolm Greenshields, *An Economy of Violence in Early Modern France: Crime and Justice in the Haute Auvergne, 1587–1664* (University Park, PA: Pennsylvania State University Press, 1994); Stuart Carroll, *Blood and Violence in Early Modern France* (Oxford: Oxford University Press, 2006). See also Claude Gauvard, *'De grace especial'. Crime, état et société en France à la fin du Moyen-Âge* (Paris: Publications de la Sorbonne, 2 vols, 1991); Robert Muchembled, *Culture populaire et culture des élites dans la France moderne, 15ᵉ–18ᵉ siècles* (Paris: Flammarion, 1991); idem, *L'invention de l'homme moderne* (Paris: Fayard, 1988).

34 Stephen Wilson, *Feuding, Conflict and Banditry in Nineteenth-Century Corsica* (Cambridge: Cambridge University Press, 1988).

35 See, for instance, the pioneering work of Howard Zehr, *Crime and the Development of Modern Society: Patterns of Criminality in Nineteenth-Century Germany and France* (Totowa, NJ: Rowman & Littlefield, 1976) and, more recently, the work of Eric A. Johnson, *Urbanization and Crime: Germany 1871–1914* (Cambridge: Cambridge University Press, 1995). See also Richard J. Evans, *Tales from the German Underworld: Crime and Punishment in the Nineteenth Century* (New Haven, CT and London: Yale University Press, 1998). For an overview of the existing historiography (with a particular emphasis on policing), see Alf Lüdtke and Herbert Reinke, 'Crime, Police and the "Good Order": Germany', in Emsley and Knafla (eds), *Crime History and Histories of Crime*, 109–37. See also the forthcoming historiographical essay by Herbert Reinke in the journal *Crime, Histoire & Sociétés/Crime, History & Societies*.

36 For a good introduction to the subject, see Peter Wettmann-Jungblut, 'Penal Law and Criminality in Southwestern Germany: Forms, Patterns and Developments, 1200–1800', in Xavier Rousseaux and René Lévy (eds), *Le Pénal dans tous ses états: justice, états et sociétés en Europe, XIIe–XXe siècles* (Brussels: Faculté Universitaires Saint-Louis, 1997). On the issue of women and the criminal justice system in early modern Germany, see Ulinka Rublack, *The Crimes of Women in Early Modern Germany* (Oxford: Oxford University Press, 1999). On capital punishment in this period and later, see Richard J. Evans, *Rituals of Retribution: Capital Punishment in Germany, 1600–1987* (Oxford: Oxford University Press, 1996).

37 See, for instance, Gerd Schwerhoff, 'Social Control of Violence, Violence as Social Control: The Case of Early Modern Germany', in Herman Roodenburg and Pieter Spierenburg (eds), *Social Control in Europe, Vol. I* (Columbus, OH: Ohio State University Press, 2004), 220–46.

38 See, for instance, Rudy Chaulet, 'La violence en Castille au XVIIe siècle à travers les *Indultos de Viernes Santo* (1623–1699)', *Crime, Histoire & Sociétés/ Crime, History & Societies*, 1, 2 (1997), 5–27; Tomás A. Mantecón, 'Popular Culture and Arbitration of Disputes: Northern Spain in the Eighteenth Century', in Louis A. Knafla (ed.), *Crime, Punishment and Reform in Europe: Criminal Justice History, Vol. 18* (Westport, CT: Greenwood Press, 2003), 39–55; idem, 'Meaning and Social Context of Crime in Preindustrial Times: Rural Society in the North of Spain, 17th and 18th Centuries', *Crime, Histoire & Sociétés/Crime, History & Societies*, 1, 2 (1998), 49–73; idem, 'Criminals and Royal Pardon in 18th-Century Spain', *Le Pardon. Cahiers de l'Institute d'Anthropologie Juridique*, 3 (1999), 477–506; Fabio López-Lázaro, '"No Deceit Safe in Its Hiding Place": The Criminal Trial in Eighteenth-Century Spain', *Law and History Review*, 20, 3 (2002), 449–78.

39 For an overview of developments, see Eva Österberg, 'Gender, Class and the Courts: Scandinavia', in Emsley and Knafla (eds), *Crime History and Histories of Crime*, 47–65; idem, 'Criminality, Social Control, and the Early Modern State: Evidence and Interpretations in Scandinavian Historiography', *Social Science History*, 16, 1 (1992), 67–98; Heikki Ylikangas, 'What Happened to Violence? An Analysis of the Development of Violence from Medieval Times to the Early Modern Era Based on Finnish Source Material', in Heikki Ylikangas, Petri Karonen and Martti Lehti, *Five Centuries of Violence in Finland and the Baltic Area* (Columbus, OH: Ohio State University Press, 2001), 1–83.

40 The British and Irish Isles would seem ideal candidates for such a study which would no doubt provide somewhat different and probably less cohesive results to those found in the Nordic countries. See Eva Österberg and Sølvi Bauge Sogner (eds), *People Meet the Law: Control and Conflict in the Courts. The Nordic Countries in the Post-Reformation and Pre-Industrial Period* (Oslo: Universitetsforlaget, 2000).

41 See, for instance, Pieter Spierenburg, *The Spectacle of Suffering: Executions and the Evolution of Repression: From a Preindustrial Metropolis to the European Experience* (Cambridge: Cambridge University Press, 1984); idem, 'Faces of Violence: Homicide Trends and Cultural Meanings, Amsterdam, 1431–1816', *Journal of Social History*, 21 (1994), 701–16; idem, 'Long-term Trends in Homicide: Theoretical Reflections and Dutch Evidence, Fifteenth to Twentieth Centuries', in E.A. Johnson and E.H. Monkkonen (eds), *The Civilization of Crime: Violence in Town and Country Since the Middle Ages* (Urbana and Chicago, IL: University of Illinois Press, 1996), 63–105.

42 John Davis, *Conflict and Control: Law and Order in Nineteenth-Century Italy* (Basingstoke: Macmillan, 1988). For an overview of the Italian historiography, see Steven C. Hughes, 'Brigands, Mafiosi, and Others: Italy', in Emsley and Knafla (eds), *Crime History and Histories of Crime*, 139–59. See also the forthcoming historiographical essay by the late Mario Sbriccoli in the journal *Crime, Histoire & Sociétés/Crime, History & Societies*.

43 Stephen P. Frank, *Crime, Cultural Conflict and Justice in Rural Russia, 1856–1914* (Berkeley, CA: University of California Press, 1999). See also Jane Burbank, *Russian Peasants Go to Court: Legal Culture in the Countryside, 1905–1917* (Bloomington, IN: Indiana University Press, 2004).

44 See, for instance, Ricardo D. Salvatore, Carlos Aguirre and Gilbert M. Joseph (eds), *Crime and Punishment in Latin America: Law and Society since Late Colonial Times* (Durham, NC and London: Duke University Press, 2001).

45 Margaret L. Arnot and Cornelie Usborne, *Gender and Crime in Modern Europe* (London: UCL Press, 1999).

46 Pamela Cox and Heather Shore (eds), *Becoming Delinquent: British and European Youth, 1650–1950* (Aldershot: Ashgate, 2002).

47 Johnson and Monkkonen, *The Civilization of Crime.*

48 For some fine examples of the work that can be carried out in this area, see Amy Oilman Srebnick and René Lévy (eds), *Crime and Culture: An Historical Perspective* (Aldershot: Ashgate, 2005) and Judith Rowbotham and Kim Stevenson (eds), *Criminal Conversations: Victorian Crimes, Social Panic, and Moral Outrage* (Columbus, OH: Ohio State University Press, 2005).

49 Barry S. Godfrey and Graeme Dunstall (eds), *Crime and Empire 1840–1940: Criminal Justice in Local and Global Context* (Cullompton: Willan, 2005).

50 Barry S. Godfrey, Clive Emsley, and Graeme Dunstall (eds), *Comparative Histories of Crime* (Cullompton: Willan, 2003).

51 For an overview, see Clive Emsley, *Crime, Police, and Penal Policy: European Experiences 1750–1940* (Oxford: Oxford University Press, 2007). See also Emsley and Weinberger, *Policing Western Europe.*

52 Foucault, *Discipline and Punish* and Norbert Elias, *The Civilizing Process: State Formation and Civilization* (Oxford: Blackwell, 1982).

53 See Knafla, 'Structure, Conjuncture, and Event', 33.

54 Bruce Lenman and Geoffrey Parker, 'The State, the Community and the Criminal Law in Early Modern Europe', in Gatrell et al. (eds), *Crime and the Law*, 11–48.

55 Martin Dinges, 'The Uses of Justice as a Form of Social Control in Early Modern Europe', in Roodenburg and Spierenburg (eds), *Social Control in Europe, Vol. I*, 174. Dinges asserts that the courts were only 'partially determined by those in charge' and that 'in general, the role of the courts was equally determined by the people'. Dinges, 'The Uses of Justice', 160.

56 For a good overview of the historiography (particularly relating to the study of homicide), see Manuel Eisner, 'Modernization, Self-Control and Lethal Violence: The Long-Term Dynamics of European Homicide Rates in Theoretical Perspective', in *British Journal of Criminology*, 41 (2001), 618–38; idem, 'Long-Term Trends in Violent Crime', in Michael Tonry (ed.), *Crime and Justice: A Review of Research*, Vol. 30 (Chicago: University of Chicago Press Journals, 2003), 83–142.

57 Lenman and Parker, 'The State, the Community and the Criminal Law', 39–41.

58 For a discussion of this issue, see Tim Harris, 'Problematising Popular Culture', in idem, (ed.), *Popular Culture in England, c.1500–1850* (London: St. Martins Press, 1995), 8–9.

59 See, for instance, the contributions of Rudy Chaulet and Richard Ireland.

60 For Malcolm Greenshields, 'physical violence was a widely accepted solution to conflict as well as the most direct personal affront in much of early modern society and, therefore, at the level of individual confrontation, violent behaviour was common'. Greenshields, *An Economy of Violence*, 2.

61 Greenshields has also noted the theatricality of violent acts in early modern France. See Greenshields, *An Economy of Violence*, 2.

62 Wiener, *Men of Blood* and Robert Shoemaker, 'Male Honour and the Decline of Public Violence in Eighteenth-Century London', *Social History*, 26 (2001), 190–208.

63 The following interpretation is very much my own and does not necessarily represent the views of the individual contributors to the volume.

64 According to Sølvi Sogner, ordinary people were less likely to bring cases of violent crime before the courts in the eighteenth century than they had been in the sixteenth century. Sølvi Sogner, 'Conclusion: The Nordic Model', in Österberg and Sogner (eds), *People Meet the Law*, 275–6.

65 See, for instance, James Sharpe, 'The Law, Law Enforcement, State Formation and National Integration in Late Medieval and Early Modern England', in Rousseaux and Lévy (eds), *Le Pénal dans tous ses états*, 79.

66 See, for instance, Mantecón, 'Popular Culture and Arbitration of Disputes'.

67 See, in particular, King, *Crime, Justice and Discretion*.

68 See, for instance, Salvatore et al. (eds), *Crime and Punishment in Latin America*.

69 Lévy, 'Crime, the Judicial System, and Punishment in Modern France', 99–100.

Chapter 1

Popular violence and its prosecution in seventeenth- and eighteenth-century France

Julius R. Ruff

Late on the afternoon of Sunday, 10 July 1785, Mathieu Robert, a cooper resident in Saint-Sulpice-de-Faleyrens in the rural Bordelais, entered a cabaret in the nearby Dordogne River valley town of Branne. There he had the misfortune to meet his hometown neighbour, the merchant Jean Bonneau, and the latter's uncle, the merchant Eyquart of Branne. These three individuals, all middle-aged men of some local standing and property, shared a contentious past that sparked a violent encounter. All three men exchanged insults and Bonneau and Eyquart, who perhaps had been consuming wine since the end of morning mass, slapped and punched Robert. In response Robert lodged criminal charges against the two merchants in the royal court for the area, the Sénéchaussée of Libourne, noting in his complaint that '... that which aggravates this action, as contemptible as it is reprehensible, is its public nature: it occurred in a cabaret.'[1] The Libourne tribunal promptly ordered a hearing and recorded sworn testimony from witnesses to the altercation. But Robert's written complaint and the hearing transcript constitute the total judicial record of this incident; its prosecution apparently stopped at this juncture, for there is no further evidence of it in either the Libourne records or those of the regional appeals court, the Parlement of Bordeaux.

At first glance the violence sustained by Robert is surprising to us. Its seemingly gratuitous nature shocks modern sensibilities, as does the fact that few persons of property today risk social station and material security in such behaviour. We will draw on almost two generations' modern research in criminal justice records, however, to find that there probably was little casual or spontaneous about this cabaret brawl. Indeed, it likely was a quite calculated event that typified much of seventeenth- and eighteenth-century French popular violence. Moreover, the apparently abrupt cessation of judicial prosecution in this case seems to have been quite common in prosecutions of crimes of this sort.[2] It, too, was a calculated move, and through examination of this case we will gain entry into the popular culture that produced the cabaret assault and its incomplete prosecution.

Popular violence

Violence was common in seventeenth- and eighteenth-century France. In this patriarchal society it began at home, where householders frequently directed physical abuse at wives, servants and children, and where infanticide was a known response to newborns delivered out of wedlock. The inadequacies of subsistence agriculture generated market riots for which royal authorities were ever watchful. Youth groups that routinely terrorised darkened streets gave free rein to their violence on festive occasions rich in the symbolism of a radical inversion of the social order. And the state's limited police resources permitted armed highwaymen to flourish almost within sight of Paris, while the streets of the capital, like those of other cities of the realm, were never free of armed robbers.[3] But the single most common form of violence in this society was that bred of quotidian human interchange in the marketplace, the workplace and, most especially, the cabaret. It appeared in the records of seventeenth- and eighteenth-century courts in the form of charges for 'insults and assault' (generally *injures et voies de fait* or *injures et excès*) largely against males; women did hurl insults, but they rarely engaged in physical violence.

This violence was a common part of the fabric of popular society, engaged in by those who did not seek to regulate their personal disputes in the highly ritualized violence of the aristocracy's duels.[4] Thus, in a study of crimes reported to the Sénéchaussée of Libourne and the neighbouring Sénéchaussée of Bazas in six sample periods of five years each over the years from 1696 to 1789, assaults similar to that in Branne constituted the most common offence reported to royal authorities. And, if we add to the reported assaults those cases alleging simple insults, we find that all such incidents represented about one half of the offences reported to the two courts. Elsewhere the incidence of this sort of physical and verbal violence was just

33

as common; in Lyon such cases accounted for almost three-quarters of all criminal complaints.[5] Robert's case thus was an example of perhaps the most common form of popular violence in both rural and urban areas of seventeenth- and eighteenth-century France.[6]

Libourne and Bazas records also show the frequency with which men of the status of Robert, Bonneau and Eyquart resorted to violence of this sort. Fully 60 per cent of the defendants for whom these documents record status came from the ranks of the region's minor officials, physicians, attorneys, merchants and skilled craftsmen. To be sure, these figures do not present a complete picture of the region's violent offenders; violence erupted chiefly between primary associates of similar social station and, as we will see, there were considerable disincentives for the reporting of crime among the poor. Nevertheless, our statistics suggest that conflicts like those of Robert were common among men of his social station.[7] The Branne cabaret altercation, moreover, typified much of Old Regime popular violence. Although at first glance it seems to be the result of a spontaneous outburst of bad temper, this was a petty violence that was almost ritualised in its patterns and that was measured out to achieve certain goals. This was a functional violence, intended to restore traditional relationships in the hierarchical and largely static society of Old Regime France, and Robert's complaint about the public character of his experience confirms that the incident chiefly involved matters of personal honour that defined those relationships. Moreover, the particularly well-documented genesis of the Branne dispute suggests that, while its violence appeared sudden, it certainly was not without deep roots, like many other such incidents. It simply represented another opportunity for all involved to continue a history of bad relations by further humiliating each other; it was the final act in a drama of at least three acts. We can understand the actions of these individuals by tracing those acts.[8]

The Branne incident began as a misunderstanding over a jest; it could just as easily have been a disagreement over a small debt or any one of the multitude of issues arising in the discourse of human relations. The first record of problems dates from September 1784, when Robert and Eyquart gathered with several other men in a cabaret, a centre of men's social relations where they conducted business, exchanged news and consumed alcoholic beverages that could inflame tempers.

Honour in this society especially rested on the esteem that a person enjoyed among friends, neighbours, co-workers and other associates. For men honour particularly depended on a reputation of honesty, professional competence and manliness; for women honour was chiefly a sexual matter, inextricably linked to their recognition for modesty, marital fidelity and general moral virtue. Male and female honour intersected when someone questioned a woman's possession of the feminine virtues, a challenge that implicitly impugned the honour of the woman's husband, father or brothers. An individual's local standing and even livelihood, in urban neighbourhoods as well as in rural small-town France, rested on a good reputation, but acknowledgement of such standing was not automatic. Honour was the currency of human relations, aptly described by one historian as a discourse in which one sought to exact from one's peers the maximum possible respect while conceding to them the bare minimum in return.[9] Because most implicitly understood this dynamic, they were alert to the most trivial slights, and when Robert joked that Eyquart had stolen a hat, the latter took immediate offence. He was a merchant and a minor legal official, the clerk of the local Branne court, whose local standing and livelihood depended on his upright reputation. Moreover, Eyquart's standing in regard to Robert, one of sufficient equality to permit socialisation with him in a public house, had been symbolically diminished. Thus Eyquart sought to deliver a blow to Robert that would restore his own honour while diminishing that of the cooper: Eyquart charged him with criminal libel. The resulting judgment required Robert to pay Eyquart damages totalling 6 *livres*, a token sum that restored the merchant's honour but which carried great symbolic cost for Robert. The loss diminished his reputation for honest dealing, and Robert readied himself for any opportunity to recoup his honour at Eyquart's expense. Not surprisingly, his seizure of such an opportunity led to violence. Many cases of assault grew out of earlier defeats in court; even in the urban sprawl of eighteenth-century Paris, fully one out of every seven honour conflicts had such origins.[10]

Eyquart and Robert inhabited a clannish society, and soon their relatives and their employees began to appear in the judicial record in a second act in this drama. Thus, on the morning of 10 June 1785, Robert observed some fowl in his wheatfield in Saint-Sulpice-de-Faleyrens. His complaint to the Sénéchaussée of Libourne, drafted with the assistance of an attorney, sought to cast his subsequent actions in the most favourable light possible by noting that he was a conscientious property owner, careful to protect his crops from the depredations of roving animals; indeed, he had asked his neighbour to confine his livestock more carefully as recently as 9 June. Significantly, the neighbour who owned the fowl was Jean Bonneau, nephew of

Eyquart and one of his supporters in the dispute with the cooper. Robert probably did not hesitate as he raised his musket and shot several of the birds. At the sound of gunfire, Bonneau, his son, his wife and one of his tenant farmers ran to the scene, knocked Robert to the ground, kicked and punched him, and left him lying amid his damaged crop. A physician's report attested to the physical effects of Robert's beating, but the victim probably felt these less acutely than he did the damage to his honour, as a closer examination of these incidents reveals.[11]

The assault sustained by Robert on 10 June, like many other cases of assault and insults, was symbolically laden for early modern French males. The symbolic nexus of male honour was the head, which, in a traditional society like that of seventeenth- and eighteenth-century France, was bowed and uncovered to express respect for another. Failure by a male ritually to remove his hat and incline his head, concomitantly, was an act of disrespect. The symbolism of the head explains why a great deal of popular violence was aimed at it. Often altercations began with slaps to the face, as Robert suffered in the Branne cabaret, and might be followed by the assailant seizing his opponent's hair and forcing him to the ground to further demean him. No longer erect, he could be kicked like an animal; symbolically he had been deprived of his manhood. This was the honorific damage that Robert sustained on 10 June. Other violence might ensue when an assailant forcibly removed an opponent's headgear, threw the hat to the ground, and symbolically enforced respect that had not been extended voluntarily by its wearer. It is noteworthy that Robert's jest involved the theft of a hat, a symbol of its wearer's elevated standing when it was not doffed. The jest could have been received as an allegation that Eyquart had deprived the hat's owner of standing and honour, or that his own honour and social position was based on theft or shady dealings, and while we lack conclusive evidence in the record, it is probable that Robert was aware of this symbolism.[12]

We can note other important elements in the violence of 10 June. Typical of most of this violence, it was the sudden result of a chance encounter. Thus it was short-lived, of limited intensity and without a fatal result. The suddenness of such violence is evident because Old Regime judges punished premeditated crime more harshly than undeliberated offences, and legal scholars of the day maintained that an assailant's employment of any sort of specialised weapon was prima facie evidence of premeditation.[13] Thus magistrates carefully recorded the weapons used in acts of violence, and we know that the assault by Bonneau and his family on 10 June, as well as the cabaret altercation of 10 July, were fairly typical acts of violence carried on without the use of lethal weapons such as firearms and swords. Indeed, 40 per cent of the assailants in the Libourne and Bazas sample simply slapped, punched or kicked their victims. An approximately equal number of persons charged with criminal assault resorted to a wide variety of implements that they found near at hand, such as tools, which by their very random nature also suggest sudden recourse to violence. Occasionally a misplaced blow with such crude weaponry might have fatal results, but the relatively rare employment of lethal armament in seventeenth- and eighteenth-century assaults certainly limited the number of violent deaths resulting from them. Our samples from Libourne and Bazas, court districts with jurisdictions encompassing a population of perhaps 165,000 persons in the late eighteenth century, yield but 36 homicides in thirty years, an annual rate of 0.72 murders per 100,000 of population that compares very favorably with that of twenty-first-century Western European societies served by modern police forces and advanced medical care. This limited incidence of fatal violence, a crime that rarely is underreported, is consistent with the findings of researchers in other regions of France, and it suggests that the real motive in many of these confrontations was not to kill or even seriously to wound one's opponent but, rather, to humiliate the person.[14]

A final aspect of the 10 June assault was its timing and location. The wheatfield assault occurred in mid-morning when many people were at work in the fields, and court records list seven eyewitnesses to the event. The presence of such an audience must have meant that local gossip quickly spread news of Robert's humiliation. As in the initial confrontation in 1784 and in the cabaret incident of 10 July, the presence of an audience seems to have been an essential component in these conflicts.[15] Assaults on the honour of an opponent had limited effect without an audience to register the humiliation of a neighbour. And the audience, some scholars suggest, played a second, vital role in such conformations. Witnesses helped to contain the violence, lest a fit of temper on the part of one of the participants threatened fatal results. In such instances, the witnesses could intervene, and victims' assertions in court documents that they would have perished at their enemy's hands without bystanders' intervention may be more than simple hyperbole intended to maximise the gravity of their suffering before a judge.[16]

Placed in these perspectives, Robert's fate on 10 July seems far more comprehensible. He must have been seeking to redress his earlier humiliations and the chance encounter with both of his opponents in the Branne cabaret provided an opportunity that Robert seized by launching a verbal salvo. He accused Eyquart of suborning witnesses in the suit of 1784, an allegation that the merchant and minor judicial official could not fail to answer without risking his own honour and reputation as an honest trader and ethical court officer. Even the best legal scholars of the day, whose writings informed the sentencing practices of judges, recognised the gravity of such insults. In a legal treatise devoted entirely to the insult, one scholar defined it this way: 'We call an insult that which is spoken, written, or done with the intent of offending the honour, person, or property of someone.'[17] Indeed, as another scholar wrote, '... the insult, which attacks the honour, is much more acute to a man of position than that which attacks his body.'[18] And, by this standard, a third jurisconsult asserted that the gravity of the insult increased with the status of its victim.[19]

The gravity of Robert's allegations of subornation thus prompted Eyquart and his nephew to respond in kind, with a torrent of insults that drew upon an established repertoire of indignities, and then with slaps and punches. Indeed, the ritualised aspect of the vocabulary of the seventeenth- and eighteenth-century insult allows modern historians to distinguish several different levels of verbal attack.[20] At a most basic level were insults that were sexual in nature. Directed chiefly at women, epithets like 'slut' (*salope*), 'whore' (*putain*), 'bitch' (*garce*) and 'bugger' (*bougresse*) and allegations of pregnancy out of wedlock impugned the moral probity so central to female honour, while also diminishing the honour and reputation of the woman's male relatives. In one case in the Libournais, the wife of a maker of spurs was alleged to have been a prostitute who slept with men for small change (2 *liards*); clearly implicit in that charge was the suggestion that her husband was a cuckold.[21] A second group of insults, aimed at both men and women, alleged that those to whom they were directed were dishonest, generally a 'thief' (*voleur*), a 'scoundrel' (*gueux, drôle, maraud*), a 'knave' (*coquin*), a 'swindler' (*fripon*) or a 'bankrupt' (*banqueroutier*), all insults designed to erode confidence in the honesty of a person. Finally, very specific allegations of professional incompetence were directed at apothecaries, physicians, attorneys and others who drew their social standing and livelihoods from the learned professions.[22] The outcome of these insults and the accompanying assault was another court case at Libourne that resulted in no verdict, a typical outcome in such trials, as we will see.

The actions of Robert, Eyquart, Bonneau and persons like them in these cases thus were hardly random. Carefully chosen insults and generally non-lethal violence were typical of incidents like this all over France and, as such, have a ritualised character to them. While most of these confrontations resulted from chance encounters, they were staged in a sense. The presence of an audience magnified the humiliation of the victim, even while it stood ready to intervene if matters got out of hand. Neither the audience nor the principals in cases of assault and insults, however, wanted such events to descend into endless cycles of ritualised attacks and counterattacks.[23] The solution lay in judicial and infrajudicial modes of dispute resolution to compel the parties to re-establish the social equilibrium upset by something like a casual jest.

Prosecution of popular violence

The ongoing conflict between Robert, Eyquart and Bonneau represented a rend in the fabric of human relations that demanded a repair comprised of two elements: restoration of the victim's honour and compensation for his medical expenses, time lost from employment and other damages stemming from the assault. These ends could be achieved through judicial action. Court verdicts routinely offered assault victims financial compensation for their expenses and remedy for humiliation in the judicial validation of their charges. Frequently, too, there were more tangible expressions of the assailant's defeat. In eighteenth-century Rouen, for example, judgments in cases like those of Robert required the posting of the verdict in public places and, occasionally, a formal act of contrition by the convicted assailant in front of the cathedral.[24] But formal judicial action was not the automatic response of many seventeenth- and eighteenth-century victims of violence. Such reticence in pursuing the route of legal redress was not the result of their unfamiliarity with legal processes. While modern scholars sometimes find perplexing the welter of some 70,000 or 80,000 tribunals operating in seventeenth- and eighteenth-century France, it seems clear that when the need arose, even illiterate peasants knew how, in the words of one French scholar, to 'play the law as a musician plays an instrument'.[25] Rather, there were significant disincentives to reporting offences and to seeking a trial; these have prompted one knowledgeable scholar to suggest that, quite possibly, the majority of criminal offences never came to the attention of the authorities.[26]

Historical research in various rural and urban locales suggests that victims sought legal redress only under conditions largely defined by local social and cultural realities. Indeed, the temptation to do nothing at all in response to violence must have been considerable. Religious considerations must have caused some to hesitate; traditional Christian teaching, after all, emphasised forgiveness. Furthermore, the plaintiff's neighbours did not welcome being drawn into the machinery of royal justice. The rural community, like the *quartiers* of many cities, was a rather closed world in which pursuit of a neighbour in law raised a number of difficulties for plaintiffs. Friends and relatives of the defendant might exact physical retribution on the plaintiff, while neighbours, less immediately interested in the crime but still disapproving of its victim's recourse to outside authority, might simply adhere to an unwritten code of silence when called to testify in court. Early modern judges were well familiar with witnesses who swore under oath that they neither heard nor saw anything pertinent to a case at law, despite the fact that, in the largely aural and visual culture of their communities, residents knew everyone else's affairs. Thus assault victims probably tolerated much before an assailant transgressed an unstated and mutable threshold of violence. A number of factors defined that threshold, and the character of the assailant was one of the most important. While cases of assault and insults largely represented conflicts between proximate social equals, it was far easier to take a marginal member of society to court than a respected figure. Thus a victim's threshold of tolerance was quite low if an assault was the work of a non-resident, an indigent or a person of diminished mental capacity. Such persons had little local standing, scant capacity to sustain a formal legal proceeding, and could be prosecuted at relatively low cost. By the same standards, a person of status equal to or higher than that of his victim, possessed of wealth and a large circle of associates, would be less likely to be the object of a complaint. The associates of such a person could make the plaintiff's life difficult, as Jean Bonneau had on 10 June 1785, and his resources could make a suit against him costly indeed.

A second determining factor was the circumstances of the assault. Law and custom both admitted alcohol abuse as a mitigating factor in criminal liability, and the inebriation of an assailant could forestall criminal charges. Moreover, because intemperate speech and a ready recourse to violence characterised much of daily life in this society, there had to have been a certain popular tolerance of behaviour that even seventeenth- and eighteenth-century elites were coming to view as quite aberrant. Nevertheless, a particularly violent, humiliating or public incident, like that Robert believed he endured, could overcome the hesitations of a victim to prosecute. But recourse to royal justice presented its own risks to plaintiffs like Robert and that also must have given him further pause.[27]

The law relegated low-grade violence like that he sustained on 10 June and 10 July to a category of offences, *injures* (assault was an *injure réelle*, while insults were simply *injures*), that posed insufficient danger to the order of which the king was guarantor to warrant prosecution at the expense of the royal domain. Indeed, the royal prosecutor at Libourne pursued only one in four of all reported offences in our samples from the period 1696 to 1789, and these were only the most grave in that official's view. They included homicide, late seventeenth- and early eighteenth-century Protestant religious dissent, offences by the dreaded vagabonds and thefts that posed signal threats to the social order, like those from churches, pilfering by domestic servants or stealing that suggested the work of a professional criminal.[28] Thus an assault victim like Robert would have had to press criminal charges, making him the *partie civile*, or prosecutor, in the case. This status encumbered him with full court costs that only could be recovered, along with medical expenses and compensation for his injuries, from the defendant upon the latter's conviction. If the court acquitted the defendant, the plaintiff sustained the costs. The full extent of these expenses largely depended on the manner in which the plaintiff chose to pursue his case, and Old Regime law provided two options in royal courts.

The plaintiff could pursue the case at the civil or ordinary level, despite the criminal nature of the offence; Old Regime law drew few of the distinctions between civil and criminal litigation common today and left the essential definition of the case up to the plaintiff. Procedurally, this was an accusatory proceeding in which plaintiff and defendant orally confronted each other, generally with legal counsel, in a public courtroom; such procedures generated scant written record. Chiefly at stake in such cases was the honour of the defendant and the civil damages for which he would be liable should he lose. A verdict in such cases could be expeditious, and in various court districts might result in relatively modest damages, court costs and perhaps an apology by the guilty party to put to rest the contest over honour that was at the root of such cases. But these proceedings left the plaintiff with all costs if the court ruled in the defendant's favour, and this reality must have deterred some assault victims from going to law.[29]

The other procedural route that a plaintiff could choose was even riskier. This was to seek a criminal judgment against the defendant, as Robert chose to do. Judges conducted criminal trials with inquisitorial procedure, that is in a closed courtroom with none of the oral interchange common in civil or ordinary procedure. The defendant faced his accusers and confronted witnesses without legal counsel, as the court scribe prepared a detailed written record of interrogations and witnesses' testimonies. Plaintiffs like Robert generally retained legal counsel, especially for assistance in crafting a complaint designed to cast his position in the best possible light while sullying the character of the defendant and undermining his justifications of his actions. The effect of this work is evident in the cases in which both parties filed complaints; their opposing versions of their encounters are almost unrecognisable as the same events. Indeed, complaints contained a good deal of the 'fiction in the archives' that Natalie Z. Davis identified in pardon requests.[30]

The judicial response to a complaint was a hearing (*information*) with witnesses testifying under oath in the absence of the defendant, followed by an interrogation of the defendant and a decision by the court as to whether the evidence warranted further criminal proceedings. A negative decision might end the matter at this juncture or prompt the plaintiff to pursue his charges at the civil or ordinary level. A positive decision elicited an extraordinary decree that moved the court to a second hearing of witnesses (*récolement*), at which the defendant had his first opportunity to challenge their sworn testimonies. Judgment then followed, as did automatic appeal to a higher court of any verdict specifying execution, corporal punishment or any penalty carrying public humiliation.[31]

Such inquisitorial proceedings could be protracted and therefore very expensive; indeed the financial stakes were high for both plaintiff and defendant if the case extended to a final verdict. Mounting rapidly as a trial dragged on were fees for the court, scribes and their supplies, *huissiers* to summon witnesses, reimbursement of witnesses for their time in testifying and troopers of the Maréchaussée (mounted police) to convey the accused to his appeal proceeding in another town. Plaintiffs incurred all of these costs if the court did not sustain their charges, in addition to such damages as the court might award to the acquitted defendant. In Rouen trials for assault and insults, court costs could range as high as 400 *livres*; the Libourne judges ordered one *partie civile* in a minor assault case to pay 150 *livres* damages.[32] But the risks did not end here. This was a criminal trial, and Old Regime law left wide latitude to judges in sentencing. A successful plaintiff, seeking to humiliate his opponent while recouping court costs and damages from him, thus could find judges ordering much more than he wanted. An unduly harsh verdict, like that in one Libourne assault case in which judges ordered a convicted merchant and his wife to pay damages and court costs of 6,000 *livres*, won the plaintiff no friends in his local community.[33]

Not only was royal justice fraught with these perils, however; it also was often inaccessible. In the main, its tribunals were in the larger provincial centres accessible to rural residents only after considerable travel over roads that could be almost impassable for much of the year. Simply lodging a complaint with such courts required a very determined plaintiff able to afford to lose time from his work. In addition, royal authorities lacked sufficient police resources to apprehend lawbreakers efficiently, to enforce their decisions and to protect plaintiffs from retribution by defendants' families and friends. The Maréchaussée had only 4,114 effectives in 1789 to police a kingdom of 25,000,000 persons, and its Bordeaux division, which policed an area of some 25,000 km² including the Libourne area, marshalled only 111 officers and men in 1780.[34]

The potential perils of royal procedure prompted many aggrieved parties to seek other modes of dispute resolution. In some parts of France, there were other judicial institutions that might assist in resolving the disputes that produced assaults. In Paris, for example, the 48 neighbourhood *commissaries* of the Lieutenant Generalcy of Police, nominally charged with initiating the investigation of crimes, also served as neighbourhood arbiters who provided dispute resolution short of a formal trial. Thus one of these officials defused a potentially nasty incident in which a local dog's aggressiveness led to an angry exchange between its owner and a neighbour; he simply laid the matter to rest by ordering the dog confined and the neighbours to speak civilly to each other.[35] In some rural areas, like the countryside of Burgundy, seigneurial courts still functioned very well and provided an accessible, quick and respected mode of resolving disputes with inexpensive, oral civil proceedings. And prior to the Revocation of the Edict of Nantes in 1685, Protestant consistories also played a very important role in accommodating disputes among their communicants and in disciplining members who refused to live in peace. But most Frenchmen did not enjoy access to such modes of dispute resolution; the seigneurial courts of parts of the southwest, for example, were quite ineffective by the eighteenth century.[36] Thus many turned to infrajudicial modes of dispute resolution that functioned alongside the king's justice and often complemented it.

In doing so they sought a peaceful compromise of their disputes, more quickly and cheaply than by judicial action, in recognition of the ironic French saying that 'A bad settlement is better than a good trial.'

Infrajudicial resolutions of disputes are far more difficult for historians to study than the criminal events and trial verdicts systematically recorded in court records. Some settlements were quite informal and left no written records. Others produced written records filed in innumerable notarial offices, making them difficult to study in any systematic way.[37] Nevertheless, we now know that many seventeenth- and eighteenth-century Frenchmen attempted infrajudicial dispute resolution in large measure because of their concern about the costs that accrued when criminal courts judicially resolved disputes. Indeed, residents of both rural and urban France seem to have initiated criminal charges primarily as a means to confront their assailants with the potential costs of litigation and thus force them to reach out-of-court settlements. This is evident in the large number of cases for assault and insults that ended after an initial hearing and the defendant's interrogation. Two out of the three cases involving Robert never reached a verdict, and in that respect they were entirely typical of this sort of litigation. In the Sénéchaussée of Libourne only 2.8 per cent of cases for assault and insult reached verdicts; in the eighteenth-century Bailliage of Mamers that figure was 7 per cent, while in the seventeenth-century court of Saint-Germain-des-Prés it was less than 1 per cent.[38] Technically legal as a settlement for only minor crimes, the sudden accommodation ending litigation was not unknown even in serious cases. Judges, indeed, facilitated it, and one magistrate in the rural Bordelais counselled a friend charged with assault and theft to 'pay money ... and everything will be settled.'[39] But money was not everything in these matters; honour remained an important issue.

At a most basic level, it seems clear that principals in cases like those of Robert simply resolved their differences privately, without any reference to a third party. This mode of dispute resolution left almost no records, but probably included a payment for damages and at least a discreet apology by the assailant to assuage his victim's honour. Better documented are settlements mediated by third parties, either prior to a trial or during litigation as all involved sought to limit their financial exposure. Settlement negotiations often opened with a ritual gesture by the assailant in extending an offer to his victim's family to assume financial responsibility for all of the damage that he had inflicted. This served notice that the assailant was ready for an infrajudicial resolution of the dispute and opened the way for negotiations over the selection of a mediator and eventually terms setting the amount of damages due the victim. These also might include a public apology to lay to rest offences to the victim's honour.[40]

Eighteenth-century legal scholars provided guidance in this process, and Joseph-Nicolas Guyot advised that 'kindly arbitrators' (*amiables compositeurs*) could be almost any male of sound mind and even, perhaps, women of exalted station.[41] With such a broad field from which to choose, Frenchmen rather consistently looked to Roman Catholic clerics, respected aristocrats, prominent members of the bourgeoisie and figures knowledgeable in the law like judges, attorneys and notaries. Jurisconsults maintained that such mediators had the same power as judges to impose settlements if necessary and offered their readers model accords to which could be added details specific to an individual dispute. In much of French society, accommodations, couched in the legal metaphors of these model settlements and signed by both sides in a dispute, were then filed with notaries to assume the legal status of a contract.[42] Failure to adhere to the agreement thus had the potential to open the assailant to additional legal action for breach of contract. The poor followed an analogous process, without official status, in which they concluded settlements in front of witnesses to avoid notarial fees.

Robert, Eyquart and Bonneau doubtlessly resolved their difference infrajudicially. Their social and economic status suggests that their mediator probably filed a copy of a written settlement with a notary, but none has yet been found. Even without such definitive resolution, however, their cabaret brawl opens much of their world to the modern researcher. The product of an ostensibly violent society, their fight emerges as a calculated event, a ritual involving honour and standing. Its probable mode of settlement tells us much about their attitudes toward the law, too. These Frenchmen viewed the law as simply one part of a complex, and complementary, range of options for dispute resolution, which also included infrajudicial solutions. Many historians have portrayed this infrajudicial dispute resolution, with its reliance on compensation rather than penalty, as an anachronism, the survival of essentially medieval practices that were being pushed aside by the growing institutions of royal justice. The case of Robert and his neighbours, however, reveals that royal institutions and infrajudicial practices hardly were in conflict; they were complementary. Frenchmen like these men of the rural Bordealais knew how to pragmatically work the law, in conjunction with mediation, to restore peace in their relations. The habits we have observed, in fact, were so deeply rooted in French society that, when the Revolution destroyed the entire edifice of Old Regime justice a mere half decade after Robert's altercation, the infrajudicial resolution of disputes not only survived but became institutionalised. Answering the demands of Frenchmen for more accessible and affordable justice, the National Assembly's Law of 16–24 August 1790 established three figures to resolve minor disputes like those of Robert. First, the law formally recognised Guyot's 'kindly arbitrator', a third party trusted by disputants to broker a non-judicial resolution of their differences. Second, the law created justices of the peace – elected, salaried officials, generally without formal legal education, whose primary function also was to mediate disputes infrajudicially. Only when these first two figures failed to resolve disputes would a case like Robert's proceed to the third figure recognised by the legislation, a judge presiding over a court of law.[43]

Notes

1 Archives départementales de la Gironde (hereinafter abbreviated as ADG), Sous-série 5B675 (Le fonds de la Sénéchaussée et siège présidiale de Libourne): 'Plainte et information à la requette de Mathieu Robert, tonnelier, contre le nommé Eyquart ...', 13 July 1785.
2 The modern historical study of French criminal records began with the students of Pierre Chaunu at the University of Caen, especially Bernadette Boutelet, 'Étude par sondage de la criminalité dans le bailliage de Pont-de-l'Arche (XVIIᵉ–XVIIIᵉ siècles),' *Annales du Normandie*, 12 (1962), 253–62, and with André Abbiateci et al., *Crimes et criminalité en France sous l'Ancien Régime, 17ᵉ-18ᵉ siècles* (Paris: Librairie Armand Colin, 1971).
3 On these varieties of violence, see: Julius R. Ruff, *Violence in Early Modern Europe, 1500–1800* (Cambridge: Cambridge University Press, 2001); Julie Hardwick, 'Early Modern Perspectives on the Long History of Domestic Violence: The Case of Seventeenth- and Eighteenth-Century France', *Journal of Modern History*, 78 (2006), 1–36; James R. Farr, *Authority and Sexuality in Early Modern Burgundy, 1550–1730* (New York: Oxford University Press, 1995); Cynthia A. Bouton, *The Flour War: Gender, Class, and Community in Late Ancien Régime Society* (University Park, PA: Pennsylvania State University Press, 1993); Frédérique Pitou, 'Jeunesse et désordre social: les coureurs de nuit à Laval au XVIIIᵉ siècle', *Revue d'histoire moderne et contemporaine*, 47 (2000), 69–92; Natalie Z. Davis, *Society and Culture in Early Modern France* (Stanford, CA: Stanford University Press, 1975), 97–123; and Olwen Hufton, *The Poor of*

Eighteenth-Century France (Oxford: Oxford University Press, 1974), 266–83. Greg T. Smith's contribution to the present volume, 'Violent Crime and the Public Weal in England, 1700–1900', demonstrates the quotidian character of early modern violence and its functions in another national context.

4 Fundamental on duelling are François Billacois, *Le duel dans la société française des XVIe–XVIIIe siècles. Essai de psychologie historique* (Paris: Éditions de l'École des Hautes Études en Sciences Sociales, 1986) and Pascal Brioist, Hervé Drévillon and Pierre Serna, *Croiser le fer: Violence et culture de l'épée dans la France moderne (XVIe–XVIIIe siècle)* (Seyssel: Champ Vallon, 2002).

5 Julius R. Ruff, *Crime, Justice and Public Order in Old Regime France: The Sénéchaussées of Libourne and Bazas, 1696–1789* (London: Croom Helm, 1984), 70; Françoise Bayard, 'Porter plainte à Lyon aux XVIIe et XVIIIe siècles,' in Benoît Garnot (ed.), *Les victims, les oubliées de l'histoire* (Rennes: Presses universitaires de Rennes, 2000), 170.

6 Benoît Garnot, *Justice et société en France aux XVIe, XVIIe et XVIIIe siècles* (Gap: Éditions Orphrys, 2000), 44; Gregory Hanlon, 'Les rituels de l'agression en Aquitaine au XVIIe siècle', *Annales: Économies, Sociétés, Civilisations*, 50 (1985), 244–68; and Hugues Lecharnay, 'L'injure à Paris au XVIIIe siècle: Un aspect de la violence au quotidien', *Revue d'histoire moderne et contemporaine*, 36 (1989), 559–85.

7 Ruff, *Crime, Justice and Public Order*, 85–7.

8 Benoît Garnot, 'La violence et ses limites dans la France du XVIIIe siècle: l'exemple bourguignon', *Revue historique*, 298, 606 (1998), 250; and Philip Uninsky, 'Violence, Honor, and Litigation: *Injures et voies de fait* in Pre-Revolutionary France', *New York University Journal of International Law and Politics*, 23 (1991), 867–904.

9 Yves Castan, *Honnêteté et relations sociales en Languedoc, 1715–1780* (Paris: Librairie Plon, 1974), 13–14. For an excellent brief presentation of these issues, see Steven G. Reinhardt, *Justice in the Sarladais, 1770–1790* (Baton Rouge, LA: Louisiana State University Press, 1991), 161–88.

10 Martin Dinges, *Der Mauermeister und der Finanzrichter: Ehre, Geld und soziale Kontrolle im Paris des 18. Jahrhunderts* (Göttingen: Vandenhoeck & Ruprecht, 1994), 178.

11 ADG, 5B675: Plainte et information à la requette de Mathieu Robert, tonnelier, contre le nommé Bonneau, père et fils, la femme dudit Bonneau et Joseph leur bordier ..., 11 June 1785.

12 Reinhardt, *Justice in the Sarladais*, 165, 170–1.

13 Ruff, *Crime, Justice and Public Order*, 78.

14 Ibid., 70; Arlette Farge and André Zysberg, 'Les théâtres de la violence à Paris au XVIIIe siècle', *Annales: Économies, Sociétés, Civilisations*, 39 (1979), 1007, found that in 1765 and 1770 about 69 per cent of all reported Parisian assaults involved no weapons. On homicide, see Frédéric Piegay, 'Les crimes de sang en Lyonnais et Beaujolais aux XVIIe et XVIIIe

siècles', in Benoît Garnot (ed.), *Histoire et criminalité de l'antiquité au XXe siècle: Nouvelles approches* (Dijon: Éditions universitaires de Dijon, 1992), 273–81.

15 On cabarets, see: Thomas E. Brennan, *Public Drinking and Popular Culture in Eighteenth-Century Paris* (Princeton, NJ: Princeton University Press, 1988) and Christine Plessix-Buisset, 'La délinquance dans les auberges en Bretagne au XVIIIe siècle', *Mémoires de la Société d'histoire et d'archéologie de Bretagne*, 73 (72) (1995), 177–94.

16 Hanlon, 'Les rituels de l'agression en Aquitaine', 255.

17 François Dareau, *Traité des injures dans l'ordre judiciaire, ouvrage qui renferme particulairement la jurisprudence du Petit Criminel* (Paris: Prault, père, 1775), i, 1–7.

18 Claude-Joseph Ferrière, *Dictionnaire de droit et de pratique* (Paris: Brunet, 1755), ii, 215.

19 Daniel Jousse, *Traité de la justice criminelle de France* (Paris: Debure, père, 1771), iii, 579.

20 On the vocabulary of the insult, see: Garnot, 'La violence et ses limites', 239; David Garrioch, 'Verbal Insults in Eighteenth-Century Paris', in Peter Burke and Roy Porter (eds), *The Social History of Language* (Cambridge: Cambridge University Press, 1987), 104–213; and Nicole Dyonet, 'Gestes et paroles de la vie quotidienne au XVIIIe siècle. Les resources des archives judiciaries', in Yves-Marie Bercé and Yves Castan (eds), *Les archives du délit: empreintes de société* (Toulouse: Éditions universitaires du Sud, 1990), 2945.

21 Examples from the following ADG *liasses*, listed by the plaintiff's name and the date of the complaint: 5B662 (Elizabeth Sabatier, 9 July 1770; Jeanne Lavigne, 27 July 1770); 5B666 (Jeanne Guillot, 28 June 1774); 5B676 (Françoise de Loubis, 5–10 August 1786).

22 Examples from the following ADG *liasses*, listed by the plaintiff's name and the date of the complaint: 5B633 (Pierre Bolay, 9 June 1741); 5B634 (Lardeau, 12 March 1742); 5B665 (André Pujol, 24 August 1773); 5B666 (Mayor and Jurats of Saint-Émilion, 9 May 1774); 5B667 (Jean Prade, 28 January 1775); 5B668 (Joseph Laveau, 28 June 1776); 5B676 (Pierre Brun, 18 July 1786); 5B679 (Arnaud Mathieu, 17 January 1789; Pierre Berthonneau, 28 February 1789).

23 Hanlon, 'Les rituels de l'agression en Aquitaine', 245.

24 Uninsky, 'Violence, Honor, and Litigation', 892.

25 François Billacois, 'Clio chez Thémis', in 'Porter plainte: strategies villageoises et institutions judiciaires en Ile-de-France (XVIIe–XVIIIe siècles)', *Droit et cultures*, 19 (1990), 10; and Garnot, *Justice et société*, 117.

26 Garnot, *Justice et société*, 22.

27 Ruff, *Crime, Justice and Public Order*, 11, 99–103; Garnot, *Justice et société*, 22–8; and on evolving behavioural standards, Robert Muchembled, *L'invention de l'homme moderne; sensibilités, moeurs et comportements collectifs sous l'Ancien Régime* (Paris: Fayard, 1988).

28 Ruff, *Crime, Justice and Public Order*, 45–7. On the law, see Pierre-François Muyart de Vouglans, *Les lois criminelles de la France dans leur ordre naturel* … (Paris: Chez Merigot le jeune, 1780), 353.

29 Uninsky, 'Violence, Honor, and Litigation', 872.

30 Natalie Z. Davis, *Fiction in the Archives: Pardon Tales and Their Tellers in Sixteenth-Century France* (Stanford, CA: Stanford University Press, 1987), 36–76. On the art of the criminal complaint: Catharine Ditte, 'La mise en scène dans la plainte: sa stratégie sociale. L'exemple de l'honneur populaire', in 'Porter plainte', *Droit et cultures*, 19 (1990), 23–48; Martin Dinges, 'L'art de se présenter comme victime auprès du commissaire de Police au XVIIIᵉ siècle: un aspect des usages de la justice', in Garnot, *Les victimes*, 141–3; and Frédérique Pitou, 'Violence et discours au XVIIIᵉ siècle: "Si je ne t'aimerais pas je te tuerais tout à fait …"', *Annales de Bretagne et des Pays de l'Ouest*, 105 (1998), 9–16. For an example of dual complaints in the same incident, see ADG, 5B623 (Philippe Coste and Jacques Lacoste, 11 December 1739).

31 Richard Mowery Andrews, *Law, Magistracy, and Crime in Old Regime Paris, 1735–1789* (Cambridge: Cambridge University Press, 1994), i, 422–93.

32 ADG, 5B700, 5B109, 5B241 (Pierre Lanouzin, 29 October 1781); Uninsky, 'Violence, Honor, and Litigation', 893.

33 ADG, 5B701 (Jeanne Bertrand, 30 September 1784).

34 Julius R. Ruff, 'Law and Order in Eighteenth-Century France: The Maréchaussée of Guyenne', *Proceedings of the Western Society for French History*, 4 (1976), 174–81; Nicole Castan, 'La justice expéditive,' *Annales: Économies, Sociétés, Civilisations*, 31 (1976), 347.

35 Martin Dinges, 'Négocier son honneur dans le peuple parisien au XVIIIᵉ siècle: la rue, "l'infrajudiciaire" et la justice', in Benoît Garnot (ed.), *L'infrajudiciare de Moyen Age à l'époque contemporaine* (Dijon: Éditions universitaires de Dijon, 1996), 397.

36 Jeremy Hayhoe, 'Neighbours Before the Court: Crime, Village Communities and Seigneurial Justice in Northern Burgundy, 1750–1790', *French History*, 17 (2003), 127–48; Anthony Crubaugh, *Balancing the Scales of Justice: Local Courts and Rural Society in Southwest France, 1750–1800* (University Park, PA: Pennsylvania State University Press, 2001); and Didier Poton, 'Le consistoire protestant au XVIIᵉ siècle: un tribunal des moeurs', in Benoît Garnot (ed.), *Ordre moral et délinquance de l'antiquité au XXᵉ siècle* (Dijon: Éditions universitaires de Dijon, 1994), 411–17.

37 The seminal work on infrajudicial dispute resolution was that of Nicole Castan, *Justice et répression en Languedoc à l'époque des Lumières* (Paris: Flammarion, 1980) and Alfred Soman, 'Deviance and Criminal Justice in Western Europe, 1300–1800: An Essay in Structure', *Criminal Justice History*, 1 (1980), 1–28. Here, again, the chapter by Greg T. Smith, 'Violent Crime and the Commonweal in England, 1700–1900', is instructive, showing the similar tendency of early modern Englishmen to avoid criminal litigation.

38 Martin Dinges, 'The Uses of Justice as a Form of Social Control in Early Modern Europe', in Herman Roodenburg and Pieter Spierenburg (eds), *Social Control in Europe, Vol. I* (Columbus, OH: Ohio State University Press, 2004), 162–4; Ruff, *Crime, Justice and Public Order*, 46; Alain Margot, 'La criminalité dans le bailliage de Mamers (1695–1750)', *Annales du Normandie*, 22 (1972), 185–224; Bruno Isbled, 'Le recours à la justice à Saint-Germain-des-Prés au milieu du XVIIe', in Bercé and Castan, *Les archives du délit*, 66–8.

39 Quoted in Iain Cameron, *Crime and Repression in the Auvergne and the Guyenne, 1720–1790* (Cambridge: Cambridge University Press, 1981), 192.

40 Garnot, *Justice et société*, 88–91.

41 Joseph-Nicolas Guyot, *Répertoire universel et raisonné de jurisprudence civile, criminelle, canonique et bénéficiale ...*, Nouvelle éd. (Paris: Visse, 1784): 'Arbitrages', 'Arbitres', I, 544–60.

42 Castan, *Justice et repression*, 26–47.

43 Jacques Godechot, *Les institutions de la France sous la Révolution et l'Empire*, 2nd edn (Paris: Presses Universitaires de France, 1968), 146–8. Recent important work on the justices of the peace include Anthony Crubaugh, *Balancing the Scales of Justice* and Jacques-Guy Petit (dir.), *Une justice de proximité: la justice de la paix (1790–1958)* (Paris: Presses Universitaires de France, 2003).

Further reading

In addition to the works listed in the notes for this chapter, the following is a list of studies which employ criminal justice records as an entry into the culture and society of seventeenth- and eighteenth-century France:

Claverie, Elisabeth and Pierre Lamaison (1982) *L'impossible mariage: violence et parenté en Gévaudan: XVIe, XVIIe, XVIIIe siècles.* Paris: Hachette.

Farge, Arlette (1993) *Fragile Lives: Violence, Power and Solidarity in Eighteenth-Century Paris*, trans. Carol Shelton. Cambridge, MA: Harvard University Press.

Farr, James M. (1995) *Authority and Sexuality in Early Modern Burgundy.* Oxford: Oxford University Press.

Farr, James M. (2005) *A Tale of Two Murders: Passion and Power in Seventeenth-Century France.* Durham, NC: Duke University Press.

Garrioch, David (1986) *Neighbourhood and Community in Paris, 1740–1790.* Cambridge: Cambridge University Press.

Greenshields, Malcolm (1994) *An Economy of Violence in Early Modern France: Crime and Justice in the Haute Auvergne, 1587–1664.* University Park, PA: Pennsylvania State University Press.

Hanlon, Gregory (1989) *L'univers des gens de bien: culture et comportements des élites urbaines en Agenais-Condomois au XVIIe siècle.* Bordeaux: Presses universitaires de Bordeaux.

Heichette, Michel (2005) *Société, sociabilité, justice: Sablé et son pays au XVIIIe*. Rennes: Presses universitaires de Rennes.

Muir, Edward (1979) *Ritual in Early Modern Europe*. Cambridge: Cambridge University Press.

Chapter 2

The containment of violence in Central European cities, 1500–1800

Joachim Eibach[1]

This article focuses on the role of violence and its containment in the cities of Central Europe between 1500 and 1800. It is possible to identify considerable continuity in both the incidence and prosecution of violence during this time. Violent ways of settling interpersonal conflicts were over the course of this period never fully rejected by all town-dwellers. There were substantial numbers of fist fights, violent assaults, manslaughters and murders in the sixteenth, seventeenth and eighteenth centuries. Throughout this period the prosecution of violent crime was also largely a joint venture between the ruling authorities of the cities and their citizens. Both sides were needed for and contributed to the containment of violence. There were, however, also significant changes in both the role of violence and in the manner in which it was dealt with. The authorities began to take a more active role and adopted a more interventionist stance in the prosecution of violent crime. They became increasingly reluctant to leave the settlement of violent conflict to the adversaries, their families or guilds to settle in a 'private' manner. The social composition of the perpetrators of violent acts also changed considerably. While men from all social backgrounds in the late Middle Ages engaged in violent disputes, by the eighteenth century the higher orders of town society had largely withdrawn from such activity and relied, to a large degree, on the courts to resolve disputes. The manner in which violent acts were carried out also altered as ritual practices surrounding violent acts came under increasing scrutiny and attack from the authorities.

Through an investigation of the interplay of continuity and change, this article seeks to illuminate the role of violence and its control in the cities of Central Europe in the early modern period. It looks at how the character and practice of violence evolved and how the authorities both drove and responded to such changes. It also demonstrates how even if the sentences of the courts became more punitive during the sixteenth and again during the eighteenth centuries, they still depended on the participation of the inhabitants to maintain order and urban stability.

The historiography of crime in German-speaking countries

To begin, it may be fruitful to explore how these developments, and the themes they evoke, fit into the wider historiography of crime and criminal justice in the German-speaking countries. The historiography of crime in Germany (and also in Switzerland and Austria) has its own distinctive history. Unlike England and the USA where crime history became an acknowledged subdiscipline in the 1970s during the heyday of social history, crime and criminal justice history in Germany were, until some 20 years ago, studied within the confines of traditional legal history. The focus was very much on the development of the criminal code and the penal system or on the reflections on the criminal law by jurists, such as Benedict Carpzov or Cesare Beccaria. The actual practice of the criminal courts constituted only a minor aspect of legal historical research.

Social history and crime history in Germany did have a brief encounter in the mid-1970s, when two monographs on robber bands and property crimes were published. Both authors were inspired by earlier Western European research, especially the English approach to 'social crime' pioneered by Douglas Hay and E.P. Thompson among others. Carsten Küther claimed that organised robbers shared popular notions of right and wrong and drew on support from the peasantry. Dirk Blasius showed that the prosecution of property crimes served the interests of the Prussian ruling classes: old landowners and the new bourgeoisie.[2] When Blasius compared statistics relating to petty theft with corn prices, he applied the methods of crime history which were developed in the classic era of social history.

After this start in 1976, crime history in Germany lay largely dormant for more than a decade. One could almost say that social history in German-speaking countries ignored crime and criminal justice history. There were some monographs on eighteenth-century poverty and vagrancy but these did not really focus on crime. In the field of early modern urban history, the contentious political constitution of towns and collective rebellions by the citizens against town councils were the preferred topics.[3]

From the early 1990s onwards, however, a younger generation of historians began to discover criminal justice records. Within a short period of time the hitherto neglected criminal and judicial records of German-speaking cities became subjects of intense investigation. The examination of the minutes of court sessions proved to be an excellent source for looking at aspects of everyday life ('Alltag' or 'Lebenswelt') in order to identify common ideas, experiences, symbolic practices and the agency of the 'faces in the crowd'. This development, not by chance, coincided with the challenge to 'classic' social history from the so-called new cultural history.[4] Many scholars, in Germany and elsewhere, found it unsatisfactory to base their arguments on evidence from quantitative material alone. Quantitative methods, favoured by many crime historians in Western Europe and the USA during the reign of social history, although not completely dismissed, were regarded with some suspicion. Micro-history became the dominant approach within German crime historiography.

The study of interpersonal violence in many ways reflects the distinctive development of crime and criminal justice history in German-speaking countries. For a long time, the debate on the role of violence in Western Europe was based solely on the analysis of homicide rates, which were taken as evidence of the validity of Norbert Elias's theory of a civilising process. On the basis of quantitative data from England, compiled by Ted R. Gurr, Lawrence Stone in 1983 stated that 'medieval English society was twice as violence-prone as early modern English society, and early modern English society at least five times more violence-prone than contemporary English society'.[5] In his response to Stone, J.A. Sharpe pointed to the importance of the 'qualitative' aspects of violent activity. Since then the 'social meaning of violence'[6] has become increasingly relevant in historical studies of violence. Robert Shoemaker has argued that the perception of violence changed drastically in eighteenth-century London. The decline of male public violence was, according to Shoemaker, fuelled by 'new understandings of masculinity' and the changing construction of honour in urban society.[7]

The investigation of the social and cultural meaning of violence has also been central in much of the German historiography of crime in recent years. In particular, the role of ritual and honour in shaping violent conflicts has become a significant theme. The examination of ritual and honour has considerably widened our knowledge about the 'how' and 'why' of violence. It has also triggered some lively debates, most notably the exchange between Pieter Spierenburg and Gerd Schwerhoff which centred on the 'highly ritualised dramaturgy' and the 'language of honour' which can often be observed in violent conflicts.[8] On the whole, we are now far better informed about the use of violence than some twenty years ago. There is also a better understanding of how early modern criminal justice systems actually worked. This is especially so for courts in urban areas, which have been prominent in the German and Swiss research.

Contexts

This article will focus mainly on findings from the criminal records of Zurich, Basle, Constance, Nuremberg, Augsburg, Cologne and Frankfurt am Main. The presence of criminal courts in these cities and towns reflected an early stage in a wider process of state formation ('Obrigkeitsbildung') and were the product of fundamental politico-social processes in urban society from the fourteenth to sixteenth centuries. These towns and cities were, especially at the outset of the period under review, dynamic places enjoying considerable economic prosperity. Merchants and craftsmen, organised in guilds, dominated the urban economy. There was also increasing social differentiation within these areas. Social life was shaped by the right of citizenship, which provided its male holders and their families with certain privileges denied to outsiders and to other city-dwellers. Political life in these cities and towns was dominated by prominent, mostly patrician families who ruled over them through the town councils. Merchants and craftsmen, who drove the economy of these urban centres, could only rarely gain access to the highest political offices. In the sixteenth century, particularly during the Reformation, the imperial towns also held considerable political power within the Holy Roman Empire, although by the eighteenth century their political influence was clearly on the wane. These urban centres, whether imperial towns or city republics, also enjoyed considerable political autonomy at this time.[9] Such autonomy meant that the town councils were ultimately in charge of all issues relating to criminal justice.

It is in these large towns and cities that we first see the emergence of a court system that produced continuous records from its court sessions. Throughout the whole period, it was not necessary to study law to become a judge on one of the numerous town courts.

There was also no clear distinction, until well into the early modern period, between criminal and civil courts. The one court could deal with both civil and criminal litigation. From the late medieval period onwards, violence was a prominent cause of concern for the urban courts. At first sight, the judicial sources reveal the often significant role that violence played in the everyday life of these cities. The very existence of court records, in some towns as early as the fourteenth century, also proves the willingness of the town council to control violence and other kinds of deviant behaviour. The uncontrolled use of violence contradicted a fundamental value of the confraternity of all citizens: the maintenance of peace and urban stability.[10] However, as will be demonstrated in this article, besides prosecuting violence through the courts there were other ways and means of controlling violent behaviour. Both town statutes and the controlled and ritualised practice of violence itself, already evident during the late Middle Ages, reflected a clear willingness to control violence. Court proceedings also cannot be adequately understood as a pure top-to-bottom process wholly prompted by the state. Willing prosecutors from below were always needed in order to prosecute criminal behaviour.

Violence and its control

Town- and village-dwellers in the late Middle Ages often resorted to physical violence as a legitimate means of defending their honour and to practise social control over neighbours, guildsmen and alien people.[11] Fist and knife fights took place in the centres of urban life: on squares and piazzas, in public taverns and in the drinking clubs of corporations. Violence was not practised secretly but, on the contrary, was performed ostentatiously in public. Honour and its defence was not a private but a public affair, which served as a link between individual and collective aspirations. The honour of the guild or the brotherhood of journeymen depended on the honourable behaviour of each individual member while individual honour was always linked with the honour of the household, the confraternity or even the town as a whole.[12] Violence in public was also, until the sixteenth century at least, by no means a marginalised or stigmatised affair among townsfolk. Gerd Schwerhoff has summarised the research of recent years: 'Even and especially the elites, the nobility and the highest representatives of urban politics cultivated violent habits'.[13]

In fourteenth-century Zurich, for example, a rich patrician by the name of Chunrat Neisideller was frequently taken to court for violent assault and in one case for manslaughter. Neisideller also acted as a witness in some cases of knife fighting. He appears again and again in the court records of Zurich as offender, prosecutor and witness. The surprising aspect, as Susanna Burghartz points out, is that Neisideller, even after he had committed manslaughter, remained an honourable member of Zurich's town council.[14] Chunrat Neisideller was no exception. The patricians and wealthy citizens of fifteenth-century Constance figure more prominently than anyone else in the recorded cases of violent disputes. Chronicles from sixteenth-century Augsburg repeatedly reveal the drinking club of the patricians and wealthy merchants as common locations for male violence.[15] In Frankfurt's criminal records from the sixteenth century we find many cases of men from well-known families who were sued for violent assault, 'excess' in taverns or the wounding of other family members.[16] None were ever sentenced to capital or corporal punishment. In most cases, the only consequence was an arrest or monetary fine, which did not affect the honour of the perpetrator. The sentences of the courts seem to have corresponded with notions of the legitimate use of violence.

A general distinction between honourable and dishonourable killings was also prevalent in the towns of Germany and Switzerland in the late medieval period. Under certain conditions, manslaughter in order to defend one's honour was tolerated. In Zurich, for example, killings were judged honourable, if the perpetrator had responded spontaneously to clear provocation from his opponent. Killings taking place in a public space in full view of witnesses were generally not understood as murder. Murder by definition of Zurich's laws was a killing which was planned and executed secretly without giving the adversary a chance to react.[17] The families of victims could seek revenge by means of a blood feud or by seeking financial compensation. The sentences of the courts in manslaughter and murder cases accommodated popular notions and distinctions between legitimate and illegitimate violence. Manslaughter was sentenced with monetary fines, murderers in contrast faced capital punishment.

The courts took account of the needs of two deep-rooted systems of norms: on the one hand, the male code of honour, on the other, the fundamental values of peace and urban stability. If the perpetrator and the family of the victim found an extra-judicial arrangement to settle the conflict, the courts would not object and would relinquish their right to impose further punishment. The findings from Zurich are similar to those from fifteenth-century Constance and Nuremberg, where reconciliation was a prominent feature in the operation of the courts. In many cases, the authorities merely supervised the 'private' settlement of conflicts, even in cases of severe wounding and manslaughter.[18] Hence, some violent behaviour was accepted by both sides: the official court system and the citizens.

Arbitrary violence, violence that was performed secretly ('bei nacht und nebel'), from behind or with uneven weapons was, however, never tolerated.[19] Perpetrators were also likely to receive severe punishments if they appeared to be a constant danger to the peace of the town or city and especially if the community of citizens withdrew their support from them. In Berlin, in the second half of the fourteenth century, a journeyman by the name of Ekart Maler was beheaded because he had continuously committed breaches of the peace without sufficient cause. At first, Maler could present guarantors ('Bürgen'), who stood surety for him. His guarantors succeeded in their petition to have him released from the town tower. However, when Maler started to cause trouble in a tavern immediately after his release, his guarantors brought him back to the tower and he was eventually executed.[20] The case of this Berlin journeyman demonstrates how the cooperation of citizens and courts could work in practice in the late Middle Ages. Whether or not violent acts were penalised as criminal offences or merely regarded as a matter of conflict regulation was decided in a process of interaction between courts and citizens.[21]

The courts were by no means the only way of controlling and containing violence at this time. A high amount of registered offences does not necessarily mean that violence took on chaotic forms in the socio-cultural sphere and was only controlled by the courts. Craftsmen's guilds in the late Middle Ages played, for instance, an active and significant role in regulating the social conduct of their members. Guild statutes contain evidence for both the frequent use of violence by journeymen and masters, but also the wish to control it. They are full of demands to avoid swearing and insults in pubs, not to bring weapons to festivities, to pull knives, to kick down doors or to fight.[22] Much of the focus of such regulation was on the pub or tavern which was central to adult male sociability in the pre-modern town.[23] In the drinking clubs of guilds and confraternities we can observe a form of social control, which originally worked without intervention from the town council or an overlord.

The social control imposed by guilds provides a clear example of an older type of social discipline before the rise of modern state institutions. So far, due to the lack of sources, the practice of conflict regulation by guilds has not been a subject of intense research. According to Rudolf Wissell, a passionate collector and scholar of old guild traditions, most of these guild regulations date from the fifteenth, sixteenth and, to some extent, the seventeenth centuries.[24] Typical sanctions imposed on those who breached the informal rules and traditions of the guilds included scolding ('Schelten'), exclusion from the craft or monetary fines which were then used by the guild to pay for candles or beer. Large trades also kept 'black books', in which they recorded the names of offenders which were read during meetings. This procedure was repeated until the offenders paid their fines and reconciled themselves with the guild. Clearly, there were ways of dealing with deviant behaviour and containing violence before the development of a monopoly of power by the modern state or, in terms of urban politics, by the town council.

The manner in which violent acts were carried out also reveals the extent to which violent behaviour was controlled even as it was being performed. Moreover, it reflected a distinction between the legitimate and illegitimate use of violence. This is evident in one significant ritual that was prominent at the outset of the period under review: the so-called 'Ausfordern aus dem Haus' (challenging out of the house). An early study by the German ethnologist Karl-Sigismund Kramer and some scattered hints in the recent work of crime historians offer some insight into the practice and meaning of this ritual.[25] Kramer has collected cases from towns mainly in Southern Germany. In the judicial books of the small Swabian imperial town of Nördlingen in the years from 1550 to 1578 he found no less than 47 such cases.[26] The general character of this ritual is underlined by the fact that the same elements with corresponding social meanings occurred in different places. Among the offenders we find men and also women from all social strata of the towns.

Essential to the ritual was the calling of one's adversary out of his house in order to settle a conflict. This laid down a challenge to one's opponent according to accepted rules of honour. Still today, the literal meaning of the German word for challenge ('Herausforderung') is to call somebody out of something. This practice had the potential to lead to acts of violence, while at the same time controlling and channelling it. When performed in the right way, it respected the 'peace of the house' and the domestic sphere of the opponent and his family. The perpetrators remained outside the house and, at worst, attacked the door or windows of the house without actually entering it.[27] Thus the settlement of the dispute was situated in the public sphere in front of the house within the view of neighbours who could act as an audience or as referees.

According to Kramer, there were four stages to this ritual.[28] The opening act was the approach of the challenger towards the house of the opponent. In most cases, the challenger appeared armed often in the evening or at night.[29] In the context of the recent discussion on the 'civilising process' it is important to note that there was very often some time between the initial dispute between the parties and the issuing of the challenge in front of the house. As in the case of Charivari, the original conflict may have occurred days beforehand. Hence, we cannot explain this ritual in terms of a lack of control over emotions, as a spontaneous, sudden outbreak or as an impulsive act of violence; rather we find elements of a consistent and planned action.[30] In the second stage, the actual challenge took place. The challenger attacked the honour of the opponent by yelling or swearing in the direction of the house. Stage three, which was closely connected to stage two, involved the pulling out of a weapon and a call to one's opponent to come out of his house. For instance, in Würzburg in 1544 the following challenge was laid down: 'If you were a pious man of honour, you should come out and fight ...'.[31] In the fourth stage the person challenged could come out of his house and confront the opponent.

In numerous cases, the 'Ausfordern' did lead to a fight in front of the house. The house-dweller did not always, however, respond to the challenge by appearing for a fight. Some just remained inside their houses or threatened to call the neighbours, which could cause the challenger to leave.[32] Another option was to appeal to the court of the town to have the opponent arrested. Again we find that the people involved reflected on their options and were able to control their temper.

This ritual shows clear evidence of a controlled use of violence, which, from the viewpoint of the town-dwellers, was legitimate. Ritualised 'Ausfordern' challenged but also respected the special legal sphere of the house and its members. In the great majority of cases, it did not have lethal consequences, but served chiefly as a symbolic means of gaining satisfaction for a real or perceived grievance. To challenge someone out of the house belonged to an accepted type of honourable violence between equal counterparts in a duel-like situation. It was not to be performed secretly or in an unfair way from behind, but face to face in public. Similar cases can be found in conflicts that started in taverns or inns. The opponents often left the tavern to settle their dispute outside on the street. The fighting was restricted to the main protagonists and the danger of the crowd in the tavern becoming involved was diminished.

Such traditional practices and means of conflict resolution were, however, also under increasing scrutiny and attack from the town councils during the early modern period. Most of the examples in Kramer's study date from the sixteenth century. During this period, before the Thirty Years War and the rise of the princely state, it was obviously still a well-known practice among town-dwellers to call an adversary out of his house. Yet, at the same time it was already penalised as an offence by the town authorities and could be taken to court by the victims or witnesses, thus producing our source material. The authorities were clearly taking an increasing interest in regulating and penalising such behaviour even by the sixteenth century. Indeed, by the eighteenth century, in Frankfurt at least, there is hardly any evidence of this ritual due to the increasing prosecution of traditional conflict regulation by the town councils.[33]

During the early modern period, guild life was also increasingly supervised by the authorities. The town councils tried to use the guilds to institute a wider programme of social control. Increasingly, the regulations of the councils were adopted by the guilds. An edict of the council of Frankfurt from 1596 reminded all artisans to stay away from 'daily boozing' in their pubs and from the frequent 'brawls' during the celebration of baptisms.[34] This edict was adopted by many trades in Frankfurt.

Of course, such policies were not wholly successful. Other sources indicate, for instance, that the attitude of the craftsmen towards violence remained ambivalent. A regulation of the shoemaker journeymen of Herborn in 1682 stated: 'Fights shall be carried out in an honest way on the journeymen's hostel, according to convention and old tradition, with the bare fist and not with murderous weapon.'[35] Violence in the workshop could still be a daily occurrence[36] and was not always restricted to the semi-public spheres of the workshop or drinking clubs of guilds. Young journeymen from all crafts remained one of the most troublesome groups in the towns throughout the eighteenth century.[37] The honour-orientated conflict regulations adopted by the guilds corresponded with some of the demands laid down by the town councils, but also clearly caused potential for more conflict and undermined the overall goal of maintaining urban stability. Despite such behaviour, however, if not directly related to the trade of the guilds, formalised ways of settling disputes and punishing deviant behaviour were increasingly abolished by the authorities. By the end of the sixteenth century criminal justice had become a matter solely for the town courts. Henceforth, only minor and purely economic offences were left to the regulation of corporations.

With the increasing capacities of town councils to intervene and to regulate urban society we witness a shift in the containment of violence. From the late Middle Ages on, the councils aspired to establish a monopoly of legitimate power. Town councils began to pass more and more edicts while officers were employed to go on patrol through the streets. Citizens were no longer allowed to bear arms. Criminal records from the fifteenth and sixteenth centuries indicate a growing willingness to impose severe corporal or capital punishments. The evidence from fifteenth-century Constance and sixteenth-century Zurich demonstrates that the council men increasingly distrusted the older 'private' type of conflict regulation and regarded it as their business to ensure peace.[38] Henceforth, at the cost of the male honour code, the concept of peace and urban stability without resorting to violence became the dominant feature of town life. The authorities finally abolished the blood feud, which by the middle of the fifteenth century was already confined to the closest relatives of the victim. The courts also no longer tolerated manslaughter for reasons of honour. Henceforth, the only acceptable reason for killing was self-defence. From around 1500 on, as urban stability became increasingly defined by courts and councils, the incompatibility of notions of male honour on the one hand, and of peace and urban stability on the other, became more and more pronounced.

The courts and the people

The question of how violence was contained is closely linked to the question of how it was perceived by different groups within urban society. Who understood certain violent actions as legitimate or illegitimate and how did the interaction between townsfolk and courts work in practice? Was the new policy of containment by the town councils repressive?

In spite of the increasing importance of the authorities (both princely state and town councils) in the regulation of social life, the prosecution of 'crime' or 'delinquency' remained a joint venture. The judicial records of the towns under examination provide clear evidence that the people throughout the early modern period were not reluctant prosecutors. The prosecution of many violent crimes also depended on the active participation of the town-dwellers. Many cases of challenging out of the house, for example, only came to the attention of the authorities because somebody decided to report the offenders. It is probable that in most cases the challenged persons themselves called the guards or went to the town hall to report incidents.[39] The claim of the courts to impose sanctions in such cases provided an alternative option to a direct response in an armed fight for those challenged. Courts could also reward the prosecutors (if they were the victims) in cases of violence by giving them a proportion of the monetary fines.[40] Compensation and different sorts of punishment imposed on the challenger were seen as a means of restoring peace. They also gave those challenged another kind of satisfaction for the insult they had suffered in the special legal sphere of their house. From this point of view, the ritual of 'Ausfordern' was not just penalised by the ruling authorities as a by-product of state formation but in a process of cooperation between the authorities and the people.

Most citizens in the early modern period did not experience the legal system as something imposed on them against their will, but rather as something which they could work with and/or use for their own interests. In sixteenth-century Zurich, the families of victims began to use the courts confidently to prosecute offenders. When deliberately taking cases of murder and manslaughter before the courts, they clearly supported the new strict policy of the town council, which led to an increase in the number of capital convictions. The statements of perpetrators in court also increasingly centred on arguments relating to the need to achieve peace in towns and of Christian virtues promoted by the Reformation, rather than on the necessity to defend one's honour.[41]

The criminal justice system was also not a major source of complaint among citizens. Even during the famous Fettmilch uprising in Frankfurt am Main, 1612–14, the popular accusation of arbitrariness against the courts of the council did not lead the rebellious citizens to challenge the prevailing legal system. While they demanded fundamental changes in all fields of urban politics, such as the participation of citizens on the council and the publication of constitutional laws and privileges, criminal justice was at the bottom of their list. Besides the demand for a special 'burgher prison', the dissenting citizens mainly asked for educated jurists to be included as judges in the courts to prevent arbitrary sentences.[42] Things were different in rural society, both in England and Germany, where we find contentious legal decisions and resistance to the courts in typical 'social crimes' such as poaching and wood-collecting.[43] In the towns, especially in city republics such as Frankfurt and Zurich, the preservation of peace and the containment of violence in contrast were understood as a common obligation of all office holders and citizens.[44] Courts were there, on the spot, and the people were ready to make use of them.

Who were the prosecutors? To determine exactly how the cases came before the courts is no easy task. It has been estimated that in late sixteenth-century Cologne at least 11.4 per cent of all proceedings were based on a private accusation which led to an 'accusation trial'.[45] Considering the weakness of policing in sixteenth-century Cologne, the actual number of indictments initiated by town-dwellers must, however, have been much higher. Unfortunately, the files from Cologne do not allow precise figures about the indictments which formed the basis for the majority of 'inquisition trials'. In contrast to the accusation trial, based on private initiative, the proceedings of the inquisition trial lay solely in the hands of the authorities. In the course of the early modern period the inquisition trial slowly replaced the accusation trial as the standard trial for all criminal offences. However, indictments and reports on crime were still needed to start the proceedings. Gerd Schwerhoff assumes that many persons who appeared as 'witnesses' in the criminal records of inquisition trials were the actual victims who also reported the offence.

The more complete criminal records of eighteenth-century Frankfurt offer more information about the indictments. Nearly two-thirds of all the cases recorded for Frankfurt's criminal court were based on the indictments of victims. Another 10 per cent were based on the indictments of witnesses. In some cases of violent crime, the information came from doctors who treated suspicious wounds. Still, a majority of 57 per cent of all cases of violent assault relied on the victims of the offence bringing the case to court and another 11 per cent of cases depended on witnesses. Information from guards and office holders only played a minor role accounting for only 8 per cent of all cases.[46]

All groups, integrated legally and socially into urban society, made use of Frankfurt's criminal court. It is no surprise, however, that those who held the right of citizenship were overrepresented with 56 per cent of all indictments.[47] Although excluded from the highest offices in town, the privileged citizens (or burghers) were the group which exerted the greatest influence on the politics of the primarily patrician council. By the eighteenth century most citizens were more likely to resort to the courts than to ritualised acts of violence to resolve disputes. The lower orders and those who lacked sufficient integration into urban society were less confident in using criminal courts as a means of conflict resolution. But it is still possible to find day labourers, servants and Jews among the prosecutors. Many charges were also brought by women. The only group completely excluded were beggars and vagrants. Alien beggars and vagrants avoided any contact with the courts and were more often looked upon as suspects. The criminal courts usually acted to repress these groups.

How were the courts used? According to Martin Dinges, 'The plaintiffs often appealed to the courts simply to improve their own chances in the extrajudicial settlements, which they fundamentally preferred.'[48] Trials often remained unfinished because the prosecutors dropped their accusations. Dinges emphasises the importance of informal means of social control in early modern societies. The state and its courts were only one player in the wider game of social control. However, Dinges underestimates the role of the courts to act on their own behalf and misses a relevant function of criminal courts in the early modern legal system. The evidence for out-of-court settlements is taken from courts that dealt with petty crime. The courts during the early modern period did not, however, only settle cases and restore peace in case of violent conflict or enhance private solutions. While dependent upon ordinary town-dwellers to bring cases to their attention, the criminal courts increasingly prosecuted deviant behaviour on their own behalf. We have to draw a line between severe and petty crime here. Already by the middle of the sixteenth century it was by no means certain that a case of manslaughter, if taken to court, would be settled by extra-judicial compensation. The example of Cologne shows that those accused of robbery, burglary or theft often received highly punitive sentences and were increasingly sent to the gallows.[49]

Another sharp distinction has to be drawn in cases of interpersonal violence between alien perpetrators and those who were integrated town-dwellers. The closer the legal and personal relationship between accuser and accused the greater the likelihood that the courts would accept an extra-judicial settlement. In this respect, Dinges makes a good point. Violence in the neighbourhood or, in particular, in the domestic sphere was very rarely punished by the courts. Beaten wives often appealed to the courts but in most cases only looked for protection and some support in their everyday life rather than to have their husbands sent to the house of correction. The primary task of the courts was to reconcile husband and wife.[50] Prosecutors still looked to the courts to get compensation from their opponents. Even in the eighteenth century, they explicitly asked for 'satisfaction' in court indicating a connection with a prior insult they had suffered. In order to gain 'satisfaction' and thus settle the violent conflict in many cases it sufficed to impose monetary compensation.[51] According to the legal and social status of the offender, non-lethal violence could still be punished either by monetary fines or in a punitive way by sentencing the perpetrator to public work or sending him/her to the house of correction.

Another significant factor in the relationship between the courts and citizens was the letters of supplication written on behalf of those convicted. Letters appealing for the mitigation of sentences were a frequent and highly characteristic element of criminal proceedings in this period.[52] In eighteenth-century Frankfurt, written supplications were sent to the council or the mayors.[53] They were included in 20 per cent of the recorded crimes against persons and in 8 per cent of the files of property crimes. They were, in many cases, sent by close relatives or masters of the accused. It was not a privilege of the housefathers to appeal for mercy. If the father or the son of the household was arrested, wives or mothers did not hesitate to send a letter of supplication to the council. The holders of the right of citizenship were, however, overrepresented. Although, ineffective in some cases, the majority of supplications were successful. They could reduce the time of imprisonment considerably or even lead to the release of the convict.

For their letters of supplication many obviously received help from educated writers. Typical arguments employed included the risk of a slide into poverty due to the imprisonment of the family's breadwinner or the good social conduct of the person prior to conviction, which was underlined with expressions such as 'moral' and 'honest' ('sittlich und rechtschaffen') or 'man of honour' ('Mensch von Ehre'). Essential to the high success rate of these letters was the fact that they were taken as evidence for a possible reintegration of the convict. As in the fourteenth-century case in Berlin of the journeyman Ekart Maler, towards the end of the early modern period it was still important for the accused persons to present someone who guaranteed better social conduct in the future.

The supplicants deliberately referred to three fundamental notions of early modern urban discourse: the right of sufficient 'nourishment', 'peace' and 'honour'. It was not in the interests of the town council to rule over impoverished people. The right of 'nourishment' ('Nahrung') is mentioned again and again in the petitions of guilds and other corporations.[54] Fathers, wives and masters of the guild guaranteed the peaceful conduct of the imprisoned person in the future. They assured the judges that the breach of the peace had merely been an accident or due to temporary insanity and the convict was portrayed as a truly honourable man who deserved mercy.

These letters of supplication show how the relationship between the courts and citizens worked in practice. The early modern criminal justice system was much more open to influence from the outside than might appear at first sight. If the accused person was an integrated member of town society, his sentence was to some degree negotiable. In this respect, towards the end of the early modern period the sentences were still influenced by lay participation.

Higher numbers of supplications – and accordingly milder sentences – for violent offenders than for thieves reflected diverging perceptions of crime. While theft and robbery were completely rejected by the authorities and town-dwellers, interpersonal violence in the public sphere could, under certain circumstances, still seem legitimate and was in many cases still settled through compensation. However, by the eighteenth century the social composition of the offenders had changed drastically. In contrast to the situation in late medieval towns, the criminal records of late sixteenth-century Cologne had already witnessed a withdrawal of the higher social ranks from violent conflict over questions of honour. It was mostly craftsmen, transport workers and peasants who were taken to court.[55] Violent perpetrators came mainly from the central strata of urban society and only four 'noblemen' appeared before the courts. This is in marked contrast to late medieval towns, where perpetrators from the highest strata were especially conspicuous. This development continued and intensified in the course of the eighteenth century. Among hundreds of violent offenders in eighteenth-century Frankfurt there were no patricians, merchants or council men.[56] The upper three of the five orders of the town no longer engaged in violent public disputes to any great extent. The great bulk of the perpetrators were artisans, gardeners and soldiers.

Not only patricians and merchants, but also artisan masters increasingly stayed away from violent disputes on the street or in taverns. In late medieval towns, the masters had been frequently prosecuted for their violent behaviour.[57] They are still present in the records of the 1740s, but seem to have disciplined their public behaviour during the second half of the eighteenth century. In contrast, journeymen, soldiers and young men from other occupations still battled fiercely against each other. Thus by looking at criminal records from the eighteenth century we can observe an increasing divergence between the lifestyles of the upper and lower strata of society. While men from the lower orders still found violent reactions to insults legitimate, the upper and middling social ranks definitely preferred to use the courts. Patricians and merchants no longer ran up to an opponent's house at night-time in order to lay down a challenge. A growing divergence in terms of lifestyle is underlined by other new habits adopted by the upper strata in urban society, such as spare time spent in the new coffee houses or, towards the end of the eighteenth century, evenings in newly erected theatres or concert halls. The new bourgeois elite of nineteenth-century society, the so-called 'Bildungsbürgertum', was deeply rooted in the urban culture of the late *ancien régime*. While public violence circa 1500 was evident in all strata of urban society, including elites, it became, during the eighteenth century, largely confined to the lower strata of urban society.

Notes

1 I would like to thank Richard Mc Mahon for his comments on earlier versions of this text.
2 Carsten Küther, *Räuber und Gauner in Deutschland. Das organisierte Bandenwesen im 18. und 19. Jahrhundert* (Göttingen: Vandenhoeck & Ruprecht, 1976); Dirk Blasius, *Bürgerliche Gesellschaft und Kriminalität. Zur Sozialgeschichte Preußens im Vormärz* (Göttingen: Vandenhoeck & Ruprecht, 1976).
3 For an overview, see Peter Blickle, *Unruhen in der ständischen Gesellschaft 1300–1800* (Munich: Oldenbourg, 1988); see also Andreas Würgler, *Unruhen und Öffentlichkeit. Städtische und ländliche Protestbewegungen im 18. Jahrhundert* (Tübingen: Bibliotheca academica, 1995). See also Mark Häberlein (ed.), *Devianz, Widerstand und Herrschaftspraxis in der Vormoderne. Studien zu Konflikten im südwestdeutschen Raum (15.–18. Jahrhundert)* (Konstanz: UVK, 1999). This collection of essays combines a history of crime with that of popular protest.
4 Joachim Eibach, 'Recht – Kultur – Diskurs. Nullum Crimen sine Scientia', *Zeitschrift für Neuere Rechtsgeschichte* 23 (2001), 102–20. For an overview of the entire field, see Andreas Blauert and Gerd Schwerhoff (eds), *Kriminalitätsgeschichte. Beiträge zur Sozial- und Kulturgeschichte der Vormoderne* (Konstanz: UVK, 2000); Gerd Schwerhoff, 'Kriminalitätsgeschichte im deutschen Sprachraum. Zum Profil eines "verspäteten" Forschungszweiges', in ibid., 21–68; Gerd Schwerhoff, *Aktenkundig und gerichtsnotorisch. Einführung in die Historische Kriminalitätsforschung* (Tübingen: Edition diskord, 1999).

5 Lawrence Stone, 'Interpersonal Violence in English Society, 1300–1980', *Past and Present*, 101 (1983), 32; see also Eric A. Johnson and Eric H. Monkkonen (eds), *The Civilization of Crime: Violence in Town and Country since the Middle Ages* (Urbana and Chicago, IL: University of Illinois Press, 1996); Manuel Eisner, 'Modernization, Self-Control and Lethal Violence: The Long-Term Dynamics of European Homicide Rates in Theoretical Perspective', *British Journal of Criminology*, 41 (2001), 618–38.

6 J.A. Sharpe, 'The History of Violence in England: Some Observations', *Past and Present*, 108 (1985), 214.

7 Robert Shoemaker, 'Male Honour and the Decline of Public Violence in Eighteenth-Century London', *Social History*, 26 (2001), 190; idem, 'The Decline of Public Insult in London 1660–1800', *Past and Present*, 169 (2000), 97–131; Shoemaker's analysis of violence in London fits well with my own findings on the decline of violence in eighteenth-century Frankfurt am Main: Joachim Eibach, 'Städtische Gewaltkriminalität im Ancien Régime. Frankfurt am Main im europäischen Kontext', *Zeitschrift für Historische Forschung*, 25 (1998), 359–82; idem, *Frankfurter Verhöre. Städtische Lebenswelten und Kriminalität im 18. Jahrhundert* (Paderborn: Schöningh, 2003), 279–86; see also the contribution of Greg T. Smith in this volume.

8 Pieter Spierenburg, 'Violence and the Civilizing Process: Does it Work?', *Crime, Histoire & Sociétés/Crime, History & Societies*, 5, 2 (2001), 87–105; Gerd Schwerhoff, 'Criminalized Violence and the Process of Civilisation – a Reappraisal', *Crime, Histoire & Sociétés/Crime, History & Societies*, 6, 2 (2002), 119; Pieter Spierenburg, 'Theorizing in Jurassic Park: A Reply to Gerd Schwerhoff', in ibid., 127–8.

9 The best overview of this process in the English language is Christopher Friedrichs, *The Early Modern City, 1450–1750* (London: Longman, 1995); for towns in late medieval Central Europe, see also Eberhard Isenmann, *Die deutsche Stadt im Spätmittelalter 1250–1500* (Stuttgart: UTB, 1988).

10 Hans-Christoph Rublack, 'Grundwerte in der Reichsstadt im Spätmittelalter und in der frühen Neuzeit', in Horst Brunner (ed.), *Literatur in der Stadt. Bedingungen und Beispiele städtischer Literatur des 15. bis 17. Jahrhunderts* (Göppingen: Kümmerle, 1982), 9–36; Peter Schuster, *Der gelobte Frieden. Täter, Opfer und Herrschaft im spätmittelalter-lichen Konstanz* (Konstanz: Schöningh, 1995); Susanne Pohl, '"Ehrlicher Totschlag" – "Rache" – "Notwehr". Zwischen männlichem Ehrencode und dem Primat des Stadtfriedens (Zürich 1376–1600)', in Bernhard Jussen and Craig Koslofsky (eds), *Kulturelle Reformation. Sinnformationen im Umbruch 1400–1600* (Göttingen: Vandenhoeck & Ruprecht, 1999), 239–83; Joachim Eibach and Raingard Esser (eds), 'Urban Governance and Petty Conflict in Early Modern Europe', *Urban History* (Special Issue), 34, 1 (2007).

11 For a discussion of the use of violence as a means of social control, see Gerd Schwerhoff, 'Social Control of Violence, Violence as Social Control:

the Case of Early Modern Germany', in Herman Roodenburg and Pieter Spierenburg (eds), *Social Control in Europe, Vol. 1: 1500–1800* (Columbus, OH: Ohio State University Press, 2004), 220–46; for the use of violence in rural communities, see Magnus Eriksson and Barbara Krug-Richter (eds), *Streitkulturen. Gewalt, Konflikt und Kommunikation in der ländlichen Gesellschaft (16.–19. Jahrhundert)* (Cologne: Böhlau, 2003).

12 The rules of honour and conflicts over honour questions have been a prosperous field of German-speaking research over the past number of years; see Klaus Schreiner and Gerd Schwerhoff (eds), *Verletzte Ehre. Ehrkonflikte in Gesellschaften des Mittelalters und der Frühen Neuzeit* (Cologne: Böhlau, 1995); Sybille Backmann et al. (eds), *Ehrkonzepte in der Frühen Neuzeit. Identitäten und Abgrenzungen* (Berlin: Akademie Verlag, 1998).

13 Schwerhoff, *Aktenkundig*, 125 ('Auch und gerade die Eliten, der Adel und die höchsten Repräsentanten städtischer Politik, kultivierten einen gewaltträchtigen Habitus').

14 Susanna Burghartz, *Leib, Ehre und Gut. Delinquenz in Zürich Ende des 14. Jahrhunderts* (Zürich: Chronos Verlag, 1990), 116–18.

15 Peter Schuster, 'Richter ihrer selbst? Delinquenz gesellschaftlicher Oberschichten in der spätmittelalterlichen Stadt', in Blauert and Schwerhoff (eds), *Kriminalitätsgeschichte*, 359–78; Mark Häberlein, 'Tod auf der Herrenstube: Ehre und Gewalt in der Augsburger Führungsschicht (1500–1620)', in Backmann et al. (eds), *Ehrkonzepte*, 148–69.

16 Eibach, *Frankfurter Verhöre*, 216.

17 For Zurich, see Burghartz, *Leib, Ehre und Gut*, 199–202; Pohl, 'Ehrlicher Totschlag', 239 (definition of manslaughter and murder) and 259–62.

18 Peter Schuster, *Eine Stadt vor Gericht. Recht und Alltag im spätmittelalterlichen Konstanz* (Paderborn: Schöningh, 2000), 146 and 156; Valentin Groebner, 'Der verletzte Körper und die Stadt. Gewalttätigkeit und Gewalt in Nürnberg am Ende des 15. Jahrhunderts', in Thomas Lindenberger and Alf Lüdtke (eds), *Physische Gewalt. Studien zur Geschichte der Neuzeit* (Frankfurt am Main: Suhrkamp, 1995), 177; Andrea Bendlage, *Henkers Hetzbruder. Das Strafverfolgungspersonal der Reichsstadt Nürnberg im 15. und 16. Jahrhundert* (Konstanz: UVK, 2003), 156.

19 Cited in Pohl, 'Ehrlicher Totschlag', 261.

20 Source from the late fourteenth century in Schwerhoff, *Aktenkundig*, 171–3.

21 For the types of penalties imposed, see Bruce Lenman and Geoffrey Parker, 'The State, the Community and the Criminal Law in Early Modern Europe', in V.A.C. Gatrell et al. (eds), *Crime and the Law. The Social History of Crime in Western Europe since 1500* (London: Europa Publications, 1980), 11–12.

22 Examples from the guild statutes of Basle, Strasbourg and Hamburg can be found in Isenmann, *Die deutsche Stadt*, 310; as regards violence among artisans in Basle, see Katharina Simon-Muscheid, 'Gewalt und

Ehre im spätmittelalterlichen Handwerk am Beispiel Basels', *Zeitschrift für Historische Forschung*, 18 (1991), 1–31.

23 Thomas E. Brennan, *Public Drinking and Popular Culture in Eighteenth-Century Paris* (Princeton, NJ: Princeton University Press, 1988); Ann B. Tlusty, *Bacchus and Civic Order. The Culture of Drink in Early Modern Germany* (Charlottesville, VA: University Press of Virginia, 2001); see also the forthcoming work on taverns in Switzerland by Beat Kuemin (Warwick) and on taverns in Saxony and France by Susanne Rau (Dresden).

24 Rudolf Wissell, *Des alten Handwerks Recht und Gewohnheit* (Berlin: Colloquium Verlag, 1971–88), vol. 2, 157–60.

25 Karl-Sigismund Kramer, 'Das Herausfordern aus dem Haus. Lebensbild eines Rechtsbrauches', *Bayerisches Jahrbuch für Volkskunde* (1956), 121–38; a case from fourteenth-century Zurich: Burghartz, *Leib, Ehre und Gut*, 133; in contrast, see the less ritualised cases from eighteenth-century Paris: Martin Dinges, *Der Maurermeister und der Finanzrichter. Ehre, Geld und soziale Kontrolle im Paris des 18. Jahrhunderts* (Göttingen: Vandenhoeck & Ruprecht, 1994), 316–20.

26 Kramer, 'Das Herausfordern', 121. It is likely that there were far more cases of this kind which did not come before the courts.

27 Whether, as Kramer maintains, a call out of the house actually constituted a breach of the peace of the house ('Hausfrieden'), as Kramer maintains, is debatable. See Kramer, 'Das Herausfordern', 121.

28 Ibid., 122. Kramer's four stages of the ritual constitute an 'ideal' scenario. We cannot always find all four elements in the cases and obviously they could be combined in different ways by those involved.

29 See the case from Zurich in the year 1382, Burghartz, *Leib, Ehre und Gut*, 133.

30 Compare the debate between Spierenburg, 'Violence', and Schwerhoff, 'Criminalized Violence', 116–17.

31 "Wer er von eren ein frumer man, so solt er herauß geen vnd sie schlagen ...", cited in Kramer, 'Das Herausfordern', 124.

32 Cases from the towns of Würzburg and Volkach, ibid., 132.

33 Eibach, *Frankfurter Verhöre*, 243–4.

34 The reason for the edict was as follows: 'des täglichen zechens uf allen und jeder zunfftstuben' and 'schlegereyen': Karl Bücher and Benno Schmidt (eds), *Frankfurter Amts- und Zunfturkunden bis zum Jahre 1612*, 3 vols (Frankfurt am Main: Baer, 1914–15, new print 1968), vol. 1, 16 f.; see also Wissell, *Des alten Handwerks Recht*, vol. 2, 157–60.

35 'Die rauf soll aufrichtig hergehen, auf der herberg, nach gebrauch und altem herkommen, mit der blossen faust und nicht mit mörderischem gewehr'; cited in Wissell, *Des alten Handwerks Recht*, vol. 2, 250.

36 For a wonderful and paradigmatic example of New Cultural History, see Robert Darnton, *The Great Cat Massacre and Other Episodes in French Cultural History* (London: Allen Lane, 1984).

37 Eibach, *Frankfurter Verhöre*, 252–66.

38 Schuster, *Stadt vor Gericht*, 146–50; Pohl, 'Ehrlicher Totschlag', 242, 250, 263–4 and 282.

39 Evidence for this assumption is presented in those sources where the challenged person refused to leave his house: Kramer, 'Das Herausfordern', 132.

40 For a case of 'Ausfordern' in fourteenth-century Zurich, see Burghartz, *Leib, Ehre und Gut*, 133; Gerd Schwerhoff, *Köln im Kreuzverhör. Kriminalität, Herrschaft und Gesellschaft in einer frühneuzeitlichen Stadt* (Bonn: Bouvier, 1991), 132; Eibach, *Frankfurter Verhöre*, 77–8 and 391–2.

41 Pohl, 'Ehrlicher Totschlag', 246 and 275.

42 For more detail, see Joachim Eibach, 'Städtische Strafjustiz als konsensuale Praxis: Frankfurt a.M. im 17. und 18. Jahrhundert' in Rudolf Schlögl, *Interaktion und Herrschaft. Die Politik der frühneuzeitlichen Stadt* (Konstanz, UVK, 2004), 192.

43 For England, see Douglas Hay (ed.), *Albion's Fatal Tree. Crime and Society in Eighteenth-Century England* (London: Allen Lane, 1975); idem, 'Crime and Justice in Eighteenth and Nineteenth-Century England', *Crime and Justice*, 2 (1980), 45–84; for Germany, see Blasius, *Bürgerliche Gesellschaft*; Norbert Schindler, *Wilderer im Zeitalter der Französischen Revolution. Ein Kapitel alpiner Sozialgeschichte* (Munich: C.H. Beck, 2001).

44 For more detail, see the contributions in Eibach and Esser (eds), 'Urban Governance'.

45 Schwerhoff, *Köln im Kreuzverhör*, 88–90.

46 Eibach, *Frankfurter Verhöre*, 74.

47 A high share of prosecutors from the upper strata and the middling sort of society is not simply a characteristic of Frankfurt or urban societies; see Martin Dinges, 'Justiznutzungen als soziale Kontrolle in der Frühen Neuzeit', in Blauert and Schwerhoff (eds), *Kriminalitätsgeschichte*, 506–7 and 525; in a shorter English version of this article Dinges comes to a slightly different conclusion: 'To have access to justice, the plaintiff's class situation or socioeconomic position hardly mattered: plaintiffs and defendants often came from the same class. An important threshold was the expenses (...).' Martin Dinges, 'The Uses of Justice as a Form of Social Control in Early Modern Europe', in Roodenburg and Spierenburg (eds), *Social Control*, 168.

48 Dinges, 'The Uses of Justice', 162.

49 Schwerhoff, *Köln im Kreuzverhör*, 343–9.

50 Heinrich R. Schmidt, *Dorf und Religion. Reformierte Sittenzucht in Berner Landgemeinden der Frühen Neuzeit* (Stuttgart: G. Fischer, 1995), 256.

51 Eibach, *Frankfurter Verhöre*, 77 and 388.

52 Gerd Schwerhoff, 'Das Kölner Supplikenwesen in der Frühen Neuzeit. Annäherungen an ein Kommunikationsmedium zwischen Untertanen und Obrigkeit', in Georg Mölich and Gerd Schwerhoff (eds), *Köln als Kommunikationszentrum. Studien zur frühneuzeitlichen Stadtgeschichte*

(Cologne: DuMont, 1999), 473–96; Karl Härter, 'Strafverfahren im frühneuzeitlichen Territorialstaat: Inquisition, Entscheidungsfindung, Supplikation', in Blauert and Schwerhoff (eds), *Kriminalitätsgeschichte*, 478–9.

53 For a further discussion of this process, see Eibach, 'Städtische Strafjustiz', 199–204.

54 Robert Brandt and Thomas Buchner (eds), *Nahrung, Markt oder Gemeinnutz. Werner Sombart und das vorindustrielle Handwerk* (Bielefeld: Verlag für Regionalgeschichte, 2004).

55 Schwerhoff, *Köln im Kreuzverhör*, 303–4.

56 Eibach, *Frankfurter Verhöre*, 211–14; for London, see Shoemaker, 'Male Honour', 205–8; see also the article by Greg T. Smith in this volume.

57 For the late medieval period, see Basel Simon-Muscheid, 'Gewalt und Ehre'; in contrast, see eighteenth-century Frankfurt, Eibach, *Frankfurter Vehöre*, 256.

Further reading

Eibach, Joachim and Raingard Esser (eds) (2007) 'Urban Governance and Petty Conflict in Early Modern Europe', *Urban History* (Special Issue) 34 (1).

Eriksson, Magnus and Barbara Krug-Richter (eds) (2003) *Streitkulturen. Gewalt, Konflikt und Kommunikation in der ländlichen Gesellschaft (16.–19. Jahrhundert)*. Cologne: Böhlau Verlag.

Friedrichs, Christopher (1995) *The Early Modern City, 1450–1750*. London: Longman.

Johnson, Eric A. and Eric H. Monkkonen (eds) (1996) *The Civilization of Crime. Violence in Town and Country since the Middle Ages*. Urbana and Chicago, IL: University of Illinois Press.

Roodenburg, Herman and Pieter Spierenburg (eds) (2004) *Social Control in Europe, Vol. 1: 1500–1800*. Columbus, OH: Ohio State University Press.

Rublack, Ulinka (1999) *The Crimes of Women in Early Modern Germany*. Oxford: Oxford University Press.

Ruff, Julius (2001) *Violence in Early Modern Europe 1500–1800*. Cambridge: Cambridge University Press.

Schlögl, Rudolf (2004) *Interaktion und Herrschaft. Die Politik der frühneuzeitlichen Stadt*. Konstanz: UVK.

Shoemaker, Robert (2004) *The London Mob. Violence and Disorder in Eighteenth-Century England*. London: Hambledon Continuum.

Ulbrich, Claudia (ed.) (2005) *Gewalt in der Frühen Neuzeit (Historische Forschungen Vol. 81)*. Berlin: Duncker & Humblot.

Chapter 3

Royal justice, popular culture and violence: homicide in sixteenth- and seventeenth-century Castile[1]

Rudy Chaulet

The working-classes are at bottom in excellent health [...] in better health than other classes; rough and unpolished perhaps, but diamonds nevertheless; rugged, but 'sterling worth': not refined, not intellectual, but with both feet on the ground; capable of a good belly-laugh, charitable and forthright. They are, moreover, possessed of a racy and salty speech, touched with wit, but always with its hard grain of common sense

This panegyric is not taken from a romantic study of popular *mentalité* during the Renaissance, but is a quotation from *The poor person's culture* in which Richard Hoggart pokes fun at bourgeois clichés of the working classes while at the same time offering an account of English working-class culture in the 1950s.[2] This quotation serves as a fine introduction to this essay which seeks to highlight the possible dangers in the use of the concept of popular culture, even when applied to the *ancien régime*.

Any historical study must run the risk of distorting or failing to capture as accurately as possible the subject of its investigation. This problem is particularly acute when investigating the *mentalité* of those who have left little by way of written material behind and whose actions and statements are often only accessible through the descriptions offered by those outside their cultural milieu. There is always the risk of both having and giving a false impression of popular practice and belief. Such images or even clichés can operate in a variety of different ways; in some cases presenting a resplendent image of the good poor, in others that of the poor as 'ugly, dirty and bad'.[3] Seen from the upper ranks of society, the common people can appear as undignified, as the orientalised noble savages or ferocious cannibals of far-off lands.

In an article written over twenty years ago, Jacques Revel highlighted the difficulties and ambiguities of studies devoted to popular culture.[4] First, the very use of the term 'popular culture' implies or even assumes that a culture which reflects the collective beliefs and actions of the mass of the people actually exists and that it can be identified above and beyond the actions of particular individuals or social groups. Second, it also presupposes the existence of an elite culture which is separate from and indeed often seen as antithetical to it. Popular culture is often defined only in terms of its opposition to elite culture; such binary oppositions can serve to distort as much as they can reveal.

Yet, as Revel also points out, it would be a mistake to totally abandon the term and to reject all that has been written about popular culture heretofore. It *is* possible to identify elements of a distinct popular culture which goes back to the Middle Ages. It is also clear that from the sixteenth century the state and the church *did* make sustained efforts to try and reshape popular behaviour and that popular culture proved largely resistant to such elite interference well into the nineteenth or twentieth centuries. In using the term, however, we must also be wary of ambiguous definitions about such a collective construct as 'the people' which, depending on context can vary from a very small section to almost the entire population. Moreover, we must be careful not to see popular culture as an arcadia which is somehow replaced by norms imposed by elite sections of society over the course of the early modern and modern periods. To go down this path would be, as Carlo Ginzburg says, to 'adhere to the unsupportable theory, by which ideas come only from the dominant classes'[5] and to forget that popular and elite culture can communicate with, and influence, each other.

If we add the question of violence to the debate, the representation of the lower orders becomes even more problematic. The historiography of violence in early modern and modern Europe has been dominated, to a large degree, by what is referred to as the 'civilising process', which is often presented as the victory of elite over popular culture. Ever since the pioneering study by Norbert Elias,[6] which has been applied by Robert Muchembled[7] in France and Pieter Spierenburg[8] in the Netherlands, this theory has been the object of several challenges and a lively discussion currently divides specialists in the history of violence.[9] Those who criticise the concept often focus on the way in which these writers use unreliable figures relating to homicidal violence, especially for the Middle Ages, and extrapolate what they consider to be the possible rates of homicide at a given time. Similar criticisms can be made of the population figures used to calculate these homicide rates as they too are unreliable for much of the medieval period. The systematic study of homicide is also placed in doubt by the fact that many of the alleged victims died for reasons that the perpetrator did not intend, such as bleeding or infection. These events do not necessarily reflect the extent of aggressive tendencies in society and cannot be compared with contemporary data from a world where the victims of aggression, for the most part, benefit from the considerable advances in medicine in the modern era.

The French court, which is a paradigm, according to Elias, of the civilising process,[10] is also far removed from many European societies where, according to the available data, a sharp decrease in the number of homicides has also been witnessed. The notion of a civilising process is also called into question if we consider the increase in homicide rates in European societies at the end of the twentieth century. Finally, the focus on the recreational and almost bestial violence, which preceded the more 'civilised' modern era, has also been called into question. Considerable focus has, in recent years, been placed on the role of honour as one of the primary causes of homicide in Europe from the close of the Middle Ages to the present day. Honour, it is argued, is a cultural construct far removed from spontaneous or impulsive violence, which proponents of the civilising process regard as the primary characteristic of violence in the late Middle Ages. In France, for instance, Claude Gauvard has shattered our vision of the medieval world as one in which violence could erupt as a result of an individual's lack of self-control. He shows how the violence of men in the Middle Ages was primarily caused by 'damaged honour' and was very much controlled in its expression.[11]

Where does Castile fit into such debates and controversies? Unfortunately, the sources available for Castile do not allow us to evaluate the level or rates of lethal violence in the sixteenth and seventeenth centuries as the records of criminal trials have all but disappeared from Castilian archives. As a result, it is necessary to eschew the attractions of quantitative analysis of incidents of homicide and focus more on the cultural context in which acts of violence both occurred and were dealt with at that time. This can be achieved through a study of the requests for pardons addressed to the monarch by those convicted of homicide.[12]

Upon receipt of a request for a royal pardon, the body in charge of justice, in this case the Council of Castile, asked the tribune who dealt with the case for a copy of the legal proceedings about the crime. Such textual records generally contained a detailed transcription of the trial or investigation. From this evidence a fairly precise idea about the circumstances of the crime can be identified.[13] These documents provide a rich source of information about the violent behaviour of a number of Castilians at this time. There is, of course, a danger in relying on pardons as our primary source as such records include only those capable of paying for a reprieve. Although the royal pardon was often granted on receipt of a large sum of money, accounting for some 54 per cent of all cases reviewed – all members of Castilian society could theoretically plead for a pardon, even those who were enslaved.[14] It is also clear that in a significant proportion of cases those involved were drawn from the lower orders, with most working either in agriculture or in craft industries. Out of a total of about 450 cases examined, the occupation of some 65 per cent of convicts, and about 73 per cent of victims, can be assessed, the difference explained by the significant number of criminals who escaped, making it difficult to gather information on them. Of these 15 per cent were peasants and about 39 per cent were craftsmen. Over half of the convicts whose occupation was recorded belonged to the lower orders of society. In examining the contexts in which these men and women resorted to violence it is possible to demonstrate that popular and elite cultures were not always at odds and that it is possible, at least in Castilian society, to find shared characteristics both in the use of violence and in attitudes to such behaviour.

Insult and honour

Is it possible to suggest that 'violence is the language of the poor'?[15] Nothing could be less certain. First, violence was by no means the preserve of the poor. Our sample shows that violent behaviour leading to homicide is also a characteristic of the privileged classes. Second, it would be a mistake to see members of the lower branches of society using weapons rather that words due to a lack of social subtlety or ability. Today[16], as in the past, linguistic eloquence is a fundamental element of popular culture. It is this street culture and its specific vocabulary that Bakhtin[17] speaks of, in which insults (a common precursor of violence) are shouted and where seemingly friendly discussions involving ritual challenges could lead to blows being exchanged.

In the context of sixteenth- and seventeenth-century Castile, the exchange of insults often preceded violent activity. Some insults were, in fact, proscribed by law. A perusal of the legal documents of the time provides us with a selection of these insults.[18] The words prohibited by the *Partidas* and later by Philip II's legislation were: *gafo* (leper), *sodomítico* (sodomite), *cornudo* (cuckold), *traidor* (traitor), as well as *puta* (whore) when this was addressed to a married woman. These insults, listed and prohibited, only account, however, for a small proportion of those used at the time; indeed, they account for only about one in every eight found in our sample.

It is 'liar' and all its variations[19] which is most prominent among the insults found in our corpus. This is not surprising, as this insult commonly and, indeed, ritually preceded swordfights.[20] All social groups in our sample used it, although it was not as common among the lower as the upper orders of society.[21] Among the lower orders, *pícaro* (rogue), undoubtedly made popular by the form of literature which borrowed the same name, *bellaco* (rascal) and *desvergonzado* (cheeky), were particularly fashionable and were ranked second, third and fourth of all insults employed in this period. Other common but prohibited expressions included *cornudo* (cuckold), followed closely by *borracho* (drunkard).

In many instances, references to the nether regions of the body appear to have appealed to people. For instance, on 3 March 1654, in a country tavern in the province of Burgos, Lázaro de Palacín, caused his friend, Felipe de Pablos, a bee-keeper, to become angry, after asking him to: 'Bésame en el trasero' (kiss my arse).[22] This shows the traditional substitution of one's face for one's posterior in order to humiliate, typical of the bodily and worldly references made in Medieval and Renaissance popular culture.[23]

The meanings behind other insults are less obvious and some exchanges could be quite obscure. In Berzosa de Bureba, 14 February 1679, a carnival day, Pedro de Pancorbo and Manuel de Quintana, two young country folk, one of whom was an agricultural worker, exchanged some rather odd insults before coming to blows. The latter shouted to the former '¡Quiebra canillas!', who replied with '¡Descula abujas!'. This pastoral, or agricultural, style abuse, the exact meaning of which seems quite odd to us today, was perfectly understood by the two young people at the time who 'from these words started to fight[24]'.

Some reactions to apparent insult reveal an acute sensitivity that would be humourous if it were not so deadly. At Valladolid, on

Maundy Thursday 1698, in the church of the Misericordia, which also served as an orphanage (*niños de la doctrina*), a 10-year-old boarder called Martín Herrero was in the playground singing the passion of Christ. Once he reached the line which goes 'Ya le atan a la columna los lobos carniceros',[25] two men started to beat him with their fists and feet so violently that he died a month later. The fight went on for so long that a witness gave evidence that: 'He said [to the most determined of the two men]: "What baseness to treat this child in such a way"', but he just continued to treat the boy in the same way and the witness added: 'and on today of all days, he was not respecting the sacredness of the place, at which he was very angry, saying that he was doing the right thing and went into the church.' The child was very badly beaten, his sides were broken and a vital organ was damaged.

What caused the savage rage of these two men? It is the hidden reference to the *carniceros* of the canticle, which in Castilian means 'carnivorous', as in the text the child was reciting, and also, more importantly, 'butchers', the profession of Ignacio González and Manuel Naval (meat cutters, *cortadores de carne*), who thought they were being insulted by Martín Herrero. There is little in the evidence given at the trial which suggests that the two men were settling an old score with the child. Their reaction is likely, therefore, to have been completely spontaneous; their brutality and the absence of discretion in their actions makes us think of the characters invoked by Huizinga[26] and Elias to illustrate the harshness and the spontaneity of former times. Yet we are dealing with a case at the very end of the seventeenth century.

We must not assume, however, that the lower orders were the only ones involved in such cases. They account for only one in two of such trials, reflecting their presence in the population as a whole. The upper echelons of society were also represented. Such violent confrontations could, in fact, even arise in the immediate vicinity of the court. This can be seen in the case of a conflict between two muleteers and a bursar who were travelling with the royal procession near Segovia in 1603. On the evening of 9 April 1603, at El Espinar, the royal procession, coming from Valladolid, paused for rest before continuing to El Escorial. Two muleteers, Alonso Poliso, 30 years old, and Francisco Pérez, 25 years old, from the royal party became angry with Luis Jacoleto, a bursar from the convoy, as he had, according to them, taken over their lodgings for the night. In response, Jacoleto barricaded himself in the house attributed to him by the servants in charge of finding accommodation for the royal procession (*aposentadores*). For over two hours, the two muleteers raged in front of the house. Here are some selected extracts:

> Get out of here faggot, damn idiot, we're going to kill you and you won't see tomorrow! [...] I don't care if he's the head bursar, he's clearly nothing other than an idiot baptised in a cauldron, seeing as he won't come out! [...] Get out of there you bloody fucking cuckold, we are not Portuguese![27]

Here, the insults are operating on three levels. First, there is the accusation that Jacoleto was homosexual or a 'faggot', which at the time was not only a very serious crime, but also *pecado nefando* (an abominable sin) punishable by the stake. Second, there was the accusation of being a complaisant husband, a character regularly the butt of community jokes at the time. Third, there was a suggestion of the clandestine practice of Judaism, which in the Spain of the new Inquisition was obviously repressed.

Other cases were based less around insults and focused more on the question of reputation and 'who was the better man'. This is evident in daily conversations during leisure or work activities, be it in agricultural or craft industries. At Valencia de Don Juan, at 4 o'clock on the afternoon of 9 May 1676, Pedro de Villares and Marcos Fernández, two day labourers, were busy clipping vines.[28] They argued about who was the best worker and the former accused the latter of not deserving his salary. Marcos Fernández asked him to stay in his vine row and not to look for an argument but at the same time pushed him vigorously. Pedro de Villares raised the tool in his hand and beat his colleague on the head, resulting in injuries from which he later died. Less than a month later, at Medina de Campo, two shoemakers were arguing over who made better shoes. After this argument got out of hand and other arguments were mixed in, the shoemaker Andrés Zamorano was killed by a blow from a sword.

Other cases extended beyond personal reputation to that of third parties. In 1600, Francisco de Vargas and Diego Iglesias, craftsworkmen from Palencia, became involved in a verbal sparring match which quickly became physical. Both were former soldiers who had served in Flanders and who were discussing the captains they had there when Diego Iglesias said he had never seen a captain as good as his own, Captain Juan de Rentería. Vargas then replied that there were other soldiers who were just as good, especially his own, Captain Ríos. Iglesias replied that what he was saying was very well said, and that Vargas's captain was not as good and was going to hell. He then picked up a tool he was working with and hit him on the head; the men eventually had to be seperated by officials.[29]

For Diego de Iglesias, affirming that one could not possibly have a captain better than his would have been of no importance if he had not known that his colleague Vargas had also served the King. Iglesias is, from the outset, set in his ways and refused any possibility of comparison. The first statement is clearly a challenge to which the person challenged must reply, which Vargas did by matching the stake of his opponent, like one might in a game of cards. Confronted by this refusal to submit (yet what else was he supposed to do?) as in accordance with strict societal rules, Iglesias was forced to resort to a more physical challenge and hit his opponent, but only symbolically. As his opponent did not react, he repeated this with a cotton reel and other workers joined in. Vargas was seriously injured and later died.

Homo ludens/homo violens

In his famous dissertation, Johan Huizinga shows how games had 'the function of creating culture'.[30] Games could also lead to violent conflict. Both individual and team games gave an opportunity for each and every person to shine publicly. But they also carried a hefty risk, inversely proportional to the given advantage: that of seeing one's prestige questioned in front of important people or even the whole village.

There was a variety of sporting events and occasions, both indoor and outdoor, in Castile at this time. There was, for instance, a number of popular indoor games – card games, pelota – which could also be played outside – and billiards. Card games, in particular, could often lead to violence. To begin with, the competitive element of the game could of itself lead to violence and the fact that money was at stake could also serve to reinforce resentment and opposition among those involved.

Even women could be drawn into such rivalry. On 16 June 1695, at Simancas, a small town near Valladolid, about twelve or so women, making the most of their Sunday, came together in the afternoon outside one of their front doors. At least five of them were playing 'fifteen',[31] with a stake of one *maravedí* for each game, a particularly modest sum. Coming towards half-past six, María Crespo got lucky and claimed, perhaps too quickly, the bets of the other players. One of them, Catalina de Mayorga, undoubtedly angered, refused to hand over her money. Furious, the winner threw her earnings in her opponent's face. There followed a dispute which soon came to blows. The others joined in and María Crespo was hit on the head, apparently not seriously. The following day, however, she died. Subsequently, a witness claimed to have seen her rival, Catalina de Mayorga, reach for a jug after the brawl, which was the weapon used to execute the crime.[32]

Outdoor games and events were also very popular; bull races were popular with all classes. These bull races were, in fact, more of a spectacle than a game. Members of the aristocracy, students, non-noble middle-class office holders and common people all went along, and sometimes fought there. Another popular outdoor pursuit was *argolla*, in which wooden balls were passed through a metal ring inserted into the ground at a point. *Argolla* was very popular in all social circles. The ring was, however, used in some cases as a weapon during a dispute. Skittles, on a Sunday afternoon, could also lead to conflict among both village- and city-dwellers. Today nine pins are arranged in three rows, which must be toppled over by throwing a ball which should not touch certain skittles or go over certain boundaries. The terminology in the past was just the same. For instance, today as in the past, a non-valid throw is called a 'cinca'.[33] This game sparked an argument in 1584 in the town of Aviñante. A witness said to Hernando de Salinas that his throw was 'cinca' as it had not crossed the border. His reply was that if it had not been stopped it would have gone over. This was too much for Gaspar de Colmenares who shouted out: 'Jesus Christ! For you it's not enough for a man to say that the throw is *cinca*, you must say the opposite. Jesus! What an idiot and a scoundrel! Do you seek to contradict what gentlemen say?' to which the other replied: 'The cuckold is you.'[34] Colmenares then threw himself upon the other man and during the brawl injured him with his spike.

A *vilorto* game which led to dispute on 2 May 1604 in the village of Aldihuela del Codonal near Arévalo, also provides an interesting insight into how inter-village tensions were handled and expressed through games. In this case, a number of local men argued with their neighbours from Aldeanueva, which was only four kilometres away. This game was either played six against six or eight against eight. Both the size of the playing field or the rules are unclear, but the disputes between players remind us more of contemporary ice hockey than croquet, although the latter is certainly closer to this game in terms of equipment. All we know is that in this case the away team probably came with malevolent intentions to start a fight. They brought *aguijadas*, similar to hockey sticks, which were very long sticks used to knock the ball through arches.

On the first hitch, one player lost his temper and started hitting his opponent with a hockey stick which he did very forcefully, for all to see, and in response, one of the referees for Aldeanueva, for no apparent reason, pushed the injured player to the ground, and then because of the people watching, they carried on and started hitting each other again so that those from Aldeanueva, which seemed to be pre-arranged, attacked those from Aldihuela and started to beat them harshly with their sticks and their fists and all were fighting vigorously which caused Bartolomé Rubio to be injured.[35]

It must be noted that on this occasion, things got even more violent than was customary: the injured player, who died, had stabbed Juan Rubio's son, from the Aldihuela team, with a knife during the general brawl, and the latter took revenge by hitting his attacker on the head with a stone.

Others and brothers

As Robert Muchembled has highlighted with regard to Artesian violence between the fifteenth and the seventeenth centuries, the other represented a figure of both fear and hatred in a world where the fight for survival lay at the heart of social life.[36] The same can be said of Castile in this period. This hatred of the other was an important element in popular culture at the time. A feeling of hatred, or at least contempt, could, in fact, serve to create a climate of fear within communities and also probably helped to strengthen ties and unite different members of the community when confronting those from outside the immediate locality.

This could manifest itself in hostility towards those in a neighbouring village. In a number of cases there could be a dispute over the boundaries between villages. As Domínguez Ortiz has pointed out:

> ... marking the boundaries of communes was a never ending task, which gave rise to endless trials and several armed confrontations, especially when breeders and butchers from neighbouring villages met in a wood where the boundaries were not clearly marked, a very frequent event at a time deprived of plans, land and property registries.[37]

83

A clear example of such a conflict occurred on 5 February 1654, around a large boundary mark on the outskirts of Aranda de Duero. According to witnesses, between 70 and 80 Fuentelcésped residents and 60 to 70 *vecinos* from Fresnillo had gathered to settle the accounts on some communal land in the *monte* of las Matas which the former were hiring out to the latter (the situation is complex as part of the land was under common ownership). This ritual was carried out every year. Once the boundaries had been settled, each group would retreat and have a great picnic in their area with bread, cheese and wine. One passer-by, a prosecutor at Fuente Espina who was going to Aranda and who stopped by because he knew both villages, commented: 'Such gatherings have ended in trials but this year the accounts have been settled peacefully.'

This situation, however, did not last long. Once the picnic had started, two men from Fresnillo, who had brought a purse of money to pay their dues, refused to pay. There was then an altercation around and on the boundary stone. A few people grappled with each other and some fell from the boundary stone. When some people from Fuentelcésped fell the wrong way, those from Fresnillo seized them. Their fellow villagers immediately took action and started throwing stones. Those from Fresnillo also began to throw stones and several blows were exchanged with harquebus. In his own words, the prosecutor from Fuente Espina said he was risking his own life by trying to calm the fracas. In the end, five or six people were injured on each side. Some even claimed that there were several deaths on both sides, not surprising considering the size of the confrontation and the means used, but only one death was reported at the trial. This was Mateo Fernández, a tailor from Fuentelcésped, who was cut by a harquebus from his groin to his kidneys.[38]

If people, who lived eight kilometres from each other, the distance which separated these two rival villages, were considered outsiders to the point of warranting the same treatment as a foreign invader during an international conflict, what can be said about those living tens or even hundreds of kilometres away from home?

Blas Manrique, resident of Alaejos, who was working on platform constructions to build a bull racing course at Segovia, a good hundred kilometres from his home, experienced the often tragic consequences of being an outsider. Having gone to Segovian Pedro de Zárate's mother to collect a debt, Pedro took offence and asked the stranger (*forastero*) why he had come to put his mother in turmoil (*alborotar*). Manrique replied he was only asking for what was his. The Segovian cut him short: 'I don't owe anything and I speak more truth than people from Alaejos.' 'People from Alaejos are honest and speak as much truth as you,' replied the other. In many cases, once such contradictory statements were uttered, the only way out would be an armed confrontation.[39] But at Segovia, on 10 July 1645, events initially took a different course. Zarate asked if Manrique had statements to prove the debt. Manrique proceeded to show the documentation. This, one witness remarked, 'calmed [Zarate] down'.[40]

Could this show a change in morals and the use of less bloody means for more bureaucratic ones? Nothing could be less certain. Shortly after this event, a witness reported that he saw a man on the Plaza Mayor being followed by six or seven others; the man being pursued fell. Another man then made his way through the crowd and delivered a fatal sword thrust to the person on the ground. The man killed was Blas Manrique.

In this case, the debtor, Zarate, also clearly looked down on the creditor, Manrique, and gave the impression that he was a nobleman,[41] thereby asserting a position of social superiority. This, combined with the fact that he was tackling an 'outsider', gave him a clear advantage in this conflict.

Yet even in a case where the social position of the protagonists was reversed, such as where the stranger was the nobleman, the result could be the same: bad fortune for the stranger. In the early afternoon of 5 May 1653, Don Benito Francisco of Bolaño Rivadeneira, knight of the order of Santiago, from Torres Dueña in Galicia,[42] accompanied by five servants, was travelling to his home town from Salamanca, where he was a student. They paused for a rest at a tavern in the village of Val de San Lorenzo de Arriba. According to one of the servants, three men came to pick a quarrel at the door of the small inn. One of the servants tried to dispatch them but things soon turned ugly. The bells were rung and the villagers came to help their own, including inhabitants of nearby villages, such as Val de San Lorenzo de Abajo and Val de San Román. Before long over one hundred people were gathered. One witness even compared this gathering to a riot and an uprising.[43] They all started throwing stones, and at the same time encouraged each other, asking who had best hit the target. They were also encouraged by the mayor (*alcalde*), Mateo Martínez, who shouted: 'Kill his dogs, I will pay.'[44] The knight was hit on the head and despite the efforts of one of his servants who crouched over him, putting his own life at risk to save his master's, 'blood flowed in abundance from his nose and mouth'. He died forty days later. The servants saw no apparent reason for this outbreak of violence as 'the deceased was a person of many qualities, courteous and measured'.[45]

This incident seems to have arisen after a rumour (*voz*) was spread that the knight and one of his servants had killed a villager after coming out of the tavern where the travellers had just dined. It was believed that a man had been pushed by one of Don Benito's servants and had fallen and died (*hizo el muerto*). In fact, it seems that at the moment of the quarrel coming out of the inn, Don Benito had already got back onto his horse, which the villager, later believed to be dead, was holding by the bridal. It is at this moment that one of the gentleman's servants intervened to push him back.

The frantic fury exhibited in this case conforms in some respects with the rules of the genre: the victim is noble and a stranger (Galicia may not be far away but is, relatively speaking, another universe) who mistreats the locals. A rumour spreads quickly and the ferocious crowd becomes uncontrollable and even encouraged by one of the main magistrates in the locality. The ringing of the bells, the solidarity of the *vecinos*, the minor local elite ensuring the smooth running of the operations, the throwing of stones, a certain anti-seigniorial feeling, are just as important as the common uprising.[46] Don Benito Francisco de Bolaño Rivadeneira had clearly got nothing to do with the difficulties or the resentment of the people of Val de San Lorenzo and its surroundings. He was rather a scapegoat in the sense that he could be substituted for a locally hated oligarch or, at least, he represented an aristocratic figure who interfered with or bothered ordinary people. He was also the victim of mimetic desire on the part of the villagers, as René Girard defines it,[47] by his status and his following of five servants who only make use of local facilities to sustain themselves, then go on to other, undoubtedly more prestigious, places. The procession of a nobleman and his servants was clearly modest seen from the perspective of Madrid or Valladolid, but in the depths of a valley far from the splendours of such big cities it was seen rather differently. This unique case in our corpus is even more worthy of interest as it shows that even in such a serious case involving a noble victim attacked by ordinary people, a pardon was granted three years later to those involved. Juan Miguélez, who was certainly not in the front row of rioters, was pardoned for the relatively large sum of one thousand ducats, but for seven of the accused, this fine was reduced by half (3,800 *reales*) due to their poverty.

Those from outside Spain could also encounter acts of violence. In the desert province of Soria, on 15 July 1647, three Frenchmen[48] were travelling the road in order to find work haymaking (one of the men, from Montpellier, said that he 'lived to cut grass'). They were nearly at the end of their travels from Galve (in the province of Teruel) to San Esteban de Gormaz (about 220 kilometres as the crow flies), and were within 20 kilometres of their destination. They made their way with their scythes on their backs, when two men jumped out in front of them, each armed with a harquebus, and demanded that they hand over their scythes and all the money they had 'threatening them a lot saying that if they did not do it they would be killed'.[49] The two Frenchmen said they didn't have any money and they refused to give over their scythes: 'We'd rather die than give up our scythes'.[50] On hearing this, the young Miguel de Antón opened fire and mortally wounded Juan de Domingo with a shot to the chest, near his left arm. The bandits escaped, the two survivors were leaning over their dying friend when a farmer and his dog appeared. This man then started to stone them and they admitted themselves that 'if they hadn't had the scythes that helped them defend themselves against the stones, he would have killed them'. He shouted at them 'I swear to God that you will die and never return to France! Tomás, Tomás, come and help me, come here and help me kill these French people'.[51]

There are two quite distinct parts to this attack. First, there was a classic bandit crime which involved an act of functional, premeditated violence. Second, there was an act marked by cruel spontaneity, which reveals strong anti-French feelings on the part of the farmer who had nothing to gain out of this business, but who attacks, not for pleasure, nothing allows us to confirm that, but rather from hostility towards foreigners or, more particularly, anti-French feelings. The man found guilty of homicide was pardoned a year later upon payment of 1,400 *reales* (127 ducats); the bandits, however, were penalised more heavily.

Other cases reveal not only the impact of xenophobia but also that of cultural differences between the parties involved. This is evident in the case of Pedro Lorenzo, a single man from Antwerp, who, along with a number of compatriots, was in Valladolid on 13 December 1646.[52] The group did not speak Castilian but were enjoying themselves and drinking wine. At one point, Lorenzo, already a bit light-headed, went with his friends to give flowers to a woman in the *corral* of the Copera, right in the centre of town. His actions, however, seem to have caused offence as he was soon confronted by Gonzalo Pérez, nicknamed *Vinagre* (vinegar).[53] Pérez arrived clutching his drawn sword with his shield in his other hand and attacked Lorenzo.

There seem to have been a number of reasons for this attack. It would appear that getting drunk was not common in Castile and the Spanish were trying to rid society of this habit. It would appear that the drunkenness of the Flemish visitors, added to by their language and their exotic dress in the eyes of Valladolid residents, must have made a strong impression on the locals. In addition, their casual and friendly approach to women undoubtedly clashed with the rigid rules of Castilian society and even offended those on the margins of society such as Pérez.

Conclusion

This essay has explored both the circumstances in which acts of lethal violence arose and the characteristics of such acts in Castilian society in the sixteenth and seventeenth centuries. Violence seems to have been woven into the fabric of Castilian culture. Violence could be used to demonstrate and express hostility towards those from outside the local community and the national polity. It could also emerge from or, indeed, be part of recreational activities and games. Violence also seems to have played a role in both elite and popular culture. Members of all classes could resort to acts of often extreme violence if they felt that their reputation or status had been called into question. In fact, an acute sense of honour, often upheld by the sword,[54] seems to have pervaded the social and cultural life of Castile at all levels of society in this period. The carrying of, and ability to use, a sword was not merely informed by a sense of duty but was also an expression of personal honour.

This cultural acceptance of violence was, in many ways, reflected in and condoned by the policies of the state at this time. The carrying of swords was not illegal: a royal edict of 1495 actually encouraged the men of the kingdom to bear arms[55] by calling on those who had abandoned their weapons at the end of the reconquest, 'the Reconquista', and civil wars to re-arm themselves. This edict reflected a concern that territory was being conceded to bandits along the roads of the kingdom and a fear that the recently instituted mounted police force, the Santa Hermandad (1476), could not fight foreign invaders effectively without the aid of well-armed civilians. The Reconquista, as René Quatrefages[56] has pointed out, also heavily influenced the military character of Spain. This period witnessed the development of a strong and loyal infantry which served as a precursor to that which later triumphed on Europe's battlefields. The country also developed a strong cavalry drawn from the mass of the people, unique in the Christian West. The popular composition of the Castilian cavalry owed its origins to the lack of men and horses in Castile which meant any cavalier was welcome, whatever their social origin. Unlike other European kingdoms, therefore, a cavalier lifestyle which was characterised by the use of swords spread throughout all social strata and developed with tacit, even explicit, royal authority.

The use of and attitudes to violence were, however, not simply rooted in the distinctive martial character of Castilian society; they were also influenced by a keen sense of Catholicism and the expression of a shared religious identity deeply rooted in both elite and popular culture. In some respects, this was a sub-product of the Reconquista. For the progressive appropriation of all the peninsular territories undoubtedly gave the Christian population of Castile a feeling of grandeur and glory. It also reflected a marked increase in intolerance towards religious minorities, and in particular towards Jews and Muslims. These two minority groups were, to a large degree, looked down upon and excluded from the wider culture which was infused with a sense of the superiority of the Catholic Church. The inferior nobleman (*hidalgo*), the peasant, the craftsman, the servant and the shopkeeper were, in a sense, bound together by a common or shared sense of belonging to a superior world to that of the non-Catholic.

Thus Castilian culture, both elite and popular, placed a great emphasis on personal honour, military preparedness and religious exclusivity. Both the use of violence and the tolerance displayed by the authorities towards violence through the pardoning process reflected this wider culture. This was a cultural outlook which had its roots in the late Middle Ages, but which was still an active element in Castilian culture at the end of the seventeenth century.

Notes

1 Translated by David Garley.
2 Richard Hoggart, *The Uses of Literacy. Aspects of Working-Class Life with Special Reference to Publications and Entertainments* (London: Chatto & Windus, 1959 [1957]), 16.
3 Robert Muchembled, who has done a lot of work to produce an accurate impression of popular culture in the modern era, calls the first chapter of his *Invention de l'homme moderne*: 'Violents, sales et méchants: Tous en scène!' ('Violent, dirty and bad: all on stage!'). Robert Muchembled, *Invention de l'homme moderne* (Paris: Fayard, 1988), 15.

4 Jacques Revel, 'La culture populaire: sur les usages et les abus d'un outil historiographique', *Cuturas populares. Diferencias, divergencias, conflictos. Actas del Coloquio celebrado en la Casa de Velásquez, los días 30 de noviembre y 1–2 de diciembre de 1983* (Madrid: Casa de Velásquez-Universidad Complutense, 1986), 223–39.

5 Carlo Ginzburg, *Le Fromage et les vers. L'univers d'un meunier du XVIᵉ siècle* (Paris: Flammarion, 1980), 176. [Translation into French of *Il formaggio e i vermi*, Turin: Einaudi, 1976.]

6 Norbert Elias, *La Civilisation des mœurs* (Paris: Calman-Lévy, 1973) and idem, *La Dynamique de l'Occident* (Paris: Calman-Lévy, 1975). [These two works are translations into French of *Über den Prozess der Zivilisation*, of which the first edition was published 1939.]

7 Robert Muchembled, *Culture populaire et culture des élites dans la France moderne (XVᵉ–XVIIIᵉ)* (Paris: Flammarion, 1978); idem, *L'invention de l'homme moderne*; idem, *La Société policée. Politique et politesse en France du XVIᵉ au XXᵉ siècle* (Paris: Seuil, 1998).

8 Pieter Spierenburg, 'Faces of Violence: Homicide Trends and Cultural Meanings: Amsterdam, 1431–1816', *Journal of Social History*, 27, 4 (1994), 701–16; idem, 'Long-Term Trends in Homicide: Theoretical Reflections and Dutch Evidence: Fifteenth to Twentieth Centuries', in E.A. Johnson and E.H. Monkonnen (eds), *The Civilization of Crime. Violence in Town and Country since the Middle Ages* (Urbana and Chicago, IL: University of Illinois Press, 1996), 63–105; idem, 'Violence and the Civilizing Process: Does it Work?', *Crime, Histoire & Sociétés/Crime, History & Societies*, 5, 2 (2001), 87–105.

9 The strongest critique is the work of Gerd Schwerhoff, 'Criminalized Violence and the Process of Civilisation: A Reappraisal', *Crime, Histoire & Sociétés/Crime, History & Societies*, 6, 2 (2002), 103–26 to which Spierenburg responded with 'Theorizing in Jurassic Park: A Reply to Gerd Schwerhoff', *Crime, Histoire & Sociétés/Crime, History & Societies*, 6, 2 (2002), 127–8.

10 Norbert Elias, *La société de cour* (Paris: Flammarion, 1985), 331. [Translation into French of *Die höfische Gesellschaft*, Neuwied und Berlin: Hermann Luchterhand Verlag, 1969.]

11 Claude Gauvard, *'De grace especial': Crime, État et société en France à la fin du Moyen Age* (Paris: Publications de la Sorbonne, 1991), 705–52 and 944.

12 For major studies based on such documents, see Robert Muchembled, *La violence au village. Sociabilité et comportements populaires en Artois du XVᵉ au XVIIᵉ siècle* (Turnhout: Brepols, 1989), 419; Gauvard, *'De grace especial'*.

13 On the royal pardon, see Mª Inmaculada, Rodríguez Flores, *El perdón real en Castilla (Siglos XIII–XVIII)* (Salamanca: Universidad de Salamanca, 1971), 280. On the documents we have studied, see José Luis de las Heras Santos, 'Indultos concedidos por la Cámara de Castilla en tiempos

de los Austrias', *Studia Histórica*, I (1983), 115–41 and Rudy Chaulet, 'La violence en Castille au XVIIe siècle à travers les *Indultos de Viernes Santo (1623–1699)*', *Crime, Histoire & Sociétés/Crime, History & Societies*, 1, 2 (1997), 5–27.

14 One example has been found in the Castilian archives (Archivo General de Simancas (AGS), Cámara de Castilla (C[a] C[a]), legajo (leg) 2659/sin número (sn): the Moorish slave Francisco (Hamete) Antonio who killed a porter (*esportillero*) called Diego Hernández, with a dagger in the stomach, during a brawl leaving a gambling den in May 1626. He was sentenced to 200 lashes of the whip, which were carried out, and ten years on the galleys. He was pardoned in 1628, 23 months after the murder.

15 Jean-Claude Chesnais, *Histoire de la violence en Occident de 1800 à nos jours* (Paris: Laffont, 1981), 409.

16 Michel Verret, *La Culture Ouvrière* (Paris, L'Harmattan, 1996 [1988]), 111–18.

17 Mikhail Bakhtin, *L'œuvre de François Rabelais et la culture populaire au Moyen Age et sous la Renaissance* (Paris: Gallimard, 1970), 148–97.

18 Marta Madero, *Manos violentas, palabras vedadas. La injuria en Castilla y León (siglos XIII–XV)* (Madrid: Taurus, 1992), 225, *passim*. For codification, 38–41.

19 *mientes, miente, mentís, remiente, miente como un cornudo.*

20 Claude Chauchadis, *La loi du duel. Le code du point d'honneur dans l'Espagne des XVIe–XVIIe siècles* (Toulouse: Presses universitaires du Mirail, 1997), 404.

21 It must be noted, however, that this does not mean that the sword and formal duels were unfamiliar to the lower orders in Castile.

22 AGS, C[a]C[a], leg. 2634/15: 'Y sobre estas palabras, se agarraron'.

23 Bakhtin, *L'œuvre de François Rabelais*, 366–74.

24 AGS, C[a]C[a], leg. 2594/14.

25 AGS, C[a]C[a], leg. 2606/5: 'The ferocious wolves tie it to the column', from the start of the flagellation of Christ.

26 Johan Huizinga, *L'Automne du Moyen Age* (Paris, Payot, 1975), 10–34.

27 AGS, C[a]C[a], leg. 2628/11: 'Sal acá, bujarrón, puto, que te hemos de matar y no has de amanecer vivo [...] que me da que sea despensero mayor, que no debe de ser sino algún puto judío bautizado en caldera pues que no sale [...] salga fuera el puto cornudo jodido, que no somos aquí portugueses.' Portuguese: referring to converted, or crypto-, Jews suspected of still practising their former religion in secret.

28 AGS, C[a]C[a], leg. 2593/10.

29 AGS, C[a]C[a], leg. 1625/18: 'Trataron cada uno de su capitán que habían tenido en Flandes y el dicho Diego de Iglesias le dijo que no había tal capitán como el suyo que era Juan de Rentería y este testigo dijo que otros había tenido tan buenos soldados y en particular el capitán Ríos y a esto el dicho Iglesias dijo que lo que decía era muy mal dicho, que

no lo hace su capitán y se fuera noramala y tomó el peine con que trabajaba y le dio en la cabeza y este testigo le dijo que mirase con quién hablaba, luego le tiró una carduza asimismo a este testigo y luego llegaron dos oficiales de Revejo que los separaron.'

30 Johan Huizinga, *Homo Ludens. Essai sur la Fonction Sociale du Jeu* (Paris: Gallimard, 1951), 86–130.

31 The number of points that one needs to win. This game is today better known as twenty-one or twenty-five.

32 AGS, CªCª, leg. 2603/9.

33 Carlos Blanco Álvaro, *De año y vez. Fiestas populares de Castilla y León* (Valladolid: Ámbito, 1993), 191–5.

34 AGS, CªCª, leg. 2610/4: 'Cuerpo de Dios, con vos, no bastará que hombres de bien digan que es cinca, y que vos digáis al contrario, cuerpo de Dios con el pícaro majadero, queréis contradecir lo que hombres de bien dicen.' 'Pícaro sois vos.'

35 AGS, CªCª, leg. 2676/27: 'A la primera pica uno de los jugadores se descompuso y sin causa a dar de palos a un adversario y se los dio muy bien dados con una aguijada, públicamente, delante de toda la gente y a esto luego un hombre que servía de juez y veedor de parte de los de Aldeanueva y sin otra razón al jugador ofendido le dio un empujón que dio con él en el suelo y después de esto por la gente que miraba, tornaron a jugar y en el mismo juego tornaron a reñir de manera que los de Aldeanueva como iban a lo que parecía de acuerdo cerraron con los de Aldihuela y les empezaron a tratar mal a palos y mojicones y unos con otros riñeron muy mal de manera que salió herido Bartolomé Rubio.'

36 Muchembled, *La Violence au village*, 86.

37 Antonio Domínguez Ortiz, *El Antiguo Régimen. Los Reyes Católicos y los Austrias* (Madrid: Alianza, 1983), 109: 'Una de las consecuencias desfavorables fue la multiplicación de los litigios por los confines; el amojonamiento de los términos era una tarea inacabable, que daba lugar a infinidad de pleitos y no pocos choques armados, sobre todo cuando ganaderos o leñadores de pueblos vecinos se encontraban en un monte de deslinde poco claro, hecho frecuentísimo en una época sin planos, catastro ni registros de la propiedad.'

38 The only person killed in this typically peasant-like quarrel was an artisan.

39 Chauchadis, *La loi du duel*, 404.

40 AGS, CªCª, leg. 1871/sn: 'No había ido más de a pedir lo que le debía.' 'No debo nada y digo más la verdad que los de Alaejos.' 'Los de Alaejos son gente honrada y decía tanta verdad como él.' '¿Qué papeles traía para pedirlo?' 'Y con esto se sosegaron.'

41 Which he may well have been – the documentation does not clarify this matter.

42   AGS, CᵃCᵃ, leg. 1916/3. We have not managed to find Torres Dueña, but the names of the victim correspond to two place names about 17 km from each other and to the east of Lugo.

43   Ibid., 'Sonada, motín y alboroto.'

44   Ibid., 'Se ayudaron unos a otros, se hablaban sobre quién había tirado la mejor pedrada al difunto y en particular el dicho Mateo Martínez, juez, que con voces altas decía: "¡Matad a esos perros, yo lo pagaré!".'

45   Ibid., 'El difunto era persona de mucha calidad, afable, compuesto y comedido.'

46   Pedro Luis Lorenzo Cardoso, *Los conflictos populares en Castilla (siglos XVI–XVII)* (Madrid: Siglo Veintiuno, 1996), 114–16, 120–4, 129–49, 192–3.

47   René Girard, *La violence et le sacré* (Paris: Hachette, 1972), 105–34.

48   Two of the men were Béarnais (the Castilians called them *Biarneses*, as they were from *Biarne*), Juan de Domingo and his brother, and Pedro Birun, from the South of France (*de la provincia de Lengua Dot* [*sic*]) near Montpellier.

49   AGS, CᵃCᵃ, leg. 1866/sn: 'Haciéndoles grandes amenazas que si no se lo daban, les quitarían las vidas.'

50   Ibid., 'antes perderemos las vidas que dar las dallas'.

51   Ibid., 'Les salió un hombre que traía un perro grande de ganado y los comenzó a apedrear y a no llevar las dichas dallas, que les sirvieron de defensa y de resistir las piedras, los matara diciéndoles: ¡Voto a Dios que habéis de morir y no volver más a Francia! ¡Tomás, Tomás, ven aquí a ayudarme! ¡Ven aquí a ayudarme a matar estos franceses!'

52   AGS, CᵃCᵃ, leg. 1877/sn.

53   A nickname which suggests both a quick-tempered character and a mediocre status in society, possibly even on the margins of society.

54   The sword was often associated with the aristocracy. It was, however, also widely used by artisans (58.2 per cent of cases) as well as by aristocrats (62.5 per cent). The use of the sword by peasants was, however, rarer (11 per cent).

55   *Recopilación de las leyes destos reynos hecha por mandado de la Majestad Catolica del Rey don Felipe Segundo nuestro señor* (Valladolid: Lex Nova, 1982 [Madrid, 1640]). Libro 6, Título 6. ley 1 fº. 121abc.

56   René Quatrefages, 'La spécificité militaire espagnole', in *Pouvoirs et société dans l'Espagne moderne. Hommage à Bartolomé Bennassar* (Toulouse: Presses universitaires du Mirail), 39–53.

Further reading

In addition to the works given in the notes for this chapter, the following is a list of studies which employ criminal justice records as an entry into the culture and society of sixteenth- and seventeenth-century Spain.

Alloza Aparicio, Ángel J. (2000) *La vara quebrada de la justicia. Un estudio histórico sobre la delincuencia madrileña entre los siglos XVI y XVII*. Madrid: Catarata.

Balancy, Elisabeth (1999) *Violencia civil en la Andalucía moderna (ss. XVI–XVIII). Familiares de la Inquisición y banderías locales*. Sevilla: Universidad de Sevilla.

Bazán Díaz, Iñaki (1995) *Delincuencia y criminalidad en el País Vasco en la transición de la Edad Media a la Moderna*. Vitoria: Servicio Central de Publicaciones del País Vasco.

Bennassar, Bartolomé (1975) *L'Homme espagnol. Attitudes et mentalités du XVIᵉ au XIXᵉ siècle*. Paris, Hachette; Brussels: Complexe, 2003.

Caporossi, Olivier (2002) 'Les Justices royales et la criminalité madrilène sous le règne de Philippe IV (1621–1665). Unité et multiplicité de la juridiction royale à la cour d'Espagne'. PhD thesis, Toulouse.

Carrasco, Raphaël (dir.) (1994) *La prostitution en Espagne de l'époque des Rois Catholiques à la IIᵉ République*. Besançon: Annales littéraires de l'Université de Besançon.

Chauchadis, Claude (1997) *La loi du duel. Le code du point d'honneur dans l'Espagne des XVIᵉ–XVIIᵉ siècles*. Toulouse: Presses universitaires du Mirail.

Dedieu, Jean-Pierre (1989) *L'administration de la foi. L'inquisition de Tolède (XVIᵉ–XVIIᵉ siècle)*. Madrid: Casa de Velázquez.

Duviols, Jean-Paul and Annie Molinie-Bertrand (eds) (1998) *La violence en Espagne et en Amérique, XVᵉ–XIXᵉ siècles, Actes du colloque international, Paris-Sorbonne, 13–15 novembre 1996*. Paris: Presses de l'Université de Paris-Sorbonne.

Fortea, José I., Juan E. Gelabert and Tomás A. Mantecón (eds) (2002) *Furor et rabies. Violencia, conflicto y marginación en la Edad Moderna*. Santander: Universidad de Cantabria.

Heras Santos, José Luis de las (1991) *La justicia penal de los Austrias en la corona de Castilla*. Salamanca: Universidad de Salamanca.

León, Pedro de (1981) *Grandeza y miseria en Andalucía. Testimonio de una encrucijada histórica (1578 a 1616)*. Granada: Facultad de Teología.

Mantecón-Movellán, Tomás Antonio (1997) *Conflictividad y disciplinamiento social en la Cantabria de los siglos XVII y XVIII*. Santander: Universidad de Cantabria.

Perez Garcia, Pablo (1990) *La comparsa de los malhechores. Valencia 1479–1518*. Valencia: Diputación de Valencia.

Perez Garcia, Pablo (1991) *El Justicia criminal de Valencia (1479–1707). Una magistratura valenciana ante la consolidación del Absolutismo*. Valencia: Generalitat Valenciana.

Perez Garcia, Pablo (1993) 'Desorden, criminalidad, justicia y disciplina en la edad moderna temprana: problemas abiertos', in León Carlos Álvarez Santaló y Carmen M.ª Cremades Griñán (eds), *Mentalidad e ideología en el Antiguo Régimen*. Murcia: Universidad de Murcia, 93–118.

Perry, Mary Elizabeth (1993) *Ni espada rota ni mujer que trota. Mujer y desorden social en la Sevilla del Siglo de Oro* [*Gender and Disorder in Early Modern Seville*]. Barcelona: Crítica.

Tomás y Valiente, Francisco (1969) *El derecho penal de la monarquía absoluta (Siglos XVI–XVII–XVIII)*. Madrid: Tecnos.

Vincent, Bernard (1987) *Minorías y marginados en la España del siglo XVI*. Granada: Diputación Provincial.

Chapter 4

Prosecution and public participation – the case of early modern Sweden

Maria Kaspersson

The historical development of the Nordic countries has generally been characterized by extensive popular support for the law and the normal judicial forums.[1]

The common perception is that the courts in the Nordic countries were able to function as significant conflict-resolving arenas in the community because of the public support they had. Österberg and Sandmo term this a 'harmony model' meaning that behind the concept of law was concealed 'not only a collection of statutes expressing prohibitions and penalties, but a general ethic, a societal ideology, the traditional patterns for handling conflicts'. Since the spirit of the law was shared by a majority of the people in Nordic society, it is also possible to talk about law and justice as 'expressions of a mentality'.[2] Österberg and Sandmo emphasise how *people met the law* and how the court, rather than being perceived as 'a theatre of power', can be seen as a 'social and discursive arena'.[3]

The Nordic countries have had written law codes ever since the Middle Ages, the oldest stemming from the twelfth century. As Sogner points out, the Nordic countries constituted a separate 'legal family', known as 'Romano-Germanic', even though the 'elements of Roman law were highly limited'. The legal system in the Scandinavian countries was also 'characterised by simple legislation and a prolonged retention of medieval law'.[4] The legal structure was tripartite – District Court, Court of Appeal and Supreme Court or the king – with an informal procedural system relying on oral proceedings. People either handled their own cases or, if they did not feel confident enough, hired someone with experience to act as a legal representative. A very large number of criminal cases depended on a private charge for the case to be heard in court and, which is important in this context, the responsibility for bringing breaches of the law to court rested with ordinary men and women, not with the authorities.[5]

The strong influence of orthodox Protestantism, in the sixteenth, seventeenth and eighteenth centuries, can also be seen as a key component in the legal and judicial development of the Nordic countries. After the Reformation in 1523, the Mosaic Law influenced the law codes. This resulted in harsher penalties, especially for extra-marital sexual relations. The state and the church combined their efforts to construct the heterosexual norm in tightening their control of marriage. The Lutheran church was closely associated with the secular power in all the Nordic countries.[6] The church passed on information from the authorities to the people by reading announcements from the pulpit – for example about changes in legislation – during Sunday service. The local clergy also participated in the disciplining and registration of the people in the local community, including the registration of deaths, births and marriages and the yearly test of the population's biblical knowledge.[7]

Community and state law

Bruce Lenman and Geoffrey Parker claim that the justice systems of Europe underwent a gradual but fundamental change between the late Middle Ages and the nineteenth century. This change involved a shift from a reliance on 'restitutive justice' and 'community law' to a greater emphasis on 'punitive justice' and 'state law'.[8] Österberg and Sandmo point out that in the case of communal and restitutive justice, 'its exercise was close to the local community and presupposed its cooperation' and the purpose of the prosecution was to gain compensation and restitution for the offended party and 'to restore the offender to the local social community'.[9] These characteristics fit well with Scandinavian justice. As an ideal type the system operating in Scandinavia in the early modern period can best be described as 'communalistic'.

The dominant feature of the 'communalistic ideal type' was justice by negotiation. The state did not adopt a particularly active role; most cases were brought by private individuals and were concerned with the resolution of conflicts and disputes between ordinary people.

Justice was rooted in the local community, the courts were close at hand and there was easy access to them.[10] For example, in Stockholm they had three subdivisions of the local District Court, one on each of the main inhabited islands (Stockholm is today spread over 14 islands). The Northern District Court had later to be divided into two further subdivisions, the Eastern and Western Northern District Court, as the population grew rapidly during the eighteenth century. In the sixteenth and seventeenth centuries, court sittings were held three days a week if needed – on Monday, Wednesday and Friday – and in the eighteenth century the number of cases meant court sittings were held every day, apart from Sunday.[11]

This 'communalistic model' worked well in Scandinavia since the society was socially homogeneous, especially in comparison to elsewhere in Europe, consisting mainly of free peasants in the countryside and craftsmen belonging to different guilds in the towns. At the same time, the social structure was vertically organised. From the latter part of the seventeenth century onward, however, the communalistic model of justice was taken over by state-controlled expert justices. The new model can be seen as the result of the judicial revolution and of what Weber termed a process of bureaucratisation.[12]

Prosecution and public participation

The element of public participation in the criminal justice system can be said to always have been substantial in Scandinavia, but the participation has not necessarily always been of the same type. The working hypothesis adopted here is that public participation has always been significant, but changed in character between the seventeenth and eighteenth centuries. One explanation is that the judicial revolution brought about changes such as professionalisation and bureaucratisation, which changed the room for and forms of public participation.

Taussi Sjöberg argues that the changes that took place in the pattern of public participation went from being actively carried out by the private prosecutor in the sixteenth century, where he or she was very much part of the proceedings, to a situation in the eighteenth century where the state took over the prosecutorial function. In the earlier period, the private prosecutor could choose the punishment, usually financial compensation. As the judicial revolution progressed it meant that people were still bringing cases to the attention of the authorities (if it was not a matter of a crime against the state), but they did not have any part to play other than that of the victim. They no longer had any say in the prosecution and choice of punishment. With growing state interest, penalties went from being in the form of compensation to being in the form of corporal punishments.[13]

One way of looking at how the public participated in the justice system is to see how active they were in bringing cases to court, i.e. to see who was prosecuting, and also which cases they prosecuted. By studying different time periods, changes in these patterns can be identified. In this chapter, the Stockholm District Court minutes for different years in the early seventeenth and eighteenth centuries will be used to investigate the pattern of prosecution. By referring to earlier studies on homicide, infanticide and suicidal murder in the eighteenth century[14] some anomalies in this model will also be highlighted and a picture painted of public participation in the prosecutorial process.

The seventeenth century

In the seventeenth century, there was not yet a division into criminal and civil cases, but all cases were dealt with by the same court. The majority of cases were actually civil or financial including matters of buying and selling properties, the execution of wills, the registering of legal representatives and loans, debts and interest matters. An estimated 160 civil cases and administrative matters were dealt with in the years 1605–8.[15] In the same period, 58 criminal cases were before the court. Twenty-four criminal cases were recorded in 1605, 12 in 1606, 14 in 1607 and a mere 8 in 1608. With a population of about 10,000,[16] this gives a ratio of 1.45 cases per 1,000 inhabitants, which is rather low. It is well known, however, that not all crimes were formally recorded in the court minute books. Other cases were dealt with privately out of court and some records have simply not survived. It is also plausible that only the more serious crimes were dealt with in this period, due to the political unrest in the country, perhaps explaining the dominance of homicide cases.[17]

In the years 1605 to 1608 the two largest categories of cases (see Table 4.1) were homicide/violence and theft. The aim of bringing these cases to court was often to claim compensation. Homicide made up 81 per cent of cases of violent crime. In these cases, the killer sometimes had to pay the victim's family compensation for the loss of income. Even if the death penalty was the most common sentence for homicide, when broken down into further categories, it

Table 4.1 Distribution of cases in the Stockholm District Court, 1605–08

Type of case	Percentages
Theft	27
Homicide/infanticide	27
Non-lethal violence	7
Sexual	7
Slander	14
Money/regulations	12
Other	6
N = 58	100

Source: Stockholm District Court Minutes 1605–1608.

was cases classified as murder that received the ultimate sentence – 73 per cent in the period 1576–1608. However, in as many as 20 per cent of homicide cases fines were imposed or compensation offered.[19] This was for cases legally classified as self-defence, involuntary or accidental manslaughter. Likewise, in cases of theft – which was sometimes prosecuted under the lesser charge of 'unlawful removal'[20] – it was not so much punishment that was sought, but the recovery of the stolen items or financial compensation. The death penalty was usually only meted out for aggravated theft or recidivist thieves.

In cases of theft it was almost always the victim, and in homicide cases the victim's family, that pressed charges. For example, in 1607[21] Mrs[22] Hansdaughter brought the killer of her husband to court and in 1605[23] Mr Nilsson accused the sawyer, Björnsson, of having killed Nilsson's brother. If the victim's family did not prosecute the killers, then it was those who had been at the scene of the crime. In 1605,[24] the city watch commander Jacobsson accused some German soldiers of rioting and killing one and seriously injuring another member of the city watch. In 1607[25] the neighbours and servant of Anders Eggert brought him to court for his 'pathetic killing' of his own wife. In 1608[26] the vicar and his clerk caught the offender who had killed a man outside the vicarage and brought him to court and in 1605[27] Halvarsson was brought to court by Jöran the Barber for having killed a sea captain in his house.

In cases of theft, it was almost always the victim who brought the case to court. In 1608,[28] a maid, Carin, was accused by her master of having stolen from him and in 1606[29] Mr Hansson brought a soldier,

Mats, to court because he had stolen silver goods from him. In some cases, where more than one person had been victimised, a group of people prosecuted the suspected thief together. This was the case in 1605[30] when several Stockholm residents brought Olsson to court accusing him of theft and unpaid debts and in 1607[31] a number of stall holders brought a boy called Daniel to court for having stolen from their market stalls.

Defamation was the third most common offence brought before the courts by private individuals. These cases were, by definition, conflicts between individuals and only the persons who were directly involved in the conflicts brought these cases to court. In 1605,[32] Mr Simonsson accused his wife's brother-in-law of having verbally insulted himself and his wife and in 1606[33] Mr Wulff accused Mr Fältmann of saying he had found Wulff drinking in a 'public whore house'. In 1607[34] Larsson was accused by Pedersson of spreading false rumours about him and in 1608[35] Mårten the Weigher brought Plös to court for having called his wife 'a whore'.

In these defamation cases and, indeed, in some homicide and assault cases a code of honour was in operation. Honour has its strongest hold on people in collective and close-knit societies[36] like seventeenth-century Stockholm. This meant that to keep your honour in other people's eyes you had to actively maintain it. For men, this meant among other things that slights to honour had to be met with violence or by bringing the case to court. Male honour was all about activity, action and reaction.[37] For women, their honour was connected to their sexual behaviour[38] and they often had no other way to counter honour slights than by bringing cases to court to prove that they were 'honourable'.[39]

How matters of honour needed to be regulated between people is not only demonstrated in cases of defamation. Since honour sometimes needed to be defended by violent means, a deep sense of honour is also often revealed in instances of assault and homicide. In 1608,[40] Mr Nublichin brought the skinner Trost to court because he had been drunk and had insulted him by refusing to drink with him. Later they fought with rapiers and eventually Nublichin was shot in the shoulder by Trost. In 1605,[41] Mrs Meiers brought Mr Höier to court and accused him of having called her a whore, assaulting her and having smashed her window.

Other cases that involve honour and the need to regulate dealings between individuals have to do with embezzlement and civil cases regarding unpaid debts. One way for the private person to put pressure on his fellow man who owed him money, or otherwise did not act according to the rules, was to bring the case to court. The publicity and threat to that person's honour, which the court case entailed, worked towards settlements being agreed. That and a wish to get his money might have been the reasons behind merchant Jonsson's bringing of innkeeper Danitz to court in 1606[42] for not having paid for a shipload of beer he had bought from Jonsson in 1600, a case that was not resolved as Danitz postponed swearing the oath he was to swear certifying that he had never received the beer.[43]

Matters that were regarded more as state business were not brought to court by private persons but by a variety of state officials. Cases of tax evasion, being illegally in Stockholm and illegal trade can be cited as examples. In 1607[44] His Majesty's Secretary, Eric Jöransson, accused Nilsson of having taken copper without permission and then having brought it into Stockholm without paying the toll. An area perhaps falling in between the private and the public was the regulation of prostitutes. In 1608[45] the vicar and other prominent burghers brought Walborg Andersson to court and testified to and investigated her 'loose' lifestyle.

Apart from this investigation of suspected prostitution the other sexual crimes were: one case of fornication – Melchior Axelsson was accused in 1606[46] of living with a woman for six years without marrying her – and two rape cases brought to court in 1605. In the first case,[47] a day labourer, Persson, accused Larsson, a peasant's son, of having seduced his relative, Karin, of keeping her with him for a year and then of having abandoned her. There is an element of honour involved, since the man had dishonoured the girl and the sought after solution was that he should marry her, thereby making her an 'honourable woman'. In the other case,[48] an unnamed 'slapper' (*sic!*) accused the boatman Phillipus of rape. The court, however, disregarded the charge since she was an unchaste woman and had previously committed fornication with the same boatman. The court could not see 'how he could take with violence something she had previously voluntarily given'. These cases indicate that women had room to act for themselves and often had to maintain honour and respectability by taking cases to court. The cases also demonstrate that once you had lost your honour, man or woman, it could be all but impossible to regain it.

Sexual crimes other than fornication and rape were dealt with by the ecclesiastical court.[49] It is therefore interesting to put the 'public participation model' to the test by studying who brought sexual crimes before the courts. Jarrick and Söderberg studied all cases dealt with in the Stockholm civil, criminal, military and ecclesiastical courts in 1681, a good deal later than the period studied here. They demonstrate that when it came to 'broken promises of marriage' (i.e. broken engagements) it was the women – commonly pregnant – that brought the cases to court. This was also the case with divorce files.[50] However, cases of fornication that were dealt with by the secular court were typically prosecuted by the rector when he discovered that an unmarried woman was pregnant or registered the birth of an illegitimate child. The fathers of these children were also prosecuted and not uncommonly sentenced for the fornication as well as the woman, and sometimes the men were also sentenced to maintain the child.[51] The only way of getting out of a fornication court case was for the two parties involved to marry.

What the cases from the seventeenth century demonstrate is that public participation was crucial in bringing cases to court. Private charges were necessary when it came to interpersonal conflicts regarding possessions, honour and money, since the state had little, if any, interest in such private matters. But even when the state and church were prominent, it was still mainly because of public participation that these cases were brought to court. This meant that the policies of the state and the church on, for example, sexual crimes had broad public support, at least with regard to certain crimes.

The eighteenth century

In the eighteenth century the effects of the judicial revolution – or evolution as Furuhagen claims is a more accurate term[52] – were more generally felt. For example, state power had become centralised and the criminal justice system had become more strictly and more hierarchically organised. At the same time, the state grew less tolerant of violence and began to punish these crimes more harshly.[53] The public element did not disappear, however, but changed in character. Homicide and theft cases were no longer prosecuted for the victim to gain compensation, but for punishment. Even if the amount of violent conflicts diminished, especially fatal ones,[54] honour still played a crucial part in all cases of defamation that were brought to court. In addition to defending your honour with violence – which still took place – you could file for defamation and slander and use the courts to restore your honour. This also meant that women had more room to manoeuvre and to defend their honour and reputation since the courts offered a feasible and accessible way for women to defend themselves. This was not a new course of action, but its use increased considerably.

One result of the judicial revolution visible in court organisation is that the District Courts were clearly defined and divided into two separate courts, the civil and the criminal. Due to gaps in the records, the Stockholm Southern and Northern District Courts were studied for 1728 and the City District Court for 1729, but are treated as representing one year. All in all 814 criminal cases were dealt with in the period. As the population had grown to 45,000 inhabitants in 1720 this gives a ratio of 18 per 1,000 inhabitants, a clear – more than tenfold – increase from the early seventeenth century. In the eighteenth century, there was also a transition from criminal cases to civil suits and the civil cases made up the vast majority of cases brought to court, but the division into civil and criminal courts meant they were not dealt with by the same court officials, as was the case in the seventeenth century.[55] This increase in criminal cases supports Lenman and Parker's observation that ordinary people demonstrated a greater willingness to participate in the prosecution of crime through the courts in the eighteenth century than had previously been the case.[56]

Table 4.2 demonstrates that violent crime was no longer the largest category, due to a dramatic decline in the middle of the seventeenth century.[57] Neither did homicide dominate as the most prevalent form of violence, as only two instances of homicide were brought to court in this period.[58] Despite these changes, it was still the victims of violence and their families that brought the cases to court and there

Table 4.2 Distribution of cases in the Stockholm District Court, 1728–29

Type of case	Percentages
Theft	21
Homicide/infanticide	0.2
Non-lethal violence	18
Sexual	20
Slander	19
Money/regulations	8
Other	13
N = 814	99

Source: Stockholm Southern and Northern District Court Minutes 1728; Stockholm City District Court Minutes 1729.

was a variety of drunken brawls, fights between men, fights between women and honour-related conflicts. As noted earlier, the number of homicides was very low, but there was a slightly larger number of prosecutions for involuntary manslaughter. These were of three main types – death by reckless driving of a horse and carriage in summer or horse and sledge in winter, accidents with firearms or child suffocation by nannies and wet nurses. They all have in common that the victims or victims' parents were the ones who usually brought the cases before the courts. For example, in 1728[59] the sea officer Anders Becker was cleaning his gun when a shot was accidentally fired and went through boatman Bökelman's head. The officer in command of the ship where Becker was stationed – as no family was present on board – brought the case to court. Likewise, in 1729[60] Maria Elisabeth Thiman was accused by her employer of having 'in her sleep suffocated the child of Mr. Colonel von Tholinius, which she was employed to breast feed'.

More interesting are the defamation and slander cases, not only because they are now as common as violence, sexual crimes and theft, but also because these are crimes in which the case still depended exclusively on private prosecutions by the individuals involved. These cases would never have been brought to court and prosecuted had it not been for the injured honour of the parties involved. In Swedish, these cases of verbal violence were tellingly named 'injuries' (*injurier*). At the same time, in comparison to the previous century, the amount of these – often seemingly petty – cases of verbal abuse had increased markedly. The slanderous epithets that were prosecuted represented a very colourful, and often highly entertaining, vocabulary. As before, men were more often accused of dishonourable acts and women's sexual reputation was repeatedly questioned. Men were called thieves, swine skins, caretaker shits, hams, drunken dogs, sausages (if you were a city guard[61]), dishonest men, kitchen bears, bloody thick bellies, peasant cats, city hall whips and whore hosts. Women were called gutter whores, night whores, bitch whores, cunts, drunken bitches, liars, thieving women, bloody things, thieving whores and very often just whores. Not uncommonly, these cases were in the shape of what was called 'vice versa charges', meaning that two persons prosecuted each other for slanderous talk. Likewise, men and women seem to have been almost equally involved in prosecuting and being prosecuted for slander and defamation.

Another category that is very informative as to what people found worthy of prosecution is what I have termed the 'other' category.

This consists of cases that were difficult to classify according to the other labels. In the Southern District Court in 1728 the majority of cases recorded in this category concerned women who were brought to trial. This might mirror the poverty and the higher ratio of women in the population of the south island (Södermalm).[62] For example, in January[63] three women were brought to trial because they had been dancing all night and in November[64] a woman was accused of having a disorderly lifestyle and of swearing. In January[65] there was an investigation into whether a man was responsible for a fire in his house, in May[66] another one was accused of bigamy and in October[67] a man was accused by his employer of being lazy in his service. In the Northern District Court more men than women were accused in this group in 1728, mirroring the higher welfare of the inhabitants and the more equal gender distribution. Among the males a man was brought to court in March[68] for having bought wine on credit giving a false name. In September[69] a rector was brought to court by a family of a recently deceased woman, accusing him of having refused to give her the last sacrament before she died. The courts functioned as coroner's inquests as well and the city physician and city surgeon could conduct autopsies on dead bodies.[70] In September 1728, we have a case of a woman who had drunk herself to death and whose corpse had been found on the square on the north island, Norrmalmstorg, which was investigated by the surgeon and physician.[71] In the City District Court, the richest part of Stockholm, men were also more common than women in 1729. A woman brought her employer to court in October[72] and demanded wages that he had not paid her. In October[73] a tailor was brought to court by a client because the tailor had refused to give back the clothes he had mended and another man[74] was charged with practising Judaism. Sometimes people were held responsible for the actions of animals in their possession. For instance, owners were commonly brought to court because their dogs had bitten children and adults. In one case, in the Northern Court[75] a man was prosecuted after his bear ran loose and mauled a man.

The city guards enforced diverse regulations. For instance, leaving or entering Stockholm without a passport, leaving employment without permission or being unemployed or wearing clothing or garments (like silk and lace for working-class women) forbidden in the 1720 Luxury and Surplus Ordinance. The city guards also enforced fire regulations, pub opening hours and curfews and prevented games and betting, fights, duels and noise in public places.[76] As mentioned above, they were unpopular and degradingly called 'sausages'.

In cases of sexual crime, which were almost exclusively cases of fornication, pregnant women dominated as private prosecutors, trying to make the fathers either marry them or pay maintenance for the child. Rectors also prosecuted such cases when they found out about pregnant women and illegitimate children, as in the case of Christina Jacobsdaughter who was brought to court by the vicar who baptised her illegitimate child in 1728.[77] The father of the child, Eric Sjöberg, a butcher's apprentice, confessed to the fornication as well as his promise of marriage and assured the court he would marry her.

From the middle of the eighteenth century onwards, the authorities, both secular and religious, began to lose the control they had had over the sexual behaviour of the population. Yet, the church still played an important part in the secular criminal justice system and cooperated with the District Court in cases of fornication, in cases of broken promises of marriage and in divorce cases. Part of the sentences for these offences could be absolved by the vicar at Sunday service by public or private repentance on the part of the offender.[78]

In Jarrick and Söderberg's study of all cases brought before the civil, criminal, military and ecclesiastical courts in Stockholm in 1780, the same pattern as in the early eighteenth century can be discerned. When it came to broken promises of marriage it was the women – pregnant or with illegitimate children – who brought their babies' fathers to court. If not for marriage, they did so at least to save their honour by making it publicly known that they had become pregnant by men who had promised them marriage but then abandoned them. For instance, Anna Örn, who had recently become a mother, turned to the court in 1778 to make the father of the child fulfil his promise of matrimony. Despite marriage being the verdict, he did not wed her.[79] In divorce cases both men and women filed for separation, usually claiming infidelity. Violence was not something the ecclesiastical court saw as grounds for divorce.[80]

Infanticide (child murder in Swedish) is also worthy of consideration in relation to public participation. The increase in infanticide cases as a response to illegitimacy may be seen as a by-product of the attempt by the church to discourage extra-marital sexual relationships in late medieval Europe. In the latter part of the sixteenth century, the Scandinavian courts had begun to develop special rules for dealing with infanticide but the number of cases did not worry the authorities until the eighteenth century.[81]

The public element in prosecuting infanticide confirms that there was probably a consensus in the general population regarding the heinousness of infanticide. It seems clear that people did not hesitate to bring these women to court. Several examples are found in eighteenth-century Stockholm. In 1729[82] two footmen in the house of Mr Sparfeldt, the mayor, found a dead infant in the baking oven. Since Maria was the only maid in the house at the time, the mayor immediately suspected her and brought her to court. Likewise, in 1765[83] female neighbours of Brita reported her since she had first gained weight and then appeared very thin after a short illness.

Another way the public participated in prosecuting women suspected of infanticide was by providing information after court enquiries, usually read in church on Sundays. In 1755[84] a dead child was found in the water in Norrström by the Butcher Bridge (Slaktarebron). There was a search for the mother and it was announced in the church. Christina's mistress reported her as she became suspicious when she heard about the baby and where it had been found. In another case, which occurred a few years earlier in 1749,[85] a skeleton of an infant was found when a new house was being built. Investigations were undertaken and it was found that the father of the child had said something about it a year earlier, and people remembered that Christina, who was not married at the time, had been 'unusually fat' nine years earlier. Cases were brought to the attention of the authorities even when the offender was not known. In 1742[86] witnesses reported to the court that they had seen a woman throw something into the water. When taken up it turned out to be a dead child with a brick tied to it.

There seems to have been considerable consensus that infanticide was something that women should not get away with. Even if it often was the public who brought these cases to court, the element of a dispute between private persons was not present. It was instead a case of actively bringing to the knowledge of the authorities cases that the state and church were left to legally process and deal with.

Concluding the results from the eighteenth century study, the influence of the judicial revolution can be found in the increased state influence on cases and how they were dealt with by the courts. There are also clear indications of the bureaucratisation of the criminal justice system – as the strict division of civil and criminal cases demonstrates – but there is still an important element of public participation in certain cases, especially in matters regarding slander and defamation and in minor disputes regarding money, debt and petty theft. In comparison to the seventeenth century, however, the character of public participation had changed, most notably in that even if you brought a case to court, you had no influence over trial and sentence. Your role had changed from an active prosecutor to becoming a prosecuting victim. That honour was still an important part of people's lives is demonstrated in the slander cases – honour had gone from being defended, in the main, by violence to being often defended in court. The judicial revolution also seems to have brought about a punitive element – justice was no longer about reconciliation and compensation but about punishment. The state's influence was also present in cases involving regulations such as the luxury and surplus ordinances.

Anomalies

There are instances that represent anomalies in the 'public participation model', namely false confessions and suicidal murders. The strong religious belief in execution as a secure entrance to heaven is worthy of consideration since it highlights different aspects of public participation in the courts. In cases of false confessions and suicidal murders the public element in the prosecution was evident, but at the same time the influence of the state and church was crucial, but in different ways.

False confessions

One challenging anomaly is the increasing number of false confessions given in court. For those who were interested in ending their own lives, suicide[87] was by no means the only available option at this time. Many tried other options; a rather popular one was to confess to heinous crimes they had not committed hoping to be sentenced to death.[88] These false confessions posed a problem and undermined the strong position confession had in the criminal justice process. More importantly, in Scandinavia it was the *voluntary* confession that held this position. Coerced confessions were considered dubious and consequently torture was very rarely in use in Scandinavia, making it stand apart from some other parts of Europe.[89] Confessions were therefore very important since people were rarely sentenced to death without one.[90]

Voluntary confessions, given on the initiative of the confessor, however, began to pose a problem for the authorities. How was the court to deal with acts committed a long time ago or without any witnesses? From the end of the seventeenth century, the authorities felt the need to investigate these confessions. The trust in the voluntary confession as strong enough evidence for a death penalty was weakened, parallel with increased feelings of the inadequacy of eyewitness and circumstantial evidence without a confession. The court consequently had to investigate if voluntary confessions originated in depression or regret.[91] It could no longer be taken for granted that a person who confessed to serious crimes did it because of guilt. The Courts of Appeal confession trials were strange in character as the roles were reversed: the suspect tried in all possible ways to demonstrate his or her guilt to a doubting court.[92]

In the Stockholm District Courts there are several examples of persons who tried to lie their lives away, ranging from confessions of murder to the gender-specific crimes of infanticide[93] and bestiality.[94] In early 1722,[95] a woman was sentenced to whipping 'because she had lied upon herself to have murdered a child'. In 1746[96] Maria Christina was in court because 'she according to her own confession has committed infanticide' but 'the Court could not consider her story as plausible.' Liliequist found that men confessed to having committed bestiality with the same purpose. When Pär fell ill in 1737[97] he confessed he had committed bestiality: 'and there was no sin or misdeed, sad event or slightest error, to which he did not confess.'

Contrary to what Foucault[98] argues, in Scandinavia executions were obviously seen as something more than the state demonstrating its power. It could be perceived as a better means of ending one's life than suicide. The immediate death following Christian preparations was an incitement for false confessions as well as an active attraction for unhappy and desperate people and for repenting sinners.[99] But false confessions of heinous acts were not the most extreme expressions of this contradiction between deterrence and reconciliation. The safest way to get executed was to actually commit murder, infanticide or bestiality with the intent of receiving the death penalty.

Suicidal murders

A suicidal murder involves the murder of someone, often a child, by a person who desires suicide, but is deterred from attempting the act by strong religious beliefs, sanctions and taboos.[100] The motive informing this kind of homicide was the desire to be executed in a way that would offer the murderer a pathway to salvation. The case of impoverished clerk widow Elisabet Runbom in 1744[101] provides an illustration of this kind of homicide. She killed her baby daughter and explained herself in the verdict as '... having been overtaken by distress, and by a spirit's impulse made the decision to take the life of her daughter, so that she as well as herself, may leave the world and all its misery.'

In explaining why people who wanted to die committed suicidal murder instead of suicide, Jansson emphasises the strong taboo against suicide prevailing in the seventeenth and eighteenth centuries[102] and Liliequist stresses the importance of the execution ceremony that was seen as providing reconciliation with God.[103] Jarrick demonstrates how committing suicide was, according to religious standards, seen as an affront against God.[104] The belief was, according to Krogh, that the act of suicide led to Hell.[105] The church strongly condemned suicide and those committing it would not get absolution from the church.

In this context, it is possible to understand the reasoning of suicidal murderers. If you seek death by getting executed, you are saved from condemnation and damnation, because you are then given the opportunity to demonstrate remorse and achieve absolution before you die. This is demonstrated in an example from Stockholm in 1733[106] when Anders Andersson Hiul, a 24-year-old boatman, stabbed his pregnant wife killing both her and the foetus. Anders stated '... that he did it on purpose and willingly, and that he did not want to live anymore, but would be pleased, the sooner the better ... to undergo the death penalty.' For despairing persons the ritual of reconciliation overshadowed the deterrence of the punishment. Death became liberation and murder the solution.[107]

The innate tension between deterrence and reconciliation subsequently resulted in ambivalence on the part of the authorities towards voluntary confessions in general.[108] This can, if one so wishes, be seen as a negative consequence of public participation in justice. If people wanted to, they could twist their roles as prosecutors for real crimes, to self-prosecution of imaginary crimes for egoistic reasons not based on a desire to see that justice was done. Worse still, they sometimes even committed these heinous crimes and willingly confessed and brought themselves to the attention of the court.

Conclusion

The working hypothesis that was adopted here – inspired by Taussi Sjöberg[109] – indicates that public participation has always been significant, but changed in character between the seventeenth and eighteenth centuries due to changes brought about by the judicial revolution. In comparison to the seventeenth century, the character of public participation changed, since the private person's influence on the case and court proceedings diminished. You went from an active prosecutor in the seventeenth century to a prosecuting victim in the eighteenth. Yet, as Sogner points out, the changes towards less laymen and more legally trained professionals brought by the judicial revolution did not mean that 'the central government triumphed over the people'.[110] The courts were still arenas for 'ongoing dialogue' between the people and those in authority.

Lenman and Parker have pointed out how the judicial revolution meant the public influence on law and justice diminished as courts became more specialised.[111] Taussi Sjöberg points out different ways of explaining the judicial revolution and the resulting changes in public participation in Scandinavia. The changes can be seen as a sign of cooperation or conflict.[112] The results from this study seem to support the former interpretation. Österberg talks about cooperation and how it characterised Scandinavian justice. The public element evident in the majority of cases, as demonstrated in this study, would not have been possible without cooperation between people – in bringing cases to court – and in the state processing them. This cooperation was demonstrated even in cases where public willingness could not always be taken for granted, such as in fornication cases.[113] The conflict theory favoured by many Finnish scholars such as Ylikangas does not apply as well to the rest of Scandinavia.[114] Public participation and the changed preconditions the judicial revolution brought for people does not seem to have caused conflicts nor were they the result of such. As Sogner points out when summarising 'the Nordic Model': 'The encounter between people and the law was an ongoing process, which involved elements of control from above and influences from below'.[115] The strength of this popular element was high before the judicial revolution but did not cease with it.[116] Instead, as was demonstrated in the eighteenth-century cases and in false confessions and suicidal murders, the interplay between the actors and lay influence in court had become more complicated even if public participation was still the crucial element. Without public participation there would not have been much crime for the state to deal with – a fact that still stands for many crimes today.

Notes

1 E. Österberg and E. Sandmo, 'Introduction', in E. Österberg and S.B. Sogner (eds), *People Meet the Law: Control and Conflict in the Courts. The Nordic Countries in the Post-Reformation and Pre-Industrial Period* (Oslo: Universitetsforlaget, 2000), 9–26 at 10.
2 Ibid., 10.
3 Ibid., 12.
4 S. Sogner, 'Conclusion: The Nordic Model', in Österberg and Sogner (eds), *People Meet the Law*, 267–76 at 267f.
5 Ibid.
6 Österberg and Sandmo, 'Introduction', 12.
7 B. Furuhagen, *Berusade bönder och bråkiga båtsmän. Social kontroll vid sockenstämmor och ting under 1700-talet* (Stockholm: Brutus Östlings Bokförlag Symposium, 1996), 191–3.
8 B. Lenman and G. Parker, 'The State, the Community and the Criminal Law in Early Modern Europe', in V.A.C. Gatrell, B. Lenman and G. Parker (eds), *Crime and the Law: The Social History of Crime in Western Europe since 1500* (London: Europa Publications, 1980), 11–48. See also Österberg. and Sandmo, 'Introduction', 16.
9 Österberg and Sandmo, 'Introduction', 16.
10 Ibid.
11 M. Kaspersson, *Dödligt våld i Stockholm på 1500-, 1700- och 1900-talen* (Department of Criminology Doctoral Thesis No. 4, Stockholm University, 2000), 34, 77f.
12 Österberg and Sandmo, 'Introduction', 18.
13 M. Taussi Sjöberg, *Rätten och kvinnorna. Från släktmakt till statsmakt på 1500- och 1600-talen* (Stockholm: Atlantis, 1996), 65.
14 Kaspersson, *Dödligt våld i Stockholm på 1500-, 1700- och 1900-talen* and M. Kaspersson, *Liberation by Murder. Suicidal Killings in Stockholm in the Eighteenth Century*. Paper presented at the International Conference of the History of Violence, Liverpool, July 2001.
15 The estimate is based on the total number of cases in the index, but since cases dealt with more than once appear as different cases, the average number of times a case was dealt with in court was calculated (three times) and the total number divided by this figure. Stockholm District Court Minutes.
16 Kaspersson, *Dödligt våld i Stockholm på 1500-, 1700- och 1900-talen*, 31.
17 Ibid., 45f. There was a state of civil war in Sweden as Karl IX took power in a *coup d'état* in 1600 and started his reign by executing high officials faithful to the former king, Sigismund.
18 Ibid, 62.
19 Ibid.
20 Sogner 'Conclusion: The Nordic Model', 272.

21 Stockholm District Court Minutes (hereafter SDCM) 1607, 22 April.
22 'Mr' and 'Mrs' are used when 'borgare' and 'hustru' (indicating they are burghers and members of the different guilds, and not labourers) are stated in the court minutes. Commonly merely the surname was given.
23 SDCM 1605, 23 October.
24 SDCM 1605, 16 September.
25 SDCM 1607, 15 July.
26 SDCM 1608, 2 January.
27 SDCM 1605, 8 April.
28 SDCM 1608, 6 April.
29 SDCM 1606, 3 November.
30 SDCM 1605, 7 October.
31 SDCM 1607, 14 November.
32 SDCM 1605, 20 March.
33 SDCM 1606, 3 March.
34 SDCM 1607, 5 January.
35 SDCM 1608, 6 April.
36 Furuhagen, *Berusade bönder och bråkiga båtsmän*, 153.
37 J. Liliequist, 'Violence, Honour and Manliness in Early Modern Northern Sweden', in M. Lappalainen and P. Hirvonen (eds), *Crime Control in Europe from the Past to the Present* (Helsinki: Hakapaino, 1999), 174–207.
38 Furuhagen, *Berusade bönder och bråkiga båtsmän*, 158.
39 Ibid., 173–7.
40 SDCM 1608, 6 April.
41 SDCM 1605, 25 September.
42 SDCM 1606, 1 September.
43 SDCM 1606, 20 September. Danitz does appear in court again, however. In 1607 he hands in a certificate stating that he will pay a boy a yearly sum in compensation for having killed his father. SDCM 1607, 15 August.
44 SDCM 1607, 24 October.
45 SDCM 1608, 28 February.
46 SDCM 1606, 12 June.
47 SDCM 1605, 9 February.
48 SDCM 1605, 19 December.
49 A. Jarrick and J. Söderberg, *Odygd och vanära. Folk och brott i Gamla Stockholm* (Stockholm: Rabén & Prisma, 1998), 98f.
50 Ibid., 102–6.
51 S. Sogner, M. Lindstedt Cronberg and H. Sandvik, 'Women in Court', in Österberg and Sogner (eds), *People Meet the Law*, 167–201 at 186.
52 Furuhagen, *Berusade bönder och bråkiga båtsmän*, 22.
53 Andersson, '*Androm till varnagel*', 22, 68.
54 M. Kaspersson, '"The Great Murder Mystery" or Explaining Declining Homicide Rates', in B.S. Godfrey, C. Emsley, and G. Dunstall (eds), *Comparative Histories of Crime* (Cullompton: Willan, 2003), 74.

55 H. Ylikangas, J.C.V. Johansen, K. Johansson, and H.E. Næss, 'Family, State, and Patterns of Criminality', in Österberg and Sogner, *People Meet the Law*, 57–139 at 102–4.
56 Lenman and Parker, 'The State, the Community and the Criminal Law in Early Modern Europe'.
57 Kaspersson, 'The Great Murder Mystery', 74.
58 Kaspersson, *Dödligt våld i Stockholm på 1500-, 1700- och 1900-talen*, 84.
59 Southern District Court (hereafter SDC) 1728, 12 October.
60 Northern District Court (hereafter NDC) 1729, Book of Verdicts, case no. 87.
61 The city guard were generally unpopular as their duty was the upkeep of public order and the guards were often former soldiers. Kaspersson, *Dödligt våld i Stockholm på 1500-, 1700- och 1900-talen*, 75.
62 Ibid., 74.
63 SDC 1728, 13 January.
64 SDC 1728, 25 November.
65 SDC 1728, 16 January.
66 SDC 1728, 9 May.
67 SDC 1728, 17 October.
68 NDC 1728, 4 March.
69 NDC 1728, 9 September.
70 Kaspersson, *Dödligt våld i Stockholm på 1500-, 1700- och 1900-talen*, 88.
71 NDC 1728, 16 September.
72 City District Court (hereafter CDC) 1729, 26 October.
73 CDC 1729, 6 October.
74 NDC 1729, 10 October.
75 NDC 1728, 27 November.
76 Kaspersson, *Dödligt våld i Stockholm på 1500-, 1700- och 1900-talen*, 75.
77 NDC 1728, 1 April.
78 Jarrick and Söderberg, *Odygd och vanära*, 141.
79 Ibid., 169f.
80 Ibid., 106–9, 172–8.
81 Kaspersson, *Dödligt våld i Stockholm på 1500-, 1700- och 1900-talen*, 133–5.
82 NDC 1729, 30 September.
83 NDC Eastern Division 1765, verdict 6 April.
84 NDC 1755, verdict 22 December.
85 NDC 1749, verdict 21 October.
86 NDC 1742, 30 June.
87 A. Jarrick, *Hamlets fråga. En svensk självmordshistoria* (Stockholm: Norstedts, 2000).
88 T. Krogh, *Oplysningstiden og det magiske. Henrettelser og korporlige straffe i 1700- tallets forste halvdel* (Copenhagen: Samleren, 2000), 229.
89 H. Munktell, 'Tortyren i svensk rättshistoria', *Lychnos*, 1939, 102–35; 1940, 132–63.

90 J. Liliequist, 'Bekännelsen, döden och makten. En studie i social kontroll med utgångspunkt från tidelagsbrottet i 1600- och 1700-talets Sverige', in *Historia Nu. 18 Umeåforskare om det förflutna* (Umeå University: Research Report from the Department of History, No. 4, 1988), 147.
91 Ibid., 169.
92 Ibid., 160f.
93 In Sweden, infanticide – or child murder as it was termed – could only be committed by an unmarried woman. Kaspersson, *Dödligt våld i Stockholm på 1500-, 1700- och 1900-talen*, 133f.
94 The clause regulating bestiality was the same regulating homosexuality and stipulated male activity only. J. Liliequist, 'Tidelagstabuet i 1600- och 1700-talets Sverige', *Historisk Tidskrift*, 105 (1985), 287–309.
95 CDC 1722, Book of Verdicts, case no. 18.
96 NDC 1746, verdict 30 June.
97 Cited in Liliequist, 'Bekännelsen, döden och makten', 160.
98 M. Foucault, *Discipline and Punish: The Birth of the Prison* (London: Allen Lane, 1977).
99 Liliequist, 'Bekännelsen, döden och makten', 162.
100 A. Jansson, *From Swords to Sorrow. Homicide and Suicide in Early Modern Stockholm*, Stockholm Studies in Economic History No. 30 (Stockholm: Almqvist & Wiksell International, 1998), 22.
101 NDC 1744, verdict 21 May.
102 Jansson, *From Swords to Sorrow*, 26–9.
103 Liliequist, 'Bekännelsen, döden och makten', 150.
104 Jarrick, *Hamlets fråga*, 87.
105 Krogh, *Oplysningstiden og det magiske*, 230.
106 NDC 1733, verdict 15 September.
107 Liliequist, 'Bekännelsen, döden och makten', 158.
108 Ibid., 164f.
109 Taussi Sjöberg, *Rätten och kvinnorna*, 62–6.
110 Sogner, 'Conclusion: The Nordic Model', 269.
111 Lenman and Parker, 'The State, the Community and the Criminal Law in Early Modern Europe'.
112 Taussi Sjöberg, *Rätten och kvinnorna*, 40f.
113 E. Österberg, 'Criminality, Social Control and the Early Modern State: Evidence and Interpretations in Scandinavian Historiography', in E.A. Johnson and E.H. Monkkonen (eds), *The Civilization of Crime: Violence in Town and Country Since the Middle Ages* (Urbana and Chicago, IL: University of Illinois Press, 1996), 35–62.
114 H. Ylikangas, 'Major Fluctuations in Crimes of Violence in Finland: A Historical Analysis', *Scandinavian Journal of History*, 1 (1976), 81–103.
115 Sogner, 'Conclusion: The Nordic Model', 276.
116 Ibid.

Further reading

The most wide-ranging and informative discussion in English of crime and criminal justice in Scandinavia is Eva Österberg and Sølvi Bauge Sogner (eds), *People Meet the Law: Control and Conflict in the Courts. The Nordic Countries in the Post-Reformation and Pre-Industrial Period* (Oslo: Universitetsforlaget, 2000). For other edited collections that contain chapters on Scandinavia, see E.A. Johnson and E.H. Monkkonen (eds), *The Civilization of Crime: Violence in Town and Country Since the Middle Ages* (Urbana and Chicago, IL: University of Illinois Press, 1996), Clive Emsley and L.A. Knafla (eds), *Crime History and Histories of Crime: Studies in the Historiography of Crime and Criminal Justice in Modern History* (Westport, CT: Greenwood Press, 1996) and M. Lappalainen and P. Hirvonen (eds), *Crime Control in Europe from the Past to the Present* (Helsinki: Hakapaino, 1999). For a more comparative perspective offering a variety of reading, see Barry S. Godfrey, Clive Emsley and Graeme Dunstall (eds), *Comparative Histories of Crime* (Cullompton: Willan, 2003). For those interested in honour and its connection to violence, see Pieter Spierenburg (ed.), *Men and Violence: Gender, Honor, and Rituals in Modern Europe and America* (Columbus, OH: Ohio State University Press, 1998), which includes chapters that debate different countries and times.

Chapter 5

Towards a legal anthropology of the early modern Isle of Man

James Sharpe

It is currently accepted as axiomatic that the law was of central importance in early modern European society. For historians of early modern England, this contention will call to mind Edward Thompson's well-known comments on the significance of law for the English people in the eighteenth century.[1] But scholars working on the histories of other countries have been equally insistent on the centrality of the law's role. Thus Aldo Mazzacane, contributing to a collection of essays on the origins of the Italian state, could comment:

> Jurisprudence has a place among the myths and values of the late Middle Ages and the early modern period. It has a central role in the anthropology of European history. It is not an artificial phenomenon, a 'superstructure' of society. It does not appear *post factum* to legitimize already established situations, to disguise interests and mediate conflicts through various sorts of private manipulation ... jurisprudence also establishes connections, determines proportions and ways to measure and settle the conflicts of society, generates expectations, and projects and creates power relations.[2]

Similarly, the authors of the introduction to an important volume of essays on the law in early modern Scandinavia have suggested that 'concealed behind the concept of the law there is thus not only a collection of statutes expressing prohibitions and penalties, but a general ethic, a societal ideology, traditional patterns for handling conflicts … law and justice can even be discussed as expressions of a mentality'.[3]

As these expressions of the importance of the law as a cultural force, and above all Mazzacone's reference to 'the anthropology of European history', remind us, the law is something which has been of considerable interest to anthropologists. There exists an extensive anthropological literature on the subject, which raises a number of important issues for historians.[4] Briefly, this literature challenges the approach to legal history which was firmly entrenched until a generation ago, and which perhaps still lingers. Anthropologists have taught historians to see law as just one form of conflict resolution; they show how other forms of conflict resolution have their own internal logic which can be as valid as that of the law; they have questioned what interpersonal interactions might underpin a law suit; they have emphasised that the law is something which people *use*. Above all, anthropologists have demonstrated how order is not something whose maintenance depends solely upon the state. Anthropology also raises questions about, and at the same time enriches, the historian's concerns with long-term change in the relationship between law, legal institutions and society. Most of the historians who have tackled this issue have adopted a model which addresses the transition from a community-based law to one operated by the state.[5] Although anthropologists are now properly cautious about the validity of overarching paradigms of this type, such models do at least provide a problematic against which individual historical case studies can be set. Moreover, as we shall see, they were once treated seriously by anthropologists.

There would therefore seem to be considerable advantages in drawing on anthropological insights when attempting to analyse the relationship between law and popular culture, or law as an element of culture more generally, in late medieval and early modern society. Indeed, one historian of such connections in fifteenth-century Florence has attempted to do so in the context of a 'legal anthropology', arguing that:

Law (itself a multifaceted entity) was implicated throughout society in an Italian city-state. Awareness of the legal rules and the operation of legal mechanisms were present on a regular (that is, daily) basis. Law's formative influence was not merely occasional. It informed most levels of activity and discourse.[6]

These comments were, of course, made about one of the most sophisticated places in the Europe of the period: this was Florence where the magnificence of the Medici court was on display, where Boticelli was painting and finding ready buyers for his work, where Giovanni Pico della Mirandola was developing the Neoplatonic world-view, and where, a generation later, Niccolo Machiavelli was to achieve lasting fame for his acerbic political insights. One would expect the law and legal institutions to flourish in such an advanced environment. But what would the law's importance be and how much validity would a concept of legal anthropology have in a society which shared none of Florence's sophistication – one which was, on the contrary, geographically marginal, culturally isolated and economically backward? A society, in fact, like the early modern Isle of Man.

I

The Isle of Man in the early modern period was indeed an economically backward and culturally isolated area, its population, the majority of them speakers of Manx Gaelic, mostly combining peasant cultivation with fishing. The island had, from 1406, been ruled by the Lancashire-based Stanley family, from 1485 earls of Derby. Despite being under the rule of an English noble family, the island was never integrated into the English polity, but retained its own laws and a peculiar secular administrative structure which owed much to pre-existing Norse institutions.[7] This peculiar administrative structure, and in particular its system of courts, generated a mass of documentation which today constitutes a rich archive. The present essay originates from two samples of court records from this archive, covering the periods 1580–1600 and 1680–1700 respectively.[8] Some idea of the richness of the documentation can be gleaned from the fact that our late sixteenth-century sample included over 10,000 cases, the second some 4,902. Of these cases, about two-thirds in each sample were non-criminal litigation rather than presentments of petty offences or indictments of serious ones: hence our focus in studying the business of the Manx courts will be primarily on civil litigation, although some mention will be made of the criminal business of those courts. It is hoped that this emphasis will provide a useful counterpoint in a collection mainly concerned with the history of crime.

Indeed, most early research into the social and cultural significance of the law in early modern England concentrated on the work of the criminal courts. More recently, however, the significance of civil litigation has been recognised. As C.W. Brooks put it in an important pioneering synthesis:

> It is arguable that the civil law is even more important than the criminal law in maintaining the social and economic relations in any society. It is certainly the case that more people in all ranks of society in early modern England came into contact with the legal system through the civil rather than the criminal courts.

Brooks adds that the civil law laid down 'the rules and legal processes by which people made and enforced agreements about property rights, contracts and debts, or sued for remedies in actions of slander or negligence'.[9] These sentiments have been reinforced subsequently by Tim Stretton, who comments that the concentration on crime among historians 'is understandable but it can be misleading ... all law deals with the peaceable ordering of society, and civil litigation plays a significant role in defining acceptable behaviour and ensuring harmony within the community'.[10] The Manx court archives offer massive support to these conclusions drawn from the English experience.

Even so, we must remind ourselves that the governmental structure and legal system of the Isle of Man was not that of England. The island was, as we have noted, ruled by the earls of Derby, but the exact nature of that rule is a little difficult to formulate. In essence, their powers in the island were regal: William Blundell, an Englishman writing about the island in the 1640s, commented that he was unable to find 'any difference at all ... betwixt a King and a Lord of Man, but only in certain formalities and not in any realities'.[11] Half a century earlier, in a legal decision of 1598, it was ruled by a panel of leading English judges that 'the Isle of Man was an ancient kingdom of it self, and no part of the kingdome of England'.[12] But, apart from a brief episode in the mid-seventeenth century, when the exigencies of the Civil War forced the royalist earl of Derby to seek refuge on the island, the Stanley Lords of Man were absentee rulers. They were also the landlords of most of the island's inhabitants, and the administration of the island looks much like that of a large and unusually potent seigneurial jurisdiction, perhaps possessing also something of the character of a middle-sized territory in the Holy Roman Empire. In the absence of the Lord, rule was entrusted to a governor. The Stanleys probably regarded the governorship of the island as a useful piece of patronage, a point reinforced by the fact that 25 of the 36 governors they appointed between 1406 and 1736 came from Lancashire.[13] But Manxmen, or men from immigrant families settled long enough on the island to be regarded as naturalised, figured prominently among the island's administrators. In particular one principal office, that of deemster, was invariably held by Manxmen. The two deemsters (one for the Northside and one for the Southside of the island) had considerable responsibilities in running the island's legal machine and hence, as William Blundell expressed it, had 'to be perfect and speak the Manks language'.[14]

The Manx legal and administrative system was, for a small island, an extremely complex one, probably because of the need to guarantee the smooth running of the island's administration and hence the efficient collection of the Lord of Man's dues and fees in a situation where the Lord was normally absent. There was, especially, an elaborate system of courts.[15] The Lord's Council, normally consisting of the governor and the four principal household officers of the island (the comptroller, the receiver, the water bailiff and the attorney general), could act as a court, while the 24 keys were also occasionally involved in decision-making in legal cases. The keys, the deemsters and the spiritual officers of the island also sat in the Tynwald Court, which met annually by the seventeenth century and, probably simply for convenience, added judicial business of a routine character to its more weighty deliberations. For normal purposes, the superior civil court was the Chancery Court. This court dealt mainly with equity cases but also had jurisdiction over cases at common law on appeal from the defendant in a common law case. The Exchequer Court had jurisdiction over all cases touching the Lord's rights and revenues. There were also deemster's courts dealing with petty matters, an Admiralty Court which had jurisdiction over maritime matters, courts of criminal and civil law for each of the four principal baronies of the island, and a debt court to assess and levy fines which had been decreed by all the temporal courts over the previous year. There was the Court of General Gaol Delivery, the equivalent of the English assizes, which dealt with serious crime. And, most importantly in terms of levels of business, the Sheading Courts, also known as the common law courts.[16]

A sheading, an administrative unit of Norse origin, was a grouping of three or (in one case) two of the island's 17 parishes, there thus being a total of six sheadings. The courts were held twice a year, within a fortnight of May Day and Michaelmas (29 September) and lasted for two calendar weeks, two days being devoted to each sheading in turn, a well-established circuit around the island being in place by the late sixteenth century. The governor and all of the principal officers could attend, but generally the Sheading Courts were presided over by the deemsters, the attorney general and the clerk of the court, with, in theory, all tenants of the Lord owing 6d or more rent being present. The Sheading Courts' business fell into two main divisions. Firstly, they would hear the presentments of petty offenders, by far the greatest number of them being accused of those assaults leading to bloodshed which Manx legal terminology termed graphically as bloodwipes.[17] Secondly, they would hear suits between parties. These cases were determined by jury, but the jury's verdict could only be implemented by the agreement of both parties. If this agreement was not forthcoming, the aggrieved party could apply to the clerk of the rolls, traverse the verdict and obtain a further trial. If a verdict was then reached which was felt to be unsatisfactory, the matter could be appealed up to the keys.

The working of the Manx legal system depended upon the active cooperation of a number of inferior officers.[18] The most important of these was the coroner, one of whom, after being appointed by the governor, was sworn for each sheading. The Manx coroner had the responsibilities of his English namesake, although it was the similarities of his duties with those of the English sheriff which struck seventeenth-century English observers.[19] The coroner was expected to empanel the numerous juries upon which the island's administration depended so heavily, while he also presented offenders to the various courts and was responsible more generally for maintaining law and order, having responsibility for arresting offenders and committing them to gaol, and for making a 'general search' each quarter for stolen goods. Coroners were normally drawn from the leading landholders of each sheading. In each parish there was a lockman, the coroner's deputy, something very like an English parish constable. Each parish also had a moar, in effect a bailiff for the Lord, who was responsible, under the coroner, for empanelling juries and summoning witnesses for the Sheading Court, as well as collecting the Lord's rent and other dues and delivering it to the receiver. Each landholder in the parish was supposed to serve for a year, in rotation, as moar, although there was some financial recompense. Another parochial office, frequently filled by the coroner, was that of Captain of the Parish, who was entrusted with command of the parish's militia or trained bands. Overall, this was a law and order and administrative system which depended very heavily on the participation of adult males in the local community.

The participatory nature of the Manx legal system was further emphasised by the frequent use of juries.[20] Nowhere was this more evident than in the proceedings of the Sheading Courts.[21] A 'Great Enquest', comprising of men representing each sheading, was returned annually, its business including screening of bloodwipe presentments made by coroners and moars. Similarly, in suits between parties, juries of six men from the sheading where the disputed land lay would be called in cases relating to real property, and juries of four men from the parish where the defendant lived in personal suits. If a case was disputed and traversed, it would be tried by a second jury, of twelve men in real actions, of six in personal disputes. Each sheading had its own Great Enquest, a jury of twelve men drawn from the constituent parishes of the sheading which presented the presence of suspicious persons such as outlaws or exiled felons, and also tried such 'manorial' matters as disputes concerning pathways, watercourses and boundaries. Each parish would also have a jury of four men, the 'setting quest', whose main duty was to assist the governor, officer and deemsters in finding a new tenant whenever a tenement fell vacant through death or alienation. Cases coming to the Court of General Gaol Delivery were tried by jury,[22] juries played a leading role in the deliberations of the Admiralty Court and the Barons' Courts, and there were also specialist juries like juries of slander, or juries of servants, the latter often involved in presenting vagrants.[23] More unexpectedly, juries were also a part of the workings of the ecclesiastical courts. In particular, cases of rape and witchcraft were screened by juries appointed by the ecclesiastical authorities whose role it was to establish if there was sufficient substance in an accusation of either of these offences to warrant taking it to the secular courts.[24]

The distinctively participatory nature of the Manx legal system was given an additional dimension by the absence of lawyers from the island. William Sacheverell, a former governor, commented favourably in 1702 on a legal system 'where every man pleads his own cause, without council or attorney, or any person that can gain by strife', adding that in Manx common law disputes, 'the ease of government, and every man's interest, draws all suits to as speedy a conclusion as possible'.[25] A less benign view was taken by George Waldron, author of a description of the island first published in 1726. Waldron commented that 'every man being allowed to plead his own cause, there is no occasion for counsellors, attorneys, or solicitors'. But he also described how the ignorance of the Manx, and 'their incapacity of speaking for themselves in publick', had provided the opportunity to some men 'to set up for a kind of lawyers, who take fees, and argue on both sides, as in the courts of justice elsewhere'.[26] In fact, analysis of the Manx common law records reveals that such men were present a century and a half before Waldron wrote. William Cowley, for example, appeared in the common law courts on 173 occasions between 1580 and 1597, representing a wide variety of mainly lowly litigants.[27] Cowley and men like him must have enjoyed a considerable reputation for knowledge of the law among their neighbours, and their presence raises some intriguing questions about how the law was perceived by the early modern Manx. Some Manxmen at least were evidently interested enough in the island's laws to prepare their own *aides-memoire* on the subject: William Blundell noted that he derived much of his information on Manx law from 'my Manksman's private booke', which his informant, a member of the keys, had 'collected for his better enablinge himself to discharge ye duty of his place'.[28]

The cases coming before the courts were numerous. On a provisional count, some 6,660 actions originating in 1580–99 were tried before the courts, and a further 2,077 dating from 1680–99.[29] Numerous presentments also came to the courts in these two periods, in each case the total of presentments running at about half those of the actions. It is striking that the number of actions is so much lower in the later period, a finding which is rather against expectations, given a simple model which would relate increasing economic development and sophistication with a greater propensity to go to law. Indeed, these Manx records suggest that, at least within the period under review, greater economic and social sophistication led to a diminution in levels of litigation perhaps indicating that high levels of litigation occurred when rules and conventions governing small-scale economic transactions were relatively fluid. Under such circumstances the decision to initiate a lawsuit might be taken to establish certainty in uncertain matters, or, conversely, the fluidity of the rules might encourage individuals to try to extract such advantages as they could from going to law.

Despite the inherent interest of such speculations, at the moment the reasons for this shift in levels of litigation remain elusive, although it is worth noting that this Manx evidence seems to run parallel with that exhibited by a number of samples of litigation in England. In both the late sixteenth- and late seventeenth-century samples of actions, two areas of litigation predominated, those concerning disputes over land and those concerning disputes over debt. In the first sample of 6,660 actions, 1,834, or 27.5 per cent, concerned land or property disputes (which, of course, incorporated a massive range of issues) and a further 4,391 cases, or 65.9 per cent, involved debt or related matters. In the 1680–99 sample, 764, or 36.8 per cent, arose from land or property disputes, and 1,072, or 51.6 per cent, from debt and related matters. Thus in both samples something like 90 per cent of actions fell into these two main categories. Obviously, deeper research is needed to try to gain a more nuanced picture of subdivisions of actions within these broad categories. Moreover, it should always be borne in mind that any attempt to categorise individual items of early modern litigation is to some extent artificial, given the way that suits were sometimes a phenomenon in which the matter allegedly at issue might symbolise a much wider range of problems.[30] Outside of these two main categories of offence, there was a trickle of actions concerning slander, disputes over labour and instances where assaults were countered by an action rather than being presented as a bloodwipe.

These overall figures mask the individual experience of litigation. Even at an initial level of analysis it is clear that there was a stratum of habitual litigants, while it seems likely that few Manxmen in possession of moderate or greater property could have avoided occasional involvement with the courts. Interestingly, the litigiousness of the Manx was noted by a number of eighteenth-century observers. George Waldron commented that 'as to their law suits, they are neither expensive nor tedious, but that draws a misfortune as bad, if not a worse consequence than either of the others; which is, that the over-cheapness renders them frequent'.[31] Towards the end of the eighteenth century, David Robertson, another observer of Manx society, writing at a time when lawyers were in business on the island, noted how 'the Manks have a culpable propensity to trifling litigation. A rash word, a choleric action, or a wound which the hand of friendship might easily have healed, is by the malicious industry of those who batten on the follies and errors of mankind, swelled into an intolerable offence'.[32] Although levels of Manx litigation over the eighteenth century have yet to be established, it is unlikely that they were higher than they had been in the late sixteenth century, suggesting that the propensity of the Manx to litigation was well established and re-emphasising the problem of interpreting the chronological pattern of litigation. In particular, the massive drop in Manx litigation between the late sixteenth and the late seventeenth century raises some interesting points of comparison with the 'Great Litigation Decline' traced over roughly the same period in England.[33]

There is also the issue of how far the nature and objectives of litigants may have changed over time. As we have noted, our two main samples of court records demonstrate that litigation was running at a much lower level in the late seventeenth than it was in the late sixteenth century. Yet surviving records suggest that the legal process could be more complicated and protracted in the later period and that this may have been related to the emergence of a number of important trading families on the island. A representative of one such was Nicholas Harley or Harloe of Castletown, late of Wexford, who was one of the most active merchants in the island in the late seventeenth century. Harley was involved in 1688 in a dispute with Nicholas Williams, also of Castletown, over freighting goods from Castletown to Liverpool and Chester, a case which proved fairly protracted and which was countered by a suit from Williams alleging that Harley and his wife Sarah had detained hops which Williams had brought over from Whitehaven.[34] Two years later, William Mercer complained that Harley and his wife had detained £16 in sterling from him.[35] At about the same time, Mr John Norris sued Harley for not paying house rent or money owed for coal.[36] In 1697, Harley, in turn, sued Norris (who had himself been involved in a number of cases in the interim) and two of his relatives for £30/10/- debt, the money having been spent by Harley in repairing the house he then rented.[37] This case is especially interesting in showing how numerous papers relating to the property in question were produced as evidence. The written word was already beginning to be seen as more reliable than oral testimony based on memory in the early modern Isle of Man.

The system was, therefore, one which was heavily dependent upon popular participation, both in the form of officials rooted in the local community and in the widespread use of juries, and was one in which some people at least were frequent litigants. It was also a system which was flexible in its workings. Here as in other late medieval and early modern legal systems, an important symbol of that flexibility was the use of arbitration. Obviously, arbitration is a term which covers a range of activities and a number of questions need to be asked about its operation.[38] It was, however, a practice which was regularly accepted in a formalised state by the Manx courts, usually involving the binding of the parties involved to accept the arbitrators' decision and the appointment of what was usually termed an umpire to make a decision if the arbitrators were unable to. Thus, in 1697, two women locked in a property dispute in Andreas, considering 'the great expence and trouble that might ensue both in prosecuting and defending the said case, the parties, with the counsel of friends and relatives', referred matters to four men, two of whom were to represent each of the women, and were bound in £40 to accept any decision the arbitrators might make, with an umpire to be chosen by mutual consent if a decision could not be made. This was clearly a case which involved a degree of familial, and possibly community, input, perhaps all the more so because the two parties were women.[39] But any discussion of arbitration must consider the exact nature and context of the matter being arbitrated, why arbitration was the preferred course of action, and who was doing the arbitrating. This last issue is of some interest, given that some Manx litigants at least were able to invoke the island's notables as arbitrators. One case of arbitration from the parish of Ballaugh involved the comptroller of the island and a deemster as the representatives of one of the litigants and the receiver of the island and another man for the other.[40] Sometimes, of course, the two parties had simply to be encouraged to reach an agreement between themselves. Hence in a Conchan debt case of 1697, John Cosnahan, acting as umpire, declared that 'I not finding throughly [i.e. truly] which of them had most right on his side, I desire both parties to agree between themselves, and through my perswation'. The court endorsed Cosnahan's 'umpihiridge'.[41] And, in a case of 1683, again from Conchan, which was appealed up to the keys, it was eventually recommended that 'for better satisfaction, peace and quiet of both parties that they should come to a friendly accommodation' based on the keys' decision.[42] On at least some occasions, harmonious agreements rather than outright victory in litigation were regarded as desirable by those involved in, or processing, Manx law suits.

Further evidence of flexibility, if we may include data from the presentments tried before the sheading courts as well as suits between parties, can be found in the use of fines by the courts. The most common reason for this was the poverty of the convicted party. A Lezayre man who disturbed the running of a court 'by wordes and otherwise' had his fine remitted to 12d 'upon mere clemency and pytie' as he was a poor man.[43] Elizabeth Moor of Arbory, plaintiff in a land detinue case and due to lose £3 for failing to prosecute a traverse, was in fact made to pay 3/4 in consideration of her poverty, 'being but a servant'.[44] Thomas Robinson, presented by the moar of Arbory for an assault on Anne Comish, was discharged by the court because he had nothing with which to pay any fine they might inflict.[45] In a similar way, a fine of £10 inflicted on a Lonan man in a case of debt was reduced to 2/-, and then to nothing, on the grounds of the man's poverty.[46] The courts might also sometimes dramatically reduce the damages claimed by plaintiffs in suits. Finlo Crane of Marown complained that John More pursued him with a stick and beat him, and claimed 40/- in damages, a sum which the court reduced to 5d. Crane also claimed £6/13/4 damages on the basis of another occasion when More beat him, the unsympathetic court awarding him nothing in this instance.[47] Evidently, the Manx secular court system was happy to accommodate its practices to individual litigants and individual circumstances.

II

What emerges from this analysis of Manx court records is a clear impression of a society where the law was an important element in everyday culture, that it was something which must have been very familiar to at least the adult male members of the island's population. The system was one which depended heavily upon local officers and jurors drawn from the local community. Launching law suits there was easy, while a suit once launched was usually carried through by the plaintiff and the defendant. This both deepened the participatory nature of the system, and ensured its cheapness, this latter an important element in a period when it was felt desirable that justice should be cheap and local. And, of course, Manx justice was local. Access to the Sheading Courts was generally easy, while even attending the higher Manx courts was not as daunting a process as that which confronted a litigant from the north or west of England contemplating litigating at Westminster. Moreover, the peculiar status of the Lord of the Isle meant that, despite a theoretical right, in practice there was no appeal from the Manx secular courts to any authority outside the island.[48] Procedures were also flexible, with the courts proving themselves willing to contemplate arbitration and showing an ability to adjust fines imposed and costs awarded to individual circumstances. Above all, these records give us a sense of what Simon Roberts has described as one of the main elements in anthropological thinking about the law, an emphasis on the actions and strategies of real people rather than a focus on rules and structure.[49]

The records of a reasonably efficiently operating legal system may not be the best place to look for hostility or indifference towards that system: nevertheless, despite the occasional presentment of critics of the courts or (more frequently) of negligent jurors, what emerges from this analysis is that the Manx were happy with their legal system and were willing to use it to settle their disputes. There is, unfortunately, little evidence of how the Stanleys imposed their system on the island in the fifteenth century, and part of the apparent success of that system in the period covered by this essay may well be explicable by the willingness of the island's new rulers to adapt an existing administrative and legal machine to their needs. But whatever the situation in the fifteenth century, by the late sixteenth the Manx common law constituted a vital element of Manx culture, evidence perhaps that the Manx had undergone a sort of legal acculturation of the type which at least some anthropologists of the law describe.[50] There might, at first sight, seem to be some parallels between the Manx situation and those described by anthropologists writing on the imposition of colonial legal systems on indigenous populations.[51] After all, the Manx legal system was presided over by a (usually) English governor working on behalf of a (usually) absentee English Lord, the records of the court were kept in Latin and English, while pleadings were (unless the party involved was not a native of the island) conducted in Manx, the first or only language of 90 per cent of the population.[52] Yet the acceptance of the system that is evident when records begin to survive regularly from around 1580, the fact that it was so widely used and the way in which it seemed to be so firmly imbricated in the culture would seem to argue against parallels between the Manx situation and that found in colonial societies studied by anthropologists. This conclusion is perhaps strengthened by the evident flexibility of the Manx legal system and its responsiveness to local concerns. A recent student of the feud in early modern France has commented, 'whereas they resented tax collectors and bureaucrats, peasants and nobles alike welcomed outsiders who could settle disputes and maintain the social equilibrium'.[53] This may well have been the attitude of the early modern Manx to the earl of Derby's administrative system in its role in settling disputes by providing legal decisions.

This apparent success of the Manx system creates problems about how to place the island in that grand transition from community to state law which we have noted earlier as the dominant paradigm in historical accounts of long-term changes in the history of law and society. This issue also brings us back to anthropology. Anthropologists are now very cautious about accepting such transitions. Norbert Rouland, addressing one aspect of this issue, has commented that 'historical and ethnographical evidence clearly demonstrates that there is no necessary chronological link between vengeance, compensation and punishment', while Peter Stein, although not an anthropologist himself, has noted that 'the main result of anthropological research is that any scheme of universal legal evolution must be rejected'.[54] Such sentiments undoubtedly demonstrate proper scholarly caution, but they also obscure the willingness of the founding fathers of the social sciences to confront the big issues. The historian authors of an important essay on the transition from community to state law in Europe begin with a nod at Durkheim's *Division of Labour in Society*,[55] while this transition has obvious parallels with the transition from status to contract so famously adumbrated by Sir Henry Maine.[56] Historians and anthropologists alike should, perhaps, be a little less reticent about confronting such meta-narratives of change. How exactly high levels of litigation should be interpreted is, of course, something of an open question. Yet it is evident that the early modern Isle of Man emerges as a surprisingly 'modern' society on the strength of any model which sees a willingness to settle disputes by official legal process as an index of modernity.

It is difficult to resolve how the Manx regarded using the law in relationship to other means of dispute settlement. There are few clues in the sources to extra-legal settlements, and this is perhaps an area where the anthropologist, who has the opportunity to observe a society at first hand, is at an advantage over the historian. It is inherently unlikely that the courts had a monopoly over conflict resolution, but demonstrating this point remains impossible, not least within the limited scope of a short essay such as this.

Certainly, there is little evidence that one obvious alternative to litigation, violence, was widely accepted as a means of dispute resolution. Contemporary observers did not include a propensity to violence among the vices of the Manx: even George Waldron, who was frequently critical of the mores of the island's native inhabitants, did not make that accusation.[57] Ironically, the most potent demonstration of this point comes from the records of the courts, which returns us to the problem of how to interpret statistics generated by any legal system. But taking the evidence at its face value, the court records do not depict the Manx as a violent people. Analysis of samples of the records of the Court of General Gaol Delivery for three twenty-year periods, namely 1580–99, 1640–51 and 1680–99, reveal only four indictments for murder and two for manslaughter, to which might be added three for infanticide, all of these last occurring in the final sample. Bloodwipes, as might be expected, were presented at the Manx common law courts at a much greater level of frequency. Yet the pattern of these presentments does not demonstrate a shift from violence to litigation, but rather runs parallel to that of non-criminal litigation. About twice as many bloodwipes were prosecuted in the late sixteenth century as in the late seventeenth. Thus there were 1,396 presentments for bloodwipes and other minor acts of violence in the 1590s, compared to 658 in the 1690s.[58] And even with these presentments, we are left wondering about the real meaning of a court case. A commentary on the island's administrative machine from c.1665 claimed that coroners or moars would frequently make such presentments upon hearsay, 'and many tymes the partie abused comes with the complaynt and shews blood, which some tymes is true, and sometimes apeares that the partie will in some maner scratt [i.e. scratch] him or herself or by some other meanes bringe forth blood, out of meere malice to give losse to the other'.[59] Thus even a bloodwipe presentment might signify, not an act of violence, but rather the willingness of the Manx to use their legal system.

But deepening our understanding of how the analysis on Manx materials might inform models of major transitions in early modern European society must be deferred to a future point. There is, indeed, much work to be done on these materials, both in terms of empirical research and in terms of conceptualising their significance. I am aware, above all, of a need to contextualise them in the Isle of Man's broader history. The wider issue of context has been stressed by historians and anthropologists alike in their study of the law. Leopold Pospisil has urged that 'law should be studied as an integral part of the cultural whole, not regarded as an autonomous institution', a sentiment echoed by the historian E.W. Ives, who has argued that the law both shapes and is shaped by society, 'a relationship of both cause and effect'.[60] I am acutely aware of these contextual issues when studying the records of the Manx legal system: but what I have done here at least is to suggest how the legal system of this small island might be analysed so as to provide, if not quite a legal anthropology, a historical account which is informed by, and profits from, some of the insights offered by the anthropology of the law. I also hope, however imperfectly, to have indicated an area where the two disciplines might enjoy a fruitful interaction. The anthropologist Norbert Rouland has claimed that there are currently some 10,000 legal systems known in the world.[61] If nothing else, this attempt to deepen our understanding of the law as a cultural entity in early modern Europe, and to demonstrate the potential for an interplay between history and anthropology, has added another, albeit historical, legal system to the list.

Notes

1 E.P. Thompson, *Whigs and Hunters: The Origin of the Black Act* (London: Allen Lane, 1975), 258–69.
2 Aldo Mazzacane, 'Law and Jurists in the Formation of the Modern State in Italy', in Julius Kirshner (ed.), *The Origins of the State in Italy 1300–1600* (Chicago and London: University of Chicago Press, 1995), 62.
3 Eva Österberg and Erling Sandmo, 'Introduction', in Eva Österberg and Sølvi Bauge Sogner (eds), *People Meet the Law: Control and Conflict in the Courts. The Nordic Countries in the Post-Reformation and Pre-Industrial Period* (Oslo: Universitetsforlaget, 2000), 10.
4 It would be impossible in the space of a note to give a full listing of even the most significant works on the anthropology of the law. Those which I have found particularly useful are: Paul Bohannan (ed.), *Law and Warfare: Studies in the Anthropology of Conflict* (Garden City, NY: Natural History Press, 1967); Leopold Pospisil, *Anthropology of Law: A Comparative Theory* (New York: Harper & Row, 1971); Simon Roberts, *Order and Dispute: An Introduction to Legal Anthropology* (Harmondsworth: Penguin Books, 1979); Norbert Rouland, *Legal Anthropology* (London: Athlone Press, 1994).
5 For an important discussion of this transition, see Bruce Lenman and Geoffrey Parker, 'The State, the Community and the Criminal Law in Early Modern Europe', in V.A.C. Gatrell, Bruce Lenman and Geoffrey Parker (eds), *Crime and the Law: The Social History of Crime in Western Europe since 1500* (London: Europa Publications, 1980). Other studies addressing this transition include: Österberg and Sandmo, 'Introduction'; Andrea Zorzi, 'The Judicial System in Florence in the Fourteenth and Fifteenth Centuries', in Trevor Dean and K.J.P. Lowe (eds), *Courts, Society and the Law in Renaissance Italy* (Cambridge: Cambridge University Press, 1994); Xavier Rousseaux, '"Sozialdisziplinierung", Civilization and Monopolization of Power: Towards a History of Social Control', in Maria Ågren, Åsa Karlsson and Xavier Rousseaux (eds), *Guises of Power: Integration of Society and Legitimation of Power in Sweden and the Southern Low Countries ca 1500–1999* (Uppsala: Uppsala University, 2003). For a perceptive analysis of changes in legal thinking in Europe, see Peter Stein, *Legal Evolution: The Story of an Idea* (Cambridge: Cambridge University Press, 1980).
6 Thomas Kuehn, *Law, Family and Women: Toward a Legal Anthropology of Renaissance Italy* (Chicago and London: University of Chicago Press, 1991), 1.
7 The Manx administrative system is described in J.R. Dickinson, *The Lordship of Man under the Stanleys: Government and Economy in the Isle of Man, 1580–1704* (Cheetham Society, 3rd series, 41: Manchester, 1996), chapter 1, 'The Government of the Isle of Man'. I am deeply grateful

to Dr Dickinson for his comments on an earlier draft of this essay. For two important contemporary sources on Manx law and administration, see: Manx National Heritage Library (hereafter MNHL), Ms 9548, John Parr, 'An Abridgement or a short Tract of the most useful Lawes, Acts and Ordinances contained in the Statute Books of the Isle of Man'; and Flintshire Record Office, Ms Nantlys D/NA/905, an anonymous account of the Isle of Man dating from c.1665.

8　These two samples were analysed and entered into a database by J.R. Dickinson in the course of a project funded by the Leverhulme Trust, F.224R, 'Crime, Litigation and the Courts in the Isle of Man, c.1550–1704'; for a preliminary report on the findings of this project, see J.A. Sharpe and J.R. Dickinson, 'Courts, Crime and Litigation in the Isle of Man 1580–1700', *Historical Research*, 72 (1999), 140–59. Further analysis of these records was facilitated by an Arts and Humanities Research Board Award, RLS AN6397/APN10423.

9　C.W. Brooks, 'Interpersonal Conflict and Social Tension: Civil Litigation in England, 1640–1830', in A.L. Beier, David Cannadine and J.M. Rosenheim (eds), *The First Modern Society: Essays in English History in Honour of Lawrence Stone* (Cambridge: Cambridge University Press, 1989), 357.

10　Tim Stretton, *Women Waging Law in Elizabethan England* (Cambridge: Cambridge University Press, 1998), 5. Apart from the works by Brooks and Stretton already noted, studies of aspects of civil litigation in the early modern period include: C.W. Brooks, *Lawyers, Litigation and English Society since 1450* (London: Hambledon Press, 1998); W.A. Champion, 'Litigation in the Boroughs: the Shrewsbury *Curia Parva*, 1480–1730', *Legal History*, 15, 3 (1994), 201–22; and Valerie J. Newill, 'Tactical Litigation and the Ideology of the Law in Late Tudor and Early Stuart Kent, c.1580–1630' (unpublished PhD Thesis, University of Kent, 2001). For parallels from another early modern culture, see Richard L. Kagan, *Lawsuits and Litigants in Castile, 1500–1700* (Chapel Hill, NC: University of North Carolina Press, 1981). Curiously, there is little sustained discussion of litigation by the various contributors to a recent overview of the significance of the law in European history published under the auspices of the European Science Foundation: Antonio Padoa-Schioppa (ed.), *Legislation and Justice* (Oxford: Clarendon Press, 1997).

11　William Blundell, *A History of the Isle of Man (1648–56)*, 2 vols, ed. W. Harrison (Douglas: Manx Society, vols. 25, 27, 1876, 1877), II, 41.

12　Cited in Dickinson, *Lordship of Man*, 18.

13　Ibid, 354–7, 'Appendix II: Governors and Deputy Governors of the Isle of Man, c.1590–c.1700'.

14　Blundell, *History of the Isle of Man*, II, 67.

15　It should be stressed that this essay is focused on the secular court system. There was also a well developed and much used system of church courts, to which the best introduction remains Anne Ashley,

'The Spiritual Courts of the Isle of Man, Especially in the Seventeenth and Eighteenth Centuries', *English Historical Review*, 57 (1957), 31–59. Jennifer Platten is currently working on a PhD at Liverpool University on the activities of the Manx church courts in the late seventeenth and eighteenth centuries.

16 On the Sheading Courts, see Dickinson, *Lordship of Man*, 68–71. Interestingly, William Blundell compared them to English courts leet: *History of the Isle of Man*, II, 65.

17 For John Parr on the bloodwipe, see MNHL, Ms 9548, ff. 28–9. For a discussion of the incidence and treatment of bloodwipes in this period, see J.R. Dickinson, 'Criminal Violence and Judicial Punishment in the Isle of Man 1580–1700', *Isle of Man Natural History and Antiquarian Society Proceedings*, 11, 1 (2000), 138.

18 This account of Manx local officials is based on Dickinson, *Lordship of Man*, 46–53.

19 For example, Blundell, *History of the Isle of Man*, II, 79.

20 This heavy dependence may have been the consequence of the Scandinavian origins of the Manx legal system: Thomas Lindkvist, 'Law and the Making of the State in Medieval Sweden: Kingship and Communities', in Padoa-Schioppa (ed.), *Legislation and Justice*, 224–5, notes the importance of juries in the medieval Swedish legal system.

21 Dickinson, *Lordship of Man*, 69–71. For some hostile comments on Manx juries from a slightly later date, see: Charles Searle, *A Short View of the Present State of the Isle of Man* (London, 1767), where it was claimed that in the island trial by jury 'becomes here the instrument of oppression, ever full of corruption and delay'.

22 Dickinson, *Lordship of Man*, 65–6; for an account of aspects of the work of the Court of General Gaol Delivery, see: idem, 'Criminal Violence and Judicial Punishment in the Isle of Man'.

23 MNHL, Ms 9548, ff. 118, 123.

24 Ibid., ff. 111, 154.

25 William Sacheverell, *An Account of the Isle of Man, its Inhabitants, Language, Soil, Remarkable Curiosities, the Succession of its Kings and Bishops, down to the Present Time* (London, 1702), sig B2.

26 George Waldron, *The History and Description of the Isle of Man* (London, 1744), 78–9.

27 Information from the database.

28 Blundell, *History of the Isle of Man*, II, 103.

29 Information from the database.

30 It might well be rewarding, for example, to compare a deeper analysis of Manx debt litigation with that given of English material in Craig Muldrew, *The Economy of Obligation: The Culture of Credit and Social Relations in Early Modern England* (London: Macmillan, 1998).

31 Waldron, *History and Description of the Isle of Man*, 78.

32 David Robertson, *A Tour through the Isle of Man: to which is subjoined a Review of Manks History* (London, 1794), 44–5.

33 A concept explored in its English context by W.A. Champion, 'Recourse to Law and the Meaning of the Great Litigation Decline, 1650–1750: Some Clues from Shrewsbury', in Christopher W. Brooks and Michael Lobban (eds), *Communities and Courts in Britain 1150–1900* (London and Rio Grande: Hambledon Press, 1997).

34 MNHL, Lib. Canc. 1688, f. 1; Lib. Canc. 1689, f. 12.

35 MNHL, Lib. Canc. 1688, f. 67.

36 MNHL, Lib. Canc. 1689, f. 14.

37 MNHL, Lib. Canc. 1697–8, inter ff. 1–2.

38 For some initial comments on this point, see Roberts, *Order and Dispute*, 70–8.

39 MNHL, Lib. Plit 1697, inter ff. 66–7.

40 MNHL, Lib. Plit. 1591, f. 96.

41 MNHL, Lib. Canc. 1697–8, ff. 69–72.

42 MNHL, Lib. Plit. 1682, inter ff. 26–7.

43 MNHL, Lib. Plit. 1581, f. 20.

44 MNHL, Lib. Plit. 1699, ff. 34, inter 34–5, 35, 36.

45 MNHL, Lib. Plit. 1688, f. 39.

46 MNHL, Lib. Plit. 1599, f. 31.

47 MNHL, Lib. Plit. 1596, f. 91.

48 Dickinson, *Lordship of Man*, 19, n. 29. John Parr, in his abridgement of the island's laws of 1679, certainly did not envisage appeal beyond the Lord: MNHL, Ms 9548, f. 12.

49 Simon Roberts, 'The Study of Disputes: Anthropological Perspectives', in John Bossy (ed.), *Disputes and Settlements: Law and Human Relations in the West* (Cambridge: Cambridge University Press, 1983), 4.

50 On this concept, see Rouland, *Legal Anthropology*, Chapter 4, 'Legal Acculturation'.

51 This issue is discussed in a number of historical contexts by Lauren Benton, *Law and Colonial Cultures: Legal Regimes in World History, 1400–1900* (Cambridge: Cambridge University Press, 2002).

52 On Manx as the language of pleading, see Flintshire Record Office, Ms Nantlys D/NA/905, f. 29.

53 Stuart Carroll, 'The Peace in the Feud in Sixteenth- and Seventeenth-Century France', *Past and Present*, 178 (2003), 115.

54 Rouland, *Historical Anthropology*, 281; Stein, *Legal Evolution*, 104.

55 Parker and Lenman, 'State, Community and Criminal Law', 12.

56 Henry Maine, *Ancient Law* (London, 1861).

57 Waldron, *History and Description of the Isle of Man*.

58 Dickinson, 'Criminal Violence and Judicial Punishment in the Isle of Man', 136–8, 128.

59 Flintshire Record Office, Ms Nantlys D/NA/905, f. 29.

60 Pospisil, *Anthropology of Law*, x; E.W. Ives, 'Law, History and Society: The Eternal Triangle', in E.W. Ives and A.H. Manchester (eds), *Law, Litigants and the Legal Profession: Papers Presented to the Fourth British Legal History*

Conference at the University of Birmingham 10–13 July 1979 (London and New Jersey: Royal Historical Society, 1983), 5.

61 Rouland, *Legal Anthropology*, 1.

Further reading

For an account of the Isle of Man in the early modern period, see J.R. Dickinson, *The Lordship of Man under the Stanleys: Government and Economy in the Isle of Man, 1580–1704* (Cheetham Society, 3rd series, 41: Manchester, 1996). For a preliminary analysis of the Manx court system and its archives, see J.A. Sharpe and J.R. Dickinson, 'Courts, Crime and Litigation in the Isle of Man 1580–1700', *Historical Research*, 72 (1999), 140–59 and, more generally, on civil litigation in the early modern period, see C.W. Brooks, *Lawyers, Litigation and English Society since 1450* (London: Hambledon Press, 1998).

Chapter 6

'For fear of the vengeance': the prosecution of homicide in pre-Famine and Famine Ireland

Richard Mc Mahon

This article explores the prosecution of homicide and in particular the role of prosecution witnesses in homicide trials in Ireland in the first half of the nineteenth century. The dominant view, if not the consensus, among many commentators of the day was that the criminal trial in Ireland was severely hampered by the fact that witnesses were reluctant to testify in open court and could face considerable dangers and difficulties if they chose to do so. Speaking before the 1839 select committee on the state of Ireland in respect of crime, Major George Warburton believed that the refusal of witnesses to come forward to give evidence against a murderer was 'constantly the result of the extraordinary intimidation that prevails; there can be no other reason for it'. This intimidation he argued was due to the actions and authority of the Ribbon society who intimidated witnesses to such an extent that they knew 'if they [gave] evidence they [would] be surely made victims'.[1] Piers Geale, crown solicitor for the home circuit, declared before the same committee on crime that 'witnesses come forward in Ireland with great reluctance, and if government did not take care of them, which they invariably do, their lives would be very unsafe'.[2] Hill Wilson Rowan, a stipendiary magistrate, also declared before the same committee that there were 'hardly any successful prosecutions unless some of the witnesses happen[ed] to be policemen'. This was particularly the case, he argued, with regard to 'waylaying, beating, and murdering, and all offences against the person'.[3] Rowan also pointed out that a number of witnesses had informed him that 'they dare not prosecute for fear of the vengeance of [the Ribbon] society or persons connected with it'.[4] Similarly, in 1852, it was claimed by Maxwell Hamilton, the crown solicitor for the north-east circuit, before the select committee on outrages, that witnesses were 'certainly' intimidated 'from fear of injury to themselves' for giving evidence.[5] James Major, the assistant barrister in Co. Monaghan, also noted before the 1852 committee that there was 'a great indisposition on the part of persons to come forward and give evidence'.[6]

These views have also found support within the historiography. Writing about the pre-Famine period, J.S. Donnelly Jr claims that there was 'extreme reluctance' on the part of witnesses to appear in open court and that this, in fact, had 'for generations been the great Achilles' heel of the Irish judicial system'.[7] For John McEldowney, 'throughout the [nineteenth] century the British administration in Dublin Castle were faced with the failure of witnesses to give evidence in court'[8] and for Carolyn A. Conley, 'the cultural sanctions against testifying for the Crown were strong'.[9]

Were ordinary people prepared to tender evidence in criminal trials and, if so, were these witnesses an isolated and unrepresentative group who defied wider social norms and cultural expectations in order to participate in the trial process? This article explores this question in the context of a study of homicide trials in a number of Irish counties for which there are adequate surviving sources. It will look at the position of prosecution witnesses and their relationships to and with the protagonists in homicide cases. It will also examine the nature of the evidence given by such witnesses, the conditions upon which they participated in the trial process and the consequences of such participation within the particular context of the criminal trial. In doing so, this article will offer both a legal and a socio-cultural history of the criminal trial in Ireland in the first half of the nineteenth century.

Such a study is, of course, by no means an unproblematic exercise. In a sense, we are attempting to satisfy two distinct constituencies and to combine their approaches to the study of legal systems. On the one hand, as J.H. Baker has pointed out, there is the lawyer whose favoured approach is 'to expound the theoretical conception, the abstract rules revealed by legal authorities'. On the other, there is the sociologist who prefers 'recorded events' to the 'theoretical explanations of the lawyer or the commands of the lawgiver'. The application of these approaches to the study of the law in history can obviously give rise to difficulties, as, in the words of Baker, the study of the law 'flits uncomfortably between intellectual and social history'. Yet, as Baker points out, the two approaches need not necessarily always be in conflict. The principles and procedures of the law can provide an essential framework within which to understand the actual operation of the system just as the operation and practices of the courts can reveal how such principles and procedures were utilised and adapted by both officials and ordinary people.[10] In adopting this approach we can also help to reconstruct and interpret the broader legal culture of the period, both official and popular, through the particular perspective offered by the prosecution of serious violent crime.[11]

This study is primarily based on newspaper reports of 141 trials and the testimony of close to 1,000 prosecution witnesses. Newspapers are, admittedly, by no means an ideal source. It is likely that some reports do not offer a complete record of all the witnesses or, indeed, all that was said by them at trial.[12] Nor do we, in most cases, get a verbatim report of either the questions asked of or the answers given by witnesses; rather such reports consist of condensed and sometimes paraphrased summaries of the evidence tendered in court. This means that we may not be able to get a wholly accurate account of the evidence tendered by witnesses in all cases. Ideally, we would be able to rely on transcripts of trials and law reports of cases but unfortunately such sources are limited for this period and those which do exist do not necessarily offer a representative sample, although they will be drawn on where relevant. Newspapers when combined with court records and various other sources do allow us, however, to trace the activities of witnesses in the courts in particular counties over a number of years and offer a more representative sample. Given, moreover, that our primary concern is to establish the nature of witness participation in the trial process, newspapers are, for this purpose at least, an adequate if not an ideal source.

Our newspaper reports are drawn primarily from Co. Armagh between 1807 and 1850, Co. Fermanagh between 1811 and 1850 and Queen's Co. from 1832 to 1850. The Armagh sample includes 50 cases and the testimony of 326 witnesses, the Fermanagh sample contains 44 cases and the testimony of 307 prosecution witnesses while the Queen's Co. sample includes 47 cases and the testimony of 344 prosecution witnesses. I also draw on evidence from another county, Co. Kilkenny, at various times throughout the article. These counties have been selected primarily because there is viable source material available for them. Fortunately, they also provide an insight into areas of the country that had somewhat contrasting rates and experiences of homicide – both southern counties, Queen's Co. and Co. Kilkenny, had reputations for unrest in this period and relatively high rates of homicide while the two northern counties, Co. Armagh and Co. Fermanagh, were less disturbed and, although rates increased in Armagh in the 1840s, had relatively low homicide rates throughout this period.[13] Finally, I have focused on the prosecution of homicide at the assizes for this study because studies of the courts in Ireland at this time have heretofore largely focused on the lower courts, in particular summary justice at petty sessions. The study of the prosecution of homicide allows us to explore the operation of the courts at a higher level and provides, therefore, an indispensable element for any broader understanding of how serious violent crime was understood and treated by the courts at this time.

I

At the outset, it is important to understand the context in which witnesses tendered their evidence. Much of the recent historiography of the criminal trial in England has focused on the increasing role of both prosecution and defence counsel in the trial process and the consequent rise of the 'adversary criminal trial' in the eighteenth century. As the prosecution of serious crime was increasingly undertaken by hired counsel so judges became more likely to allow defence counsel to represent the accused and began to develop new safeguards for those who stood accused of felony.[14] Unfortunately, the history of both the role of counsel and more generally the criminal trial in Ireland remains obscure. There is certainly no equivalent of Langbein's study of the English criminal trial in the eighteenth century in the Irish historiography.[15]

What is certain is that the participation of counsel in the prosecution of homicide at the assizes was firmly established in Ireland in the first half of the nineteenth century. Indeed, their participation in the prosecution of felony generally at the assizes probably increased appreciably in this period with the development of the system of public prosecution in the early 1800s. Under this system, many and, by the end of our period, most prosecutions at the assize courts were carried out by counsel paid by the state and supported by state-appointed solicitors.[16] There were still cases where the family of the alleged victim could employ their own counsel alongside that of the crown,[17] but this was rare and could only be done if the counsel carrying out the prosecution on behalf of the crown was agreeable.[18] There were also, it seems, some cases where private prosecutors took a case before the assizes but this was, in the words of the former

Attorney-General, Joseph Napier, 'not very usual, because it [was] considered that the case, having been rejected by the Attorney-general', was not 'a fit case, or one with sufficient materials for a prosecution'.[19]

The counsel for the crown was essentially the Attorney-General's representative at the assizes and was 'considered as having the power of the attorney-general' in conducting prosecutions.[20] They were appointed by the Attorney-General, who had, technically at least, the power to remove them from office. This was, however, a power which was never exercised in our period.[21] Counsel were not paid a salary but a fee by the central government for each brief they took on.[22] The general practice seems to have been to have two permanent counsel on each circuit who were responsible for all crown prosecutions at the assizes. There was a senior prosecutor, who was generally a Queen's Counsel, and a 'permanent prosecutor' who assisted the more senior counsel and whose duty it was to aid in the preparation of the indictment and to 'see that the evidence [was] all correct'. These two lawyers were then supplemented by more junior barristers in each county. These additional or 'supernumerary' prosecutors assisted the more senior men and, at times, undertook prosecutions themselves, albeit under the control and supervision of the senior prosecutor.[23] Those appointed were predominantly, although not exclusively, Protestant.[24]

The reputation of those who practised in the criminal courts seems not to have been high. According to Garnham, in many cases, in the eighteenth century, counsel 'were perceived as meddlesome incompetents'.[25] Greer has also noted the 'low professional status' of criminal practice in the nineteenth century.[26] Practice in the civil courts was undoubtedly seen as an altogether more respectable pursuit and those who operated in the criminal courts were not regarded and, in some cases did not regard themselves, as the cream of their profession.[27] We should not, however, wholly dismiss the credentials of those who did practise in the criminal courts. Joseph Napier declared, in 1855, that counsel for the crown were 'men of considerable eminence; a high class of men'.[28] Whatever their merits, and any proper assessment must await a more in-depth analysis than can be provided here, counsel played a central role in and were vital to the prosecution of homicide in the nineteenth century.

In setting out the case for the prosecution, the prosecuting counsel had two main tasks: to examine the witnesses for the prosecution and, if he chose to do so, to state the case to the jury. Stating the case was done at the very beginning of the trial and was the exclusive preserve of counsel.[29] Its use was, however, it seems, restricted to certain cases. Counsel might, for instance, address the jury where the case was based entirely on circumstantial evidence. In stating the case at the trial of Lucy Keefe at the Fermanagh spring assizes of 1838, Mr Schoales 'observed that a statement from him would not be necessary only that the case rested on circumstantial evidence'.[30] In such cases, it was probably thought necessary or at least advisable for counsel for the crown to offer a plausible narrative of what he believed occurred which would provide the jury with a context or framework within which to interpret the evidence given by the witnesses.[31] Counsel could also state the case in situations where there was a particularly unusual aspect to the case. At the trial of Peter Magill at the Armagh summer assizes of 1845, Sir Thomas Staples 'in stating the case for the prosecution, dwelt on its importance because it involved the life of a fellow creature; and its painfulness, because the Crown would be obliged to produce some of the prisoner's own children as witnesses against him'.[32] There were also those cases which were probably seen as having a wider public significance and which, therefore, warranted an opening speech.[33] Finally, counsel could also take the opportunity of stating the case in order to clarify a point of law for the jury. In homicide trials, this often involved an explanation for the petty jury of the distinction between murder and manslaughter.[34]

When addressing the jury, counsel were also expected to adhere to the practice, established both in Ireland and England in felony cases at this time, the so-called 'duty of restraint'. The precise origins of this practice are unclear but the reason cited for such restraint on the part of prosecution counsel was the fact that defence counsel in both countries were prohibited up to 1836 from addressing the jury on behalf of the accused in homicide trials (and felony cases generally).[35] In such circumstances, it was felt that the prosecution counsel should not unduly press his case when making an opening address and was not to 'struggle for a conviction'.[36] In particular, counsel were expected to restrict themselves to an account of the evidence to be tendered by the witnesses for the prosecution.[37]

In our sample, counsel often adopted an apparently neutral position when giving an address to the jury, tending to stress the degree to which they were impartial and concerned only with discovering the truth of the case. At the trial of Lucy Keefe for the murder of her husband at the Fermanagh spring assizes of 1838, Mr John Schoales QC 'entreated the jury if he stated any thing that might make an unfavourable impression on them, and that should not be borne out by the clearest testimony, to discharge it from their minds. His object was not to excite a prejudice against the unfortunate prisoner, but to elicit the truth only; and he would be cautious in his statement, to confine himself to what alone should appear in evidence'.[38] Others could be almost apologetic in their opening pronouncements. At the trial for the murder of William McCreery at the Fermanagh summer assizes of 1824, Mr Johnston, in addressing the jury, pointed out that the accused stood accused of murder but that 'he hoped they would acquit themselves'. He also concluded the speech by stating that 'it would be far from him to aggravate any offence. But he thought it his duty to submit an outline of the case.'[39]

There were, of course, times when counsel appeared less solicitous to the position of the accused and took the opportunity to stress the importance of finding a murder verdict. My impression, however, is that such practices were rare and, if anything, probably more likely after the passing of the Prisoner's Counsel Act of 1836 than before.[40] It may be that counsel, after 1836, felt they had greater leeway in stating the case when counsel for the defence was also afforded the opportunity of addressing the jury. Indeed, where counsel for the crown appeared to overstep the mark, defence counsel could be quick to draw it to the attention of the court during their address to the jury and even, at times, during the opening address by the prosecuting counsel.[41]

Such confrontations, however, appear rare, probably reflecting not only that prosecution counsel were generally restrained in stating the case but also the relative rarity of addresses by counsel to the jury. Counsel seem, indeed, to have restricted the extent to which they would address the jury and the available evidence suggests that in the majority of homicide cases they refrained from doing so altogether.[42] Given the seemingly limited use made by counsel of an opening address, even in homicide trials; it is likely that they preferred or perhaps even felt obliged to make the examination of witnesses the primary and sometimes the only focus of the prosecution case.

The examination of prosecution witnesses was to be conducted by counsel within certain established rules, the most important of which was that leading questions were not, as a general rule, to be put to witnesses. These were questions which, as Purcell put it, '... plainly suggest to [the witness] the answer he is expected to make'.[43] The evidence provided by prosecution witnesses was also to be 'relevant', in the strict legal sense of the word, to the case at hand[44] and, at the risk of being deemed inadmissible by the judge, was to be consistent with the established rules of evidence. There were, as Langbein has demonstrated, considerable changes to the rules of evidence governing the prosecution of those accused of felony over the course of the eighteenth century. In particular, Langbein identifies the development of four primary rules: the character rule, the corroboration rule, the hearsay rule and the confession rule – all of which served, to some degree at least, to afford greater protection to the accused.[45] Such developments had by the nineteenth century come to have a significant bearing on the trial process in England which meant, as Bentley has demonstrated, that 'throughout the nineteenth century the protection conferred upon the accused by the law of evidence was substantial'.[46] These rules of evidence were also firmly entrenched in the criminal trial in Ireland by the first half of the nineteenth century. This is evident in the legal literature of the day and in the actual conduct of trials as revealed in the available sources.[47]

What effect did such rules have on the conduct of criminal trials? To begin, the prosecution could not introduce evidence on the character of the accused and would generally only produce such evidence as a rebuttal when evidence of the good character of the accused was raised by the defence.[48] Similar fact evidence, that is evidence that the accused had committed a similar but distinct offence, also could not, as a general rule, be given in evidence. As Purcell puts it, 'it is not competent, ... for the prosecutor to give evidence of facts tending to prove another distinct and unconnected offence'.[49]

Another area of key importance (and of some controversy) in the field of criminal evidence was the law surrounding the admission of the evidence of accomplices (generally referred to as approvers). In our period, it was clearly established that approvers were competent witnesses and that the degree of credit to be given to such witnesses was 'a matter exclusively within the province of the jury'. Thus, if the jury saw fit to convict solely on the basis of the evidence tendered by an approver, they were, in law, entitled to do so.[50] In practice, however, the presiding judge was to advise the 'jury not to convict a prisoner upon the testimony of an accomplice alone, and without corroboration' and if the judge failed to so caution the jury, it was regarded as an 'omission of duty' on his part.[51]

It is unclear, however, to what extent juries were even given the opportunity in this period to decide whether or not to convict on the uncorroborated evidence of an approver. I have only come across one case in which the prosecution sought to secure a conviction based on the uncorroborated evidence of an approver. This was a case for administering an illegal oath at the Fermanagh summer assizes of 1826. In this case, the judge remarked that 'it was the first time in his experience that he had seen a charge of felony *brought forward* resting on the uncorroborated testimony of an accomplice'. He went on to warn the jury that it would 'not be safe on [their oaths] to find the prisoners guilty' and that there was 'no instance in modern times where a charge of this nature has been sustained, solely upon the testimony of an approver, without any corroborating circumstances'. He did concede that the law allowed them to find a guilty verdict but warned that such a verdict 'would be unsafe'.[52] The unwillingness of the prosecution to pursue a case solely on the basis of accomplice evidence was also acknowledged in the opening address to the jury by Mr Tickell QC at the trial for the murder of William Carter in Queen's Co. in 1835, where he pointed out that 'if the [prosecution] case depended alone on [the approver's] testimony, it would never have been brought before a court of justice' and that it was for the jury 'to see if his testimony would not be corroborated by unimpeachable witnesses'.[53]

The extent and nature of the corroborating evidence which was required for the jury to convict was also a matter of some considerable debate.[54] The judges themselves were divided on the question of whether such corroboration was sufficient if it related only to the circumstances of the case or whether the corroborating evidence had to relate to the actual participation of the accused in the crime. In *R v. Sheehan* five of the eleven judges who considered the case concluded that 'a corroboration in the circumstances of the crime charged, though entirely unaccompanied by any circumstance applicable to the prisoner on trial, or to any other person charged by the accomplice, was a substantial corroboration, fit to be examined and weighed'. It was also their opinion that 'there ought not to be any rule of practice, by which juries should be advised to disregard, or to pay slight attention to, such circumstances of corroboration ...'. In contrast, the majority of the judges were of the opinion that 'the accomplice being supported in his narrative of the transaction only, without corroboration as to any person charged, was so slight a confirmation, as to be entitled to very little, if any, attention, and that a jury should generally be so told.'[55]

There was also some uncertainty as to whether an approver could be corroborated by the evidence of another approver if they were held separately before trial and were unable to communicate with each other. Such evidence was allowed at the trials arising from the burning of Wildgoose lodge and the practice was also referred to in *R v. Aylmer, Aylmer and Behan* (1839) where Judge Bushe noted that if 'there could have been no communication between the approvers, the testimony of one might be brought forward to support the evidence of another'.[56] By the end of the period under review, however, it seems to have been settled that 'if two or more accomplices are produced as witnesses, they are not deemed to corroborate each other; but the same rule is applied and the same confirmation is required as if there were but one' with no allowance for the fact that the approvers may have been held separately before trial.[57] Such restrictions on the use of accomplice evidence were clearly intended to, and, as we shall see, probably did limit the extent to which the prosecution could resort to or rely upon accomplice evidence in order to secure a conviction.

The rules of criminal evidence also held that hearsay was, as a general rule, to be deemed inadmissible. This was evidence of a statement or assertion made by someone other than the witness giving oral evidence of it in court.[58] Such evidence was generally excluded on the basis that the person whose assertion or statement was being relayed to the court was not under oath at the time the statement was made and also was not subject to cross-examination at trial.[59] There were, however, some instances in which the rule did not apply. This could occur, for instance, where the evidence related to the state of mind of the accused before the alleged crime, where the fact that the statement was made and not whether it was true or not was the issue at stake, where it was necessary to prove pedigree and where the statement formed part of the *res gestae*.[60] Such evidence, in particular that relating to the state of mind of the accused, could, as we shall see, be crucial at times in homicide cases.

There were also a number of exceptions to the hearsay rule, most notably the admission of the dying declarations of the accused and evidence of a confession.[61] Even here, however, there were clear restrictions placed on the admission of such evidence.[62] A dying declaration was only admitted if the judge was satisfied that the deceased had a settled expectation of death when making the declaration.[63] There were, for instance, cases in our sample where evidence relating to statements made by the alleged victim were deemed inadmissible. In its report of the evidence of Bernard Moley during the trial of six men at the Armagh spring assizes of 1819 for the murder of Patrick Moley, the *Belfast Newsletter* pointed out that 'any conversation [the witness] had could not be given in evidence, it not appearing the deceased considered himself in danger at the time'.[64]

Another exception to the hearsay rule was the admission of confession evidence. The rules governing the admission of such evidence were again strict. A confession was admitted as evidence on 'the presumption that a person will not make an untrue statement militating against his own interest' and included 'not only explicit and express confessions of crime, but all those admissions of the accused from which guilt may be *implied*'.[65] It had, however, to be the entire statement made by the accused and, most crucially, had to be 'freely and voluntarily made'. Confessions obtained by temporal inducements in the form of a threat, a promise or hope of favour were to be deemed inadmissible.[66]

A strict definition of what constituted a threat or a promise was applied in the first half of the nineteenth century[67] and the judges in Ireland, like their counterparts in England, certainly seem to have erred on the side of caution.[68] For instance, at the trial of Patrick Carberry at the Armagh spring assizes of 1826, the chief constable of Drogheda, John Armstrong, gave evidence that he had asked the accused 'how he thought the case would go with him at Armagh' to which the accused replied 'he believed there was a strong case against him'. At this point, Judge Vandeleur stopped the witness from giving any further evidence 'it being the opinion of the court that the words of Mr. Armstrong implied a *threat*, and that consequently any subsequent confession could not be received'.[69]

Although, it was generally accepted that a confession was inadmissible if it was obtained by a person in authority, or a person sanctioned by a person in authority, holding out temporal inducements to the accused,[70] there was considerable debate on whether a confession was also inadmissible if obtained by inducements held out by 'private persons'.[71] There were diverging views on this question in the early decades of the century. According to Bentley, however, by 1840 it was settled that 'only an inducement held out by, or with the sanction of, a person in authority (that is a person in a position to influence the conduct of the prosecution) would exclude'.[72] Yet, there were, even in the 1840s, diverging opinions in Ireland on the position of the person who held out the inducement. Joy, writing in 1842, claimed that a confession could not be deemed inadmissible if obtained by inducements held out by a person having no authority over the accused.[73] Writing in 1849, however, Purcell was less convinced, suggesting that the admissibility of confessions obtained by inducements held out by 'private persons' was (properly) a matter for judicial discretion rather than an established rule.[74] The evidence that is available to us would also suggest that some judges, even as late as the 1840s, still exercised their discretion in excluding confession evidence tendered by private persons. This is evident at the trial of Patrick Price for the murder of John Mahon at the Queen's Co. summer assizes of 1848. In this case, a painter called John Connor gave evidence that he had been painting at the jail and that he told Price that he had heard another man, called Whelan, say the accused had confessed to the murder. This drew a strong reaction from Price who 'stamped his foot on the ground and said "*I am guilty of the murder, and I do not care about Whelan or the Devil*".'[75] At this point, the judge intervened and said that he 'did not think there was authority for the admission of the evidence now offered to court'.[76]

The rules governing the admission of confessions, of course, did not, as Bentley points out, always favour the accused.[77] Aside from confessions obtained by 'temporal inducements' those obtained through all other methods, 'however reprehensible and improper', were admissible as evidence. This included cases where the confession was obtained by 'artifice' or 'deception', by acting on the feelings of the accused, by making the accused drunk, by making a solemn promise of secrecy to the accused, by putting questions which assumed the guilt of the prisoner or by reporting confessions which were overheard.[78] The discussion of the admissibility of confessions, which was generally carried out in open court in front of the jury rather than on the *voir dire*, may also have been detrimental to the accused.[79] Yet, despite such leeway, the impression remains that the judges were still quite strict in their enforcement of the confession rule and that the rule itself probably inhibited the police and the authorities in eliciting or tendering evidence of confessions before the courts.[80]

Indeed, the judges were not too keen and, if anything, became increasingly wary of the questioning of suspects by the police at this time. The rules governing the admission of evidence garnered during police questioning were, in fact, not quite settled. In the early decades of the century, answers given by the accused to questions posed by the police were usually admissible in court,[81] often with the proviso that the officer had cautioned the accused beforehand.[82] By the late 1830s, however, judicial hostility in Ireland towards such police questioning was becoming more evident. For instance, in *R v. Glennon, Toole and Magrath* (1840) Judge Doherty declared that 'the questioning of persons in custody by policemen and others, within the scope of whose duty such questioning does not fall, is not to be permitted'.[83]

These then were the primary conditions governing the conduct of the prosecution case and it is in the context of such procedural norms and evidentiary rules that we shall now examine the role of prosecution witnesses and the nature of the evidence tendered by them.

II

Who were the prosecution witnesses in homicide cases? In all three counties, officials working within or employed by the official legal system constituted a minority of prosecution witnesses – accounting for less than one in five prosecution witnesses in Queen's Co., just over one in eight in Armagh and only one in ten in Fermanagh.[84] The only group of officials who made any significant impact as prosecution witnesses were the police. They were the most prominent group of officials in all three counties in our sample and their participation served to increase significantly the proportion of cases in which officials gave evidence.[85] In Queen's Co., 50 policemen accounted for 76.92 per cent of all officials and appeared as prosecution witnesses in 33 of the 47 cases in our sample (70.21 per cent). The high participation rate in Queen's Co., is perhaps not too surprising, given that it was the second most heavily-policed county in Ireland in the 1830s and 1840s.[86] Participation by the police, although high compared to other officials, was, however, less pronounced in the northern counties.[87] Their participation did increase over the course of the period under review but this was from a position where there was little or no police involvement. Even by the 1840s their role seems to have been minimal in these counties.[88]

Other prominent local officials such as magistrates played only a minor role as prosecution witnesses in all three counties – they accounted for just over 2 per cent of witnesses and gave evidence in less than one in six cases.[89] The role of other officials such as coroners was even more limited. The evidence given by the coroner was only reported in three homicide cases over a 40-year period in Fermanagh, in only two out of 50 cases in our sample from Armagh (1807–50) and in only one case, over a 19-year period, in Queen's county.[90]

A more prominent group of witnesses were the relatives of the deceased. In Queen's Co., the deceased's family acted as prosecution witnesses in 31 of the 47 reported cases – 65.95 per cent. They also accounted for 51 of the 344 witnesses whose testimony was reported over this 19-year period (14.82 per cent). In Fermanagh, the deceased's relatives played a somewhat less significant role. They only acted as witnesses in 12 out of the 44 cases in our sample – 27.27 per cent of cases, accounting for only 23 out of the 307 prosecution witnesses (7.49 per cent), while in Armagh members of the family of the deceased appeared in 21 of the 50 cases in our sample (42 per cent) and made up 41 of the 326 prosecution witnesses (12.57 per cent). The majority of these witnesses were members of the deceased's immediate family – making up *c*.70 per cent, in all three counties, of those relatives of the deceased who gave evidence for the prosecution.[91]

Other witnesses were related to both the accused and the deceased.[92] They generally gave evidence in cases arising from family disputes and the majority of them were more closely related to the deceased than the accused.[93] It was relatively rare for those who were only relations of the accused to tender evidence for the prosecution. In all three counties they accounted for circa one per cent of all witnesses and only appeared in around one in 20 cases.[94] Most of these were distant relations or were related through marriage to the accused. Only one was definitely a member of the accused's immediate family and in this case the witness gave evidence as an approver.[95]

An interest in acting as witnesses extended beyond the direct relations of the principal protagonists as the majority of witnesses in all three counties were not related to the parties involved.[96] These witnesses could be local authority figures such as members of the clergy or local landlords or land agents. The participation of such witnesses was, however, rare.[97] The majority of the witnesses were ordinary people.[98] Some were neighbours of the deceased. At the trial of Patrick Price, a young servant boy, for the murder of his master's son, John Mahon, no less than eight neighbours of the deceased gave evidence, adding to that already given by the father, brother and sister of the deceased.[99] Neighbours of the accused also gave evidence in a number of cases. Sarah Keenan, a prosecution witness at the trial of Francis Graham at the Fermanagh summer assizes of 1829, lived in a house opposite to Graham's where she had 'a little grocery shop and an eating house'.[100] Bridget Kelly, a prosecution witness at the trial of Patrick Fannan at the spring assizes of 1835 in Queen's Co., pointed out that she and 'the prisoner were reared children together in the same neighbourhood'.[101]

Others were neighbours of the accused and the deceased. This was often the case in homicides arising from domestic disputes. In the trial of Alexander Smyth for the murder of his wife in Fermanagh in 1845, their neighbour, Sarah Robinson, was the main prosecution witness.[102] At the trial of Lucy Keefe for the murder of her husband at the spring assizes of 1838 in Co. Fermanagh, no less than nine neighbours of the couple, five men and four women, gave evidence. Neighbours could also give evidence in situations where members of the deceased's immediate family were reluctant to provide information. For instance, in Armagh in 1843, the police noted in the case of the murder of Sarah Smith by her husband, Samuel Smith, that it was 'evident the children [did] not wish to prosecute their father'.[103] A number of neighbours did, however, provide the police with strong evidence against Smith.[104]

Employees of the accused could also give evidence for the prosecution. At the trial of Jeremiah Dooley at the Queen's Co. summer assizes of 1832, Mary Morton, a servant woman, who had 'lived more than five years' with the accused, testified for the prosecution.[105] In other cases, the relationship between the witness and the parties involved was not so close or direct. In some cases, the witnesses were simply acquaintances of the protagonists. In her testimony at the trial of Patrick Whelan, John Malone and Joseph Abraham for the murder of John Larkin at the spring assizes of 1835 in Queen's Co., a Catherine Bergin claimed that one of the accused, Whelan, was 'one of the men who beat [the] deceased' and that she 'often saw Whelan before [and was] quite sure he was one of the party'. This evidence was also corroborated by the witness's mother.[106] John Cleary was convicted of murder at the Kilkenny spring assizes of 1838 on the basis of circumstantial evidence provided by a number of women whose houses he had visited on the night of the murder. These women seem to have known the accused quite well and the daughter of one of them was 'in the habit' of washing Cleary's clothes for him.[107]

Other witnesses had no previous relationship with the deceased. A prosecution witness at the trial of Francis Graham for the murder of Michael Nolan at the Fermanagh summer assizes of 1829 testified that he was 'never acquainted with deceased, nor never saw him till [the day of the killing]'.[108] There were also some witnesses who at least claimed that they had no previous knowledge of either the deceased or the accused. For instance, at the Queen's Co. summer assizes of 1832, during the trial for the murder of Peter Dowling, one of the witnesses claimed that he 'was a stranger and did not know any of the men' but had seen the accused give three blows to Dowling and had 'desired the men who attacked [the deceased] not to kill the man'.[109]

Finally, there were those who had no previous relationship with the accused and the deceased but who offered 'expert' testimony at the trial. These were doctors and surgeons, who accounted for around one in eight witnesses in our sample[110] and their testimony was reported in over 70 per cent of cases in all three counties.[111]

III

What was the nature of witness participation? There was considerable scope, despite the restrictions upon the tendering of evidence noted earlier, for prosecution witnesses to tender evidence against the accused. This could include evidence of the alleged homicide itself and the role of the accused in it as well as on events before and after the alleged incident.

Before the homicide

Despite restrictions on what could be revealed by the prosecution about the character and previous conduct of the accused, prosecution witnesses could tender valuable evidence relating to events, activities and statements made before an alleged homicide. In some cases, officials such as police and magistrates provided a description of events or local conditions before the alleged incident. In Fermanagh in 1830, two magistrates and a policeman gave evidence at the trials for the murders of Robert Mealy and Edward Scarlet of an encounter between a large group of Catholics and some Orangemen which occurred on the morning of the alleged murder. This confrontation was seen as a precursor to and contributing factor in the fight in which the two men lost their lives.[112]

More commonly, information on events before the alleged homicide were provided by ordinary people. A number of witnesses, for instance, could offer circumstantial evidence on the appearance and/or the movements of the deceased and the accused before the alleged violent attack. At the trial of John Keys and Peter Evans for the murder of Daniel Delany at the Queen's Co. spring assizes of 1847, Alice Delany, who knew both the accused and the deceased, testified that upon leaving a fair on the night in question she 'passed Dan Delaney on the road near Ballycoolan' and shortly afterwards 'passed [Keys and Evans] on the road'. When she passed them they were about 40 yards behind Delany but when she 'looked behind, after passing them, [she] saw all three together'. A number of other witnesses also testified that they had seen the accused near the scene of the alleged homicide on the night in question.[113]

Others gave evidence not only of the actions but also the statements of the accused before the alleged homicide. Such statements were tendered at homicide trials as evidence of the state of mind of the accused before the alleged offence. Evidence was given by a witness at the trial of Dennis Rooney for a murder arising from a sectarian affray in Fermanagh in 1824 that he heard Rooney say before the affray that 'he would not leave the meadow till he would have a Lisbellaw man's life'.[114] Another heard him say 'he would be stopped by no *budda … for that he would have blood for blood!'*[115] Conversations with the accused were also given in evidence. At the trial for the murder of Brian McCresh at the Armagh summer assizes of 1839, Michael McCresh, brother of the deceased, gave evidence of a conversation he had with Ellen McMahon, who was charged with soliciting a number of men to kill Brian McCresh. He recounted how McMahon told him that she had £4 and how she would use it to hire someone to kill Brian and 'if the £4 should not be sufficient, she had a stripper cow, and she would leave herself without either cow or calf forever, to have Brian's life taken or, in case she had not means to do it, her brother would get it done'.[116]

The statements and actions of the accused could also be used to establish a clear motive for the crime. This is evident, for instance, at the trial of a 17-year-old servant boy called Patrick Price who was tried at the Queen's Co. summer assizes of 1848 for the murder of his master's son, John Mahon. In this case, Eliza Doolan, another servant in the house, gave evidence of a conversation she had with Price two days before the killing of Mahon in which the accused not only expressed personal animosity towards John Mahon but also a desire to secure enough money to travel with his sister to America. This was significant as the case also involved the robbery of a sum of money.[117]

The homicide and the identification of the accused

Evidence relating to the actual homicide and the identification of the accused was often crucial to the prosecution case. Such evidence played a very prominent role in the prosecution of homicide at this time and unlike other areas of the law of criminal evidence, the conditions governing the admission of such evidence were not, relatively speaking, a major area of concern for the judges in this period.[118] In a majority of cases in all three counties one or more witnesses gave direct evidence in which they identified one or more of the accused – in over three-quarters of cases in Queen's Co., in around 70 per cent of cases in Armagh and in just under 60 per cent in Co. Fermanagh.[119]

Who identified the accused? It was extremely rare for those who had an official role within the legal system to offer direct evidence in which they identified the accused. In our sample of 141 cases there was only one homicide trial in which an official identified the accused as the perpetrator of a homicide. This was Martin Bergin, a bailiff, who gave evidence at the trial of Edward Phelan at the Queen's Co. spring assizes of 1849 for the murder of another bailiff called John Dunphy.[120] There were no cases in which the police or magistrates offered direct evidence against the accused. This, it must be admitted, is hardly surprising as most homicides were, perhaps sensibly, not carried out in the presence of the police or magistrates.

It was more likely that the relatives of the deceased would identify the accused – over one in four of the witnesses who identified the accused were members of the deceased's family.[121] Some were drawn from the deceased's extended family. At the trial of John Maguire for the murder of Henry McNiece at the Armagh summer assizes of 1825, a cousin of the deceased identified the accused as the man who attacked McNiece and pointed out that he had been drinking with him on the night in question.[122] More commonly, they were members of the immediate family.[123] At the summer assizes of 1832, Margaret Dowling both described the circumstances leading to her husband's killing and identified those responsible. In her testimony, Dowling claimed that the accused, Richard Connor senior and Richard Connor junior 'beat [her] husband across the road: they broke all his fingers, as he held up his hands [and] they left him senseless'. Her son also corroborated her testimony.[124]

There were cases where the members of the deceased's family were the only witnesses to identify the accused. For instance, at the trial for the murder of Denis Flanagan at the Queen's Co. spring assizes of 1835, the only witnesses to identify the accused as the perpetrator were the father and sister of the deceased.[125] Such cases were, however, the exception. In only a minority of cases did the identification of the accused depend solely on the participation of the deceased's relatives[126] and those from outside the deceased's family identified the accused in a very high proportion of cases.[127] In some cases, ordinary members of the public could add to the evidence given by the deceased's relatives.[128] At the trial of two men for the murder of Patrick Salmon at the Queen's Co. spring assizes of 1839, the evidence of two members of the deceased's family was added to by two men and one women who also witnessed the incident. One of these witnesses, Walter Moore, described how one of the accused chased Salmon down the street and then beat him with a stick.[129] Moore also described the clothes the accused had on the day of the attack and recounted how he had run up the street in pursuit of the men crying out 'murder' and that 'the big fellow ... had killed a man'. He also identified both of the accused in court.[130]

More commonly, the identification of the accused depended solely on the evidence of those from outside the deceased's family.[131] These witnesses could often have some form of (non-familial) relationship with or connection to the deceased. There were those witnesses, for instance, who shared a clear communal or group affiliation with the deceased. This is evident in those cases which arose from factional quarrels or sectarian animosity where those who came from the same group as the deceased could often be enthusiastic witnesses for the prosecution.[132] Other witnesses knew the deceased through their work. At the trial for the murder of Owen Drum at the Fermanagh spring assizes of 1835, an apprentice employed by the deceased gave evidence in which he both described the homicide and identified the accused.[133] Some witnesses were neighbours of the deceased. At the trial for the manslaughter of Patrick Ward at the Armagh spring assizes of 1850, Philip Duffy, a neighbour of Ward's, gave evidence in which he described the incident and identified the accused as the perpetrator.[134]

There were also those witnesses who had some form of relationship with or connection to the accused. John White, the employer of Henry Convere who was charged with manslaughter at the Armagh spring assizes of 1846, gave evidence against his employee in which he identified him as the perpetrator of the homicide.[135] At the trial of Thomas and Rose Gormley for murder at the Fermanagh summer assizes of 1835, a neighbour of the accused, John Corrigan, gave evidence that he 'saw Gormley strike Lang [the deceased] with the stick and his wife [Rose] also strike him with a stone at the same time'. He also saw 'Thomas give more than one blow, several on the body and one on the side of the head', and claimed that Gormley was a 'principal leader' in the affray.[136] There were even cases, albeit rare, where the relatives of the accused were willing to identify the accused. This is evident, for instance, in the prosecution of Patrick Kennedy for the manslaughter of Charles Kelly at the spring assizes of Queen's Co. in 1839. In this case, a relative of the accused was one of the main prosecution witnesses at his trial and he seems to have willingly given evidence against him. He had been present at the fight that led to the death of Kelly and pointed out that the accused was the aggressor in the dispute.[137]

Of course, the prosecution was not able to produce evidence identifying the accused as the perpetrator in all homicide cases brought before the courts.[138] It is likely, however, that this reflects more the inability rather than the unwillingness of witnesses to identify the perpetrator. In the vast majority of these cases there is also little evidence that fear of retribution from a secret society or popular hostility inhibited witnesses from identifying the accused. In some cases, the fact that the offence arose in the private sphere (often taking place in the family home) restricted the number of witnesses who were in a position to identify the accused as the perpetrator. Of the 18 cases in Co. Fermanagh in which no direct evidence was tendered against the accused, nearly half arose from disputes within families while in Armagh over one-third of such cases arose within the family.[139] This does not, however, necessarily reflect an unwillingness to tender evidence as in most cases the prosecution was able to produce strong circumstantial evidence against the accused. For instance, during the prosecution of Lucy Keefe for the murder of her husband at the Fermanagh spring assizes of 1838, a neighbouring woman recounted a conversation during which the accused told her that 'she could not get rid of [her husband]' and that the 'first news' the witness would hear would be 'that one will kill the other, or be hanged for the other'.[140] In some cases also the prosecution was clearly instigated by those who knew the deceased rather than by the authorities.[141]

It was probably also far more difficult to secure direct evidence in those cases in which there was a high degree of premeditation on the part of the accused. For instance, it was difficult to secure direct evidence against the accused in homicide cases arising from robberies as in such cases the perpetrator probably took care not to carry out the deed in front of witnesses. This is certainly evident in our sample of cases from Queen's Co. where there were three trials arising from homicides involving robberies. In none of these cases was direct evidence tendered identifying the accused as the perpetrator. There were, however, numerous witnesses who were willing to offer strong circumstantial evidence against the accused.[142]

There were also those homicides that arose in the course of a general affray between opposing groups and in which it could be difficult for witnesses to identify those who carried out the act. For instance, at the Fermanagh summer assizes of 1824, a Robert Maxwell described a riot in which William Ingram received a fatal injury but could not 'identify any of the attacking party, there was a great number of them'.[143] Although unable to identify whether or not the accused was the perpetrator in such cases, witnesses were often willing and able to place the accused at the scene of the crime. At the trial of Patrick Nellis for manslaughter at the Fermanagh spring assizes of

1842, three witnesses, although they could not directly identify the accused as the perpetrator, were able to identify him as being present and as participating in the affray in which the victim lost his life.[144] Thus, even though the accused was not directly identified as the perpetrator, a description of the homicide could be offered and the accused placed at the scene.

After the homicide

Evidence of events, activities and statements made after an alleged homicide also played a part in the prosecution case. Evidence of the movements of the accused in the aftermath of the alleged homicide were tendered in some cases. At the trial for the murder of Hessy Rodgers at the Fermanagh summer assizes of 1839, Hanna Malone recounted how she saw the accused carry a bundle to a local river and then open the bundle and throw its contents in the water. A number of witnesses also gave evidence of finding the body of the deceased in the river. Eliza Connor, for instance, gave evidence that she saw the body 'floating on the water' and that with the aid of her husband she removed it and found 'marks on [the deceased's] neck and body, and blood flowing out of her mouth'.[145]

While much of this kind of evidence was tendered by ordinary people, the authorities and expert witnesses could also play a prominent role in providing evidence concerning events after an alleged homicide. In many instances, the police offered a pretty straightforward account of the accused's arrest.[146] They could also, however, offer evidence on finding or taking possession of the alleged murder weapon or of other evidence found upon the person of the accused. James Carson, a police constable, gave evidence at the trial of Philip Fitzpatrick in which he recounted how he took possession of a knife after it was dropped by the accused during his arrest.[147] At the trial of Patrick Meagher at the Queen's Co. summer assizes of 1833, David Baldwin, a policeman, testified that he saw the accused on 'the morning after the murder [and that there] was blood on his trousers'. He then produced a piece of material from the accused's trousers in court.[148]

Forensic evidence was also provided by 'expert' witnesses. In most cases, doctors provided evidence on the cause of death. Such evidence was not always conclusive and, on occasion, could aid the defence case but at most trials doctors provided a fairly straightforward account of the deceased's injuries and concluded that the injuries inflicted caused or at the very least accelerated the death. Doctors could also, on occasion, make connections between the injuries inflicted and weapons found in the possession of the accused. During the case of Patrick Meagher at the Queen's Co. summer assizes of 1833, a Dr Lawlor gave evidence that he had 'made experiments' on blood found on a spade belonging to the accused and was satisfied that it was the blood of the victim, Alexander Tweedy. He also compared hair found on the spade with that on the victim's neck.[149]

Evidence of statements made by the accused and the deceased in the aftermath of an alleged act of violence was also tendered by prosecution witnesses. Witnesses gave evidence or at least attempted to give evidence of the dying declaration of the deceased in a number of cases.[150] In some, the dying declaration was relayed to the court by an official. At the Armagh summer assizes of 1828, Mr Olpherts, the local magistrate, gave evidence of the dying declaration of James Hagan, a Catholic, in which he identified the accused, Thomas Hayes, a Protestant, as the person who struck him on the head with a stone.[151] More frequently, relatives of the deceased relayed the dying declaration of the deceased to the court. This probably reflects the fact that the family of the deceased would have cared for the victim before he or she died and, in many cases, would have been in close proximity at the time of death. At the trial of Thady Conrahy for the manslaughter of John Graham at the Queen's Co. spring assizes of 1840, the father of the deceased gave evidence that on the day his son died he declared 'Thady Conrahy, Thady Conrahy, you have taken me from my father'.[152] At other times, those who were unrelated to the alleged victim but who were in the proximity of the incident gave evidence of the dying words of the victim. For instance, Owen Magee, a prosecution witness at the trial of John Corrigan, gave evidence that he was 'about forty perches off, when he heard a noise, and when he went over found the deceased dying. [He] took him up in his arms, and [the victim] said "Oh John Corrigan, you killed me". He died in five minutes'.[153]

In a number of cases, prosecution witnesses also tendered or at least attempted to tender evidence of confessions made by the accused in the aftermath of an alleged homicide.[154] In a number of these cases, evidence was given by a policeman or a magistrate who recounted a conversation with the accused. At the trial of John Darcy for the murder of Michael Smith at the Queen's Co. spring assizes of 1848, evidence was given that, when arrested and cautioned by the police, Darcy said that if the witnesses were to 'swear against me … I'll be hanged'.[155] The authorities could also succeed in obtaining a confession 'by acting on the feelings of the prisoner'. Catherine

Moore, for instance, made an explicit confession to the murder of her husband in Queen's Co. at the spring assizes of 1850 in order to exculpate the rest of her family who had been taken into custody after she had absconded.[156]

In other cases, the accused could probably see a distinct advantage in admitting to his actions. Such a course of action could, for instance, give the accused the opportunity to give his side of the story through a prosecution witness which might lead to a mitigation of the sentence imposed by the court. For instance, at the trial of John Mooney, 'a respectable farmer', at the Queen's Co. spring assizes of 1847, a policeman testified that the accused voluntarily gave evidence that he had stabbed Mathew Hogan while the latter was in the act of stealing turnips. The accused was found guilty but when it came to sentencing the defence counsel pointed out that the accused 'was in gaol for two months before he had been admitted to bail'. The judge, in this case, then sentenced him to 'be imprisoned for two calendar months from the date of his committal' which effectively meant that, despite confessing to and being found guilty of manslaughter, the accused was discharged immediately after the trial.[157] There were also cases where the accused confessed to the police and seemed quite willing and even pleased to undergo the sentence of the court. Joseph Ryan confessed to the manslaughter of Michael Carroll and was convicted at the Queen's Co. spring assizes of 1835. In this case, the *Express* noted that at the trial 'the sentence [transportation for life] gave great satisfaction to the prisoner who seemed much pleased when it was pronounced'.[158]

Such cases were, however, not very common. In most cases, it is likely that the accused was unwilling to confess to the authorities while he or she was in their custody and that the authorities themselves were restricted in the methods they could use to glean admissible evidence from the accused. There is also, to be fair, little evidence that the police or magistrates misreported or misrepresented, whether intentionally or not, what the accused had said voluntarily to them. This may, however, have been due more to lack of opportunity than to probity of practice.[159]

Those who did not have an official function within the criminal justice system were somewhat more likely to offer confession evidence.[160] At times, evidence of statements made by the accused while in custody were relayed by these witnesses to the court. At the trial of James Spencer at the Armagh summer assizes of 1824, the Revd Silver Oliver, rector of Loughgall, gave evidence that the accused, who was one of his parishioners, confessed to the murder in

Armagh jail shortly after the killing had occurred.[161] More commonly, these statements were made by the accused in the aftermath of the homicide and before he had been taken into custody. During the prosecution of Thomas Todd at the Armagh spring assizes of 1837, for the murder of Henry Gillespie, the brother of the deceased, Richard Gillespie, gave evidence of a conversation in which he declared to the accused 'you villain you have kilt my brother' to which the accused was reported to have replied 'by J---s I cut half of the head off him, and I'm sorry I didn't cut the whole head off him'.[162] At the trial for the manslaughter of George Latimer at the Fermanagh spring assizes of 1842, William Magee tendered evidence that the accused came into his house 'a few evenings after the fight [and] took up a pair of tongs and shook them, saying if he had them he could fight with them'. The witness then asked him if he would strike a man with tongs, to which the accused replied that 'he would, and that he struck Latimer in the fight with the tongs'.[163] Thus, it is evident that prosecution witnesses could tender valuable and strong evidence relating to homicides and to events, statements and activities before, during and after such incidents. This leaves the question as to upon what conditions such witnesses participated in the trial process and the consequences for those who did so.

IV

The consequences of participation could be severe. There were occasions where witnesses in homicide trials and their families were subject to reprisals involving acts of interpersonal violence and attacks on property. In April 1835, the house of a Richard Power was 'maliciously set fire to' because he appeared for the prosecution in the case of James Murphy who was executed for the murder of Lundy Foote esq., a local landlord. Moreover, in May of the same year, Power's son, Martin, was attacked by four men who 'beat him severely', seemingly because his father had taken an active part in the prosecution of Murphy.[164] In Queen's Co. in 1835, Eleanor Bergin, the niece of a prosecution witness, who gave evidence leading to the conviction and subsequent execution of Patrick Whelan, was 'assaulted in the chapel ... by Judith and Maria Whelan who threw her down, tore her bonnet and ribbons [and] told her she was dressed with the blood money of Patrick Whelan'.[165]

Instances of reprisals against witnesses may also be found in the northern counties in our sample. In Armagh, in August 1835, a party of around twelve men fired several shots and broke the windows and doors of houses belonging to six men who had been 'actively engaged in carrying on the prosecution against the persons now confined in the gaol of Armagh for the murder of Hugh Donnelly' during a sectarian affray.[166] In Fermanagh in 1835, a turf stack owned by William Crawford, a Protestant, was burned because both Crawford and his son had acted as witnesses in the trial of a number of men accused of the murder of a Catholic farmer called Cowan who had taken land from a previous tenant. The main suspect in this trial was a Protestant, Andrew Crawford, who had elicited the support of both local Protestants and Catholics in his attack on Cowan's house.[167]

Retribution was not restricted to homicide cases. In the counties in our sample, those who participated in the prosecution of other offences could leave themselves open to acts of lethal violence. The most striking example of lethal violent retribution against a witness comes, somewhat surprisingly, from Co. Fermanagh. At the spring assizes of 1826 in that county, Dominick Noon gave evidence that led to the conviction of a man named Maguire for administering an illegal (Ribbonman) oath. Noon lived in the jail for his protection before and after this trial and was due to give evidence against a man called Owen Cox at the next assizes. In June 1826, however, he disappeared while away from the jail, and was not seen again until his badly beaten body was found in August of the same year in a cave in the county.[168] More prosaically, perhaps, in Queen's Co. in June 1839, Mary Keating was killed by the blow of a stone thrown from a crowd who assembled outside her house. The crowd had gathered to taunt Mary's son who had participated in a prosecution for riot at the local petty sessions earlier in the day.[169]

On a national level, between 1843 and 1845, there were also nine reported cases in which witnesses/prosecutors or their relations were killed for participating, or planning to participate, in a criminal prosecution while in a 14-month sample drawn from the years 1847 to 1849 there were a further nine such cases.[170] In June 1845, John Lundrigan was 'brutally beaten, and his skull [was] fractured, in a tent on the racecourse of Ballina' in Co. Tipperary because he was 'related to persons who were prosecutors in a case of murder'.[171] In Cork in July 1847, 'the putrid and mutilated remains of Daniel Mahony, aged 11 years, [were] found in a ditch … where he had been murdered'. This killing was carried out to 'prevent [Mahony's] brother, (for whom he had been mistaken), prosecuting in a case of sheep stealing'.[172] Criminal prosecutions for relatively minor offences could also provoke acts of serious violence. In Co. Londonderry in

October 1845, Edward McGill died following a beating he received from people he had charged with stealing his grass.[173]

The authorities had to afford police protection to some witnesses. In Armagh in 1837, in the case of the murder of George McFarland it was believed that the life of the victim's son-in-law and 'that of his wife and daughter from having given the evidence they did [were] in very great peril in fact not worth twenty-four hours purchase unless some protection [was] afforded them'. It was recommended that the lord lieutenant authorise the removal of the witnesses to a 'comfortable slated house' that would be 'protected by police until after the assizes, otherwise the persons who [were] in custody [would] never ... be prosecuted'.[174] Witnesses were also sometimes held in the county jail or in Dublin in order to protect them before they gave evidence. Following the fatal shooting of Eliza Dowling, a young girl, in Queen's Co. in 1844, the stipendiary magistrate, Thomas Cannon, reported that he had 'taken the liberty of bringing William Dowling and his wife into Maryborough for protection as crown witnesses ... as [he] was perfectly satisfied, from the prisoner's connections in the county their lives would not be safe if not protected'.[175]

There were also a number of cases in which witnesses, claiming to live in fear of reprisals, requested aid from the government to assist them in leaving the country after they had given evidence. In Co. Kilkenny in 1850, Patrick Costello was convicted for the manslaughter of his wife and sentenced to transportation for life. According to a report of the case by the crown solicitor, 'the conviction [could be] mainly attributed to the unimpeachable evidence of Judith Keefe the convict's servant maid who in consequence thereof, is so much afraid to live in the country that [he] considered it [his] duty to have her supported ... at the public expense'. He also recommended that she receive £30 to allow her to emigrate. The government, in this case, agreed although they only gave her £13.[176] In 1848, following the conviction of John Darcy at the spring assizes in Queen's Co., a number of witnesses applied to the government for assistance to emigrate.[177] Some of these applications were supported by the crown solicitor, William Elliot, who did not consider it 'prudent or safe' for a number of the witnesses to remain in the country. In the case of an approver in the trial he also declared that it was 'not *customary* nor would it be safe he should be suffered to remain in this country'.[178]

Witnesses also claimed to find it difficult to maintain or secure employment after giving evidence. In Fermanagh in 1846, Patrick Cleary, a stonemason, sent a memorial to the government requesting financial aid to emigrate, claiming that 'he and his family have been reduced to a state of the greatest distress in consequence of being deprived of his usual employment his fellow tradesmen refusing to be engaged in the same employment with him'. He was also fearful that both he and his family would receive 'some bodily harm from the connections' of the accused in the case.[179] In Kilkenny in 1848, James Brennan, a shoemaker, claimed that, after giving evidence against those accused of killing his brother, he had lost his job and was 'much abused after testifying'.[180] The state also allowed for compensation to be paid in cases where someone, whether civilian or official, was killed or injured for aiding in the prosecution of offenders against the public peace.[181]

Given such evident difficulties and dangers it is perhaps no surprise that some witnesses had to be either encouraged by the prospect of a reward or put under pressure by the authorities to tender evidence for the prosecution. The offer of a reward could certainly encourage prosecution witnesses to tender evidence. At the Queen's Co. spring assizes of 1834, William Tuck, a witness at the trial for the murder of Daniel Stones, admitted that he 'did not tell at the inquest, as he was afraid he would be beaten' and only gave information after he 'heard of the reward'.[182] John Cole, a 16-year old servant boy in a local hotel and a key prosecution witness in the case of the murder of William White at the Fermanagh summer assizes of 1836, admitted under cross-examination that he 'heard of the reward before he said anything about the affair'. He also revealed that he had been in Dublin for protection before the trial and that he 'got plenty to eat and drink in Dublin, and got his hat from a policeman, and his coat from another'. He also pointed out that he didn't expect a reward 'but would take it all, and more, if he could get it'.[183] Witnesses in a number of cases were also keen to receive their expenses. According to the newspaper report of the trial of Joseph Horsefield in Co. Fermanagh in 1827, one of the main prosecution witnesses, James Howell, was said to have 'hesitated considerably to take the book until he was paid what he called his bill of expenses' and had to be 'at length prevailed on to be examined'.[184]

It is clear that, in some cases, the witnesses gave evidence under pressure from the authorities. Michael Meredith, a key prosecution witness at the trial for the murder of Daniel Stones at the Queen's Co. spring assizes of 1834, admitted that he had not attended the coroner's inquest but was now 'afraid he would be put in gaol if he did not tell'.[185] The police may also have put pressure on witnesses by arresting them in the hope that they would offer up evidence useful to the prosecution. William Lartley, a prosecution witness at the trial of Edward Gannon at the Queen's Co. spring assizes of 1839, revealed, under cross-examination, that he had originally been 'taken for this murder' and was examined by the local magistracy.[186] At the trial of John Darcy at the Queen's Co. spring assizes of 1848, John McCormack, a prosecution witness, admitted under cross-examination that he had spent 17 days in jail for the murder and that he had been taken up by the police after mentioning that he knew details of the case to a man called Michael Fitzpatrick.[187]

A number of prosecution witnesses made it clear to the court that they were unwilling participants in the trial process. At the Fermanagh summer assizes of 1839, Alice Smith, a prosecution witness in the trial of six members of the Murphy family who were accused of killing a young woman called Hessy Rodgers, claimed that her initial informations were not true 'because she did not swear all she knew, not wishing to have a hand in any one's death ...' and that 'she would not now prosecute if she was not obliged'.[188] Similarly, in Armagh at the summer assizes of 1836, Mary Daly, a Catholic, admitted, under cross-examination, that she had not been willing to give evidence against three Protestant men who were accused of murdering her husband 'because she was a stranger in the country, and if the gentleman [magistrate] had let her alone, she would never have told'.[189]

There were also those witnesses, generally referred to as approvers who admitted to being accomplices to the accused and who gave evidence in order to avoid being prosecuted for the offence themselves. At the trial for the murder of William Lalor in Queen's Co. in 1834, Samuel Judge claimed that he only gave evidence 'to save his life'.[190] A degree of emotional blackmail may also have been applied by the authorities in order to secure evidence. This is evident at the trial of Thomas Wilson, Thomas Kerr and Robert Cathcart at the Fermanagh summer assizes of 1849 when Margaret Cathcart, probably a relative of one of the accused, gave evidence which both described the incident and identified Thomas Wilson as carrying out the murder with the other two men assisting. The accused were convicted in this case but only Thomas Wilson and Thomas Kerr were executed while Cathcart earned a reprieve. It is not inconceivable that the reprieve was one of the conditions upon which Margaret gave her evidence in the first instance.[191] Thus, both pressure from and inducements offered by the authorities could clearly have a bearing on witness participation in homicide trials.

V

Yet, it is important not to exaggerate the degree to which witnesses gave evidence under such circumstances or the extent of the threat of reprisal against those who testified. To begin, the relative rarity of cases in which the defence raised the issue of undue pressure to testify during cross-examination would suggest that witnesses bullied into participating in the trial process were not all that common. In some cases also such witnesses were often already in a vulnerable position. Of the two female witnesses in our sample who admitted that they were only testifying under pressure from the authorities, one was a stranger in the country and the other was a labouring woman who had had an illegitimate child.[192] Such witnesses were not typical of those who acted as prosecution witnesses. Moreover, it should be remembered that such tactics are by no means unique to the Irish criminal justice system in the first half of the nineteenth century and there is little to suggest the entire system relied on such pressure being exerted.

Witnesses such as approvers also seem to have played a minimal role in the prosecution of homicide cases. In our sample of cases from Fermanagh there was only one reported case involving an approver between 1811 and 1850 – accounting for less than 0.5 per cent of all prosecution witnesses. In a sample of 50 cases from Co. Armagh, between 1807 and 1850, there were only three in which approvers gave evidence and they accounted for less than one per cent of prosecution witnesses. There were also only four cases in a sample of 47 in Queen's Co. between 1832 and 1850 where approvers were used by the crown – accounting for just over one per cent of prosecution witnesses. Even at the height of disturbances in the county, the use of approvers was minimal. At the special commission held in Queen's Co. in 1832, when the county was at its most disturbed, the *Leinster Express* noted that 'in no instance has the law been sustained by the evidence of an approver; and it is an additional corroboration of the verdicts [given by the jury], that they have been founded on evidence not contaminated by criminal participation'.[193]

It is also important not to exaggerate the extent to which witnesses were motivated by the prospect of a reward. H.J. Brownrigg, at the 1852 select committee on outrages, stated that it was 'very seldom' that the offer of a reward encouraged witnesses to come forward even where a large reward was on offer.[194] Brian Griffin has also demonstrated that it was extremely rare for rewards to be claimed in homicide cases and in cases of serious crime generally.[195] Some witnesses were keen to stress that they were not motivated by the prospect of a reward. Edward Gorman, a prosecution witness at the trial of two men at the Queen's Co. spring assizes of 1847, declared that he 'would not take £5,000 as a reward; would take no reward for telling the truth'.[196] Others stressed the importance of the oath they had taken. For instance, at the trial of Richard Malone at the Queen's Co. spring assizes of 1847, a prosecution witness, Michael Delaney, identified the accused in court claiming that he had 'no doubt but that is Dick Malone' and that he would not 'damn [his] soul for any one'.[197] Of course, such assertions should be taken with a grain of salt but the fact that the accusation that the witness was motivated by a reward was a relatively rare device employed in the cross-examination of witnesses would also seem to suggest that most prosecution witnesses participated for reasons other than financial ones.

Witnesses were, of course, entitled to be paid expenses for attending the assizes but those who sought to benefit financially from their participation in the trial process were not, it seems, engaging in a particularly lucrative line of work.[198] H.W. Rowan believed such expenses were 'inadequately paid and obtained with considerable difficulty, and ... as compared with former times, penuriously paid; ... [as the] sums allowed are not adequate to compensate the risks, expenses and difficulties necessarily encountered'.[199] They were, he pointed out, paid 'very little ... beyond the mere expenses incurred'. This he felt was little compensation for the risk that witnesses ran of reprisals for giving evidence as well as 'the expenses they incur, and the inconveniences they are subject to at the assizes ... towns from the difficulty of getting lodgings; and also from their being obliged to leave their farms and businesses unattended to during their absence'.[200]

The extent of the threat of retribution against witnesses also should not be exaggerated. The killing of witnesses and/or prosecutors in the four counties in our sample was either non-existent (in the case of Co. Kilkenny and Co. Armagh between 1835 and 1850) or extremely rare (in the case of Co. Fermanagh, 1811–50, and Queen's Co. between 1835 and 1850).[201] Those cases which did arise were generally isolated incidents and there is little evidence of popular support for such killings. Given the high number of witnesses and prosecutors who would have participated in criminal trials, not only at the assizes but also at quarter and petty sessions in this period, it is clear that the risk of lethal violent retribution against witnesses and prosecutors was extremely low and, more crucially perhaps, did not, in the vast majority of cases, unduly inhibit participation in the trial process.[202]

It is likely, indeed, that some witnesses exaggerated the extent and nature of the threat they faced in their communities. Doubts about the nature and extent of the threat faced by individual witnesses could, for instance, be raised at trial. At the Armagh summer assizes in 1839, the evidence of James McMahon that he had been intimidated from identifying the accused at an inquest was strongly contested by a local Catholic curate, who claimed that 'McMahon had no right to apprehend danger from disclosing the names of the murderers, in that part of the country; he would on the contrary, get praise for so doing'. It is, moreover, unlikely that the curate was simply wishing to aid the case of the accused on sectarian grounds as the accused were Presbyterian while the family of the deceased, who acted as prosecution witnesses, were Irish-speaking Catholics.[203]

In a number of cases, the government also refused to grant money to emigrate to crown witnesses because they believed that these witnesses exaggerated the danger they were in. In response to the application of two prosecution witnesses, James and Jeremiah Twomey, for assistance to emigrate, the government replied that they could find 'no sufficient reason for complying with [their] application'.[204] The abovementioned memorial of James Brennan in Kilkenny, in 1848, was rejected on the advice of the crown solicitor, who did not believe that Brennan was in any real danger and noted that the magistrate who took the informations in the case had not even signed Brennan's memorial.[205] Similarly, in response to an application for assistance to emigrate in the spring of 1849 made by John McCormack, a witness at the Queen's Co. assizes of 1848, the crown solicitor pointed out that he did 'not consider [the witness's] life to be in any danger' and saw no reason why he could not 'continue to live at home'.[206] Such doubts may have been well-founded. In the abovementioned case of Cleary in Co. Fermanagh, it is worth noting that after successfully applying to the government for money for himself and his family to emigrate he changed his mind and decided to keep the money and stay in the country.[207] The majority of witnesses who testified at the assizes did not, in fact, require support from the government afterwards. Following the spring assizes of 1849 in Queen's Co., for instance, only four witnesses required government assistance.[208] Of the four, three were from the abovementioned trial for the murder of Michael Smith and were again in a particularly vulnerable position.[209] In this case, moreover, the threat of retribution was probably from associates of the man convicted rather than a product of widespread popular hostility. Indeed, there was little popular sympathy for John Darcy, the accused in this case. In its report of his execution, the *Leinster Express* reported that 'there were comparatively few spectators of this execution, and no commiseration was manifested for the unfortunate young man by any of the persons assembled'.[210]

VI

In conclusion, it seems that there could be clear resistance to the participation of witnesses in the trial process. Those who tendered or intended to tender evidence on behalf of the prosecution could leave themselves open to acts of violent retribution and there were clearly those who attempted, in individual cases, to thwart the operation of the courts. There is, however, little evidence of a coordinated or at least a successful strategy on the part of secret societies to intimidate witnesses or of a coherent and pervasive popular hostility towards witnesses. It is clear that resistance was limited and did not unduly inhibit participation in the trial process. Rather the prosecution of homicide depended on the participation of ordinary people including those who were related to the parties involved and those who appear to have no direct or apparent relationship with either the accused or the deceased.

There were restrictions placed upon the evidence which could be tendered and the questions asked of such witnesses which both limited and shaped what could be said by them in open court. The effect of such restrictions should, however, not be exaggerated. The evidence provided by ordinary people was often direct and strong. The accused was identified in the majority of cases and witnesses provided often crucial and compelling circumstantial evidence relating to events before, during and after the alleged homicides. Such restrictions which did exist also probably served, in some respects, to limit the role of officials and to reinforce the importance of the evidence tendered by ordinary men and women at trial. In particular, the relative lack of stringent controls on the admission of evidence in which the accused was identified probably bolstered the role of ordinary people in the trial process while the rules such as those governing the admission of confession evidence may have restricted the scope for officials to tender evidence for the prosecution. It was, in many respects, therefore, left largely to ordinary people to provide evidence for the prosecution and this was a role which they fulfilled in the overwhelming majority of cases.

There was, though, no blind allegiance to or all-encompassing acceptance of the courts and the law. Not all witnesses were willing participants in the trial process and the authorities had to put considerable pressure on some witnesses in order to get them to tender evidence in court. These cases, indeed, serve to remind us that participation was by no means always unconditional but rather was negotiated through a complex array of different influences and pressures. In some cases, such influences and pressures came from the authorities in the form of inducements or threats. More commonly, however, it was probably communal, familial and personal influences, which combined with a belief that in most cases the courts were the most appropriate or at least the most practical forum to deal with acts of lethal violence, which shaped witness participation. Moreover, given such participation, and combined with the fact that there was also widespread participation in and use of the lower courts in this period, it is difficult to dismiss those who participated in the courts as an isolated group who defied wider social norms and cultural expectations in order to participate in the trial process.

Notes

1   *Minutes of Evidence taken before the Select Committee of the House of Lords appointed to enquire into the State of Ireland since the year 1835 in respect of Crime and Outrage, which have rendered Life and Property Insecure in that part of the Empire,* p. 91, HC 1839 (486) xi, xii, 1 (hereafter cited as Crime and Outrage Committee, *Minutes of Evidence, 1839*).

2   Ibid., 669.

3   Ibid., 361.

4   Ibid., 154.

5   *Report from the Select Committee on Outrages (Ireland) together with the Proceedings of the Committee, Minutes of Evidence, appendix and index,* HC 1852 (438), xiv, 1 (hereafter cited as Select Committee on Outrages, *Minutes of Evidence, 1852*), 149.

6   Ibid., 273.

7   J.S. Donnelly, Jr, 'Factions in pre-Famine Ireland', in A.S. Eyler and R.F. Garratt (eds), *The Uses of the Past: Essays on Irish Culture* (London: Associated University Presses, 1988), 126.

8   J.F. McEldowney, 'Crown Prosecutions in Nineteenth-Century Ireland', in Douglas Hay and Francis Snyder (eds), *Policing and Prosecution in Britain 1750–1850* (Oxford: Clarendon Press, 1989), 433.

9   Carolyn A. Conley, *Melancholy Accidents: The Meaning of Violence in Post-Famine Ireland* (Lanham, MD: Lexington Books, 1999), 148.

10   J.H. Baker, 'Criminal Courts and Procedure at Common Law, 1550–1800', in J.S. Cockburn (ed.), *Crime in England, 1550–1800* (Princeton, NJ: Princeton University Press, 1977), 15.

11   For a useful summary of the role of histories of legal cultures, see Willibald Steinmetz, 'Introduction: Towards a Comparative History of Legal Cultures, 1750–1950', in idem (ed.), *Private Law and Social Inequality in the Industrial Age, Comparing Legal Cultures in Britain, France, Germany, and the United States* (Oxford: Oxford University Press, 2000), 3–4. Steinmetz claims that the 'history of legal cultures is not traditional lawyers' legal history as it is not restricted to the inner life of the legal system – norms, doctrines, institutions, and professions. The notion of "legal culture" comprises more. It includes the attitudes and practical experience of laymen and laywomen who became involved with the law. What has to be investigated is the mutual interference, as well as the distance between a legal system and those who appealed to it or were drawn into it.'

12   To take but one example, the trial of Jeremiah Dooley at the Queen's Co. summer assizes of 1832 lasted 13 hours. There is a fairly extensive report of this trial but there is little to suggest that we have been given 13 hours' worth of court proceedings as the report covers just over three columns of a page of the *Leinster Express* (*Leinster Express*, 4 August 1832).

13   See Richard Mc Mahon, 'Homicide, the Courts and Popular Culture in pre-Famine and Famine Ireland' (PhD thesis, University College Dublin, 2006), chapter 1.

14   See, in particular, J.H. Langbein, *The Origins of Adversary Criminal Trial* (Oxford: Oxford University Press, 2003). According to Langbein, lawyers 'came to dominate the felony trial' over the course of the eighteenth century. This happened slowly initially but became 'ever more visible in the later eighteenth century' (Langbein, *Adversary Criminal Trial*, 3).

15   The evidence that is available suggests that the role of counsel in criminal trials in Ireland was, before the nineteenth century, limited. Neal Garnham claims, for instance, that the role of counsel 'in criminal proceedings was … probably small' in the eighteenth century and it remains uncertain to what degree their role developed or evolved over the course of that century (Neal Garnham, *The Courts, Crime and the Criminal Law in Ireland, 1692–1760* (Dublin: Irish Academic Press, 1996), 101).

16   Mc Mahon, 'Homicide', 232–8.

17   For instance, at the trial of Thomas Neal for the murder of John Simmington at the Armagh summer assizes of 1846, Sir Thomas Staples QC and Mr Hanna, who were described as the 'ordinary crown prosecutors', were joined by a Mr Ross Moore, who 'appeared for the next of kin' (*Armagh Guardian*, 14 July 1846).

18   See, for instance, the opinion of Baron Smith in the case of the murder of William Carter which was tried at the Queen's Co. summer assizes of 1836 (*Leinster Express*, 23 March 1836).

19   *Report from the Select Committee on the Public Prosecutors Bill; together with the Proceedings of the Committee, Minutes of Evidence, Appendix and Index*, 141, HC 1854–5 (481), xii, 1 (hereafter cited as Select Committee on Public Prosecutors, *Minutes of Evidence, 1854–55*).

20   Ibid., 143.

21   Ibid., 147.

22   Ibid., 143 and 146. Both the crown solicitors and counsel for the crown were paid from the consolidated fund.

23   Ibid., 148.

24   Crossman has pointed out that of the 38 barristers who acted as counsel for the crown in 1833, only seven were Catholics (Virginia Crossman, *Politics, Law and Order in Nineteenth-Century Ireland* (Dublin: Gill & Macmillan, 1996), 66). For an account of the barristers who operated as counsel for the crown in the counties from which the sample used in this article is drawn, see Mc Mahon, 'Homicide', 278–9.

25   Garnham, *The Courts, Crime and the Criminal Law*, 101.

26   D.S. Greer, 'Crime, Justice and Legal Literature in Nineteenth-Century Ireland', *Irish Jurist*, 37 (new series) (2002), 249 and generally 246–9.

27   Randal Kernan, a Catholic barrister from Enniskillen, explained that he did not practise in the civil courts for a variety of reasons including 'the loss of [his] teeth' which meant he 'never could bear to go into the civil courts, from the defect in [his] speech'. Such a defect, however, obviously did not inhibit him from taking an active part in criminal cases at the assizes. *The Third Report of the Select Committee appointed to inquire into the Nature, Character, Extent and Tendency of Orange Lodges, Associations or Societies in Ireland*, 93, HC 1835 (476), xvi, 1.

28   Select Committee on Public Prosecutors, *Minutes of Evidence, 1854–55*, 143. Napier himself would have acted as a supernumerary prosecutor for Co. Louth in the 1840s.

29   According to T.A. Purcell, 'a prosecutor who conducts his case in person and who is to be examined as a witness in support of the indictment has no right to address the jury' (T.A. Purcell, *A Summary of the General Principles of Pleading and Evidence, in Criminal Cases in Ireland: With the Rules of Practice Incident Thereto* (Dublin: Grant & Bolton, 1849), 191).

30   *Enniskillen Chronicle and Erne Packet*, 15 March 1838. At the Fermanagh summer assizes of 1845, Mr Schoales 'briefly stated the case' at the trial of Alexander Smith but did not go into detail 'as it was not a case for circumstantial evidence' (*Enniskillen Chronicle and Erne Packet*, 24 July 1845). The practice of only stating the case in cases involving circumstantial evidence can also be found in England at this time. For instance, Cairns notes that on the 'Midlands Circuit there was a strong feeling against opening speeches: counsel only opened in cases of

intricate circumstantial evidence'. Also 'on the Oxford circuit counsel "scarcely ever" began with a speech'. In contrast, on the Northern Circuit the practice 'was for counsel "always" to make an opening address to the jury, though this rarely lasted for longer than quarter of an hour' (D.J.A. Cairns, *Advocacy and the Making of the Adversarial Criminal Trial, 1800–1865* (Oxford: Clarendon Press, 1998), 38).

31 See, for instance, the report of the opening address of Mr Edward Tickell QC at the trial of Thomas Hogan for the murder of Alexander Tweedy at the Queen's Co. spring assizes of 1834 (*Leinster Express*, 22 March 1834).

32 *Armagh Guardian*, 22 July 1845.

33 See, for instance, the opening speech of the Attorney-General at the trial of John Kennedy for the murders at Carrickshock during the Kilkenny spring assizes of 1832 (James Mongan, *A Report of the Trials of John Kennedy, John Ryan, and William Voss, for the Murder of Edmund Butler, at Carrickshock, on the 14th December, 1831. Tried before the Hon. Baron Foster, at the Spring and Summer Assizes of Kilkenny, 1832* (Dublin: R. Milliken, 1832), 7–15). It was also common for counsel to state the case in trials arising from sectarian animosity. See, for instance, the opening address of Mr McCartney KC at the Armagh spring assizes of 1824 (*Belfast Newsletter*, 16 March 1824).

34 At the trial for the murder of William McCreery at the Fermanagh summer assizes of 1824, Mr Johnston in stating the case 'read the law as laid down in 1st Russell, page 174, minutely distinguishing murder and manslaughter, according to the lawfulness of the act, and the intention of the party'. He then went on to tell the jury that it was their duty to determine whether or not the case was one of manslaughter or murder 'if they believed the evidence to be true' (*Enniskillen Chronicle and Erne Packet*, 19 August 1824).

35 *An act for Enabling Persons indicted of Felony to make their Defence by Counsel or Attorney* (6 & 7 Will. 4, c. 114).

36 For a discussion of the 'duty of restraint' in an English context, see Langbein, *Adversary Criminal Trial*, 287–91 and Cairns, *The Making of the Adversarial Criminal Trial*, 38–46. According to Langbein, the duty of restraint 'developed to mitigate the unfairness of the continuing restrictions on the scope of defence counsel's activity in felony cases' (Langbein, *Adversary Criminal Trial*, 287–8). In an Irish context, Purcell points out that in felony cases it was 'the duty for the prosecution to be assistant to the court in the furtherance of justice and not to act as counsel for any particular person or party' (Purcell, *Pleading and Evidence in Criminal Cases*, 190). According to Joseph Napier, 'it [was] considered to be the duty of those who represent[ed] the Attorney-general to administer justice in a becoming way, and never unduly to press a case, and never to exercise any severity which the purposes of justice do not require' (Select Committee on Public Prosecutors, *Minutes of Evidence, 1854–55*, 146).

37 Writing in 1849, Purcell set out the conditions upon which counsel was to state the case. Counsel was to 'state declarations proposed to be proved, as well as the facts' upon which such declarations rested. Counsel was to avoid citing 'any particular expressions supposed to have been used by the prisoner, nor the precise words of any confession', although he could 'state the general effect of what the prisoner said'. See generally Purcell, *Pleading and Evidence in Criminal Cases*, 190–1.

38 *Enniskillen Chronicle and Erne Packet*, 15 March 1838. He made a similar point the following year at the summer assizes when stating the case at the trial of Patrick Murphy for the murder of Hessy Rodgers (*Enniskillen Chronicle and Erne Packet*, 25 July 1839).

39 *Enniskillen Chronicle and Erne Packet*, 19 August 1824.

40 See, for instance, the opening address of Sir Thomas Staples at the trial of Philip Fitzpatrick during the Armagh summer assizes of 1848 and that of Mr John Corballis at the trial of Edward Phelan at the Queen's Co. spring assizes of 1849 (*Armagh Guardian*, 24 July 1848 and *Leinster Express*, 17 March 1849).

41 See, for example, the address to the jury by defence counsel at the trial of Edward Phelan at the Queen's Co. spring assizes of 1849 (*Leinster Express*, 17 March 1849). See also the trial of Bryan Hanratty at the Armagh summer assizes of 1850, where the Attorney-General in stating the case observed that hair found on the alleged murder weapon 'was found to correspond exactly with the hair on the head of the prisoner'. This led the defence counsel, Mr O'Hagan, to interject and ask the Attorney-General if he was intending to produce evidence to support 'all the statements he [was] making to the jury' (*Armagh Guardian*, 15 July 1850).

42 In Queen's Co. between 1832 and 1850, the stating of the case by counsel was only reported in 14 out of 47 cases (29.78 per cent). In Armagh between 1841 and 1850, the stating of the case was only reported in nine out of 23 cases (39.13 per cent) while it was reported in ten out of 44 cases in Co. Fermanagh between 1811 and 1850 (22.72 per cent). This evidence is also consistent with the views of Edmund Hayes who claimed that it was relatively rare for counsel in Ireland to state the case at the outset of the trial. See Edmund Hayes, *Crimes and Punishments, or a Digest of the Criminal Statute Law of Ireland, Alphabetically arranged, with Ample Notes*, 2nd edn (Dublin: Hodges & Smith, 1842), 847. Also cited in Greer, 'Crime, Justice and Legal Literature', 260.

43 Purcell, *Pleading and Evidence in Criminal Cases*, 196–7. There were, however, some exceptions to this. For instance, leading questions could be put in order to identify the accused in court, in order to contradict a former witness or in examining an adverse or reluctant witness. Leading questions could also be asked if they were 'merely introductory' and were not 'conclusive on any of the points of the issue'.

44 As Purcell puts it, 'the evidence offered must correspond with the allegations, and be confined to the points in issue' (Purcell, *Pleading and Evidence in Criminal Cases*, 244–55).

45 See Langbein, *Adversary Criminal Trial*, 178–80.

46 David Bentley, *English Criminal Justice in the Nineteenth Century* (London: Hambledon, 1998), 205.

47 See, for instance, Purcell, *Pleading and Evidence in Criminal Cases*. How such rules of evidence developed in Ireland in the eighteenth and nineteenth centuries is, to say the least, a subject worthy of further study.

48 As Bentley points out, 'if the accused did not give evidence of good character, it was not normally open to the crown to adduce evidence of his bad character' (Bentley, *English Criminal Justice*, 239). The origins of this rule are discussed by Langbein. See Langbein, *Adversary Criminal Trial*, 190–203.

49 Purcell, *Pleading and Evidence in Criminal Cases*, 245. There were, however, certain exceptions to this rule, see generally Purcell, *Pleading and Evidence in Criminal Cases*, 245–53 and Bentley, *English Criminal Justice*, 241–9.

50 In an Irish context, this was confirmed by the unanimous decision of the eleven judges in *R v. Sheehan* (1826) who concluded that 'in point of law, the testimony of an accomplice, though altogether uncorroborated, was evidence to be submitted to a jury, and that a conviction upon it would be legal'. See Robert Jebb, *Cases, chiefly relating to the Criminal and Presentment Law, Reserved for Consideration, and Decided by the Twelve Judges of Ireland, from May, 1822, to November, 1840* (Philadelphia: T. & J.W. Johnson, 1842), 56. See also Henry Joy, *On the Evidence of Accomplices* (Dublin: Milliken, 1836), 2 and Purcell, *Pleading and Evidence in Criminal Cases*, 355. This was, in fact, not a very contentious point and merely confirmed, in an Irish context, what was from the early eighteenth century an established rule in the English criminal courts. See Langbein, *Adversary Criminal Trial*, 159.

51 As a consequence, according to Purcell at least, it was the 'settled practice' for the jury not to convict 'a prisoner in any case of felony upon the sole and uncorroborated evidence of an accomplice' (Purcell, *Pleading and Evidence in Criminal Cases*, 356). For a discussion of the development of the corroboration rule in eighteenth-century England, see Langbein, *Adversary Criminal Trial*, 203–17 and for a nineteenth-century critique of its operation, see Joy, *On the Evidence of Accomplices*, 3–8.

52 The jury, in this case, failed to reach a verdict (*Enniskillen Chronicle and Erne Packet*, 27 July 1826 [my italics]).

53 *Leinster Express*, 18 July 1835. See also the evidence, before the 1839 Select Committee, of the crown solicitor for the Connacht circuit, Edward Chadwell Hickman, who claimed that he would not instigate

a criminal prosecution 'on the evidence of an approver, unless he was supported' (Crime and Outrage Committee, *Minutes of Evidence, 1839*, 654). It should also be noted that the decision not to pursue a case on the basis of such evidence was not simply that of the crown solicitor or the prosecuting counsel. As Purcell points out, the admission of an accomplice to give evidence for the crown was at the discretion of the judge who 'usually considers not only whether the prisoners can be convicted without the evidence of the accomplice, but also whether they can be convicted with his evidence'. The practice in such cases was for the counsel for the prosecution to request that 'the accomplice be allowed to go before the grand jury, pledging his own opinion, after a perusal of the facts of the case, that the testimony is essential'. If the approver had already been included in the indictment with the accused, the practice was, with the consent of the court, to apply to have him acquitted before the trial of the others. This, according to Purcell, was 'an application which the court, if it sees no cause to the contrary, will grant almost as of course, relying on the discretion of the counsel who conduct the prosecution' (see Purcell, *Pleading and Evidence in Criminal Cases*, 354–5).

54   Joy, *On the Evidence of Accomplices*, 8–99 and Hayes, *Crimes and Punishments*, 7–9.

55   *R v. Sheehan* (1826) in *Jebb's Reserved Cases*, 54–8. In *R v. Carberry* (1826) it was also held that 'a corroboration as to the facts of the transaction is not sufficient, unless there be some proof connecting the prisoner with the transaction' (George Crawford and E.S. Dix, *Report of Cases Argued and Ruled on the Circuits, in Ireland, During the Years 1839 and 1840; together with Cases Decided at the Nisi Prius Sittings, and in the Courts of Criminal Jurisdiction at Dublin, a Table of Cases, and an Index to the Principal Matters, Volume I* (Dublin: Hodges & Smith, 1841), 160–1). The majority position of the judges also became established practice in the English courts (see Bentley, *English Criminal Justice*, 256).

56   This, he pointed out, 'was done in the *Wild Goose Lodge Case* where the approvers had been confined in separate gaols, so that there could have been no communication between them'. In the case before him, however, the judge noted that 'the approvers have had an opportunity of concocting a story among themselves' (*1 Crawford and Dix's Circuit Reports*, 116).

57   Purcell, *Pleading and Evidence in Criminal Cases*, 356. See also *R v. Magill* (1842), George Crawford and E.S. Dix, *Report of Cases Argued and Ruled on the Circuits, in Ireland, During the Years 1840, 1841, and 1842; together with Cases Decided at the Nisi Prius Sittings, and in the Courts of Criminal Jurisdiction at Dublin, a Table of Cases, and an Index to the Principal Matters, Volume II* (Dublin: Hodges & Smith, 1843), 418. It does seem, however, that an accomplice's wife could offer corroborating evidence. See *K v. John Casey and Sarah McCue* (1827), *Jebb's Reserved Cases*, 203–8.

58 Writing in 1849, Purcell pointed out that the term hearsay referred to 'that which is written, as well as to that which is spoken, and, in its legal sense, ... denotes that kind of evidence which does not derive its value solely from the credit to be given to the witness himself, but also in part on the veracity and competency of some other person' (Purcell, *Pleading and Evidence in Criminal Cases*, 285).

59 For the development of this rule in the eighteenth century, see Langbein, *Adversary Criminal Trial*, 233–47. See also Purcell, *Pleading and Evidence in Criminal Cases*, 286.

60 Purcell, *Pleading and Evidence in Criminal Cases*, 286–92.

61 While dying declarations and confessions were perhaps the most important exceptions to the hearsay rule, other exceptions did exist. See Purcell, *Pleading and Evidence in Criminal Cases*, 292–4.

62 The restrictions placed on the admission of dying declarations actually increased in the nineteenth century. See Bentley, *English Criminal Justice*, 214–18.

63 Baron Smith, summing up a case for the jury at the Queen's Co. spring assizes in 1832, made clear the conditions upon which a dying declaration was to be admitted as evidence: 'No evidence was admissible in a court of Justice, unless delivered upon oath, or under sanctions equivalent to the sacred obligation of an oath. These sanctions the law considered to be supplied by the awful situation of a man standing on the brink of eternity, and aware of his position; on whom virtually this life and its concerns were closed; whose thoughts were wholly fixed on that which was to come; and whose sentiments were suited to so solemn a cast of thought' (*Leinster Express*, 24 March 1832). See also Purcell, *Pleading and Evidence in Criminal Cases*, 295–300. According to Purcell, dying declarations were admitted as evidence 'on the general principle that they are declarations made in extremity, when the party is at the point of death, and when every hope of this world is gone, when every motive to falsehood is silenced, and the mind is induced by the most powerful considerations to speak the truth. A situation so solemn and so awful, is considered by the law as creating an obligation equal to that which is imposed by a positive oath in a court of justice' (Purcell, *Pleading and Evidence in Criminal Cases*, 295). See also Hayes, *Crimes and Punishments*, 228–30.

64 *Belfast Newsletter*, 19 March 1819. This restriction applied equally to the defence. For instance, at the Armagh spring assizes of 1848, a defence witness 'being about to detail a conversation which he had with the deceased, his Lordship put a stop to the examination' (*Armagh Guardian*, 6 March 1848).

65 Purcell, *Pleading and Evidence in Criminal Cases*, 300.

66 Ibid., 301–2. This rule had its origins in developments which occurred in the English criminal courts over the course of the eighteenth century. See Langbein, *Adversary Criminal Trial*, 218–33.

67 The judges were to determine whether a temporal inducement was held out to the accused before he confessed and were to decide this with regard to the particular circumstances of the individual cases. According to Joy, '... the threat or inducement held out must have reference *to the prisoner's escape from the charge*, and be such as would lead him to suppose, it will be better for him to admit himself to be guilty of an offence, which he never committed'. See H.H. Joy, *On the Admissibility of Confessions and Challenge of Jurors in Criminal Cases in England and Ireland* (Dublin: Milliken, 1842), 13 and Purcell, *Pleading and Evidence in Criminal Cases*, 302–7. According to Bentley, however, 'any ... inducement was commonly treated as sufficient to exclude, without the need for any inquiry as to whether the inducement was one which in the particular circumstances would have been likely to lead the particular accused to make a false confession' (Bentley, *English Criminal Justice*, 222).

68 Bentley, *English Criminal Justice*, 222. According to Bentley, such judicial caution was due to 'the difficulty of assessing the influence of an inducement on a prisoner's mind' and the 'need for great caution before admitting confessions in evidence'. On the credit to be given to confessions, see Joy, *On the Admissibility of Confessions*, 100–9 and Purcell, *Pleading and Evidence in Criminal Cases*, 301.

69 *Belfast Newsletter*, 24 March 1826. Armstrong was aware of the confession rule and was keen to stress that at the time of the arrest he 'held out no inducement to get any confession from him'. See also *R* v. *Graham and Boyle* (1839) 1 *Crawford and Dix's Circuit Reports*, 99. In this case, the constable said to the accused 'I have enough against you' after which the accused confessed to a robbery. It was held that the words of the constable were 'tantamount to a threat' and that any confession made after such words were used would not be permitted as evidence.

70 According to Joy, 'a confession is not admissible in evidence where it is obtained by *temporal* inducement, by threat, promise, or hope of favour held out to the party, in respect of his escape from the charge against him, by a person in authority, or where there is reason to presume, that such person appeared to the party to *sanction* such threat or inducement' (Joy, *On the Admissibility of Confessions*, 5). For an example of a case where a confession was deemed to have been made in consequence of inducements held out by someone under sanction from a person in authority, see *R* v. *Moody* (1841) in 2 *Crawford and Dix's Circuit Reports*, 347–8.

71 A person in authority was generally regarded as one who had authority over the accused and/or the conduct of the prosecution. Joy defined a person in authority as (1) a master, (2) a mistress, (3) a prosecutor, (4) a magistrate and (5) a constable (Joy, *On the Admissibility of Confessions*, 5). Purcell, however, offered a more wide-ranging group of persons in authority. He claimed that 'if the inducements were offered by

the prosecutor, the prosecutor's wife, the prosecutor's attorney, by a constable or other officer having the prisoner in custody or by any person assisting a constable or prosecutor in the apprehension or detention of a prisoner or by a magistrate, magistrate's clerk, gaoler or chaplain of a gaol or indeed by *any one having authority* over him, or over the prosecution itself or by a private person in the presence of one having authority, with the assent of the latter whether direct or implied; the confession will not be deemed voluntary, and will be rejected' (Purcell, *Pleading and Evidence in Criminal Cases*, 307–8).

72 Bentley, *English Criminal Justice*, 221.

73 Joy, *On the Admissibility of Confessions*, 23. For Joy, 'a confession is admissible in evidence, although an inducement is held out, if such inducement proceeds from a person not in authority over the prisoner'.

74 Purcell, *Pleading and Evidence in Criminal Cases*, 308–9.

75 *Leinster Express*, 29 July 1848.

76 *Leinster Express*, 29 July 1848. It is difficult to see why the judge deemed this evidence inadmissible as no apparent inducement seems to have been held out to the accused. Mr Corballis for the crown argued that the evidence was legal but when the judge 'said his opinion was against admission', Corballis decided not to press the matter but simply noted that 'the evidence was tendered to him, and understanding the witness to be respectable, he produced him'. It should be noted that the judge did point out that 'Mr Corballis might, if he thought proper, take the verdict on it'. By this he probably meant that the point at issue could be referred to the twelve judges for decision. For an outline of this procedure, see Mc Mahon, 'Homicide', 427–30.

77 See Bentley, *English Criminal Justice*, 225–9.

78 Purcell, *Pleading and Evidence in Criminal Cases*, 311–12. See also Joy, *On the Admissibility of Confessions*, 42. According to Joy, 'a confession is admissible, although it is elicited in answer to a question which assumes the prisoner's guilt, or is obtained by artifice or deception'.

79 See Bentley, *English Criminal Justice*, 226.

80 This will be discussed in greater detail later.

81 See *R* v. *Gibney* (1822), *Jebb's Reserved Cases*, 15–19.

82 See, for instance, the evidence tendered by a policeman at the trial for the murder of Daniel Deegan at Queen's Co. spring assizes of 1835 of the warning given to the accused before he was questioned (*Leinster Express*, 21 March 1835). It should be noted, however, that in some cases confessions were admitted without such warnings and that such evidence was, in law, admissible. According to Joy, 'A confession is admissible, although it is elicited by questions put to a prisoner by a magistrate, constable, or other person' (Joy, *On the Admissibility of Confessions*, 34). Joy was, in fact, by no means a fan of the practice of policemen questioning witnesses and noted that 'it may be proper

that the police authorities should forbid the practice of questioning a prisoner by a constable; and it might reasonably induce caution, and perhaps, suspicion, and a scrutinizing jealousy in jurors, in investigating the credit of a confession obtained by such person through such means …' (Joy, *On the Admissibility of Confessions*, 38–9). See generally Joy, *On the Admissibility of Confessions*, 34–41.

83   1 *Crawford and Dix's Circuit Reports*, 362. See also Bentley, *English Criminal Justice*, 229–35.

84   Only 33 of the 307 witnesses (10.74 per cent) in Fermanagh were officials employed within or by the official legal system. In Armagh, only 44 out of a total of 326 witnesses (13.49 per cent) were officials. In Queen's Co., 65 of the 344 witnesses were officials (18.89 per cent).

85   Officials did participate in a significant proportion of cases. In Queen's Co., their evidence was reported in 35 of the 47 cases (74 per cent). In Armagh, their evidence was reported in 20 of the 50 cases in the sample (40 per cent). In Fermanagh, their evidence was reported in 17 of the 44 cases in our sample (38.63 per cent).

86   See K.T. Hoppen, *Elections, Politics and Society in Ireland 1832–1885* (Oxford: Clarendon Press, 1984), 371.

87   In Fermanagh, their testimony was reported in nine out of the 44 cases (19.56 per cent of cases) and in Armagh, the evidence of policemen was reported in 15 out of 50 cases (30 per cent).

88   In the 11 cases in Fermanagh, from the period 1841 to 1850, the evidence of the police was only reported in three cases while in Armagh in the same period their evidence was reported in only eight out of 22 cases.

89   In Fermanagh, between 1811 and 1850, the evidence of a magistrate was only reported in six out of 46 cases (13.04 per cent) and they accounted for only eight out of a total of 307 prosecution witnesses (2.60 per cent). In Armagh, only seven magistrates gave evidence (2.14 per cent of witnesses) in seven out of a total of 50 cases (14 per cent of cases). Similarly, in Queen's Co., between 1832 and 1850, nine magistrates gave evidence (2.6 per cent of witnesses) in eight out of 47 cases (17.02 per cent).

90   The other officials (excluding the police) who gave evidence for the prosecution at these trials were: (a) in Armagh – one clerk of the court, two surveyors and one governor of the jail; (b) in Fermanagh – three clerks of the court, one bailiff, a sub-sheriff, one surveyor and one governor of the jail; and (c) in Queen's Co. – three surveyors, one bailiff and one employee of the jail.

91   In Armagh, 29 of the 41 prosecution witnesses (70.73 per cent) were members of the deceased's immediate family. In Fermanagh, 16 out of 23 (69.56 per cent) and in Queen's Co., 37 out of 51 (71.15 per cent). There may, of course, have been cases where it was not made clear that a witness was related to the deceased, although it is likely that counsel

would have been keen to establish this fact in most cases.

92 In Armagh, six out 326 witnesses (1.84 per cent) were related to both the accused and the deceased and they appeared in five out of 50 cases (10 per cent). In Fermanagh, they accounted for ten out of 307 witnesses (3.25 per cent) and appeared in six out of 44 cases (13.63 per cent). In Queen's Co., they accounted for three out of 344 witnesses (0.87 per cent) and appeared in one out of 47 cases (2.12 per cent). The higher rate of participation by such witnesses in the northern counties may reflect the fact that family or domestic disputes constituted a higher proportion of homicide cases in those counties. See Mc Mahon, 'Homicide', table 3.1.

93 Of the 19 witnesses who were related to both the accused and the deceased, nine were more closely related to the deceased than the accused, five were more closely related to the accused and five witnesses were as closely related to the accused as to the deceased.

94 In Queen's Co., relatives of the accused accounted for five out of 344 witnesses (1.45 per cent) and appeared in only three out of the 47 cases (6.38 per cent). In Fermanagh, they accounted for only two out of 307 witnesses (0.65 per cent) and appeared in only two out of 44 cases (4.25 per cent). In Armagh, they accounted for four out of 326 witnesses (1.22 per cent) and appeared in three out of 50 cases (6 per cent).

95 This was the case of Peter Magill who was charged with the murder of Christopher Jordan at the Armagh summer assizes in 1845. In this case, the son of the accused gave evidence, as an approver, against his own father (*Armagh Guardian*, 22 July 1845).

96 In Armagh, these witnesses accounted for 57.05 per cent of all witnesses, in Fermanagh 66.77 per cent and in Queen's Co. 50.58 per cent (these figures do not include officials, doctors and surgeons).

97 In Armagh, only three members of the clergy gave evidence and in both Fermanagh and Queen's Co. only one clergyman testified for the prosecution. The participation of land agents was even rarer accounting for only one prosecution witness in Fermanagh and one in Armagh.

98 These witnesses were predominantly male: in Armagh 76.34 per cent were male, in Fermanagh 68.29 per cent and in Queen's Co. 75.28 per cent.

99 *Leinster Express*, 29 July 1848.

100 *Enniskillen Chronicle and Erne Packet*, 20 August 1829. She also declared, under cross-examination, that the accused was a 'civil neighbour' and that she was 'sorry for him'.

101 *Leinster Express*, 21 March 1835.

102 *Enniskillen Chronicle and Erne Packet*, 17 July 1845.

103 This may also have been because the children themselves were involved in the affray which led to their mother's death.

104 NAI, outrage papers, Armagh, 1843/16211.

105 *Leinster Express*, 4 August 1832. She gave evidence that a bag found on the head of the deceased was 'very like' a bag which 'held two stones of potatoes' and which had been in Dooley's house.

106 *Leinster Express*, 28 March 1835.

107 *Belfast Newsletter*, 20 March 1838.

108 *Enniskillen Chronicle and Erne Packet*, 20 August 1829.

109 *Leinster Express*, 4 August 1832.

110 In Armagh 13.8 per cent of witnesses were medical practitioners, in Fermanagh 11.4 per cent and in Queen's Co. 13.37 per cent.

111 In Fermanagh, a doctor or surgeon gave evidence in 31 out of 44 cases (70.45 per cent), in Armagh in 39 out of 50 cases (78 per cent) and in Queen's Co. in 40 out of 47 cases (85.10 per cent).

112 *Enniskillen Chronicle and Erne Packet*, 25 March, 1 April and 15 April 1830.

113 *Leinster Express*, 13 March 1847. It was, it seems, a common tactic for the prosecution to try and build a case around circumstantial evidence provided by a large number of witnesses. In Fermanagh, at the trial of William Bleakley in 1844 no less than 24 witnesses gave evidence, on behalf of the prosecution, concerning the movements of the accused and deceased on the day of the alleged incident (*Enniskillen Chronicle and Erne Packet*, 7 March 1844).

114 *Enniskillen Chronicle and Erne Packet*, 19 August 1824. A number of the opposing party were from Lisbellaw.

115 Ibid. According to the *Chronicle* the word 'budda' was 'Irish for a rich, full country man'.

116 *Belfast Newsletter*, 2 August 1839.

117 *Leinster Express*, 29 July 1848.

118 Unlike the rules governing confessions and dying declarations, where quite stringent rules applied, it seems that the judges took a more generous view when it came to evidence in which the accused was identified. See Bentley, *English Criminal Justice*, 264–5. For the scope afforded to witnesses when identifying the accused in criminal trials in Ireland, see, for instance, *R* v. *Tobin* (1839), *1 Crawford and Dix's Circuit Reports*, 298–9 and *The Queen* v. *Burke and Kelly* (1847) in Edward W. Cox (ed.), *Reports of Cases in Criminal Law: Argued and Determined in all the Courts in England and Ireland, Volume II* (London: J. Crockford, 1848), 295–6.

119 In 98 out of 141 cases in our sample (69.50 per cent) the accused was identified as the perpetrator. The accused was identified as the perpetrator in 37 out of the 47 cases (78.72 per cent) in Queen's Co., in 35 out of the 50 cases (70 per cent) in Armagh and in 26 out of 44 cases (59.09 per cent) in Fermanagh. Overall, in our sample, 183 witnesses identified the accused as the perpetrator, 70 in Armagh, 48 in Fermanagh and 65 in Queen's Co.

120 *Leinster Express*, 17 March 1850.

121 Of the 183 witnesses who identified the accused, 53 (28.96 per cent) were relatives of the deceased.

122 *Belfast Newsletter*, 29 July 1825. The witness claimed that he was 'certain as to the prisoner Maguire [as he had] drank at the table with him that night'.

123 Of the 53 relatives of the deceased who identified the accused, 33 were members of the immediate family.

124 *Leinster Express*, 4 August 1832.

125 Ibid., 21 March 1835.

126 Of the 98 cases in our sample in which the accused was identified as the perpetrator, only 15 (15.30 per cent) depended solely on the identification of the accused by relatives of the deceased.

127 In Armagh those from outside the deceased's family identified the accused in 33 out of the 35 cases where there was an identification of the accused (94.28 per cent), in Fermanagh in 21 out of 26 cases (80.76 per cent) and in Queen's Co. in 29 out of 37 cases (78.37 per cent).

128 In Armagh the identification of the accused by members of the deceased's family *and* those from outside the family occurred in 11 out of 35 cases, in Fermanagh in two out of 26 cases and in Queen's Co. in eight out of 37 cases.

129 According to Moore, the victim ran down the street crying 'murder, murder, are you going to kill a gossoon' (*Leinster Express*, 23 March 1839).

130 Ibid.

131 In Armagh, the accused was identified by witnesses drawn solely from outside the deceased's family in 22 out of 35 cases, in Fermanagh in 19 out of 29 cases and in Queen's Co. in 21 out of 37 cases.

132 See, for instance, the evidence given at the trial for the murder of William McCreery, a Protestant, at the Fermanagh summer assizes of 1824 (*Enniskillen Chronicle and Erne Packet*, 19 August 1824).

133 *Enniskillen Chronicle and Erne Packet*, 19 March 1835.

134 *Armagh Guardian*, 11 March 1850.

135 Ibid., 10 March 1846.

136 *Enniskillen Chronicle and Erne Packet*, 30 July 1835. This case arose from a sectarian affray in which William Lang, a Protestant, was killed and for which the Gormleys, both Catholics, were tried. It is likely that Corrigan, the witness, was also a Catholic as he lived in a predominantly Catholic area of the town known as Beggar Street and he had also known the accused for some time (since 1829) and, in fact, gave Thomas a good character.

137 *Leinster Express*, 16 March 1839.

138 The prosecution had the greatest difficulties in getting direct evidence against the accused in Fermanagh, where in 18 out of 44 cases (or 40.90 per cent) direct evidence against the accused was not tendered. In Armagh, there were 15 cases out of 50 (30 per cent) in which

the witnesses did not identify the accused as the perpetrator and in Queen's Co. there were ten such cases (21.27 per cent).

139 Of the 18 cases in Fermanagh where the prosecution did not produce direct evidence against the accused, eight arose from family-based disputes, eight arose from personal disputes, one arose from a land dispute and one arose from a sectarian dispute. In Armagh, of the 15 such cases, six arose within the family, three arose from sectarian disputes, three from land disputes, one from a robbery, one from a personal dispute and one where a policeman was accused of homicide arising from a riot. In Queen's Co., of the ten such cases, three arose from robbery, two from work disputes, one from a family dispute, one from a factional dispute, one from a land dispute, one from a property dispute and one from a personal dispute.

140 *Enniskillen Chronicle and Erne Packet*, 15 March 1838.

141 See, for instance, the prosecution of Thomas Maguire for the murder of his wife at the Fermanagh spring assizes of 1836 (*Enniskillen Chronicle and Erne Packet*, 17 March 1836, and cited in Mc Mahon, 'Homicide', 86).

142 See, for instance, the trial for the murder of Daniel Deegan at the Queen's Co. spring assizes of 1835, the trial for the murder of Edward Gannon at the Queen's Co. spring assizes of 1839 and the trial for the murder of John Mahon at the Queen's Co. summer assizes of 1848 (*Leinster Express*, 21 March 1835, 23 March 1839 and 29 July 1848).

143 *Enniskillen Chronicle and Erne Packet*, 12 August 1824.

144 Ibid., 10 March 1842.

145 Ibid., 25 July 1839.

146 For some examples, see Mc Mahon, 'Homicide', 247–8.

147 *Armagh Guardian*, 24 July 1848.

148 *Leinster Express*, 20 July 1833.

149 Ibid., 20 July 1833.

150 Evidence of a dying declaration was given in just over one in ten cases in our sample. In Armagh, a dying declaration was given in five out of 50 cases (ten per cent), in Fermanagh, in four out of 44 cases (11.34 per cent) and, in Queen's Co., in eight out of 47 cases (17.02 per cent).

151 *Belfast Newsletter*, 1 August 1828.

152 *Leinster Express*, 13 March 1841.

153 *Enniskillen Chronicle and Erne Packet*, 12 March 1849. Of the 22 witnesses who tendered evidence of a dying declaration, five were magistrates, two were policemen, one was a clerk of the court of petty sessions, one was a doctor, one was a reverend, eight were relatives of the deceased and four were ordinary men and women who were unrelated to the deceased.

154 Such evidence could, it should be remembered, include explicit confessions or statements from which the guilt of the accused could be implied. In Queen's Co. between 1835 and 1850, there were 12 cases out of 47 in which confession evidence was tendered by prosecution

witnesses (25.53 per cent), in Armagh such evidence was tendered in eight out of 50 cases in our sample (16 per cent), and in Fermanagh in nine out of 44 cases (20.45 per cent).

155   *Leinster Express*, 11 March 1848.

156   Ibid., 16 March 1850. See also *R* v. *Nolan* (1839) – in this case the accused had confessed to the murder after being informed that his neighbours had accused his father of the crime (*1 Crawford and Dix's Circuit Reports*, 74–6).

157   *Leinster Express*, 13 March 1847.

158   *Leinster Express*, 21 March 1835. Thomas Kelly, a policeman, gave evidence that the accused when in custody 'exclaimed "it was I who struck Carroll, but I am sorry I did not sink the hammer to his shoulders for preventing me from killing Bergin"'. Kelly also produced the dying declaration of Michael Carroll. The actions of the policeman in this case won the praise of the judge who 'commended the correctness' of Kelly's actions.

159   The only case in our sample where such practices seem evident is at the trial of Joseph Horsefield for the murder of his son at the Fermanagh summer assizes of 1827. In this case, three policemen and the brother-in-law of the accused gave contrasting statements concerning conversations with the accused at the scene of the alleged crime. Two of the policeman claimed that the accused confessed to the killing of his son while another policeman and the brother-in-law of the accused pointed out that the accused merely acknowledged that his son was dead (*Enniskillen Chronicle and Erne Packet*, 9 August 1827). The confused nature of the evidence in this case certainly suggests that judicial suspicions about confession evidence tendered by those in positions of authority may have been well-founded and that the relative rarity of such evidence may have been a positive aspect of the administration of justice in Ireland at this time.

160   Of the 44 witnesses in our sample who tendered evidence of a confession, 28 (63.63 per cent) did not have an official function within the criminal justice system.

161   *Belfast Newsletter*, 26 August 1824. During the conversation, the accused admitted 'that he committed the murder, and that he did it with a bill hook'. He also related to the witness how he had carried out the act.

162   *Belfast Newsletter*, 21 March 1837.

163   *Enniskillen Chronicle and Erne Packet*, 10 March 1842.

164   NAI, outrage papers, Kilkenny, 1835/32 and 56.

165   NAI, outrage papers, Queen's Co., 1835/55.

166   NAI, outrage papers, Armagh, 1835/29. The accused in this case were Protestant while the deceased was a Catholic.

167   NAI, outrage papers, Fermanagh, 1835/48. See also *Enniskillen Chronicle and Erne Packet*, 24 July 1834.

168   *Enniskillen Chronicle and Erne Packet*, 16 August 1827.

169   *Leinster Express*, 25 July 1840.

170 Chief Secretary's Office, constabulary returns, monthly returns of outrages, 1843–45 and 1847–49, NAI, 3/7/2. See also Mc Mahon, 'Homicide', appendix one.

171 *Returns of outrages, 1843–45.*

172 *Returns of outrages, 1847–49.*

173 *Returns of outrages, 1843–45.*

174 NAI, outrage papers, Armagh, 1837/144.

175 NAI, outrage papers, Queen's Co., 1844/20341.

176 NAI, outrage papers, Kilkenny, 1850/236.

177 See NAI, outrage papers, Queen's Co., 1849/48/49/60/166/207.

178 NAI, outrage papers, Queen's Co., 1849/99 [my italics].

179 NAI, outrage papers, Fermanagh, 1846/6417.

180 NAI, outrage papers, Kilkenny, 1848/70/92.

181 For legislation governing the payment of compensation for injuries arising from prosecutions of felony, see *An Act for the more Effectually Preventing the Administering and Taking of Unlawful Oaths in Ireland; and for the Protection of Magistrates and Witnesses in Criminal Cases* (50 Geo. 3, c. 102, s. 6). The provisions of this act were reaffirmed by the 1836 grand jury act (see *An Act to Consolidate and Amend the Laws Relating to the Presentment of Public Money by Grand Juries in Ireland* (6 & 7 Will. 4, c. 116, s. 106)). See generally D.S. Greer, *Compensation for Criminal Injury* (Belfast: SLS Publications, 1990), 8–13.

182 *Leinster Express*, 22 March 1834.

183 *Newry Examiner*, 27 July 1836.

184 *Enniskillen Chronicle and Erne Packet*, 9 August 1827.

185 *Leinster Express*, 22 March 1834.

186 Ibid., 23 March 1839.

187 Ibid., 11 March 1848.

188 *Enniskillen Chronicle and Erne Packet*, 25 July 1839.

189 *Belfast Newsletter*, 29 July 1836.

190 *Leinster Express*, 22 March 1834.

191 *Armagh Guardian*, 23 July 1849.

192 *Enniskillen Chronicle and Erne Packet*, 25 July 1839 and *Belfast Newsletter*, 29 July 1836. The authorities, in fact, may, on occasion, have discouraged such witnesses from coming forward. At the trial for the murder of Hessy Rodgers during the Monaghan summer assizes of 1838, a prosecution witness revealed that she had told a Mr Gregg of Clones what she had seen on the night of Rodger's death but he advised her not to come forward with her evidence. According to the witness, Gregg 'said there were witnesses enough against the prisoners, and for her not to mind as she was lonely and desolate'. This was confirmed by Mr Gregg who admitted that he had 'advised her to tell nobody'. *Belfast Newsletter*, 10 August 1838. This case was tried later in Fermanagh at the summer assizes of 1839.

193 *Leinster Express*, 2 June 1832.

194 Select Committee on Outrages, *Minutes of Evidence 1852*, 188. Also cited in Brian Griffin, 'Prevention and Detection of Crime in Nineteenth-Century Ireland', in N.M. Dawson (ed.), *Reflections on Law and History: Irish Legal History Society Discourses and Other Papers, 2000–2005* (Dublin: Four Courts Press, 2006), 108.

195 Griffin, 'Prevention and Detection', 108–9. Griffin estimates that rewards were claimed in less than 4 per cent of cases of serious crime in which they were offered by the government in 1836 and 1837. He also estimates that rewards were claimed in only 20 of 402 cases of homicide (and attempted murder) between January 1842 and February 1846 (just under 5 per cent of cases).

196 *Leinster Express*, 13 March 1847.

197 Ibid., 20 March 1847.

198 Witnesses were entitled, by statute, to claim expenses for tendering evidence in cases of felony. See *An Act for the Payment of Costs and Charges to Prosecutors and Witnesses, in Cases of Felony in Ireland* (55 Geo. 3, c. 91) and *An Act to Explain and Amend an Act of the Fifty-fifth Year of King George the Third, for the Payment of Costs and Charges to Prosecutors and Witnesses in Cases of Felony in Ireland* (1 Will. 4, c. 57). According to, H.W. Rowan, the crown solicitor 'on each circuit decide[d] what may be the reasonable expense for the payment of witnesses, and [paid] them accordingly'. The solicitor would pay witnesses 'for the most part as soon as he thinks they have effected the object for which they are required; if the prosecution is abandoned, or from any circumstances they are sooner discharged, he pays them as soon as the necessity for their attendance ceases' (Crime and Outrage Committee, *Minutes of Evidence, 1839*, 163).

199 Crime and Outrage Committee, *Minutes of Evidence, 1839*, 163.

200 Ibid.

201 See Mc Mahon, 'Homicide', appendix one.

202 For the high level of participation in the lower courts in this period, see D.J. McCabe, 'Law, Conflict and Social Order: County Mayo, 1820–45' (PhD thesis, University College Dublin, 1991) and Richard Mc Mahon, 'The Court of Petty Sessions and the Law in pre-Famine Galway', in Raymond Gillespie (ed.), *The Remaking of Modern Ireland 1750–1950: Beckett Prize Essays in Irish History* (Dublin: Four Courts Press, 2004), 101–37.

203 *Belfast Newsletter*, 2 August 1839. He went on to claim that the parish had not been disturbed and that a murder had not been committed there 'during the last seven years'.

204 NAI, outrage papers, Queen's Co., 1847/27809.

205 NAI, outrage papers, Kilkenny, 1848/87.

206 NAI, outrage papers, Queen's Co., 1849/70.

207 NAI, outrage papers, Fermanagh, 1846/8259.

208   At the Carlow spring assizes of the same year no witnesses required the support of or preferred claims against the government. NAI, outrage papers, Queen's Co., 1849/99.
209   Of the three witnesses one was an approver and railway worker called John Cahill while the other two witnesses were women who ran a tent of ill-repute near the railway works. Again such witnesses were very much from the lower levels of Irish society and were probably in a particularly vulnerable position after testifying with little means of supporting themselves. The other witness at the assizes who needed assistance after testifying was Anastasia McEvoy who gave evidence in an arson case. She was described by the crown solicitor as 'a young woman without friends' (NAI, outrage papers, Queen's Co., 1849/99).
210   *Leinster Express*, 25 March 1848.

Further reading

Bonsall, Penny (1997) *The Irish RMs: The Resident Magistrates in the British Administration of Ireland*. Dublin: Four Courts Press.

Broeker, Galen (1970) *Rural Disorder and Police Reform in Ireland, 1812–36*. London: Routledge & Kegan Paul.

Carroll-Burke, Patrick (2000) *Colonial Discipline: The Making of the Irish Convict System*. Dublin: Four Courts Press.

Clark, Samuel and J.S. Donnelly, Jr (eds) (1983) *Irish Peasants: Violence and Political Unrest*. Manchester: Manchester University Press.

Conley, Carolyn A. (1999) *Melancholy Accidents: The Meaning of Violence in Post-Famine Ireland*. Lanham, MD: Lexington Books.

Connolly, S.J. (1988) 'Albion's Fatal Twigs: Justice and Law in the Eighteenth Century', in Rosalind Mitchison and Peter Roebuck (eds), *Economy and Society in Scotland and Ireland 1500–1939*. Edinburgh: John Donald, 117–25.

Connolly, S.J. (1999) 'Unnatural Death in Four Nations: Contrasts and Comparisons', in S.J. Connolly (ed.), *Kingdoms United? Great Britain and Ireland since 1500*. Dublin: Four Courts Press, 200–14.

Crossman, Virginia (1996) *Politics, Law and Order in Nineteenth-Century Ireland*. Dublin: Gill & Macmillan.

Eiriksson, Andres (1992) 'Crime and Popular Protest in Co. Clare 1815–52'. Unpublished PhD thesis, Trinity College Dublin.

Garnham, Neal (1996) *The Courts, Crime and the Criminal Law in Ireland, 1692–1760*. Dublin: Irish Academic Press.

Garnham, Neal (1997) 'How Violent Was Eighteenth Century Ireland?', *Irish Historical Studies*, 30 (119): 377–92.

Griffin, Brian (2005) *Sources for the Study of Crime in Ireland, 1801–1921*. Dublin: Four Courts Press.

Griffin, Brian (2006) 'Prevention and Detection of Crime in Nineteenth-Century Ireland', in N.M. Dawson (ed.), *Reflections on Law and History: Irish Legal History Society Discourses and Other Papers, 2000–2005*. Dublin: Four Courts Press, 99–125.

Hickey, Éanna (1999) *Irish Law and Lawyers in Modern Folk Tradition*. Dublin: Four Courts Press.

Johnson, D.S. (1985) 'The Trials of Sam Gray: Monaghan Politics and Nineteenth-Century Irish Criminal Procedure', *Irish Jurist*, 20 (new series): 109–34.

Johnson, D.S. (1996) 'Trial by Jury in Ireland, 1860–1914', *Journal of Legal History*, 17: 270–93.

Kilcommins, Shane, Ian O'Donnell, Eoin O'Sullivan, Barry Vaughan (2004) *Crime, Punishment and the Search for Order in Ireland*. Dublin: Institute of Public Administration.

McCabe, D.J. (1991) 'Law, Conflict and Social Order: County Mayo, 1820–45'. Unpublished PhD thesis, University College Dublin.

McCabe, D.J. (1991) '"That Part that Laws or Kings Can Cause or Cure": Crown Prosecution and Jury Trial at Longford Assizes, 1830–45', in Raymond Gillespie and Gerard Moran (eds), *Longford: Essays in County History*. Dublin: Lilliput Press, 153–72.

McDowell, R.B. (1964) *The Irish Administration, 1801–1914*. London: Routledge & Kegan Paul.

McEldowney, J.F. (1989) 'Crown Prosecutions in Nineteenth-Century Ireland', in Douglas Hay and Francis Snyder (eds), *Policing and Prosecution in Britain 1750–1850*. Oxford: Clarendon Press, 427–57.

McEldowney, J.F. (1990) 'Some Aspects of Law and Policy in the Administration of Criminal Justice in Nineteenth-Century Ireland', in J.F. McEldowney and Paul O'Higgins (eds), *The Common Law Tradition: Essays in Irish Legal History*. Dublin: Irish Academic Press.

Mc Mahon, Richard (2004) 'The Court of Petty Sessions and the Law in pre-Famine Galway', in Raymond Gillespie (ed.), *The Remaking of Modern Ireland 1750–1950: Beckett Prize Essays in Irish History*. Dublin: Four Courts Press, 101–37.

Malcolm, Elizabeth (2002) 'Investigating the "Machinery of Murder": Irish Detectives and Agrarian Outrages, 1847–70', *New Hibernia Review*, 6 (3): 73–91.

Malcolm, Elizabeth (2005) *The Irish Policeman, 1822–1922: A Life*. Dublin: Four Courts Press.

O'Donnell, Ian (2002) 'Unlawful Killing: Past and Present', *Irish Jurist*, 37 (new series): 56–90.

O'Donnell, Ian (2005) 'Lethal Violence in Ireland, 1841–2003: Famine, Celibacy and Parental Pacification', *British Journal of Criminology*, 45: 671–95.

Palmer, S.H. (1988) *Police and Protest in England and Ireland, 1780–1850*. Cambridge: Cambridge University Press.

Chapter 7

Violent crime and the public weal in England, 1700–1900

Greg T. Smith[1]

This essay considers the role of, and responses to, violent crime in eighteenth- and nineteenth-century England and its impact on the public weal. It has become something of a canonical statement to assert the prevalence and apparently high tolerance for physical violence in early modern England.[2] Paul Langford has argued that the English abroad bore an unjustified reputation as a people who were unusually tolerant of 'disproportionate and gratuitous violence', yet it seems fair to say that before the eighteenth century, men and women were not particularly concerned with the familiar place of violence in everyday life.[3] There were many familiar or mundane forms of violence that formed a part of quotidian experience. Street and neighbourhood quarrels, pub brawls, domestic fights, the invasion of one's personal space by harsh hands or tongues, all were part of the familiar experiences that one came to expect as an occasional part of daily intercourse. Beyond the interpersonal violence that will form the principal focus of this essay, we might also speak of a culture of violence, suggesting the familiar place of violence in other realms of everyday life in the early modern period. Throughout the eighteenth and well into the nineteenth centuries, the exercise of power by the British state in the form of military aggression, suppression of revolts and disturbances or the punishment of criminals each involved violence in various ways. Deaths from violent accidents were also familiar events and probably increased in the nineteenth century as industrialization spread and heavy industries such as coal mining expanded.[4] As well, many popular sports and entertainments were very violent, for example cudgelling, cock fighting, bull and bear baiting, and bullock hunting.[5]

Violence was at the core of rituals of popular culture as well. As E.P. Thompson and others revealed in their studies of shaming rituals for cuckolded husbands (and occasionally wives), public humiliation and deep embarrassment triggered by physical assaults upon the body of the offender were considered acceptable and even elemental to the success of the ritual in question.[6] As John Beattie suggested in a seminal essay on early modern violence, such punishments were predicated on an 'acceptance of violent behaviour that was more domesticated and closer at hand'. In other words, violence was much more of a quotidian reality in the past than it is today; this is confirmed by evidence from a range of contemporary sources that reveal a high threshold of tolerance for violent behaviour in many facets of daily life. Violence was considered an acceptable means of maintaining discipline in both public and private spheres.[7] It is also important to note that it was not until the late eighteenth and early nineteenth centuries that men and women began increasingly to articulate sustained concerns over the role of such behaviour in daily life. This transformation in attitudes towards violence in society was less an event than a very long process, and one that continued into the twentieth century.

That interpersonal violence in the past was gendered is becoming increasingly clear. Qualitative evidence found in pamphlets, newspapers and so on and the surviving court records suggest both lethal and non-lethal violence must be seen as a more prominent feature of male life experience than female. In the London courts of the seventeenth and early eighteenth century, men appeared up to four times more frequently than women in trials for violent acts, particularly when weapons were involved.[8] Men were conditioned to violence from an early stage of life and the use of violence in situations where a boy's or man's normative gender role was under threat was 'part of accepted codes of masculine behaviour'.[9] Recent studies have begun to expose how both the nature of violence, and trends in attitudes towards it, were deeply imbricated in evolving ideas about gender roles. Indeed, the decline in public violence by the later eighteenth century has been linked to the evolution of conceptions of masculinity and the withering place for violence within constructions of the manly man, a development which continued into the nineteenth century.[10] Such studies reveal just how complicated and multivalent violence – as an issue in social interactions – could be.

Here I would like to survey attitudes towards violent crime in England as a cultural artefact in the eighteenth and nineteenth centuries, and try to sketch out the relationships between violence in society and violent criminal behaviour in particular. I am especially interested in shedding greater light on attitudes towards non-lethal interpersonal violence, in other words assaults, an aspect of the historiographical debates on violence in the past which has received only limited attention.

Violent crime in English society

Let us consider first the forms of interpersonal violent crime that are known to historians. What do historians know about such crimes in the past? The answer is still not as much as they want to. One major obstacle to writing the history of violent crime is that very often confrontations involving physical force did not come to be recorded, let alone make it to a court of law. That a large number of potential 'crimes' are absent from the historical record is certainly true for crimes against property, but is especially the case for crimes of violence. If the victims of violence did not pursue legal action, then there is unlikely to be any historical record of the event ever taking place. Occasionally, diaries, memoirs or other personal accounts will relate violent experiences, but these are rare – perhaps in itself a sign that either violence was considered 'unremarkable' except in the most extreme circumstances, or rare among those in a position to diarise their lives. The most extreme form of violence – homicide – is the most likely to leave a historical record because of the fact that someone died. It is for this reason that historians have privileged the statistical record of homicide as the most reliable measure of levels of violence in the past. But it is precisely this privileging of homicide statistics that, for a long time, diverted attention from larger questions about violence in its multifarious forms in early modern society.

Homicide

Though attitudes towards many offences changed markedly over the course of the eighteenth and nineteenth centuries, and though a range of violent experiences may have been a common feature of life in the past, some forms of violence were never acceptable. Attitudes towards homicide have remained constant over time, and murder was universally condemned and reported to the authorities. It is the one crime that attracts general reproach and widespread support for harsh punishment, including the death penalty. In the mid-eighteenth century, Parliament passed a statute that was designed to amplify the terror attached to the punishment for murder by ordering the swift execution of the condemned and anatomisation by surgeons.[11] Roughly eighty years later, in the 1820s and 1830s, even some of those who campaigned to remove the death penalty from property offences were willing to retain it for murder. Indeed, well into the nineteenth century, amid calls for legal reform removing the death penalty from all property offences, many believed with the solicitor general that the most serious crimes of violence, those which threatened life, 'must continue to be under the painful necessity of visiting with death' as only the most severe punishment in such cases 'accorded with the natural feeling of man'.[12]

Homicide is often used as an index for violence, and clearly a sudden and sustained increase in the murder rate is a telling comment on the role of violence in interpersonal relationships. But one must remember that compared to all other offences involving violence (burglary, assault, robbery) it remains one that is relatively rare. Between 1660 and 1802, Beattie calculated 314 homicide indictments presented at the Surrey assizes, a little more than three per year. Of murder trials proceeding to conviction, one study calculated the average annual number from London and Middlesex in the period 1749–71 to be four, and a search of murder convictions among the proceedings of the Old Bailey for the ensuing period 1772–99 results in 52 convictions or roughly two per year.[13]

Although property offences formed the overwhelming bulk of all offences that came to the attention of the authorities in eighteenth- and nineteenth-century England, it was offences against the person that provided the most spectacular headlines and the most terrifying images of criminality. But, as is borne out in today's statistics, although people feared they would be murdered during a robbery or by a vicious member of the 'dangerous classes', in fact most homicide victims knew their attacker and many were related by blood or marriage. In 77 convictions of men for murder committed against women found at the Old Bailey between 1695 and 1820, trial evidence suggests that at lest 73 of the victims were known to the accused. Of those 73 women, 51 (70 per cent) were killed by their husbands or intimate partners. Similar conclusions for the intimacy of homicide hold true for the late nineteenth century as well.[14]

Whether homicide was growing more intimate over time may only be speculated here. What is clear, however, is that official trends in prosecuted violence have shown a long-term decline in roughly the two centuries preceding the First World War (see Figure 7.1).[15] Manuel Eisner, who has recently summarised the available literature on historical trends in homicide, confirms what earlier studies have stated for England and places the decline of homicide within a larger pan-European trend.[16] The steady pattern of decline in homicide continued throughout the nineteenth century and was disturbed significantly only once, in 1865, when the homicide rate – which had been moving down from an average of 1.5 per 100,000 in the late 1850s and early 1860s to 1 per 100,000 at the turn of the century – increased to 2.[17]

Common assault

Lethal violence, then, constituted a rare but significant issue in early modern England and was always subject to more rigorous attention by both the public and the authorities. But what can be said of the comparatively less serious forms of interpersonal violence? Overall there seems to have been a rather high threshold of tolerance for the use of non-lethal violence in the course of daily life. That said, the frequency with which men and women suffered rough usage or ill treatment at the hands of another person in the eighteenth and nineteenth centuries is very difficult to gauge with any sort of accuracy because of the ambiguous and individual thresholds for

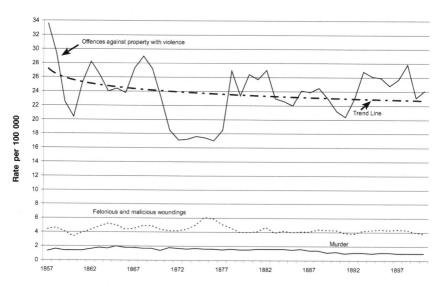

Figure 7.1 Violent offences known to police in England, 1857–1900

violence and conflict that people set for themselves. The extent to which these early modern folk subscribed to a concept of 'personal space' is difficult to discover and impossible to generalise. And when that imaginary circle just inside arm's length was violated by another's rough behaviour, going to law in order to seek some sort of recompense was but one reaction well along the spectrum of possible responses to the hurly-burly of life, especially, one might guess, in the exceptionally crowded and busy capital of London. To bring another person before an authority – a magistrate in the eighteenth century, a police constable in the later nineteenth – was clearly indicative of one individual's threshold of tolerance for violence having been crossed, of someone having taken offence, even if the alleged wrong was in no way understandable as a criminal offence. It is also important to bear in mind that both custom and law acceded to a certain level of violence in a number of social situations. Evidence for this includes the leniency shown to combatants involved in informal boxing matches (working-class duels) or the licence given to husbands and masters to correct their wives, children and servants with moderate physical violence.[18]

Common assault was by far the most familiar species of violent crime. Assault charges could arise from an extremely wide range of events, and for that reason it is difficult to draw specific conclusions about the nature of violence in society simply from the patterns of assault prosecutions.[19] Counting assault indictments across time as an index of levels of interpersonal violence might, then, seem highly problematic, given that the so-called 'dark figure' of unrecorded crime is potentially so huge that it may engulf the comparatively small number of assault cases that did make it to court. However, as recent studies of assault have shown, conclusions drawn from conviction patterns can suggest underlying attitudinal changes towards interpersonal violence. Also, the wide discretion permitted in the prosecution of misdemeanour offences meant that many prosecutors avoided trial by settling their assault cases at pre-trial examinations before a magistrate. Even in cases that proceeded to trial, the power and authority of the courts could be manipulated to broker a private settlement, frequently with the courts' assistance.[20]

Incidents in which some sort of injury was sustained were more likely to result in a formal indictment and a trial, as in the case of Elizabeth Lorain who was charged by Ann Bromley in October 1747 with 'violently assaulting and beating her and cutting her in the head with a knife'.[21] Lorain was committed to jail to await trial. But even when one person felt they had been ill treated or even injured, the guardians of the peace, especially the local JPs, were inclined to read into the context of physical disputes a certain latitude for the exercise of violent behaviour before drawing a formal indictment. Thus in November 1761, when Catherine Dawson, a servant, was roughly turned out of her master's shop when she refused to leave of her own will, she brought a charge of assault before one of London's sitting magistrates at the Guildhall. But the JP decided that 'ye Assault being justifiable he [the defendant] was Discharged.'[22] The specifics of the alleged violence done are vague but there is no suggestion that there was any serious physical injury. Still, physical injury was by no means the benchmark for a charge being made and an indictment sworn, and many trifling disputes did make it to trial before they were sorted out.

Provocation was understood as a cause of escalating violence and perhaps a mitigating circumstance, even if it was not always accepted as a legitimate excuse, if courtroom evidence can be taken as indication of such values. In April 1791, when Thomas Parsen was charged by Thomas Daniel with violently assaulting him and 'knocking him down under a Cart Wheel which put him in imminent Danger of being run over', the JP permitted a private settlement and discharged the case rather than sending it to quarter sessions as 'there was great Provocation'.[23] The resort to violence in situations where one's honour or standing was challenged continued to receive popular justification well into the nineteenth century. Carolyn Conley cites a number of examples from the Victorian Kentish courts where verbal taunts incited physical hostility. And though the magistrates criticised the turn to violence in interpersonal disputes, the common defence of provocation indicates 'the persistence of a belief in the right to respond physically when verbally provoked'.[24]

There are countless indications that alcohol was a factor in a good many public and private rows. Eighteenth-century depositions for assault cases heard before the Court of King's Bench in London also confirm that public houses could be very violent places. One case describes how a woman who, while drinking at the Sugar Loaf, was attacked by a man who 'laid hold of a stick which was then on the Fire in the Grate there and threw [it at her] and struck [her] therewith on the Face' and then proceeded to strike her 'several Violent Blows on her Face with his Double Fists so that the Blood Gushed out of [her] nose and mouth.'[25] Historians have suggested that interpersonal violence was more likely to follow the fluctuations in social conditions and economic cycles so that in times of prosperity, when there was more disposable income available for alcohol, assault rates increased.[26] Drink was frequently offered as a mitigating circumstance in cases of violence and contemporaries were never surprised to learn that the consumption of alcohol and acts of violence were frequently linked events. Mr Justice H.S. Keating of the Court of Common Pleas argued in a letter to an 1874 parliamentary committee that in his experience, 'nine-tenths of the crimes of violence committed throughout England originate in public houses, and are committed under circumstances which exclude all reflection.'[27] Violence came easily to men and women who were drunk and angry, and stiffer legislation was not necessarily going to deter such behaviour in others. Still, the available statistics for the late nineteenth century do suggest a strong correlation between declining rates of drunkenness and declining rates of interpersonal violence. This may well be due to the success in reforming the morals of Victorian society and marginalising the acceptability of drunkenness as an excuse for unwelcome behaviour. Martin Wiener has shown how such attitudes became reflected in the courts. By the late Victorian era it became much less likely that drunkenness would serve as a mitigating circumstance in cases of murder, as the standards for personal responsibility in controlling violence were ratcheted upwards.[28]

Domestic violence

Drink was often a factor in cases of both public and domestic violence but even sober husbands and masters were known to threaten and beat their subordinates with a certain degree of impunity. The use of reasonable violence to control and discipline subordinates was an acceptable practice throughout the eighteenth and nineteenth centuries, though by the mid-1800s we can begin to see a more concerted effort to curb and contain excessive violence against women and children. But for most of our period, 'moderate physical correction' of wives, children, servants or apprentices was permitted in law and condoned in practice. Justicing manuals stated that a charge of assault and battery would not be sustained in the case of a parent chastising a child 'in a reasonable and proper manner' or 'a master his servant being actually in his service at the time, or a schoolmaster his scholar, or a gaoler his prisoner or even a husband his wife'.[29] This cultural tolerance for a modicum of violence in the domestic sphere makes it difficult to discover how widespread the systematic abuse of subordinates was as there were, understandably, considerable risks involved in making private violence a public issue.

For a long time then, the master of the household was free to use physical violence to 'correct' wives and children, as well as servants and apprentices.[30]

Records from magistrates' courts reveal how domestic violence might come to light through the intervention of a third party. In 1791, Thomas Bond was hauled before the JP presumably by his landlord and his wife for 'disturbing the Neighbourhood' and beating his wife. Bond agreed 'to leave the Lodging and promises not to beat [his wife] in future' for which he was simply discharged.[31] But although lenient solutions to domestic violence can be found throughout the eighteenth and nineteenth centuries, there is some evidence to suggest that attitudes towards domestic violence were hardening even in the mid-eighteenth century. The courts made some attempts to halt such abuse by detaining abusive spouses and by issuing peace bonds, even if they were ultimately powerless to prevent its recurrence. When Judith Abrahams charged her husband Abraham with assault for 'frequently assaulting beating abusing and threatening her' she brought a witness, Reba Levi, to confirm the complaint. The magistrate was satisfied too. Noting that 'it appearing ye Woman was in danger' Abraham was committed to Wood Street Compter to await trial. Some abusive husbands were committed to trial for want of sureties to keep the peace, such as Samuel Simpson in 1782, whose wife Elizabeth charged him with assaulting and beating her.[32] Still others, however, were able to reach an amicable arrangement, as in the case of Sarah Rottam whose husband Thomas was charged in 1761 with a violent assault and with 'running away and leaving her whereby she is likely to become chargeable' – in other words a financial burden on the parish. To prevent this, the justice initiated some kind of discussion which resulted in the husband agreeing to pay Sarah an allowance of 3s. 6d. per week 'to which she was contented' and he was discharged.[33] Such cases are unmistakable examples of court officials finding a way to curb the violence, to separate the parties and to prevent the wife from becoming a financial burden upon the parish by arranging for something approximating modern maintenance payments.

Women could terrorise their households with violent outbursts too. In one deposition for an assault case that came before the court of King's Bench in 1798, it appears that Sarah Kingsworth, a London servant, carelessly left a milk delivery in a spot where the household cat was able to help herself. When the lady of the house, Mary Black, discovered the oversight she 'threw herself into a violent rage and not only very much abused this deponent by calling her approbrious [*sic*] names but violently assaulted her by thrusting a candle and Candlestick in her face.' According to Kingsworth, her employer then 'violently jammed [her] Arm between the door of a large folding press ... so as to render her Arm totally useless ... and so much bruised ... lamed disabled and hurt that [she] expected she should be obliged to have her arm amputated.'[34] Clearly, gender was not in itself an impediment to the use of violence to dominate others in the home, though perhaps servants and children suffered worse than did husbands. Among the records of the London sessions of the peace, there are occasional examples of husbands prosecuting their abusive wives, though such cases are exceptional.[35]

The explicit classification of domestic violence as an issue more prevalent among the lower orders or specifically 'working classes' was more of a nineteenth-century construct. An 1853 Act endorsed flogging as a suitable punishment for those convicted of assaulting women and children, a sub-group – it was widely assumed – of the labouring classes and the poor.[36] Frances Power Cobbe tried to explode this Victorian myth – that domestic violence was an issue only among the poor – with limited effect, and so the misperception that middle- and upper-class families enjoyed domestic peace persisted throughout much of the succeeding century. However, she was successful in pushing for legally empowering women caught in the cycle of domestic violence to break free of those abusive relationships. In her powerful essay 'Wife Torture in England', Cobbe called on Parliament to take more aggressive steps to protect women and children against violence, even drafting a bill which would permit wives whose husbands had been convicted of beating them to be granted a legal separation.[37] The result was the 1878 Matrimonial Causes Act.[38] Despite this and other progressive legislation that opened up the summary courts to female victims of spousal violence, there were yet larger gulfs between the law in theory and the nature of social and gender relationships in practice, which prevented women from exercising the power of the law without either considerable expense or, worse, dangerous risks to themselves.

There is much evidence to support the claim that violence in the home continued to be an accepted part of working-class life well into the twentieth century. Thus the changes in legislation from the mid-nineteenth century may well suggest a hardening of attitudes towards intimate violence among middle-class legal theorists and legislators. So the question is to explain the reasons for the hardening of attitudes towards domestic violence among the middle class and elites. No longer content to chalk up another victory for Victorian civility, historians are now coming to understand the complicated relationship between the law and the culture that created and sustained it in its daily operation. In what Martin Wiener has styled the 'Victorian criminalization of men' he argues that the trend towards more public and official ways of encouraging self-discipline and repressing violent behaviour has much to do with the long-term 'reconstruction of gender' which began in earnest around the middle of the eighteenth century. As women's gender roles transformed, especially in the nineteenth century, and as women emerged in normative Victorian discourses as the group most in need of protection from men, two things happened: the veil of secrecy surrounding violence and abuse committed on them in private was pierced and gradually pulled back; and second, having exposed the horrors of intimate violence, the nation's legislators crafted new statutes to remedy the problem and to better protect women.[39] But the target of such reforms was male violence first and female suffering second.

The responses to violent crime

Victims of interpersonal violence had a range of strategies open to them should they seek to reproach their assailant's behaviour. Immediate reprisal, of course, was one route, and countless acts of retaliatory violence must have occurred without any resulting comment or reaction, especially if the retributive violence left the initial victim feeling he or she had received satisfaction. Occasionally, evidence survives to reveal how third parties intervened in attacks or affrays from an immediate, visceral reaction to the violence before them. This, I think, suggests something of a common understanding at work: that when possible, such behaviour should be contained and controlled. At times, witnesses and passers-by intervened in disputes in order to check the escalation of violence. For example, John Showers, a tavern keeper in Long Lane, West Smithfield, 'interfered' when Rachel Reynolds challenged Ann Wood to a fight over a pot of ale. But when he did, he recounted, 'both flew upon me like Tygers' and 'fell breaking my toes with their fists'. Only with the assistance of his wife and another person was he able to expel them from his premises.[40] One study has suggested that interventions into violent disputes may have been increasing over the eighteenth century, perhaps signalling a growing intolerance for public violence, but more evidence is needed to confirm this.[41]

Victims who chose to make the authorities aware of their complaint could go to law, and many did. But it is unlikely we shall ever know the true extent to which victims of violence pursued legal action, even if a criminal charge could be sustained. Unlike property offences, where the possibility of the return of the goods stolen, or perhaps a reward, motivated prosecutors, in assault cases the motives for laying a charge were more complex. Leaving aside those cases where a charge was laid for malicious reasons, the initial decision to go to law was motivated out of a sense of having suffered a wrong or a physical hurt. As Norma Landau has shown, the peculiar nature of the early modern criminal justice system, so dependent on both private prosecutors to initiate a case and upon fees to see it through the process, encouraged many, for merely pecuniary reasons, to seek an alternative settlement in their assault cases in a way that shut the state out of making a comment on the violence inherent in the initial charge.[42]

But the exclusion of the state from the effective punishment of thousands of episodes of interpersonal violence over the eighteenth century was not seen as a particular failing on the part of the authorities to control such behaviour. That is because, before the early 1800s, assault was regarded in terms similar to a civil dispute. This meant that the state frequently took a back seat to the plaintiff in exacting some kind of restitution for the wrong done by way of physical violence. Though the court was, in theory, a representative of the king and people, and clearly had a large stake in maintaining order in society, in the vast majority of cases of interpersonal violence where the harm done was reasonably slight, the courts exercised the considerable discretion accorded to them to settle such matters extra-legally. The range of action enjoyed by the magistrates is especially clear in the manner in which they dispatched cases of interpersonal violence. As other historians have noted, it is at the summary level that we see the considerable discretionary power accorded to these justices.[43] For instance, when Thomas Wetherall and Robert Bound charged one James Ottoway with assault in September 1782, the magistrate permitted the parties the chance to settle the matter themselves. The clerk records that the parties 'withdrew and agreed' and all were discharged.[44] In managing such matters and maintaining the peace, the local magistrate played an especially significant role. JPs were not only permitted but encouraged in procedural manuals to facilitate a mutually-negotiated settlement whenever possible.[45] The courts would sanction this semi-private settlement by imposing only a minor fine, a symbolic marker of the conclusion of the legal proceedings. There is good evidence that lone justices did this in their parlours and justice rooms, and it is also clear that they moved in a similar way when they sat together at regular quarter sessions of the peace.[46] Table 7.1 shows the frequent imposition of the 1s. fine at two quarter-sessions courts in the eighteenth century, suggesting that the desire to avoid state-imposed sanctions in cases of assault was fairly common before the 1790s. By the turn of the century, however, larger fines were being imposed in more cases and imprisonment was also being used more frequently. Peter King's figures suggest the change was more dramatic in Essex. With Middlesex's larger population, and a shortage of space in the jails or house of correction, it is perhaps understandable that the rate of imprisonment might rise less dramatically when stiffer fines and orders for convicts to enter into recognizances to keep the peace might yet serve as an appropriate punishment.

That JPs had wide latitude to manufacture settlements in cases of assault involving a range of violence was a function of the law of assault itself. It is frequently noted that the crime of assault in the eighteenth century had both a public and private nature to it. William Blackstone, England's pre-eminent legal theorist, outlined the fact at the time, and the familiar procedure manuals for JPs,

Table 7.1 Punishments for assault, Middlesex and Essex Quarter Sessions, 1748–1835

Known sentences	Middlesex			Essex		
	1760–75	1790–1805	1820–35	1748–52	1793–97	1819–21
	%	%	%	%	%	%
Not guilty	19.8	45.4	55.1	12.5	18.7	20.8
Fine 1s. or less	62.3	21.1	2.1	73.2	34.1	13.2
Fine over 1s.	9.8	17.3	11.8	5.4	7.7	13.2
Imprisoned	7.8	15.0	20.6	3.6	31.9	51.6
Other	0.3	1.1	10.3	5.4	7.7	1.1
Total known (%)	100.0	99.9	99.9	100.1	100.1	99.9
(Sample size)	(902)	(1014)	(1313)	(56)	(91)	(91)

Sources: Middlesex: London Metropolitan Archive, Sessions Rolls MJ/SR; Essex: adapted from evidence in Peter King, 'Punishing Assault: The Transformation of Attitudes in the English Courts', *Journal of Interdisciplinary History*, 27, 1 (1996), table 1.

like Burn's ubiquitous *Justice of the Peace and Parish Officer*, similarly noted the fact that crimes against the person were of both public and private interest. Before 1803 laws regarding assault were either very vague or narrowly conceived. Statutes existed to punish very specific forms of interpersonal violence, maiming for example, but it was only with the 1803 Malicious Shooting or Stabbing Act that (despite its precise title) individuals were granted statutory protection from less specific forms of violence to the person.[47] For the most part, magistrates in summary hearings or sitting at quarter sessions simply put into practice what Blackstone had stated in his *Commentaries*, by classifying most manifestations of interpersonal violence as 'private wrongs, or civil injuries, for which a satisfaction or remedy is given to the party aggrieved'.[48] Although there was a 'public light' to these matters too, England's highest and lowest justices were encouraged where possible to facilitate private settlements. Though many historians have suggested the frequency of this practice in assault prosecutions, using anecdotal evidence, Landau's work demonstrates that in fact it was overwhelmingly the norm. Her careful examination of quarter sessions procedure shows that the 1 shilling fines noted in a large proportion of assault cases prosecuted at the Middlesex quarter sessions were, indeed, as others have only speculated, simply the court's way of signifying that the matter had been dealt with privately and that the criminal prosecution had come to an end.[49]

Judges and magistrates in London and elsewhere were agreed in the desire to see the parties to an assault charge leave their courts with a reconciliation rather than an indictment. Speaking in 1819 before a Parliamentary Committee, the clerk to the magistrate at Guildhall, William Payne, testified that whenever the magistrate sensed that the prosecutor might be willing to permit the defendant to be discharged 'with an admonition from the magistrate; there always has been on the part of the magistrates of the city, a great anxiety to have such persons discharged rather than to commit them.'[50] As the clerk noted, the magistrate was careful not to upset the 'public interest' and so made some inquiry into the character of the accused and no doubt into the nature and circumstances of the alleged offence. And sensitive magistrates were careful to balance the court's limited time with a duty not to encourage the prosecutor to drop a serious case. Thus, in June of 1792, when Mary Green was brought before the sitting alderman for striking Ann Holland 'a violent Blow on her Breast', he did not encourage any settlement and left Holland 'to indict if she thinks proper'.[51] But, by allowing those litigants who were willing to settle their disputes out of court to do so, the courts were, to some extent, implicitly legitimising the use of violence in certain situations.

What was finally agreed to when settlements were reached was unique to each case. It could have been as simple as an apology and a handshake, while in other cases the magistrate may have imposed some form of financial restitution. Again, at the City's magistrates' courts, some of the accused were 'reprimanded' without any fine, especially in cases where only violent threats were made, or if the defendant was poor, or upon their 'begging pardon' from the prosecutor.[52] Sometimes the apology itself was the punishment and in some cases it was made public, appearing in the daily newspapers.[53] In many other cases, including at quarter sessions, if the issue could be settled and the parties discharged, the defendant almost always paid some compensation to the victim or at least his or her costs. They also paid the small 1s. fee to the court, symbolising that the case had ended.[54] But, if we set aside the cases in which the court imposed minor fines as essentially civil remedies for assault, as Landau urges us to do, what are we to make of the remainder of assault cases that were in fact punished by the courts? If we concentrate on those cases actually prosecuted and punished by the courts, we can begin to examine the behaviour of judges and juries and from that information it is possible to speculate about how their decisions may have been shaped by larger cultural forces. The records of assault prosecutions reveal a change in penal strategies beginning around the 1770s in London, Middlesex and other counties such as Essex.

By the 1770s, we can begin to detect a change in penal practice reflecting the state's growing interest in punishing interpersonal violence. Table 7.1 demonstrates the shift in punishments away from the simple fine and towards imprisonment in both Middlesex and Essex. At both the Middlesex and Essex quarter sessions, at least until the end of the eighteenth century, the vast majority of those convicted of assault faced a small fine. Table 7.1 shows that in Middlesex in the period 1760–80, only around 17 per cent of cases of interpersonal violence were punished with any sort of severity, meaning more than a nominal fine or a term of imprisonment. The same was true in less than 10 per cent of Essex cases in the period 1748–52. In Middlesex for the sample period 1760–65, of 135 assault convictions only twelve resulted in terms of imprisonment, four of which were for assaults with intent to ravish. By the period 1810–30, 47 per cent of those convicted of assault at the Middlesex quarter sessions were sentenced to some term of imprisonment, a pattern replicated in the London sessions of the peace. By the period 1820–30, magistrates in the City of London were relying on imprisonment in nearly 58 per cent of convictions, while simple fines had declined to around 33 per cent.[55] Clearly there was a growing willingness among metropolitan judges to impose a greater public voice when punishing assault, to see interpersonal violence punished with a sentence more severe than a simple fine, and a term of imprisonment in either the jail or house of correction was the new punishment of choice.

The recourse to imprisonment in the punishment of assault seems to speak to a growing understanding of the social causes of violence, and also suggests something about changing attitudes to the nature of criminal (or at least anti-social) behaviour more generally. If judges and juries (who understood the consequences of their verdicts) were beginning to see such behaviour as socially induced – that is as learned behaviour in a culture with a high toleration for violence – then imprisonment offered the authorities the chance to address the most egregious examples of that behaviour with a new regime of social reform. Support for this argument comes from the evidence of where Middlesex assault convicts were imprisoned. Though a few were sent to Newgate jail or the New Prison at Clerkenwell in the 1780s, by 1820 virtually all were sent to the House of Correction. Judges could also specify punishment at hard labour during their confinement.[56] It is possible that judges were holding out hope for the reformation of these people by imposing a period of stern correction.

Another penalty that gained favour as a response to interpersonal violence – one which was sensitive to both the public and private nature of assault – was the use of recognizances to keep the peace. Once an indictment was sworn for the alleged assault, following an unsuccessful attempt at reconciliation before a magistrate, the parties would usually be bound over in a recognizance to appear at the next session of the peace for that county to prosecute the case. The recognizance constituted an agreement to appear, backed by monetary sureties, and failure to appear at the trial would mean that the sureties that the defendant and his or her supporters put up would be escheated to the crown. In most instances, the recognizance served only this limited purpose, and when the parties appeared for trial their recognizances were discharged.[57] But in cases of assault, recognizances were used as an instrument for maintaining order in English society.[58] One possible explanation for the growing use of recognizances is that it answered public desires for justice and for the state to use its power to restrict violence, without the considerable cost and burden of custodial sentences. Moreover, it moved the courts away from what Blackstone identified as the 'dangerous practice' of allowing litigants to broker private settlements. The state, he argued, did in fact have an interest in the prosecution of interpersonal violence, and in such cases, 'the right of punishing belongs not to any one individual in particular, but to the society in general, or the sovereign who represents that society.'[59] It was the public interest that was most threatened by the casual punishment of violent behaviour characteristic of the private settlements.

Middlesex quarter sessions compelled defendants to enter into a recognizance to keep the peace and/or to be of good behaviour (both terms were used) as a court-imposed sentence in cases of assault only rarely in the mid-to-late eighteenth century. But in the 1820s and 1830s, there was a noticeable increase in the application of this sanction in such cases, either on its own or in conjunction with a fine. At the London sessions of the peace for the City, the use of recognizances to keep the peace increased in the 1820s too, but to a lesser extent. Only about 10 per cent of City assault cases were settled using a recognizance for good behaviour.[60] The recognizance was a more inclusive instrument of social control than a fine and a cheaper option than imprisonment. It required guarantors or sureties from the community itself to put up significant amounts of money to guarantee the peaceful behaviour of one of their kith and kin, often for an extended period of time. By employing the recognizance as a punishment for assault, the judges found a way to actively involve members of the common weal in the control and repression of violence while reserving scarce prison space for more serious offenders.

The fact that these changes in sentencing in the metropolis were also taking place at roughly the same time in both Essex and Surrey (as the work of King and Beattie has shown) suggests strongly that these patterns do not reflect the unique proclivities of local magistrates but are rather indicative of a more general change in sensibilities and attitudes towards the punishment of interpersonal violence in the last decades of the eighteenth and early decades of the nineteenth centuries.[61] Unfortunately, there is virtually no direct record of the motives that inspired these magistrates to make the sentencing decisions they did. Our best evidence that such a transformation in the punishment of assault had occurred over this period comes from the records of the courts themselves which show that, over the three or four decades after about 1770, when it came to violent offences against the person, both metropolitan and rural justices were moving in the direction of greater penal severity. Peter King has tied the changes he detected in assault prosecutions in Essex to the prison-reform initiatives that 'complemented' the reformation of manners movement of the 1780s.[62] There is much merit in that claim, though I would suggest that all of these changes can be linked by an even more general shift in attitudes or sensibilities towards violence in multiple forms – in public displays of violence, in the treatment of prisoners and in the punishment of interpersonal violence. These changes were more obvious among the elite and middle classes than among the lower orders, but over time the ideas and rhetoric that underpinned them began to circulate more widely. The other important development regarding the prosecution and punishment of assault is the expanding role for summary courts in the trial of petty offences. While negotiated settlements may have characterised the actual process for many assault cases appearing at eighteenth-century quarter sessions, by the nineteenth century such improvisation was seen as more acceptable in the less formalised structure of the summary courts. My suspicion is that by the 1810s, at the increasingly busy metropolitan courts of quarter session, cases of trifling import were being steadily filtered out of the calendars and quickly dismissed, permitting the court to concentrate on those cases involving more serious violence, cases which merited the more severe punishment of imprisonment available to the court. As well, as King suggests for his Essex data, not guilty verdicts may mask the high number of cases which were settled privately before the trial began and before the accused would be pressured to change his or her plea to guilty.[63] With sentences in assault cases growing stiffer, accused offenders may have been more obliged to settle than to take their chances with a jury. To facilitate this and to end the case in a manner that would be recorded as an acquittal, the prosecutor simply would not appear at trial. These factors may account for the exceptionally high rate of acquittals in Middlesex cases with known outcomes, revealed in Table 7.1.

Over the two centuries surveyed here, perhaps the most remarkable change in attitudes towards interpersonal violence came in the way that it was recognised in law. Not surprisingly, the most serious forms of violence had long been legislated against. Some statutes had appeared in the early modern period to address specific acts of violence involving knives, and before the nineteenth century, as the technology of killing evolved, the law too was modified towards repressing violence involving firearms.[64] However, it was not until the early nineteenth century that lawmakers in England gave serious thought to the formal codification of interpersonal violence. Lord Ellenborough's 1803 Act was the first piece of legislation to reframe the legal definition of various violent acts, followed by the more comprehensive Lansdowne's Act of 1828, the first Offences Against the Person Act.[65] These acts marked the first comprehensive statements, in law, of violent crimes against the person below murder, and enshrined in law what had been going on in practice for nearly a generation previous: that is, the summary punishment of minor acts of violence was extended, while serious crimes of violence were to be punished with greater severity.

That the state was taking greater cognisance of the problem of interpersonal violence after about 1850 seems clear from a string of legislation that appeared throughout the second half of the century.[66] Concerns about a perceived escalation of particular or apparently innovative forms of public violence triggered parliamentary commissions and sometimes new legislation. The moral panic over street crime – violent muggings – in 1862, led to stiffer penalties in the 1863 Garotter's Act, a reactionary piece of legislation that attempted to quell the public fears over an apparent surge in violent street robberies.[67] This turn towards greater severity in the laws dealing with interpersonal violence confirmed a growing revulsion against public violence, particularly violence among men, and the rise of middle-class notions of polite, respectable, civilised behaviour.

By the 1870s, Parliament was responding swiftly to public anxieties over particular acts of violence. In October 1874, the Home Secretary Sir Richard Assheton Cross, canvassed the opinion of the country's leading judges, magistrates and police officers with an eye to strengthening the law as it related to crimes of violence. In particular, Cross inquired of these men whether the existing law pertaining to assaults of brutal violence 'as distinguished from trifling assaults' was 'sufficiently stringent'. He sought their advice about upgrading certain kinds of assaults from misdemeanour offences, punished summarily, to indictable offences and pressed the desirability of increasing the maximum fines and jail terms for summarily punishable assaults. The responses, though mixed, tended to support a turn to more severe sanctions. At the one extreme, Lord Chief Justice Cockburn opined that 'the Penal Law against assaults of brutal violence is not sufficiently stringent.' He supported stiffer penalties all round, adding that 'flogging may well be authorised for violence in cases of brutal assault', particularly in cases of 'personal violence of an outrageous character' where bodily injury was clearly intended by the accused.[68] But Alex Knox, one of the magistrates in the Metropolitan Police Court at Marlborough Street, cautioned against extending the use of flogging. To do so, he believed, would extend 'quite an improper power' to a lone magistrate, and warned 'a reaction against the law would be the certain consequence of any such provision.'[69] Justice Keating agreed, adding that he would be surprised 'if a case could be found where a flogged man became less violent'.[70]

Conclusion

Throughout the eighteenth and nineteenth centuries then, violence played a visible and pervasive role in daily life. Both the early modern state and its citizens held few qualms about exercising violence in order to control and discipline others, and popular culture legitimised the use of violence in a number of social contexts. Though violence would not (and could not) be legislated against in all of its manifestations, what is evident over the two centuries considered here is a growing desire, especially among the middling sorts and elites, to curb and control interpersonal violence in various spheres of daily life. Violence that transcended social classes or in which the power or authority of a social superior was implicitly or explicitly challenged was more likely to bring strict censure throughout our period, while infra-class violence – including assault generally and domestic violence in particular – was undergoing tighter legal framing and clearer codification in law, and was being punished more harshly in practice.

Until the mid-eighteenth century, the authorities did not see the punishment of interpersonal violence as one of their central tasks. Most cases of assault were settled privately, with little or no public sanction involved. However, over the course of the late eighteenth and early nineteenth centuries, violent activity appeared and reappeared as a frequent subject of popular concern and increasingly authorities were entrusted with the job of circumscribing and repressing that activity. Records of assault prosecutions suggest that magistrates and juries were at the forefront of these changes, ensuring from about the 1770s, and with greater certainty by the early nineteenth century, that public accountability and community involvement came to the fore in the repression of interpersonal violence, with the growing use of recognizances to keep the peace and terms of imprisonment serving as two indications of this trend. The data from the metropolis seems to confirm the trends uncovered by Beattie and King for other parts of England.[71]

This change in sentencing was not the result of any particular legislative development, or other concerted initiative, but had its roots in much less tangible forces. I would speculate that the judges and juries inferred from more general changes in social and cultural attitudes that the threshold of toleration for acts of violence was sinking lower and lower as tastes, beliefs and standards of public behaviour became more 'civilised'. In the emerging 'polite and commercial' society of late eighteenth-century Britain, there was less tolerance for behaviour that was cruel, vicious and offensive to shared cultural norms. These changes mirrored larger anxieties about the place and role of violence in everyday life in the metropolis. The courts were the venue in which such aspects of life's darker side regularly came to light, and it was there that some of the first steps were taken to minimise, marginalise and regulate the problem of violent behaviour.[72] Though the metropolis was considered by many contemporaries to be a more violent place at the end of the eighteenth century, there were, nevertheless, significant developments in the official and public levels of intolerance of violence within that very context.

By the first third of the nineteenth century, the official responses to interpersonal violence changed markedly, resulting in an increased role for the state in the maintenance of order through changes in the punishments meted out for violent behaviour. This was followed in the mid-to-late nineteenth century by a string of legislation that attempted to spell out in law and seriously punish a range of violent acts, in many cases for the first time. By the mid-nineteenth century, the power to police such behaviour was more firmly ensconced and the will of Parliament to legislate against such behaviour was a reflection of the extent to which cultural norms had shifted and permeated a wide section of society.

If these changes in the punishment of interpersonal violence do indeed reflect larger cultural shifts in the attitudes and anxieties about violence and thereby the thresholds of what was tolerable and what was not that were occurring in this period, then the data also demonstrates that the metropolis was very much at the centre of this apparently widespread – if yet halting and uneven – change in attitudes towards violence in English society. The contours of that change within the criminal justice system may be traced using the data described here. But the driving forces behind that change are extremely complex and thus are much harder to pinpoint. Explanations of those broad cultural changes and their impact on interpersonal violence have yet to be fully worked out, though others may have something to add to our understanding of the historical changes I have sketched here.

Notes

1 I would like to thank John Beattie, Chris Frank and Richard Mc Mahon for their comments and helpful suggestions on an earlier version. I am grateful to the Social Science and Humanities Research Council of Canada and to the University of Manitoba for research support.

2 Lawrence Stone, 'Interpersonal Violence in English Society, 1300–1980', *Past and Present*, 101 (1983), 22–33; James A. Sharpe, 'The History of Violence in England: Some Observations', *Past and Present*, 108 (1985), 206–15; Lawrence Stone, 'Rejoinder', ibid. 216–24; James Cockburn, 'Patterns of Violence in English Society: Homicide in Kent, 1560–1985', *Past and Present*, 130 (1991), 70–106.

3 Paul Langford, *Englishness Identified: Manners and Character, 1650–1850* (Oxford: Oxford University Press, 2000), 137.

4 John Rule, 'A Risky Business: Death, Injury and Religion in Cornish Mining, c.1780–1870', in A. Bernard Kapp et al. (eds), *Social Approaches to an Industrial Past: The Archaeology and Anthropology of Mining* (London: Routledge, 1998), 155–73; idem, 'The Misfortunes of the Mine: Coping with Life and Death in Nineteenth-Century Cornwall', *Cornish Studies*, 2nd ser. 9 (2001), 127–44.

5 Robert Malcolmson, *Popular Recreations in English Society, 1700–1850* (Cambridge: Cambridge University Press, 1973).

6 E.P. Thompson, *Customs in Common: Studies in Traditional Popular Culture* (New York: New Press, 1991), ch. 8.

7 J.M. Beattie, 'Violence and Society in Early-Modern England', in Anthony Doob and Edward Greenspan (eds), *Perspectives in Criminal Law* (Aurora, ON: Canada Law Book, 1985), 36–60; Greg T. Smith, 'Civilized People Don't Want to See That Sort of Thing: The Decline of Physical Punishment in London, 1760–1840', in Carolyn Strange (ed.), *Qualities of Mercy: Justice, Punishment, and Discretion* (Vancouver, BC: UBC Press, 1996), 21–51; Robert Shoemaker, 'Streets of Shame? The Crowd and Public Punishments in London, 1700–1820', in Simon Devereaux and Paul Griffiths (eds), *Penal Practice and Culture, 1500–1900: Punishing the English* (London: Palgrave Macmillan, 2004), 232–57.

8 Robert B. Shoemaker, *Prosecution and Punishment: Petty Crime and the Law in London and Rural Middlesex, c.1660–1725* (Cambridge: Cambridge University Press, 1991), 213.

9 Robert Shoemaker, 'Male Honour and the Decline of Public Violence in Eighteenth-Century London', *Social History*, 26, 2 (2001), 200.

10 Shoemaker, 'Male Honour', *passim*; Martin Wiener, 'The Victorian Criminalization of Men', in Pieter Spierenburg (ed.), *Men and Violence: Gender, Honor, and Rituals in Modern Europe and America* (Columbus, OH: Ohio State University Press, 1998), 197–212; idem, *Men of Blood: Violence, Manliness, and Criminal Justice in Victorian England* (Cambridge: Cambridge University Press, 2004), ch. 1.

11 25 Geo. II, c. 37. On this act, see J.M. Beattie, *Crime and the Courts in England 1660–1800* (Princeton, NJ: Princeton University Press, 1986), 78, 529–30.

12 *Parliamentary Debates* (1833) 3rd ser. xvii: 164, cited in Randall McGowen, 'Punishing Violence, Sentencing Crime', in Nancy Armstrong and Leonard Tennehouse (eds), *The Violence of Representation: Literature and the History of Violence* (London: Routledge, 1989), 148.

13 Beattie, *Crime and the Courts*, table 3.2, 90. Note that Beattie's numbers are drawn from a complete count of all homicide indictments for a 95-year time period between 1663 and 1802 (see Appendix, 641); John H. Langbein, 'Shaping the Eighteenth-Century Trial: A View from the Ryder Sources', *University of Chicago Law Review*, 50 (1983), 44–6. Results from the period 1772–99 were derived from *The Proceedings of the Old Bailey*, http://www.oldbaileyonline.org (16 March 2008).

14 Clive Emsley, *Crime and Society in England 1750–1900*, 3rd edn (London: Longman, 2005), 42–44; Carolyn Conley, *The Unwritten Law: Criminal Justice in Victorian Kent* (New York: Oxford University Press, 1991), 59.

15 For the eighteenth century, see Beattie, *Crime and the Courts* and Peter King, *Crime, Justice, and Discretion in England 1740–1820* (Oxford: Oxford University Press, 2000); for the nineteenth, see V.A.C. Gatrell, 'The Decline of Theft and Violence in Victorian and Edwardian England', in V.A.C. Gatrell, Bruce Lenman and Geoffery Parker (eds), *Crime and the Law: The Social History of Crime in Western Europe since 1500* (London: Europa Publications, 1980), 238–365; Emsley, *Crime and Society*, 41–9.

16 Manuel Eisner, 'Modernization, Self-Control and Lethal Violence: The Long-Term Dynamics of European Homicide Rates in Theoretical Perspective', *British Journal of Criminology*, 41, 4 (2001), 618–38.

17 Gatrell, 'Decline of Theft and Violence', table A1, 350.

18 Beattie, 'Violence and Society', 46–7; Shoemaker, 'Male Honour', 194–6. On domestic violence, see Margaret Hunt, 'Wife-Beating, Domesticity and Women's Independence in Eighteenth Century London', *Gender and History*, 4, 1 (1992), 187–206; A. James Hammerton, *Cruelty and Companionship: Conflict in Nineteenth-Century Married Life* (London: Routledge, 1992); Maeve Doggett, *Marriage, Wife Beating and the Law in Victorian England* (Columbia, SC: University of South Carolina Press, 1993); Anna Clark, 'Domesticity and the Problem of Wife Beating in Nineteenth-Century Britain: Working-Class Culture, Law, and Politics', in Shani D'Cruze (ed.), *Everyday Violence in Britain, 1850–1950: Gender and Class* (London: Longman, 2000), 27–40; Wiener, *Men of Blood*.

19 On the problems surrounding the study of assault indictments, see Beattie, *Crime and the Courts*, 75–6; Peter King, 'Punishing Assault: The Transformation of Attitudes in the English Courts', *Journal of Interdisciplinary History*, 27, 1 (1996), 43–74; Gregory T. Smith, 'The State and the Culture of Violence in London, 1760–1840' (PhD thesis, University of Toronto, 1999), ch. 2.

20 King, 'Punishing Assault'; Smith, 'State and Culture of Violence', 281–304; Norma Landau, 'Indictment for Fun and Profit: A Prosecutor's Reward at Eighteenth-Century Quarter Sessions', *Law and History Review*, 17, 3 (1999), 507–36.

21 Guildhall Library Manuscripts, MS 8959.

22 London Metropolitan Archives [LMA], Guildhall Justice Room Minute Book, CLA/005/01/002, 18 November, 1761.

23 LMA, CLA/005/01/048, 6 April 1791.

24 Conley, *Unwritten Law*, 49.

25 The National Archive [TNA] KB 1/22 Michaelmas, 20 Geo. III, No. 1, pt. 2, Affidavit of Elanor Hurley.

26 Emsley, *Crime and Society*, 48–9; V.A.C. Gatrell and T.B. Hadden, 'Criminal Statistics and their Interpretation', in E.A. Wrigley (ed.), *Nineteenth-Century Society: Essays in the Use of Quantitative Methods for the Study of Social Data* (Cambridge: Cambridge University Press, 1972), 336–96; Wiener, *Men of Blood*, 255–88.

27 *Reports to the Secretary of State for the Home Department on the State of the Law Relating to Brutal Assaults, &c.*, Parliamentary Papers [PP], 1875, LXI, 12.

28 Wiener, *Men of Blood*, 288.

29 Richard Burn, *Justice of the Peace and the Parish Officer*, 22nd edn (1814), I, 181.

30 For an example of the court condoning the 'violent beating & abusing' of a baker's servant by his master for 'neglecting ye Business', see LMA, CLA/005/01/003, 3 May, 1762.

31 LMA, CLA/005/01/048, 28 April, 1791.

32 LMA, CLA/005/01/003, 6 May, 1762 (Abrahams); CLA/005/01/018, 17 September 1782 (Simpson).

33 LMA, CLA/005/01/002, 17 November 1761 (Rottam). See also the case of Alexander English whose wife's assault charge was dismissed by the magistrate on their agreement to separate and on his promise to 'allow her 5s. a week' (CLA/005/01/018, 10 September 1782).

34 Public Record Office [TNA] KB 1/29 Hilary 38 Geo. III, pt. 2 (1798), Affidavit of Sarah Kingsworth.

35 LMA, CLA/047/LJ/06/009 9 (September 1829), Alfred Alfredius v. Margaret Alfredius. She was convicted, fined 1s. and committed to jail until the fine was paid.

36 16 & 17 Vict., c. 30. Hammerton, *Cruelty and Companionship*, 27, 59–62.

37 Frances Power Cobbe, 'Wife Torture in England', *Contemporary Review*, (April, 1878).

38 41 & 42 Vict., c. 19.

39 Hammerton, *Cruelty and Companionship*, 52–67; Wiener, 'Victorian Criminalization of Men', *passim*; idem, *Men of Blood*, 3.

40 LMA, CLA/005/01/0056, 21 March 1796.

41 Shoemaker, 'Male Honour', 205–6.

42 Landau, 'Indictment for Fun and Profit', 517–20, 525–33.
43 Norma Landau, *The Justices of the Peace, 1679–1760* (Berkeley, CA: University of California Press, 1984), 173–4; King, *Crime, Justice*, 86; Smith, 'State and Culture of Violence', 70–81.
44 LMA, CLA/005/01/018, 23 September 1782.
45 Richard Burn, *The Justice of the Peace and Parish Officer*, 2nd edn (1756), II: 425. The same advice was still appearing in the early nineteenth century. See Burn, *Justice of the Peace*, 22nd edn (1814), III, 185.
46 King, 'Punishing Assault', 46; Smith, 'State and Culture of Violence', 292–8; Landau, 'Indictment for Fun and Profit', 521, 527.
47 The Act, 43 Geo. III, c. 58, was dubbed Lord Ellenborough's Act after its principal sponsor.
48 Sir William Blackstone, *Commentaries on the Laws of England* (Oxford: Clarendon Press, 1765–9), IV, 217.
49 Landau, 'Indictment for Fun and Profit', *passim*; Beattie, *Crime and the Courts*, 76; King, 'Punishing Assault', 49.
50 PP 1819 viii, 84.
51 LMA, CLA/005/01/051, 16 June 1792.
52 LMA/CLA/004/02/001, Mansion House Justice Room, 24 November 1784; 1 December 1784; CLA/004/02/069, 16 December 1802; CLA/005/01/033, 6 November 1786.
53 Donna T. Andrew, 'The London Press and Public Apologies in Eighteenth-Century London', in Norma Landau (ed.), *Law, Crime and English Society 1660–1830* (Cambridge: Cambridge University Press), 208–29.
54 See the records of the Mansion House and Guildhall Justice Room generally. Also, see Rachel Margaret Short, 'Female Criminality 1780–1830' (MLitt thesis, Oxford University, 1989), 105 for similar settlements in Bedfordshire.
55 Smith, 'State and Culture of Violence', table 6.3.
56 LMA, MJ/SR 4246, ind. 9, February 1831. It would appear that imprisonment with hard labour was used for particular types of violent offenders. When William Terrard was convicted of an attempted rape of an eight-year-old girl, he was sentenced to be imprisoned for six months in the house of correction with hard labour.
57 See Joel Samaha, 'The Recognizance in Elizabethan Law Enforcement', *American Journal of Legal History*, 25, 3 (1981), 189–204; Landau, *Justices of the Peace*, ch. 6; Shoemaker, *Prosecution and Punishment*, chs 2, 5. Landau, 'Appearance at the Quarter Sessions of Eighteenth-Century Middlesex', *London Journal*, 23, 2 (1998), 33–41.
58 Smith, 'State and Culture of Violence', 309–14.
59 Blackstone, *Commentaries* IV, 357. Blackstone was quoting from Beccaria's *On Crimes and Punishments* (1764), first published in English translation in 1767.
60 Smith, 'State and Culture of Violence', table 6.3.
61 Even the rural JP Richard Wyatt was turning to imprisonment as a suitable punishment for assault. See Elizabeth Silverhorne (ed.), *Deposition Book*

of Richard Wyatt, J.P. 1767–1776 (Guilford: Surrey Record Society, 1978), 22, no. 116, case of George King.

62 King, 'Punishing Assault', 68.

63 Ibid., 50–2.

64 Malicious shooting 'in a dwelling house or other place' was covered under the infamous Black Act 1723, 9 Geo. II, c. 22, s.1. For other legislation regulating the use of firearms, see 5 Geo. IV, c. 83, Vagrancy Act 1824; 9 Geo. IV, c. 69, Night Poaching Act 1828; 1 & 2 Will. IV, c. 32, Game Act 1831. Ellenborough's 1803 Act was officially styled the 'Malicious Shooting Bill' during its progress through Parliament.

65 43 Geo. III, c. 58 (1803); 9 Geo. IV, c. 31 (1828).

66 Act for the Better Prevention of Aggravated Assault Upon Women and Children 1853 (16 Vict. c. 30); Criminal Law Amendment Act 1861 (24 & 25 Vict. c. 95); Offences Against the Person Act 1861 (24 & 25 Vict. c. 100); Infant Life Protection Act 1872 (35 & 36 Vict., c. 38).

67 26 & 27 Vict., c. 44; Rob Sindall, 'The London Garotting Panics of 1852 and 1862', *Social History*, 12 (1987), 351–9.

68 *Reports to the Secretary of State for the Home Department on the State of the Law Relating to Brutal Assaults, &c.*, Parliamentary Papers [PP], 1875, LXI, 5, 6.

69 Ibid., 114.

70 Ibid., 12.

71 Beattie, *Crime and the Courts*, 609; King, 'Punishing Assault', 53. I will examine these changes in greater detail in my forthcoming book.

72 Joshua White, an American visitor to England in 1816, perceived a certain English reverence for the law which he felt helped to keep violence under control: 'Personal injuries dare not be inflicted with impunity', he noted, and 'individual rights, so far at least as they regard exemption from violence and assault, are most carefully preserved and protected.' Joshua E. White, *Letters on England: Comprising Descriptive Scenes; with remarks on the State of Society, Domestic Economy, Habits of the People, and Conditions of the Manufacturing Classes Generally. Interspersed with Miscellaneous Observations and Reflections* (Philadelphia: William Fry, 1816), 320.

Further reading

In addition to the works cited in the notes, the following studies examine other aspects of the history of violent crime in eighteenth- and nineteenth-century England:

Amussen, Susan D. (1995) 'Punishment, Discipline and Power: The Social Meanings of Violence in Early Modern England', *Journal of British Studies*, 34 (1): 1–34.

Andrew, Donna T. (1980) 'The Code of Honour and its Critics: the Opposition to Duelling in England, 1700–1850', *Social History*, 5 (3): 409–34.

Beattie, J.M. (2001) *Policing and Punishment in London, 1660–1750: Urban Crime and the Limits of Terror*. Oxford: Oxford University Press.

Carroll, Stuart (ed.) (2007) *Cultures of Violence: Interpersonal Violence in Historical Perspective*. Basingstoke: Palgrave Macmillan.

Clark, Anna (1987) *Women's Silence, Men's Violence: Sexual Assault in England, 1770–1845*. London: Pandora.

Clark, Anna (1992) 'Humanity or Justice? Wifebeating and the Law in the Eighteenth and Nineteenth Centuries', in Carol Smart (ed.), *Regulating Womanhood*. New York: Routledge, 187–206.

Cockburn, J.S. (1994) 'Punishment and Brutalization in the English Enlightenment', *Law and History Review*, 12 (1): 155–79.

Conley, Carolyn A. (1986) 'Rape and Justice in Victorian England', *Victorian Studies*, 29 (4): 519–36.

Davis, Jennifer (1980) 'The London Garotting Panic of 1862: A Moral Panic and the Creation of a Criminal Class in Mid-Victorian England', in V.A.C. Gatrell, Bruce Lenman and Geoffrey Parker (eds), *Crime and the Law: The Social History of Crime in Western Europe since 1500*. London: Europa, 190–213.

Doody, Margaret (1984) '"Those Eyes Are Made So Killing": Eighteenth-Century Murderesses and the Law', *Princeton University Library Chronicle*, 46: 49–80.

Edelstein, Laurie (1998) 'An Accusation Easily to Be Made? Rape and Malicious Prosecution in Eighteenth-Century England', *American Journal of Legal History*, 42 (4): 351–90.

Forbes, Thomas R. (1977) 'Inquests into London and Middlesex Homicides, 1673–1782', *Yale Journal of Biology and Medicine*, 50: 207–20.

Forbes, Thomas R. (1978) 'Crowner's Quest', *Transactions of the American Philosophical Society*, 68 (1): 5–52.

Gatrell, V.A.C. (1990) 'Crime, Authority and the Policeman-State', in F.M.L. Thompson (ed.), *Cambridge Social History of Britain 1750–1950. Volume 3: Social Agencies and Institutions*. Cambridge: Cambridge University Press, 243–311.

Gatrell, V.A.C. (1994) *The Hanging Tree. Execution and the English People 1770–1868*. Oxford: Oxford University Press.

Gilmour, Ian (1992) *Riot, Rising and Revolution: Governance and Violence in Eighteenth-Century England*. London: Pimlico.

Gurr, T.R. (1981) 'Historical Trends in Violent Crime: A Critical Review of the Evidence', *Crime and Justice: An Annual Review of Research*, 3: 295–353.

Hair, P.E.H. (1971) 'Deaths from Violence in Britain: A Tentative Secular Survey', *Population Studies*, 25 (1): 5–24.

Hindle, Steve (1996) 'The Keeping of the Public Peace', in Paul Griffiths, Adam Fox and Steve Hindle (eds), *The Experience of Authority in Early Modern England*. London: Macmillan, 213–48.

Jackson, Mark (1996) *New-Born Child Murder: Women, Illegitimacy and the Courts in Eighteenth-Century England*. Manchester: Manchester University Press.

Jackson, Mark (ed.) (2002) *Infanticide: Historical Perspectives on Child Murder and Concealment, 1550–2000*. Aldershot: Ashgate.

Johnson, Eric A. and Eric H. Monkkonen (1996) *The Civilization of Crime: Violence in Town and Country since the Middle Ages*. Urbana and Chicago, IL: University of Illinois Press.

King, Peter (2006) *Crime and Law in England, 1750–1840: Remaking Justice from the Margins*. Cambridge: Cambridge University Press.

MacDonald, Michael (1986) 'The Secularization of Suicide in England 1660–1800', *Past and Present*, 111: 50–100.

MacDonald, Michael and Terrence R. Murphy (1990) *Sleepless Souls. Suicide in Early Modern England*. Oxford: Oxford University Press.

McGowen, Randall (1989) 'Punishing Violence, Sentencing Crime', in Nancy Armstrong and Leonard Tennenhouse (eds.), *The Violence of Representation: Literature and the History of Violence*. London: Routledge.

McGowen, Randall (1994) 'Civilizing Punishment: The End of the Public Execution in England', *Journal of British Studies*, 33: 257–82.

Malcolmson, R.W. (1977) 'Infanticide in the Eighteenth Century', in J.S. Cockburn (ed.), *Crime in England, 1550–1800*. Princeton, NJ: Princeton University Press, 187–209.

May, Allyson N. (1995) '"She at First Denied It": Infanticide Trials at the Old Bailey', in Valerie Frith (ed.), *Women and History: Voices of Early Modern England*. Toronto: Coach House Press, 19–49.

May, Margaret (1979) 'Violence in the Family: An Historical Perspective', in K.P. Martin (ed.), *Violence in the Family*. New York: John Wiley & Sons, 135–68.

Philips, David (1977) *Crime and Authority in Victorian England*. London: Croom Helm.

Rudé, George (1985) *Criminal and Victim: Crime and Society in Early Nineteenth Century England*. Oxford: Oxford University Press.

Ruff, Julius R. (2001) *Violence in Early Modern Europe, 1500–1800*. Cambridge: Cambridge University Press.

Sharpe, J.A. (1981) 'Domestic Homicide in Early Modern England', *Historical Journal*, 24 (1): 29–48.

Sharpe, J.A. (1984) *Crime in Early Modern England 1550–1750*. London: Longman.

Shoemaker, Robert (1991) *Prosecution and Punishment: Petty Crime and the Law in London and Rural Middlesex*. Cambridge: Cambridge University Press.

Shoemaker, Robert (1999) 'Reforming Male Manners: Public Insult and the Decline of Violence in London, 1660–1740', in Tim Hitchcock and Michele Cohen (eds), *English Masculinities, 1660–1800*. London: Longman.

Shoemaker, Robert (2002) 'The Taming of the Duel: Masculinity, Honour and Ritual Violence in London, 1660–1800', *Historical Journal*, 45: 525–45.

Shoemaker, Robert (2004) *The London Mob: Violence and Disorder in Eighteenth-Century England*. London: Hambledon Press.

Simpson, Anthony E. (1988) 'Dandelions on the Field of Honor: Dueling, the Middle Classes, and the Law in Nineteenth-Century England', *Criminal Justice History*, 9: 99–156.

Sindall, Rob (1990) *Street Violence in the Nineteenth Century: Media Panic or Real Danger?* Leicester: Leicester University Press.

Smith, Greg T., (2007) 'Expanding the Compass of Domestic Violence in the Hanoverian metropolis', *Journal of Social History*, 41: 31–54.

Spierenburg, Pieter (1998) 'Masculinity, Violence and Honor: An Introduction', in Pieter Spierenburg (ed.), *Men and Violence: Gender, Honor, and Rituals in Modern Europe and America*. Columbus, OH: Ohio State University Press, 1–36.

Thompson, E.P. (1972) '"Rough Music": Le Charivari anglais', *Annales: Economies, Sociétés, Civilisations*, 27 (2): 285–312.

Tilly, Charles (1969) 'Collective Violence in European Perspective', in H.D. Graham and Ted Robert Gurr (eds), *Violence in America*. Toronto: Bantam, 5–34.

Tomes, Nancy (1978) 'A "Torrent of Abuse": Crimes of Violence between Working-Class Men and Women in London, 1840–1875', *Journal of Social History*, 3: 328–45.

Walkowitz, Judith (1992) *City of Dreadful Delight: Narratives of Sexual Danger in Late-Victorian London*. Chicago: University of Chicago Press.

Wiener, Martin (1998) 'The Victorian Criminalization of Men', in Pieter Spierenburg (ed.), *Men and Violence: Gender, Honor, and Rituals in Modern Europe and America*. Columbus, OH: Ohio State University Press, 197–212.

Wood, J. Carter (2003) 'It's a Small World After All? Reflections on Violence in Comparative Perspectives', in B. Godfrey, C. Emsley and G. Dunstall (eds), *Comparative Histories of Crime*. Cullompton: Willan, 36–52.

Wood, J. Carter (2004) *Violence and Crime in Nineteenth-Century England: The Shadow of Our Refinement*. London: Routledge.

Zedner, Lucia (1991) *Women, Crime, and Custody in Victorian England*. Oxford: Oxford University Press.

Chapter 8

Atonement and domestic homicide in late Victorian Scotland

Carolyn A. Conley

By 1867 Scotland had been part of the United Kingdom of Great Britain for over a century and a half and in many ways the Scots had accepted their identity as Britons. However, according to Article XIX of the Treaty of Union of 1707, the Scots had kept their own judicial system and laws.[1] The Union also left the Scots with their distinctive state religion. Scotland also had a stronger and broader tradition of education. Domestic homicide trials in Scotland reflected the distinctive aspects of the country's institutions. Scottish criminal procedures differed from those of the English system. Instead of a coroner's jury, homicide investigations were begun by the Procurator Fiscal. The investigation was carried out in secret. If no charges were brought the details of the investigation were not disclosed. If the Procurator Fiscal thought that the evidence made a conviction likely then charges were brought and the accused was tried before a judge and a 15-man jury in the Scottish criminal courts.[2] A simple majority of the jury could render a verdict. Scottish juries also had three possible verdicts – guilty, not proven and not guilty. While the latter two both freed the accused, juries clearly felt the distinction was significant. In crimes in which more than one defendant was involved, the same jury might find one of the parties not guilty while the verdict for another was not proven. The not proven verdict would seem to have served two purposes. It reinforced the concept that guilt had to be proven, thereby protecting the rights of the accused. But the defendant who was released on a verdict of not proven returned to the community with a very different reputation than one who had been found not guilty. In practice, the not proven verdict also provided an option for juries in cases in which the defendant was probably guilty but not someone the jurors wanted to see as a criminal.

The traditions of Calvinism also influenced the courts. Scottish judges often spoke in terms of sin and atonement. The sentiments were made explicit in 1876 when Jane Docherty, a widow of good character, was accused of killing a man who had assaulted her. The presiding judge explained that 'the prisoner appeared to have been the subject of an unprovoked assault by a man who struck her a violent blow in the face and knocked her down.' Docherty had then grabbed a poker and struck him on the head. The judge explained that 'the crime was apparently not meditated by her, but no one could excuse, even under such provocation the use of such an implement.' But he insisted that the Scots law was merciful. 'If a woman was attacked by a man or struck violently and knocked down one would not be disposed to beat her again with many stripes because she yielded to an impulse of passion. It was not excused but the pain of imprisonment which she had already suffered (four months) went well to atoning in the way of punishment for the guilt which she had committed.'[3] Yielding to a passionate impulse was committing a sin and atonement was required, though the degree of atonement might be mitigated by circumstances. These circumstances were often influenced by matters of class (most often defined in terms of education) and gender.

Another trait emerging from Scotland's religious history is the faith in honest, reasoned discourse. Scottish courts preferred not to deal in euphemism. While quite willing to show mercy to those who had momentarily succumbed to passion, the Scots insisted on an honest accounting of the consequences of those actions. Pretence and appeals to sentimentality often met with a cold response. Further, the Scottish courts did not usually see drunkenness as an excuse for crime. Though alcohol might make it harder to control one's passion, the decision to become drunk was often seen as a rational one. In fact persons accused of committing a murder in Scotland while intoxicated were over twice as likely to hang as sober killers.[4]

The belief in atonement tempered by mercy as a response to an honest assessment of a crime influenced the Scottish courts as they dealt with domestic homicide cases. Cases in which the victim and killer were related either by blood or marriage made up between one-third and one-half of all homicide trials in Scotland between 1867 and 1892. If the count includes the killings of newborn infants domestic cases are 47 per cent of the total. If neonates are not included, domestic cases are 37 per cent of the total. The high percentage of domestic homicide in part reflects the fact that Scotland had a low rate of homicide. Generally the rate of family homicides tends to fluctuate less than other sorts of homicide so the lower the overall rate the higher the percentage of family killings.[5] But Scottish judges were probably unaware of the statistical pattern and frequently commented on how often they heard such cases. Minor children and spouses were the victims in over 85 per cent of homicides within the family.

Infanticide

The killing of a newborn by its mother accounted for over a third of all domestic homicides. Scottish courts demonstrated great flexibility in cases involving the murder of a newborn. Under English law cases in which a newborn was killed by its mother could be dealt with under the charge of concealment of birth – a crime with a maximum penalty of two years.[6] Even English judges sometimes acknowledged that these incidents were technically murders but juries were not willing to treat them as such.[7] In English neonaticides, jurors who believed the mother had actually killed the child usually had to choose between a murder conviction which meant a mandatory death sentence or the legal fiction of concealment of birth. Scottish law also had a concealment provision. Women could be charged with concealment of pregnancy.[8] However, Scottish courts showed greater flexibility than their English counterparts. In cases where the woman had deliberately killed the child, the Scottish courts were much more willing to accept the plea of culpable homicide, the Scottish equivalent of manslaughter.[9] Even in cases where the methods used implied intent, Scottish jurors were encouraged to return a lesser verdict based on the notion of diminished responsibility. For example, a woman who had given birth on a cattle road while on her way to work was charged with having violently thrown the infant to the ground and then trampled it to death. The defence argued that 'it may have been in her terror and dismay that she committed the crime.' The judge accepted the plea of culpable homicide, 'as counsel said at time of crime you were probably in great bodily torture and mental anguish and your reason not unlikely somewhat disturbed.'[10]

Of the 141 Scottish women tried none were convicted of murdering a newborn, but over a third of those tried were convicted of culpable homicide and 16 of them (nearly a third of the culpable homicide convictions) resulted in sentences of five or more years of penal servitude. Thirteen of these women had pled guilty to culpable homicide presumably because they feared a murder conviction. After the prosecution recommended accepting Elizabeth McClure's plea of culpable homicide in the death of her newborn, the presiding judge said that in accepting the plea the prosecutor had taken 'a merciful view of the case ... her conduct was exceptionally cruel, for the prisoner had cut her own child to pieces and thrown it into a loch. He should be wanting in his duty towards the protection of infant life if he did not send her to penal servitude for five years.'[11]

Scottish judges stressed that the offence was not simply the concealment of an illegitimate pregnancy. When Margaret Anderson, a domestic servant, was charged with strangling her newborn, she pled guilty to culpable homicide. The defence argued that 'she bore an excellent character, and had filled many good situations ... The courtship which preceded the seduction seemed to have been a bona-fide one and that was proved by the fact that her lover was allowed by her master to visit her.' The attorney also pointed out that she had not attempted to conceal the pregnancy but had gone to a lodging house to give birth 'in her despair and to spare her father's feelings'. Given her respectable character her suffering was more intense. 'Could it be wondered at that suffering severe agony both of body and of mind, tortured by the heartless betrayal of her seducer, the loss of her situation, and the knowledge that she had outraged the feelings of her father and friends, and her own shame she was almost beside herself, scarcely accountable for her own actions and was driven to this rash deed.'

But the judge rejected the argument. He insisted that this was not about concealing a shameful pregnancy, it was about homicide. 'I am not going to address you upon the impropriety of your conduct as a young unmarried woman having an illegitimate child; that is no matter concerning my duty. In that matter you may have been more sinned against than sinning. It is not for immorality of that kind that I have got to sentence you.' Instead the judge stressed that the sin for which she must atone was 'being an unnatural mother. Other girls have fallen before you, with more or less excuse, generally with a good deal of excuse, so that one would make allowance for their transgression. But unnatural mothers who violently put an end to the life which they themselves have given are, I am happy to say, of rare occurrence in this country.' The judge was willing to praise her choosing to give birth alone, 'I dare say you had good impulses upon you in trying to keep the thing secret – the respectability of your and your father's house. These impulses are intelligible enough;

but you brought forth a living child and put it to death. That is not a mere transgression of immorality in a young woman yielding to temptations.'[12]

Children

Scottish authorities were also unflinching in cases in which parents killed older children. Scotland had the highest rate of reported child homicide in the United Kingdom. It is probable, however, that rather than being more prone to filicide, the Scots were simply more likely to bring charges in such cases. In Scotland, the Society for the Prevention of Cruelty to Children was active and the press printed statistics on the Society's prosecution of cruel or neglectful parents.[13] Generally Scottish courts were more ready to interfere between parent and child than courts in England and Wales and gave heavier sentences to parents who killed their children. Sixty-six Scottish parents were tried for killing children between 24 hours and 14 years old. Though none were executed, nearly two-thirds were convicted of culpable homicide and over half the convicted served more than five years.

One of the most significant factors in determining the outcome of child homicide cases was whether the child had been legitimate. Killing a legitimate child was often seen as an irrational act. Nearly a third of parents who killed legitimate children were found insane. After hearing a case in which a woman whose husband had brought her home from a lunatic asylum had murdered her children, 'Lord Neames said it was a striking illustration of the injudiciousness of people taking their friends out of lunatic asylums before they are in a condition to be readmitted to society.'[14] Lord Neames' concerns would seem to have been valid. Often these cases involved mothers who were suffering from what would now be diagnosed as post-partum psychosis. In another case, a miner asked his mother to come stay with his wife and their two young children because his wife had not recovered from childbirth. Despite the grandmother's presence his wife murdered their seven-month-old daughter and attempted to kill the two year old. Her physician said, 'If I were told that she killed a child who was lying in bed by throwing it at another child of two years old I would think that it was not impossibility.'[15]

On the other hand, killing an illegitimate child was a rational act and never led to a verdict of insanity. When Helen Brown, a 24-year-old unwed mill worker in Dundee, was accused of drowning her two-year-old son, she pled insanity. Her attorney pointed out that Brown's mother was in a lunatic asylum and that Helen had been so depressed since discovering that she was pregnant again that a doctor had recommended she not have custody of her child. A physician testified that 'Pregnancy sometimes acts as an exciting cause to insanity.' But the prosecuting attorney argued that Brown's 'was an intelligible act and committed from intelligible motives by a person of some intelligence.' Nevertheless, the jury chose to convict of culpable homicide rather than murder. The presiding judge, Lord Deas, said the 'verdict was a very merciful one. Such crimes as that of which the prisoner had been found guilty could not be tolerated in a civilized country.' He sentenced her to only seven years penal servitude.[16] Though the insanity defence was not a particularly viable option for single mothers wishing to avoid conviction, Scottish courts might recognise mental distress as mitigation. In a case from Inverness in which a 19-year-old woman had drowned her toddler, Lord Kingsborough told the jury 'if they thought she was sane then the crime was murder, but on the other hand, if they thought her mind was afflicted by the unhappy treatment to which she had been subjected, it might only be culpable homicide.' The jury quickly concurred and Lord Kingsborough, noting that 'the verdict was a great relief', sentenced her to seven years.[17]

Still, the mothers of illegitimate children were often described as 'more sinned against than sinning.' When a 20-year-old domestic servant was convicted of drowning her child after being abandoned by her 45-year-old lover, the judge expressed his sympathy. 'The Court shrinks from sending a comparative child like you into penal servitude but suffering of an exemplary kind must be inflicted on you. I therefore sentence you to two years.'[18] Eighty-three per cent of Scottish single women accused of killing their children were convicted.

After insanity the most common cause in cases where parents killed minor children was poverty. The SPCC acknowledged the problem. 'On the whole it was only by thrift, industry, and sobriety that the majority of the people would be able to bring up their children in such a manner as was desirable in the interest of the whole community and until these qualities reached the lower circles of society they must be prepared to cope in the best possible way with the evil.'[19] The pattern of Scottish courts insisting on atonement but mitigating punishment with mercy could be seen in cases where homicidal parents cited poverty as their motive. Killing a child to escape poverty was a rational act – criminal certainly, but with extenuating circumstances. Not a single Scottish woman who offered poverty as an explanation for killing her child was found insane. This is striking since in England, Ireland and Wales married women who explained that they had killed their children for fear of starvation were often ruled insane. For example, Elizabeth Reid Jones, described as 'a poor, silly-looking woman', had murdered her two-week-old daughter after the husband deserted her. A physician testified that the prisoner 'was weak in mind and body and incapable of taking care of either herself or her children.' Nevertheless she was convicted of culpable homicide.[20]

Seventy per cent of Scottish parents who claimed poverty as the motive for killing their child were sentenced to penal servitude. In a typical case, Elspet Duncan, an unmarried domestic worker, had tried to find child care for her infant but the costs were more than her wages. She had begged the local constable's wife to take the child and then applied to the poor house but found no help in either place. In desperation she had drowned the child. Though the jury convicted her only of culpable homicide the judge said, 'The crime was murder. It is proof how dangerous it is to leave the path of virtue.' He sentenced her to eight years penal servitude. The sentence was heavy but in cases with almost identical circumstances courts in England and Ireland had convicted women of murder.[21]

Though unwed mothers were likely to be convicted and usually served long sentences, when both parents were involved fathers were more likely to be convicted of culpable homicide than mothers. Accused fathers were nearly 75 per cent more likely to be convicted when charged with killing a minor child than were mothers. Once convicted, fathers were also likely to receive longer sentences. The heaviest sentence given to a parent accused of killing a child went to Andrew Wallace, a collier in Ayrshire who killed his two-year-old daughter while in a drunken rage. He was convicted and sentenced to 20 years in prison. The only judicial comment was that he probably deserved more.[22] But a young unwed mother who pled guilty to culpable homicide after dashing her three-week-old daughter's head on the pavement and beating her with a stick was sentenced to just six years.[23]

Concerns with gender and responsibility may also be reflected in the outcome of the three cases in which grandmothers were charged with killing illegitimate grandchildren. Elizabeth Gillies was charged with poisoning her 19-month-old granddaughter. Gillies had kept the four illegitimate children of her daughter. The daughter told the court that her mother 'did not care much for the deceased child' and Gillies told neighbours and the police 'I am the criminal.' Nevertheless the jury returned a verdict of not proven by an eight to seven vote. The verdict was met with loud cheers in the courtroom.[24] In another case an Irish woman was charged with strangling her three-day-old illegitimate grandson. She had refused to allow her daughter to nurse the child because she wanted her daughter to work. The grandfather had said that his daughter could come home but he would not have the illegitimate infant in the house. Even though the judge charged for a guilty verdict once again the verdict was majority not proven.[25] In both cases it seems that the jurors were not comfortable with the idea that the grandparents should be responsible for the results of their daughter's moral failings.

The third case was different. Mary Boyd had stabbed her two-year-old illegitimate granddaughter but in this case the grandmother had been receiving support payments to keep the child but had insured the child for 30 shillings and filed for the insurance money two hours after the child's death. She also obtained a death certificate before a physician saw the child but the physician went to the police to report the stab wound. Boyd was convicted of murder though her death sentence was commuted. Grandparents were not held accountable for the support of illegitimate grandchildren, but trying to profit through murdering one was a step too far even for an elderly woman.[26]

Wives

Spousal homicides accounted for slightly over 15 per cent of all homicide trials. Scottish judges lamented that such deaths were common. Lord Deas complained 'I am sorry to see that savage treatment by a husband towards his wife is not uncommon. There is a great deal too much of it and the way in which these poor women are treated would wring the heart of any man that has a spark of humanity in him.'[27] For the Scots, wife murders were a social problem which threatened their perception of themselves. It was the sort of thing that foreigners or drunken workers might do. But it was not credible that a respectable Scot might be guilty of killing his wife. In three cases in which highly respectable men were tried for killing their wives the verdict was 'not proven'. In one of these cases the victim had been disembowelled while she and her husband were alone in a locked room and her husband was found to have two knives in his pockets. The family had always been respectable and the defence produced a great many character witnesses. The judge said that 'it was hard to understand why the accused could not explain what happened but a man of good character deserved the benefit of the doubt.' On leaving the court the public outside gave the accused another 'hearty cheer'.[28] When a 'respectable-looking engineer', was convicted of beating his wife to death on Christmas Day the presiding judge said: 'It was exceedingly difficult for him to pronounce sentence.' He consulted with another judge and as 'they were somewhat moved by the consideration that the prisoner being a man of education might regain his character the sentence was mitigated.'[29]

As one judge told a man convicted of killing his wife it was his duty 'to protect innocent life and weak and feeble women from having their lives sacrificed by such ruffianly hands as yours.'[30] But what constituted 'innocent life' and which husbands were ruffians were both still open to debate in the press and among the public. In an editorial, in 1878, *The Scotsman* assured its readers that 'brutality to wives is a survival to be found only in the lowest classes of the population ... What is wanted is to rouse and quicken in the class prone to wife-beating the sense of shame and disgrace already attendant in all round public opinion upon assaults by men upon women. These feelings of shame in respect of attacks by husbands upon their wives are non-existent in the class from which the brutal wife-beaters come.'[31]

Working-class Scots who killed their wives were nearly twice as likely to be convicted as men from the middle or upper classes. However, once convicted working-class wife killers were more likely to receive a light sentence. Judges seemed to believe that working-class men were less capable of self-control and foresight. In 1878, a common labourer in Glasgow was accused of punching and kicking his wife to death by rupturing her intestines. The presiding judge announced after the verdict that he felt 'it was a single, reckless act attended probably with consequences which the prisoner never anticipated and which were not so palpable at the time as to lead one to suppose that death would be the result.' Apparently, the judge intended to send a message to the working classes that by mastering their impulses they could improve their lot. He concluded his speech by noting that 'there were no more respectable people in the country than the working men if they behave themselves as they ought.' He sentenced the man to just 18 months.[32]

Alcohol was cited as a factor in over 75 per cent of Scottish spousal homicides. After hearing the trial of a wife murder which followed a holiday party, the judge noted, 'I am sorry to say that savage treatment by a husband towards his wife is not uncommon. There is a great deal too much of it generally attributable to that poison called whiskey.'[33] The same insistence on atonement and accountability also made Scottish courts unlikely to accept a verdict of insanity. Only 5 per cent of the men accused of killing their wives between 1867 and 1892 in Scotland were found insane and all of them were so seriously deranged as to be unable to even make a coherent statement.

However, issues of class had an impact as well. In a precedent-setting case in 1867, Lord Deas heard a murder charge against Alexander Dingwall, a well-connected man who had retired from the Indian Navy. Dingwall and his wife had both been hospitalised for alcoholism and though his estate had an income of nearly £600 a year neither Dingwall nor his wife were ever allowed to handle money. A lawyer in Aberdeen managed his finances and his landlord was entrusted with keeping an eye on the couple. On New Year's Eve, Dingwall had gone out and been able to obtain alcohol by appealing to the spirit of the holiday. When the landlord heard screams he ran to the Dingwall's apartment and found Dingwall sitting fully dressed and announcing quite calmly: 'I have murdered Mrs. Dingwall.' When the police arrived, Dingwall told them he had been provoked because his wife had hidden the whisky bottle and laughed when he asked for it. Since there was no question he had killed her, his defence attorney attempted to plead insanity. In his charge to the jury, the presiding judge argued that Dingwall could not be found insane; however, he suggested that Dingwall's intoxicated state could be an indication of diminished responsibility and indicated that culpable homicide would be an acceptable verdict. Dingwall was convicted of culpable homicide and sentenced to ten years.[34] The case is cited as precedent-setting in that it meant that even in cases where the legal definition of insanity was not met, alcohol and other factors might legally limit culpability in homicide cases.[35] However, the precedent was often ignored.

The defence of diminished responsibility seemed to be available only to the well-connected. A tinker who murdered his wife that same year while both were drunk was found guilty of murder and sentenced to death.[36] In another case, the judge announced 'he had no doubt that unlucky night when the prisoner was much intoxicated and [k]new little of what he was doing, he had no intention of taking his wife's life. But that did no[t] go very far to palliate the offence of which he had been found guilty. He had the want of manliness, as well as the inhumanity to strike his wife with a pair of tongs and a crowbar, utterly reckless of what the result might be.'[37]

Generally, men who were drunk at the time they killed their wives were eight times more likely to be convicted and five times more likely to be executed than men who had been sober. But in 1890 a case similar to Dingwall's had a similar outcome. A pubkeeper pled guilty to beating his wife to death. They had been drinking and he got angry because she failed to share her bottle of whisky. Explaining that his leniency was based on the fact that the couple had been happily married for 22 years but the wife had become a drunkard after he bought the pub, the judge sentenced him to just 18 months. Here, the lesser charge was allowed because the wife had 'been of dissipated habits and led her husband into dissipated habits'.[38]

While the Scottish courts insisted that criminals should atone for their crimes, they often allowed for the possibility that violence towards a wife might itself be a form of chastisement. As a judge explained before sentencing in one homicide case, 'there had been some explosion of temper for which in the first instance the accused might not have been to blame.'[39] A series of articles in *The Scotsman* in 1878 suggested that violence against women might be understandable. 'The criminal at the bar has often been goaded into his crime by provocations of domestic misery caused by his wife's faults. Which on review seem almost too much for a frail human nature to bear.' The editorial suggested that men who resorted to violence against wives who were drunks or scolds were not really criminal. 'It is only after putting aside cases like these that the devilry of brutes given over to drink and all evil passions is reached.' Finally, it acknowledged that occasionally 'decent, well-doing women' were mated with savage brutes but insisted 'Such men be few and exceptional.'[40] The Scots were not given to rhetorical flourishes regarding the plight of abused wives. In a letter to the editor a man asked, 'what would a husband be entitled to from his wife were he to prove that three times she pawned his effects for the sake of getting drunk. In short all this American style of sentimentality in regards to women's wrongs and rights is simply absurd.'[41]

Any sign of improper conduct on the part of the victim might be mentioned on behalf of the accused. In one case a carpenter had beaten his wife, who was nine months pregnant, with an axe handle because she was drunk and had not prepared his supper. The woman died five days later. In a post-mortem examination surgeons determined her death was the result of violence and that the beating was the direct cause of her death. Nevertheless, by a vote of 14–1 the jury ruled the charge of culpable homicide had not been proven. They did find him guilty of assault 'but unanimously recommend leniency on account of great provocation'. He was sentenced to 18 months.[42]

Provocation could be nothing more than irritating comments. *The Scotsman* warned of 'scolds, who without being quite abandoned to drink contrive to produce perpetual worry by the constant use of a bad tongue. The slatternly scold is often the terror of her neighbours and if her husband is a dull heavy fellow, his hands do for him some time or other what his head is unable to accomplish.'[43] In 1873, the defence attorney for a man who had strangled his wife pointed out that the victim had been given to drink and 'had the upper hand of spouse and an aggravating tongue when she drank.'[44] A man who remembered nothing about beating his wife to death with a brass brush admitted 'she had a bad tongue and I am rather quick in the temper.'[45] Even family members might blame the victim. After watching him beat her daughter to death with fire tongs, one woman explained to the police that her daughter had begun 'to flyte on the prisoner. She was casting up things to him and he got angry.'[46]

A woman's failure to meet the standards for a good wife – i.e. obedience, housekeeping and sobriety – mitigated the penalty for violence by the husband. When a labourer in Glasgow threw a paraffin lamp at his wife during a drunken fight, the lamp ignited and burned the woman to death. She had crawled under a bed to escape his blows and he used the lamp to look for her and then threw it at her. He had made no attempt to extinguish the fire or to rescue his wife. Nevertheless, after hearing evidence that the deceased 'was hardly a pattern woman', the judge sentenced the man to just 18 months explaining that he preferred 'to err on the side of leniency and was assuming that he had picked up the lamp with no intention of burning her.'[47]

John Young who beat and kicked his wife to death aroused considerable sympathy. His wife was 'a notorious drunkard who neglected her family and sold everything of her husband's property to buy drink'. When he found her in 'a house of bad moral reputation in company of a man who was the prisoner's own servant, Young, who was naturally irritated struck his wife a blow ... she died within minutes.' Young's character references included the chairman of the local magistrates who said he was a 'civil and obliging man whose life had been ruined by domestic trouble'. The prosecution pointed out that Young had also been drunk and that he had beaten the victim about the head and face for 20 minutes before she died. After the jury returned a verdict of culpable homicide, the judge expressed his own sympathy for the prisoner: 'You found her helplessly drunk upon the floor of a very bad home in company of one of your servants. That was enough certainly to arouse anger in any man and almost to deprive him for the moment of reason and that you should have struck her in those circumstances is not really greatly to be wondered at.' Young's punishment was light (six months) since he had already atoned for his sin. 'You did give way to passion ... therefore you must suffer punishment although the punishment which you have suffered at her hands and must have suffered since her death is greater.'[48] Even relatives of victims might accept that drinking a man's wages was grounds for assault. Robert Paul's mother-in-law asked why he was so hard on her daughter 'who never spent or drank his means'.[49]

Though Scottish juries sympathised with men driven to violence the requirement for atonement remained. No man in Scotland was convicted of murdering a wife who had been drunk or had provoked him. However, wife killers, even when provoked, were more likely to be convicted than other Scots accused of culpable homicide and husbands convicted of culpable homicide received higher average sentences than other male killers. Scottish courts shared the general Victorian assumption that masculinity depended on control of the wife and that female provocation might be beyond endurance. However, even when the victims were not 'pattern women' men who gave way to passion had to atone.

Husbands

There were over ten times more cases of men killing their wives than of wives killing their husbands. Even though in two-thirds of these cases the women had suffered years of abuse at the hands of their victims, wives who killed their husbands were almost inevitably required to atone for their guilt. Scottish women who had killed their husbands were over twice as likely to be convicted as women accused of other sorts of homicides.

But wives who killed husbands were treated less harshly by judges than men who killed their wives. All of the cases in which Scottish women were convicted of killing their husbands involved violent struggles and only one out of a total of eleven cases resulted in a murder conviction. Isabella Grant, described as a 'frail-looking elderly woman', had stabbed her husband to death. *The Scotsman* noted that the couple's domestic life had been 'extremely wretched.' Four months earlier she had been punished for hitting her husband on the head with a pot. 'After stabbing him she refused to offer any aid.' The presiding judge charged for murder and the jury voted nine to six to convict her of the full offence. However, the jurymen immediately signed a petition for mercy and her sentence was commuted to life in prison.[50] The only other sentence of more than ten years went to a miner's wife who was accused of murdering her abusive, drunken husband. He was found with a pick in his chest. She claimed he had threatened her with the pick and then fallen on it. There were no witnesses and the defence argued that the evidence was circumstantial and even if she had held the pick it had been in self-defence. But in this case the judge was not willing to give her the benefit of the doubt. 'It was not usual for murders to be committed before a human eye, if a man or woman was not to be convicted unless they had been seen to commit the crime by a human eye there would be an end to conviction altogether.' Twenty minutes later the men of the jury found her guilty of culpable homicide. The judge sentenced her to 20 years.[51] Of the other two Scottish women who were sentenced to penal servitude, one had used a knife and the other had set her husband on fire with a paraffin lamp. In the remaining cases, involving women who had struck violent husbands in the head with tongs, clothes-line poles, chairs or other household items, the sentences were less than a year and in some cases the women were allowed to plead guilty only to assault.

The courts recognised a clear distinction between defence and retaliation. As a judge told a woman who had thrown vitriol on her drunken abusive husband, 'You state that your husband was a very ill-living man. Were he one of the worst men in the world the law cannot permit you to retaliate in a way of this kind.' He sentenced her to five years penal servitude for the assault.[52] Guilty parties must be punished, even when the victim had been violent.

In addition to the cases in which women tried to defend themselves, there were two Scottish cases in which men killed to avenge the abuse of a female relative. The state's insistence on personal accountability was a cruel bind for those caught in a violent household. For seven years, John Curran, described by police as a 'quiet, sober man', had watched his brother-in-law Dennis McFayden abuse his wife, their children and Curran's mother. The police had refused Curran's request for intervention. After witnessing another round of brutality, Curran went home, got a knife and stabbed McFayden in the neck. Because he had told the arresting officer that his 'heart had been in it for seven years' the trial judge claimed that he was guilty of premeditated murder. The jury concurred and he was sentenced to death though the sentence was commuted to life in prison.[53] Even though the police were reluctant to interfere among family members, Curran had to atone for killing the abuser. The court was more sympathetic to Walter Battison who shot his stepfather when he found him kneeling on his mother's chest beating her face. He had aimed at his stepfather's arms but the bullet struck his lung. At his trial, the judge accepted a petition signed by over 1,400 people supporting his good character. Since the death was apparently an accident, he was sentenced to just twelve months to atone for his crime.[54] In similar cases in England and Ireland, no punishment was given at all.[55]

Other relatives

Only 13 Scottish homicides involved in-laws or step-relatives, compared to 43 involving adult blood relatives. Except for cases involving the defence of abused women, the homicides involving adults related by marriage all grew out of drunken brawls. The conviction rates and sentences were no different from those in drunken brawls between non-relatives.

In homicides between adult blood relatives there were significant gender differences. Even though Scottish women were the accused in 30 per cent of Scottish homicide trials, Scottish women were accused in less than 15 per cent of Scottish family homicides outside the nuclear family. Only two Scottish women were accused of killing adult male relatives and both were found insane. Of the six Scottish women accused of killing adult female relatives, five were convicted but not a single one served over two years. Since the cases usually involved drunken brawls, apparently the loss of the victim was not considered worthy of serious atonement. Jane Corrigan, a paper worker in Glasgow, was accused of murder for killing her mother 'with a hatchet, delft and a kettle'. Both the killer and victim were drunk at the time and the defence attorney pointed out that the room had been so dark that the prisoner had not been able to tell whether the items she was throwing at her mother were having an impact or not. She pled guilty to culpable homicide and was sentenced to ten months hard labour 'so she could become sober and industrious'.[56]

Almost all cases in which men killed adult male blood relatives also stemmed from drunken brawls and the sentences usually were relatively light. But Scottish men who killed adult relatives were actually over 50 per cent more likely to kill females than males. A quarter of these men explained that the violence had been punishment for lapses in behaviour or housekeeping. Women who were not submissive and did not perform housekeeping duties were liable to violence from the men in the household regardless of the relationship. When James Sandilands beat the woman he lived with to death because she did not have dinner ready when he got home, he was arrested and charged with killing his wife. Sandilands angrily responded that she was his sister. The exact nature of the relationship does not seem to have mattered to the court. Sandiland was sentenced to seven years for culpable homicide.[57] A widower who cut his female cousin's throat with a razor explained that he 'had been provoked to do it because she was teaching the children bad.'[58] Agnes Smith was beaten to death by her father and brother. According to neighbours, Agnes, who was 'frail and weak', had managed her father's pub. But the defence warned the jury not to convict a 'weak old sorely tired man who had made full atonement for the death of a favourite daughter'. The jury convicted both father and brother of assault only and the father was released for time served.[59]

Fifteen Scotsmen were accused of killing their mothers, more than twice as many as were accused of killing their fathers. Several had been provoked by the fact that the mother had been too drunk to attend to housekeeping duties. In a case in which a young man had kicked his mother to death because she was drunk and would not get up and make his supper, he claimed he was too drunk to remember what happened. The defence argued that the fatal injuries were the result of a drunken fall. The jury returned a verdict of not proven.[60] Two other men pled guilty to culpable homicide but were given relatively light sentences because the victims had been drunk. One labourer who had beaten his mother to death was given a lighter sentence on account of his 'excellent character' and the fact that the victim 'was a woman so addicted to drink that she made his home not so comfortable.'[61]

Drink was actually a factor in two-thirds of the matricide cases, though in different ways. When a veteran of good character beat his mother to death, the concept of diminished responsibility was again introduced. The judge said, 'the question to consider was whether it was possible, consistent with what was required for the vindication of the law, to stop short of a sentence of penal servitude.' He decided it was and sentenced the man to just 18 months.[62] Five young men had killed their mothers during drunken family brawls – circumstances which judges found particularly deplorable. After hearing a case in which a drunken 17-year-old was convicted of stabbing his mother to death in a drunken family melee on new year's day the judge 'said certainly no picture of domestic life could be more terrible that that presented in this case, and that it would be difficult for the imagination to shape a more sad and deplorable tragedy.' When the jury returned a verdict of culpable homicide the judges said it was a 'very merciful view of the case' and sentenced him to ten years. The sentence was clearly meant to be a time for reflection: 'During that time he had no doubt, the recollection of that dreadful night and the part he took in it would not depart from him. He was a young man now and when his penal servitude was ended he might have years before him. Let him see that he made good use of them.'[63] Like other Scottish killers, the young man could atone for his crime.

Notes

1 Known in England as the Act Ratifying and Approving Treaty of the Two Kingdoms of Scotland and England (6 Anne, c. 11). Regarding the Scottish legal system and its links to Scottish national identity, see Lindsay Farmer, *Criminal Law, Tradition and Legal Order: Crime and the Genius of Scots Law 1747 to the Present* (Cambridge: Cambridge University Press, 1997).

2 The Court of Justiciary was the supreme criminal court in nineteenth-century Scotland. It was located in Edinburgh but the High Court judges (like their English counterparts) went out on circuit to the assizes. The Court of Justiciary held exclusive jurisdiction over treason, murder, attempt to murder and rape. Though lesser offences could also be heard in Sheriff's Courts, the Court of Justiciary was empowered to hear them as well. All males between the ages of 21 and 60 with property to the yearly value of £5 were qualified to be jurors (6 Geo. IV, c. 22).

3 All statistics for Scottish homicides are based on the National Archive of Scotland (NAS) AD14 Records of High Court of Justiciary and the Minute Books JC8, JC11, JC12, JC13 and JC14 for the years 1867 to 1892. Case of Jane Docherty AD14 76/285; *Glasgow Herald*, 10 May 1876. Statistics for England and Wales are based on all homicide trials reported in *The Times* between 1867 and 1892.

4 Martin Wiener has pointed out that English courts during the nineteenth century were becoming increasingly less tolerant of drunkenness as an excuse for violence (Martin Wiener, *Men of Blood: Violence, Manliness, and Criminal Justice in Victorian England* (Cambridge: Cambridge University Press, 2004), 255–77). Since my study only covers the years 1867 to 1892, I am not able to say whether the Scottish lack of sympathy with drunken offenders was a nineteenth-century evolution. However, during the period 1867 to 1892, the average sentences given to persons convicted of homicide while intoxicated in Scotland were higher than those given

in English courts. For more on the comparisons, see my book, *Certain Other Countries: Homicide, Gender and National Identity in Late Nineteenth Century England, Scotland, Ireland and Wales* (Columbus, OH: Ohio State University Press, 2007).

5 Martin Daly and Margo Wilson, *Homicide* (New York: Aldine de Gruyter, 1988), 50 and *passim*.

6 43 Geo. 3, c. 58.

7 For example, see *The Times*, 8 April 1886, 12c or the testimony of Justice Stephen before the Capital Punishment Commission (*Report of the Capital Punishment Commission; together with the Minutes of Evidence and Appendix*, 291, [3590], HC 1866, xxi, 1).

8 Scotland Statute, 49 Geo. 3, c. 14.

9 Fewer than six per cent of neonaticide trials reported in *The Times* led to manslaughter convictions.

10 AD 14 84/280; *Dundee Advertiser*, 15 January 1884.

11 *The Scotsman* (Edinburgh), 10 June 1879.

12 *The Scotsman*, 18 May 1886; AD14 86/22.

13 *The Scotsman*, 16 October 1884; 21 February 1891.

14 AD 14 67/118; *Glasgow Herald*, 27 December 1867.

15 AD 14 76/67; *Glasgow Herald*, 4 September 1876.

16 AD 14 82/345; *Dundee Advertiser*, 12 April 1882.

17 AD 14 90/18; *Inverness Courier*, 9 May 1890.

18 AD 14 74/92; *Times*, 19 November 1874, 4f.

19 *The Scotsman*, 16 October 1884.

20 AD 14 88/118; *The Scotsman*, 11 May 1888.

21 AD 14 76/306; *Daily Free Press* (Aberdeen), 6 April 1876.

22 AD 14 74/92; *The Times*, 19 November 1874, 4f.

23 AD 14 76/171; *Glasgow Herald*, 31 March 1876.

24 AD 14 77/224; *Glasgow Herald*, 13 September 1877; *The Scotsman*, 13 September 1877.

25 AD 14 71/237; *Galloway Advertiser and Wigtownshire Free Press*, 11 May 1871.

26 AD 14 88/119; *Glasgow Herald*, 25 October 1883.

27 *Glasgow Herald*, 7 September 1881.

28 AD 14 73/23; *The Scotsman*, 24 April 1873.

29 AD 14 75/148; *The Scotsman*, 22 April 1875.

30 AD 14 87/74; *Glasgow Herald*, 24 February 1887.

31 *The Scotsman*, 12 April 1878. The assumption that violence towards wives was a working-class problem was also common in England and Wales. See Wiener, *Men of Blood* and Greg T. Smith's article in this volume.

32 AD 14 80/119; *Glasgow Herald*, 7 May 1880.

33 *Glasgow Herald*, 7 September 1881.

34 AD 14 67/192; *The Scotsman*, 21 September 1867.

35 Nigel Walker, *Crime and Insanity in England*, Vol. I (Edinburgh: Edinburgh University Press, 1973), 142.

36 AD 14 67/264.
37 *The Scotsman*, 19 March 1878.
38 *Glasgow Herald*, 28 November 1890.
39 AD 14 87/131; *Glasgow Herald*, 26 June 1887.
40 *The Scotsman*, 12 April 1878.
41 *The Scotsman*, 17 April 1878.
42 AD 14 72/127; *Glasgow Herald*, 24 December 1872; *The Scotsman*, 29 October 1872; 24 December 1872.
43 *The Scotsman*, 12 April 1878.
44 *Glasgow Herald*, 23 December 1873.
45 *Glasgow Herald*, 31 August 1882.
46 *Glasgow Herald*, 19 August 1881.
47 *Glasgow Herald*, 29 October 1890.
48 AD 14 86/216; *Dundee Advertiser*, 20 January 1886.
49 *Glasgow Herald*, 19 August 1881.
50 AD 14 78/244; *The Scotsman*, 21 June 1878; *Glasgow Herald*, 5 and 6 September 1878.
51 AD 14 73/363; *The Scotsman*, 26 May 1873; *Glasgow Herald*, 2 October 1873.
52 *The Scotsman*, 20 October 1882.
53 AD 14 83/2; *The Scotsman*, 13 March 1883.
54 AD 14 77/116; *Glasgow Herald*, 25 April 1877.
55 For Irish cases, see Carolyn A. Conley, *Melancholy Accidents: The Meaning of Violence in Post-Famine Ireland* (Lanham, MD: Lexington Books, 1999), 72.
56 AD 14 91/122; *Glasgow Herald*, 8 May 1891.
57 *Glasgow Herald*, 8 September 1878.
58 *Glasgow Herald*, 10 May 1892.
59 AD 14 82/319; *Dundee Advertiser*, 2 February 1882.
60 *The Scotsman*, 14 November 1882.
61 *Glasgow Herald*, 19 January 1886.
62 AD 14 85/88; *Glasgow Herald*, 20 October 1888.
63 *The Scotsman*, 28 April 1881.

Further reading

Breitenbach, Esther and Eleanor Gordon (eds) (1992) *Out of Bounds: Women in Scottish Society 1800–1945*. Edinburgh: Edinburgh University Press.
D'Cruze, Shani (2000) *Everyday Violence in Britain, 1850–1950: Gender and Class*. London: Longman.
Devine, T. M. (1999) *The Scottish Nation*. New York: Viking Press.
Ferguson, Rona and Yvonne Galloway Brown (eds) (2004) *Twisted Sisters: Women, Crime and Deviance in Scotland Since 1400*. Edinburgh: Tuckwell Press.

Lynch, Michael (1991) *Scotland: A New History*. London: Pimlico.
Smout, T.C. (1986) *A Century of the Scottish People 1830–1950*. New Haven, CT: Yale University Press.

Chapter 9

'A second Ireland'?
Crime and popular culture in
nineteenth-century Wales

Richard W. Ireland

The identification of 'popular culture' is, of course, a difficult business. The second word of the term implies a concept (or concepts) of learned and expected social practice and belief while the first component is tacitly oppositional – these norms are 'popular' as distinct from, presumably, 'unpopular' culture. The ambiguity of this latter term alerts us to some of the messages which lie hidden in our invocation of an idea of 'popular culture'. It speaks of both mass participation and also of dislocation from other normative systems, those of minorities or elites (individuals are, no doubt, excluded by the social context of 'culture'). But what are the qualifications for membership of that 'popular culture'? How firmly held, how universal do its tenets have to be? How inconsistent, if at all, with politically dominant concerns? Isn't 'popular culture' merely the academic gloss that we put on historical stereotyping? 'The Scots are mean' is an unacceptable statement. 'The nineteenth-century Scot showed a commitment to principles of domestic frugality' could possibly pass, supported by a couple of diary entries and a manuscript account book or two, as a statement (admittedly bad and, I stress, entirely a product of my imagination) of social history![1]

I have chosen, rather mischievously, to start with this idea of stereotyping because I want to explore some attitudes (generally, but not exclusively, of English writers) towards the Welsh in the nineteenth century, specifically in relation to attitudes towards law and order. Not the least significant aspect of the material to be considered is the bringing together of 'the Welsh' and 'the Irish' in discussions of crime. The next part of this article will reflect upon the factors which may have informed such attitudes, investigating archival sources to consider whether the Welsh records support the allegations of a specific cultural orientation towards criminality and its consequences. Finally, for the preceding two matters involve rather broad assessments, I wish to sharpen the focus a little and consider the participation of the crowd (often, though not unproblematically, taken as the manifestation of 'popular' consciousness) in nineteenth-century criminal trials and punishment. My reason for so doing is to stress the porosity of the boundary between 'official' and 'unofficial' penal realms, stressing the role of the 'audience' participating in, commenting on and sometimes influencing the nature of the performance of the law. Paradoxically, in this final section, though my sources are taken still from rural Wales, I hope to use them to ask a number of broader questions which have, I think, been neglected in many historical accounts of the 'penal revolution' which marked the century between 1777 and 1877. Not the least important of these questions is: 'Whatever happened to the execution crowd?'

'... and Wales'

With some notable exceptions, the most important of which is the pioneering work of David Jones,[2] the social history of crime in Wales has attracted little attention. It may be that the Welsh experience has been regarded as unique, to be left to its own historians and therefore exempted from discussion of more general developments in criminal justice history in the British Isles on that account.[3] But I suspect that another, rather different, assumption may also be operative, namely that there is nothing particularly distinct about that history and that the conjunction, so often to be found under statistical figures and tables, 'England and Wales', indicates a cultural homogeneity which renders separate consideration of the smaller country's position redundant. Neither the hypothesis of utter singularity from or utter similarity to its neighbours, particularly that to the East, will bear scrutiny. Moreover, I believe that in the history of the nineteenth-century transformation of the criminal process (with the changes in the mechanics of prosecution, trial and punishment, all of which were premised on an assumption of uniformity of treatment) the position of Wales, jurisdictionally the same as England, culturally different, is of some significance. It need hardly be added that the same essential tension suggests that to those interested in the space between 'official' and 'popular' perceptions of law and order a consideration of the Welsh evidence may be productive.

For those unaware of the political and legal history of Wales a few words will be necessary to explain its jurisdictional status.[4] Employing a variety of indigenous customary law in the Middle Ages, generally referred to as the law of Hywel Dda after a tenth-century king, Wales had seen some assimilation of legal process in 1284 after the suppression of the insurgency of Llywelyn ap Gruffudd.[5] Under legislation of 1536 and 1543 the substantive law applicable in Wales was declared to be the same as in England, though a distinct court, the Court of Great Sessions, exercised jurisdiction over a variety of matters, including the trial of cases of serious crime, until 1830.[6] Thereafter, in theory at any rate, the legal systems of the two countries were the same. In the views of nineteenth-century commentators there is an evident ambiguity when it comes to the Welshman's attitude towards the criminal law. On the one hand, Wales had a reputation, particularly among the judiciary who went on circuit there, for freedom from serious crime. The presentation of a pair of white gloves on a 'maiden' assize was a sufficiently common event to elicit fulsome praise for the Principality from the judges and to allow of a proud self-identification as a country largely unacquainted with felony, or at least with trials for felony.[7] On the other hand, Taffy was, poetically and axiomatically, both Welshman and thief, whose nationality by the mid-nineteenth century had apparently provided the English with a verb indicative of untrustworthiness in a bargain.[8] The words of one of the Education Commissioners, whose Report we will consider later, brought the two components of the stereotype together. The Welsh, said Jelinger Symonds, were 'peculiarly exempt from the guilt of great crimes', before continuing: 'On the other hand, there are, perhaps, few countries where the standard of minor morals is lower.'[9]

This apparent ambiguity concerning attitudes towards crime was connected to a wider cultural uncertainty. The Welsh, we have seen, were legally and constitutionally no different from their English neighbours. Yet in many respects the cultural differences remained marked, at least among those lower down the social hierarchy. The tradition of a separate legal regime had not been entirely overwhelmed and manifested itself in the popular belief that the 'ceffyl pren' ('wooden horse' – a type of 'riding' to punish the breach of social mores not uncommon in early modern communities both within and outside Wales) was sanctioned by the laws of Hywel.[10] More obviously the crucial indicators of cultural cohesion, language and religion, marked the Welsh out as something distinctly other than Anglophone, Anglican, Anglo-Saxons.[11]

The same could be said of course of the Irish.[12] It was unsurprising to find the Welsh compared to the Irish, and in particular when attitudes to law and order fell short of required standards. The starkest dislocation between ideal and reality in this respect was manifested in the serious outbreak of rural disorder which began in South West Wales in 1839 and lasted until 1844. Taking its name from a biblical character, the Rebecca Riots were immediately provoked by unease over road tolls but drew upon a much wider rural discontent which embraced the operation of the legal system and the New Poor Law.[13] It was the Home Secretary, James Graham, who had voiced the fears that Wales might then become 'a second Ireland'.[14] The same idea clearly troubled a local estate manager, recently appointed from England, who wrote to his brother in December 1843 that 'Wales is still an agitated country and I fear it will too likely remain so, and we think it getting more and more like Ireland *daily*'.[15] The archetypal Rebecca attack, with its torches and costumes, was rooted in the *ceffyl pren* tradition which had itself been described in evidence to the Commission on the Constabulary in 1839 in terms which raised the spectre of disorder further West: 'The principle is perfectly Irish, and though the practice falls short of the manners of that country in atrocity, it equally contains the germ of resistance to local order.'[16] This attitude towards authority, according to the author ('F.P.C.') of a remarkable essay 'The Celt of Wales and the Celt of Ireland' written nearly forty years later, was rooted in a shared ethnic deficiency:

> To an Anglo-Saxon living in a Celtic country it always appears that there is an unaccountable lack among his neighbours of the spirit so familiar to him at home, which cannot rest till *justice be done* – till a crime be detected or encroachment resisted, or any act of oppression exposed and stopped. On the contrary, of such abstract sentiments as these he perceives no trace; but every *personal* consideration of kinship, friendship, common sectarianism, or politics, are freely and even unblushingly cited as motives for neglecting or overriding justice.[17]

Later he adds, in the context of an attitude to domestic arrangements, the more general assertion that 'The fact seems to be that a Rule, even if he had a voice in making it, is, to the Celt, *per se* a hateful thing to be broken at once. So far from being "law-abiding" like the Saxon, the Celt cannot abide a law.'[18] Lest it should be thought that the Irish parallel is one employed in the nineteenth century only by English commentators, it should be pointed out that it is to be found also at times within the Welsh press.[19]

Yet if the Rebecca disturbances were important in suggesting parallels between the Welsh and the Irish in respect of their attitudes to public order in the 1840s, other events in the same decade served to make the relationship between nationality and crime rather more complex. The highly critical *Report of the Education Commissioners* of 1847, which a great many Welsh people saw as a calumny upon the morality of their kind, had, I believe, an important effect on the relationship between Wales and England in respect of the enforcement of the criminal law. I have argued elsewhere that this 'Brad y Llyfrau Gleision' ('Treachery of the Blue Books'), as it came to be known, may have helped to maintain, or even harden, a reluctance to bring offences, and in particular offences of a 'moral character', before the courts of law. To have done so would have been to bring evidence of vice against a community, not simply an individual.[20] In respect of the relationship between Wales and Ireland, the Famine, which deposited large numbers of poor Irish people in Wales, seems to have helped promote a self-supporting definition of Welshness which placed the blame for such criminality as was conceded upon outsiders. As Paul O'Leary argues:

> In order to strengthen its own identity after the strictures of the Education Reports of 1847, Nonconformist Wales needed to be able to point to a group which personified the opposite of everything it purported to stand for. By unhappy coincidence, the Great Famine deposited large numbers of destitute men and women on Welsh shores just as the heated controversy was getting under way, and they fitted the polemicists' bill.[21]

The Irish were portrayed, in particular, as being at the heart of the vagrancy problem in Wales.[22] They certainly did appear in court charged with a range of offences. In Carmarthenshire, the county which I have studied most closely, somewhere around 8 per cent of those remanded for felony in the period 1844–71 were reckoned to have been born in Ireland,[23] although this was held to be a county generally much less 'infected' by immigration than the industrial areas of North East and South East Wales.[24] Defendants who spoke Irish could further complicate the linguistic complexity of a Welsh trial,[25] while the Chaplain of the Carmarthen Gaol expressed himself pleased to have received no fewer than six copies of the New Testament in

Irish for the use of inmates in 1875.[26] It should be pointed out that statistical evidence of the number of any particular group prosecuted for, or punished for, crime is no safe indicator of differential involvement in criminality, but may be evidence only of a differential employment of the criminal justice system in response to it.[27] Nor do I think the argument that the self-identification of Wales, or perhaps *real* Wales, as relatively innocent of crime is incompatible with the bringing together of the Irish and Welsh as similar in their respect to order. The paradoxes of the Welsh experience of criminality are here again being exploited to serve rather larger rhetorics around national identity. Save perhaps in the hands of a committed Celtophobe like 'F.P.C.' the argument would seem to be that the Welsh are generally good. It is only when they are bad that they resemble the Irish! An internal refinement of the position is that those who are bad in Wales may not even be *really* Welsh at all.

Rhetoric and reality

An attempt to go behind the stereotype and to investigate the 'real' levels of crime in nineteenth-century Wales and the attitudes of 'the people' thereto is an enterprise fraught with difficulty. If we restrict our survey for a moment to offences which feature prominently in this volume as a whole, crimes of violence, then David Jones's detailed analysis of the criminal statistics for Wales over the course of the nineteenth century would seem to offer support to the hypothesis that relatively little took place, at least at the more serious end of the scale.[28] My own work on Carmarthenshire in South West Wales, upon which this article will, for the most part be based, though it reveals a routine procession of cases of common assault before magistrates, shows the cases of violent felony over a period of nearly thirty years almost buried in the routine catalogue of property crime.[29] There is a range of offences relating to the deaths of others, though not all allege deliberate violence, which do come to court but for which it is exceptionally difficult to secure a conviction. These are offences concerning neonatal or young children.[30] Serious violent crime, and particularly that resulting in conviction, was, apparently, not particularly common.

I want to leave to one side for a while my deeply held conviction that an undue emphasis on the serious (it is tempting to say the 'glamorous') end of the spectrum of criminal behaviour has grossly distorted our historical narratives of crime and punishment.[31] Nor do

I wish simply to assert that official statistics tell only part of a story, for that should be more than obvious to all who read this volume. Rather I want to explore, by using evidence primarily drawn from Carmarthenshire, some of the reasons English judges found their attendance at assizes sometimes little more than an occasion to hear a good Welsh sermon.[32] The following is not, however, a quantitative survey but an attempt to pursue attitudes. As such, as the introduction to this article suggests, it runs the risk of concealing the complexity of the particular behind the assertion of the general. It is a risk we will have to take.

There were instances of a communal failure to provide evidence, even in the most serious of cases. It was the silence, despite handbills in Welsh and English advertising a £50 reward and a pardon for accomplices in return for information, which followed the death of Ruth Jones in Blaencwm in 1851 which made the Tory, Anglican *Carmarthen Journal* turn upon the residents of the locality: 'That a foul murder has been perpetrated there can be no doubt, and that some of the neighbours are cognizant of the circumstances, which, if honestly revealed, might further the ends of justice, is also probable', before expressly invoking the familiar parallel with the 'Irish peasantry' and commending a Welsh translation of Mrs S.C. Hall's tale from Ireland: 'Do you think I'd inform.'[33] It is from Parry-Jones's 'internal' narrative of a similar event which did come to trial that we learn something of the social attitudes around the proceedings. While stressing that those who withheld information 'had no sympathy with the murderers', Parry-Jones reflects that 'the trial was in an alien tongue and men became mute as they thought of it'. He suggests, however, that an informal, financial settlement was a consequence of the event.[34]

This last piece of information is important. It is perhaps not too fanciful to see in this tale an invocation of the ancient legal tradition of the primacy of 'conciliation and compromise' as enshrined in the laws of Hywel. As Llinos Beverley Smith has suggested, such a tradition seems to have had continuing weight, extending at least into the sixteenth century.[35] But even if it *is* too fanciful the case at least alerts us to the existence of other, extra-curial means of dispute settlement in nineteenth-century Welsh communities.

There is plenty of other evidence to support the contention that an invocation of the law was not the only possible response to behaviour which might constitute a breach of it. Parry-Jones himself relates the potency of social ostracism, the men obliged to move to industrial areas for work and sociability invisible in criminal statistics and hidden within demographic ones.[36] Another Carmarthenshire memorialist, D.J. Williams, reveals that the Chapel could operate as a forum for arbitration, relating the consequence of 'a bit of a skirmish' in Rhydcymerau around 1873 when 'the scrappers were wise enough to keep clear of the court of law, But ... they took the matter to chapel to make it a matter of church discipline.'[37] He too had noted the linguistic and cultural distance from the assizes ('the judge, an Englishman, came on circuit, and in his armoury all the pomp and authority of English law imposed on the almost monoglot Welsh people'[38]).

The most dramatic form of both community judgment and punishment can be seen, as has been noted, in the survival in rural Wales of the *ceffyl pren* tradition. Rosemary Jones indicates a link not only with the tradition of medieval law but also with the chapel-centred community, congregations being told of proposed action as they assembled outside their places of worship.[39] Records show that the proceedings continued to be an integral part of social regulation at mid-century, indeed one which still apparently enjoyed widespread support. It was of course a form of activity officially incompatible with the law. In 1853, James Jones was fined and a further twelve boys reprimanded by the Bench on charges of riot after a disturbance accompanied by the blowing of horns outside the house of Gwenllian Rees. 'They intended carrying me' was her laconic explanation.[40] But the tension between the social and legal forms of process was evident in both directions, for just as the 'popular' judgment could receive its own commentary in the law court, so too could the process be reversed. In 1851, Elizabeth Gibbs was acquitted on charges of poisoning at the assizes. She was nonetheless burned in effigy outside her house on one night, and on the next a funeral procession made its way along her street, which had been given the new name of 'Scape the Gallows'. Gibbs took the hint and disappeared.[41]

This last case raises starkly another issue of importance in assessing the connection between 'legal' and more broadly 'social' attitudes towards criminality. The jury's reasons for acquitting Gibbs are not known, though it would be premature to assume that it necessarily meant that they simply thought she was not guilty.[42] Even if in this case the jury can, on one view of the subsequent events, be seen to be out of step with other 'popular' opinion (rather than possibly complicit with it) there are others where the jury's actions seem well attuned to local circumstances. I have analysed the material in detail elsewhere.[43] It suffices here to say that rural juries, sometimes unable to understand the language of trial, mindful of the danger of washing dirty linen in public and aware that, in a society in which shame remained as important a weapon as guilt, sanctions could be minutely regulated, gained in Wales a well merited reputation for (depending upon the point of view) 'independence' or 'perversity'.

Yet the role of the jury as representative of broader public attitudes is perhaps not too surprising. Less well explored, I think, is the role of 'public' participation in the trial process where juries are not involved.[44] It is clear that many summary proceedings were concluded by financial settlement between the parties, and sometimes evidence emerges that the process of encouragement of this outcome went beyond the covert or the merely culturally anticipated. In a case before the magistrates in Carmarthen in 1852, Amelia Thomas settled the prosecution after an intervention by 'kind individuals present'.[45] Not long before this there had been another example of the involvement of members of the public in a summary case, in which Margaret Davies's husband had been convicted of an assault upon her. 'At the conclusion of the ordinary business', the newspaper report reads, 'Mr Jeremy of Cwmdu, Mr Howells, and several other respectable farmers put in a written statement in Welsh, to the effect that the defendant was not to blame in the assault of which he was convicted, as the complainant had, owing to her bad conduct, been the means of "breaking her former husband's heart".'[46] This bizarre, but probably not unique,[47] exchange raises, I think, some interesting question concerning the interplay between official and popular participants in the Victorian penal system.[48]

Trial, punishment and the audience

Work by legal historians on what, for want of a better term, I will here refer to as the 'audience'[49] in the criminal justice system, those that is whose participation is not formally a part of the process, has been restricted largely to the role of the 'crowd', and in particular the execution crowd. While I do not wish to survey that body of work which takes the crowd as its starting point, it may be surprising to the modern reader to learn that Le Bon, the nineteenth-century pioneer of such work, chose to include the criminal jury within that description, indicating (in a similar fashion to the analysis offered above) the porosity of the membrane between the 'official' and the 'unofficial'.[50] The execution crowd has been the topic of particular analysis. Whether conceived of as a vicious mob or support for the condemned, as motivated by feelings of carnival or consent, all seem agreed that the execution crowd plays an important role in the

247

story of the history of crime and, in particular, in the account of the changing nature of punishment.[51]

Of the 'other' crowds, the audiences which attended trials rather than punishments, we hear much less, certainly at the level of analysis.[52] Moreover, of the crowd and its role in punishment when hanging became uncommon and then, after 1868, conducted only in 'private', we hear almost nothing at all. The 'execution' crowd, by definition, has gone. But was it always so utterly singular in the criminal justice system?[53] And what happened to its members? Did they simply go home to wait for the invention of television and *Big Brother*? Or, like good Foucauldians, did they shrug wearily in their acceptance of the interpenetration of discipline into the social body and agree to redefine themselves as objects rather than subjects within the carceral archipelago? It will perhaps be no surprise to learn that I will offer a negative answer to these questions. Again my comments are limited to experiences within Wales, particularly Carmarthenshire. While some of my observations apply particularly well to the cultural conditions of the Principality, some may have resonance further afield. On this matter I am not sufficiently well qualified to comment. But I want to raise the question here, for it is not simply the fault of Anglocentrism but also the more general distortion inherent in a preoccupation with serious crime which are the obstacles to be circumvented at this point.

Even after 1868 the arrival of the executioner in town to perform his now hidden task could still be the occasion of excitement, the 'great crowds' who attended to see Berry disembark from the train in Carmarthen in 1889 being only one example among many.[54] I should perhaps point out that this was the first execution in the county for sixty years and that the account that follows here is coloured by this de facto absence of public hanging for two generations.[55] My point is that even cases in which the penal stakes were relatively low could be mass events. They were played out before groups of formally, but not actually, 'uninvolved' observers. If we restrict the metaphor of the theatre only to the scaffold and restrict our analysis of audience participation similarly, we will miss an awful lot of important repertory performances.

Some of these were farces. In starting my discussion of the mass attendance at selected criminal trials with the case of Mrs Poole in Carmarthen in 1868 I am probably doing no more than indulging the same taste for the comic as drew the crowds in the first place. Mrs Poole, an 'electro-biologist', was prosecuted for commanding the 14 mesmerised subjects of her public performance to attack a sceptical newspaper editor who had arrived armed with a hat pin! So great was the public desire to see the trial that it was necessary to move the court to a larger venue above the normal courtroom.[56] I am sure that it is possible to offer elaborate analyses of the popular sentiment here, but for myself I am content to remark that in some cases the criminal trial could simply be understood as free entertainment. But it is not always so clear why particular trials attracted large audiences. Anne Matthews's trial in the town in 1849 caused great public interest and public attendance.[57] The case was in many ways unusual. The female defendant, charged with stealing items consigned to the post, was from a respectable family but evidenced signs of personal eccentricity. The offence, uncovered by a specialist investigator, was sufficiently serious to result in a sentence of transportation. It is difficult to know which elements were the most potent in turning this case into a cause célèbre, but, if I were pressed, I would be tempted to say that the combination of sex and class made Anne Matthews almost as exotic a specimen as Mrs Poole. It is possible that the interest the case provoked reveals simply the tacit cultural assumption as to what sort of person was the 'natural' participant in the criminal process.

Other factors seem to be at play in respect of the appeal of one kind of crime which seems to have drawn crowds to the courtroom, and indeed outside it. Cases of bigamy seem to have been among the biggest draws. It may be that the tales of seduction they often involved were titillating without being considered 'indecent' (as was the case in some prosecutions for concealment of birth where women were removed from the public gallery, the only examples I have discovered of attempts to control public access to trials[58]). But this cannot be the whole explanation for, as will be seen, the excitement extended outside the courtroom. Other forces seem to have been at play. Bigamy was, in origin, an offence against marriage and morality. Compulsory registration in the nineteenth century had made it, as Keating J told the Carmarthen assizes in 1867, one easy to prove,[59] for it had become, in part, an offence against bureaucracy. Had that not been the case it was, I suggest, the kind of offence which was traditionally well suited to the flexibility of the judgment and punishment (marital 'offences' were commonly the occasion for 'ridings') of the local community. It was one in which they might have found it difficult to abandon their role in passing judgment entirely, as the applause which greeted the conviction in the case just mentioned seems to suggest.[60]

It was not only within the court but also in the liminal space between that building and the county jail that Carmarthen's bigamy followers assembled. In 1851, Mary Callis, rumoured to be four times married, most recently to a local policeman, appeared for trial. 'Great crowds assembled around the Town Hall to obtain a sight of the prisoner and for some time the Guildhall Square was almost impassable and a large concourse of people followed the prisoner to the Gaol.' At the conclusion of the trial ('packed to suffocation'), Callis seems to have taken an active role in her resignation to her punishment: 'A very great crowd followed her to the County Gaol, on the steps of which the prisoner coolly turned to the spectators, thanked them for their attendance, and bounded into prison with all the agility of a young lady going down a country dance with an amiable partner.'[61] It is a simple spontaneous moment, perhaps unfitted to bear the weight of analysis, but the description reminds me just a little of the 'good deaths' of the bride or bridegroom-attired victim of the Bloody Code.[62] Perhaps a wider appreciation of the role of popular interaction with offenders has been partially concealed by the assumption that the 'last great act' of the law took place in an otherwise deserted theatre.

The Callis case leads us to consider more generally the role of the crowd and the prison. In what has become a modern orthodoxy the narrative of criminal punishment runs something like this: the old regime of the Bloody Code with its public punishment of the body is displaced (for reasons which various authors dispute) by the more regular and uniform punishment of the mind in prisons. Penality becomes essentially private, and its focus, its 'gaze', is primarily characterised as directed inward, to the offender. There is much truth in this shorthand account of the transition in punishment between the eighteenth and nineteenth centuries, though it is necessarily an oversimplification which can conceal important continuities and ignore other interesting dimensions of change.[63] But I want to consider the question of imprisonment a little further here, and in particular its relationship to its own crowd.

In one sense the crowd was always part of the prisons. The new, purpose-built (or rebuilt) institutions of the late eighteenth and nineteenth centuries, county jails probably even more so than convict establishments, were paradoxical monuments to ostracism in the heart of the communities they served. Their outsides were as architecturally considered as their insides. In Carmarthen the county jail dominated the town, appearing centrally in the topographical prints produced for and by tourists to the town. And the regime of prisons too was less than hermetically sealed from outside eyes, as rocks and rope were taken inside the gates and stone and oakum passed out. Even non-productive labour could be visible. The huge sails which rotated when the treadwheel operated could be seen above the perimeter walls of at least some prisons. In Carmarthen itself the rotating, life-size, pewter model of a prisoner attached to the wheel mechanism made the internal hard labour visible to the town.[64] It may have been this, or an earlier device, that the 'thimble gentry' operating at a local fair were shown as a warning before being moved on in 1833, not long after the wheel had been installed.[65] The spectacle of punishment was not, then, removed with the abolition of public corporal punishment. It had been made permanent and normalised. It is rather like the domestication of electricity, where the occasional bolt of lightning gives way to the constant glow of the 40-watt bulb.

It may be objected that this argument misses the point, for not only has the method of punishment changed completely but so too has the nature and role of the audience. Populations going about their daily business are not 'crowds' in the sense that we have been using that term in relation to executions. It is in that very difference, it may be suggested, that the significance of the penal transformation may be measured. But even if we accept that, the case of Mary Callis reminds us that specifically assembled masses of people drawn together to participate in the process of trial and punishment (even if we are to conceive of that participation as formally restricted to the level of observation and commentary) does not disappear with the pillory and the public execution. This fact was known to contemporary observers and it made them uncomfortable. The close proximity of jail and courtroom in Carmarthen led the local justices to investigate the possibility of connecting the two by an underground tunnel.[66] Elsewhere the use of the closed prison van, a vehicle now so familiar to us that we forget that it was once an innovative design, hoped to head off this possibility of an unscripted performance of 'popular culture'. It was not to be so easily circumvented. In 1847, the Governor of Carmarthen Gaol, Henry Westlake, waited up late into the night on two successive occasions for the arrival of a prisoner, Mary Hughes, who finally was brought in at 2.30 in the morning. Hughes had hanged her three children and the early reports made no mention of the insanity which was evident at her trial. It was, I have no doubt, the threat of the involvement of 'the crowd' in the events which led to Westlake's disturbed sleep.[67] A month later a drunken sheriff's officer, with whom the Governor had had an argument, apparently had no trouble in raising 'a mob of the lower orders' who proceeded to beset the jail.[68] The evidence adduced here is admittedly not vast, though I suspect more could be discovered. There is sufficient, however, to allow of the suggestion that participation in and around the institutions of trial and punishment is a tradition still alive in mid-nineteenth-century West Wales.

Conclusions

This article has dragged together a number of apparently different themes, linked by the almost infinitely elastic term 'popular culture' as related to crime. What, beyond the sometimes entertaining details of specific cases, can we take out of it which might be of any interest to those readers, and I am sure that they form the vast majority, for whom the legal history of rural Wales hardly demands a central place in their attention? A review of our findings may clarify matters.

Consideration of the position of Wales in the nineteenth century warns us against the assumption that social change and the paradigms of legal process which are linked with them did not occur simultaneously and to the same extent throughout the jurisdiction. Only an idiot, it might be thought, could argue otherwise. But to accept this as an intellectual proposition is one thing, to build it into the fabric of one's understanding of the process is something quite different. Rural Wales was not rural Devon and was not urban Manchester or metropolitan London. As new ideas, of policing and prosecution, procedure-governed trials, regular and predictable punishments and the like, are advanced and refined in the nineteenth century they are projected not onto a blank landscape but on to a variegated one. When one of the key tenets, I would argue *the* key tenet, of a reformed criminal justice system within that century was a movement towards a concept of uniformity within the jurisdiction, then this local variance becomes not simply a background to change or its recognition a motor for it. It also becomes a problem for that movement, as differences in popular culture become sites of resistance and contention.

In this respect Wales was a particularly knotty problem, or would be if it made its differences too apparent. It had done this in the days of Rebecca, but thereafter its divergence from legal and cultural norms was largely played out away from official scrutiny. It had different traditions, a different language and a different religion from those who made, and often enforced, the laws within it. Yet the differences in respect of law and order in Wales could be presented as unthreatening in their essence. The Principality's failure to prosecute crime could look very much like a freedom from it. Its allocation of guilt as general to the offender rather than specific to the offence might seem to be a result of perverse or ignorant juries rather than the assertion of another way of dealing with things. When it was caught out in these differences, however, Wales appeared rather alarming. English when it was good, it became Irish when it was bad. Cultural differences to those of the dominant political jurisdiction which were patent and problematic in Ireland were occasionally glimpsed in Wales.[69] Mostly, however, they could be ignored. In this respect modern legal historiography largely shares the attitude of nineteenth-century government!

Another regrettable tendency in the writing of the history of crime and punishment has prompted an exploration of the role of the popular audience in the second part of this article. The overemphasis on serious crime has led to many distortions in our understanding. The persistent but unsustainable assumption that incarceration is a modern punishment derives from it, for example, as does the historians' relative neglect of the fine, the bind-over and the licence as methods of social control. I have suggested here that, in Wales at any rate, intervention by 'unofficial' actors outside the courtroom and within it, in minor cases as well as serious ones, later in the nineteenth century as well as earlier, was part of a spectrum of activity available to persons not formally involved in the criminal process. It was not restricted to cases of capital punishment and neither did it disappear alongside it. It was, of course, to be officially condemned, as all encroachments on procedural fairness and uniformity were condemned. Even the jury, though politically inviolable, could be a little suspect as the extension of summary jurisdiction suggests. But the crowd remained, certainly in Carmarthenshire. An embarrassment it may have been, distanced by tunnels, vans and prison walls, but it was still waiting in the pub round the corner. Like the beer it was drinking, it depended upon a complex but persistent strain of culture.

Notes

1 This is no place to undertake a detailed investigation of such a concept. More subtle analyses can be found elsewhere in this volume and, for example, in Tim Harris, 'Problematising Popular Culture', in idem (ed.), *Popular Culture in England, c.1500–1850* (London: St. Martin's Press, 1995). My own views are addressed at rather greater length in Chapter 1 of '*A Want of Order and Good Discipline': Rules, Discretion and the Victorian Prison*

(Cardiff: University of Wales Press, 2007). My intention here is not to explore all the difficulties which inhere in the term 'popular culture', still less to resolve them, but merely to ensure that the reader is as worried about them throughout the argument which follows as the author is. Incidentally, it seems to me a little strange that the search for *mentalité* within historical analysis has survived so well in the current climate of fracture and individualisation promoted by postmodern critique.

2   See, in particular, David J.V. Jones, *Crime in Nineteenth Century Wales* (Cardiff: University of Wales Press, 1992).

3   This has been, I suspect, the general attitude to both Scottish and Irish criminal justice history outside those jurisdictions, although only the most blinkered commentator could write a history of policing or of prisons without some recognition of developments in Ireland as contributing to a wider narrative of development (see S.H. Palmer, *Police and Protest in England and Ireland 1780–1850* (Cambridge: Cambridge University Press, 1988); Shane Kilcommins, Ian O'Donnell, Eoin O'Sullivan and Barry Vaughan, *Crime, Punishment and the Search for Order in Ireland* (Dublin: Institute of Public Administration, 2004), 18–20). I think, however, that the antithetical assumption, of a lack of a distinct experience, is less marked in relation to those jurisdictions than is the case with Wales.

4   For a brief overview, see J.H. Baker, *Introduction to English Legal History*, 3rd edn (London: Butterworths Law, 1990), 30–1.

5   Statute of Wales, 12 Ed. I (1284).

6   27 Hen. VII c. 6, 34 and 35 and Hen. VIII c. 26. For the Great Sessions, see Glyn Parry, *A Guide to the Records of the Great Sessions in Wales* (Aberystwyth: NWL, 1995), Introduction.

7   For the rhetoric of the *Gwlad y menyg gwynion* ('land of white gloves'), see Jones, *Crime in Wales*, ch. 1; R.W. Ireland, 'Putting Oneself on Whose Country? Carmarthenshire Juries and Crime in the Mid-Nineteenth Century', in T.G. Watkin (ed.), *Legal Wales: Its Past, Its Future* (Cardiff: Welsh Legal History Society, 2001), 63–87.

8   The traditional verse is apparently attested first in 1780 (see Iona and Peter Opie (eds), *Oxford Dictionary of Nursery Rhymes* (Oxford: Oxford University Press, 1997) 477–8). The *OED* officially gives the etymology of 'welsh' as a verb as 'obscure', but records it as in use in the 1850s.

9   *Reports of the Commissioners on the State of Education in Wales*, 1847 [871.] xxvii Part II 56–7.

10 On the subject of 'ridings' and cognate practices in general, see E.P. Thompson, 'Rough Music', in his *Customs in Common* (London: Penguin, 1991), 467–538. For the Welsh practice, see Jones, *Crime in Wales*, 11–13, and R.A.N. Jones, 'Popular Culture, Policing and the Disappearance of the *Ceffyl Pren* in Cardiganshire c.1837–1850', *Ceredigion*, 11, 1 (1988–9), 19–39. The link with Welsh law is considered at 27. Compare also Parry-Jones's reference to 'tribal law' cited in Jones, *Crime in Wales*, 11, and for the contrast between 'lynch law' and the 'Old English Law' in the letter

from 'D' of Builth following the Elizabeth Gibbs disturbances (*infra*), see *The Welshman*, 4 April 1851.

11 I have discussed these differences at some length in Chapter 1 of *A Want of Order*.

12 I should perhaps make it clear to those unfamiliar with the subject that the Welsh and Irish languages, though related, are distinct, while the popular religion in Wales was Non-Conformism rather than Catholicism. Both countries of course had a politically important class of English-speaking, Anglican landowners.

13 For the riots, see, for example, David J.V. Jones, *Rebecca's Children* (Oxford: Clarendon, 1989); Pat Molloy, *And They Blessed Rebecca* (Llandysul: Gomer, 1983) and David Williams, *The Rebecca Riots* (Cardiff: University of Wales Press, 1955).

14 See David J.V. Jones, 'Rebecca, Crime and Policing: A Turning Point in Nineteenth-Century Attitudes', *Trafodion Anrhydeddus Gymdeithas y Cymmrodorion* (1990), 105.

15 C. Davies, 'The Rebecca Riots – Letters from the Front', *The Carmarthenshire Antiquary*, 40 (2004), 100.

16 *Report of the Constabulary Force Commissioners*, 1839 [169.] xix 44.

17 The piece appears in the *Cornhill Magazine* for 1877, 661 at 673. Italics as in the original.

18 Ibid., 677.

19 See *The Welshman*, 24 November 1877 reproducing the letter of Lewis Morris sent to *The Times* which *inter alia* commented on the potential of Carmarthenshire and Cardiganshire to have reached 'the level of Tipperary and Westmeath' following Rebecca, and the comments of the *Carmarthen Journal* following the murder of Ruth Jones in 1851, for which, see Ireland, 'Whose Country', 71.

20 Ireland, 'Whose Country', 78–80.

21 Paul O'Leary, *Immigration and Integration: The Irish in Wales 1798–1922* (Cardiff: University of Wales Press, 2000), 185.

22 See David J.V. Jones, '"A Dead Loss to the Community": The Criminal Vagrant in Mid-Nineteenth-Century Wales', *Welsh History Review*, 8 (1977), 317–18.

23 I have taken this figure from an analysis of the Felons' Register (Carmarthenshire Record Office, hereafter CRO, Acc. 4916). There are huge problems with this figure, however. It depends on accurate gathering and recording of information which cannot be guaranteed. It applies to instances (generally) of custodial remand rather than to separate individuals (i.e. the same person may be remanded on more than one occasion). Some records are incomplete.

24 Note the defensive position of some Welsh writers who regarded levels of criminality in these areas distorted by the effects of immigration (see O'Leary, *Immigration and Integration*, 165).

25 See the case of Bridget Dowd (*Carmarthen Journal*, 21 October 1853) discussed in Ireland, 'Whose Country', 77, n. 40. Three languages and two translators were used at trial.

26 See the Gaol Chaplain's Report for 1875 in CRO QS Box 20. The books were supplied by the British and Foreign Bible Society.

27 I mean, of course, that an inclination not to prosecute or to acquit might be lacking where 'outsiders', particularly those perceived as troublesome, were concerned. Such individuals may also have come more readily to the attention of the police, although the evidence, where available, does not always support these hypotheses, at least without some qualification. So, for example, the evidence from the diary of PC David Williams, 1857–8 (CRO Mus. 112), suggests that not all fights involving such 'outsiders' would necessarily result in prosecution; see, for example, 26, 27 December 1857. See too the comments of the Superintendent of Police to the Bench that 'there were disturbances almost every night Under-the-Bank [an area of Carmarthen] with a horde of Irish who lived in a most disgraceful and disgusting manner in a house in that neighbourhood' (*Carmarthen Journal*, 2 April 1852).

28 'It is not easy ... to make a final, definitive, statement about the level of violence in nineteenth-century Wales. The amount of homicide and grievous bodily harm was, when compared with the rest of the British Isles, low' (Jones, *Crime in Wales*, 101). Jones's analysis includes a discussion of regional and temporal variation in the figures of a kind not undertaken here. See too his statistical analyses of other types of offence. For a discussion of crime in Merioneth 1860–5, see R. Gwynedd Parry, 'Trosedd a Chosb ym Meirionydd yn Chwedegau Cynnar y Bedwaredd Ganrif ar Bymtheg: Tystiolaeth Cofnodion y Llys Chwater', in T.G. Watkin (ed.), *The Trial of Dic Penderyn and other Essays* (Cardiff: Welsh Legal History Society, 2002), 77.

29 For a variety of reasons, some practical, some intellectual, I have avoided the statistical analysis of the felony figures here. As I have suggested elsewhere ('Whose Country', 72) the seductive certainty of computer analysis is not always an unalloyed benefit to understanding.

30 For an analysis of the cases, see R.W. Ireland, ' "Perhaps My Mother Murdered Me": Child Death and the Law in Victorian Carmarthenshire', in C.W. Brooks and Michael Lobban (eds), *Communities and Courts in Britain 1150–1900* (London: Hambledon, 1997), 229–44.

31 Though the evidence just reviewed merits some thought on this score. It might be suggested that the more serious the offence the greater the consensus between 'unofficial' and 'official' attitudes might be. Let us leave aside for a moment the fact that any attempt to establish this proposition requires as much concentration on the less as upon the more serious offences. The evidence presented here suggests to me that a 'serious' offence like homicide can attract different responses depending on the qualities and behaviour (at the time and subsequently) of the

killer, the identity and qualities of the victim (child, spouse, lover, unpopular gamekeeper, local stalwart?) and the circumstances of the act. I see the same sorts of issues being considered important in cases of common assault and petty theft too. The issues touch the question of the extent of the 'wrong' involved, but importantly also that of the propriety of the response to that wrong. This is not to argue that serious offences should not receive our attention, or indeed that their relative gravity is incapable of acting as a significant variable in the response, but only that that attention be properly balanced and contextualised.

32 I wish to consider in particular here the cultural factors which may account for offences which were committed not resulting in successful prosecutions. It is no part of my contention that cultural factors had no effect on levels of offending in the first place.

33 *Carmarthen Journal*, 12 September 1851.

34 See D. Parry-Jones, *A Welsh Country Upbringing*, 2nd edn (London: Batsford, 1949), 98, and note that Jones remains, in his omission of details, complicit in the suppression he describes; see also Ireland, 'Whose Country', 86. Note also the discussion by Jones, *Crime in Wales*, 73.

35 See Llinos Beverley Smith, 'Disputes and Settlements in Medieval Wales: The Role of Arbitration', *English Historical Review*, 106 (1991), 839.

36 Parry-Jones, *Country Upbringing*, 134.

37 D.J. Williams, *Hen Dy Ffarm*, translated by Waldo Williams as *The Old Farmhouse* (Carmarthen: Golden Grove, 1987), 84. Compare the intervention of the Catholic priest in disputes in Swansea's Irish Greenhill district (see Jones, *Crime in Wales*, 9).

38 Ibid., 39.

39 Jones, *'Ceffyl Pren* in Cardiganshire', 23.

40 *Carmarthen Journal*, 3 December 1852.

41 *The Welshman*, 4 April 1851.

42 It is possible that the jury felt that the crime was more *appropriately* punished extra-curially (see the argument advanced in Ireland, 'Perhaps My Mother').

43 Ireland, 'Whose Country', *passim*.

44 Here and below, when discussing the 'participation' of the non-official actors in the trial process, it should be borne in mind that, although overt action by the public may be noticeable as an input into the trial process the mere presence of a body of persons, though they may appear passive or leave no trace of their activity, may still affect the behaviour of others involved in the process.

45 *Carmarthen Journal*, 9 January 1852.

46 *Carmarthen Journal*, 16 January 1852.

47 Compare the petition raised after conviction of David Thomas by a Glamorganshire jury in 1853, Gareth Hughes (ed.), *A Llanelli Chronicle* (Llanelli: Llanelli Borough Council, 1984), 47–9.

48 Among the more far-reaching speculation invited by considerations of such interaction would be the extent to which the existence of the 'new police' as a prosecuting authority might be changing a more traditional framework of practice of extra-curial compromise, or, on the other hand, the extent to which the prosecution is pursued or encouraged by victims instrumentally seeking to pressure defendants into settlement. The evidence I have is too slight to allow any claims to be made with confidence.

49 I hope that it will become clear that I conceive that the role of the 'audience' may extend well beyond simple passivity. Its presence alone is an act of participation, and that participation may extend well beyond that.

50 Gustave LeBon, *Crowd: A Study of the Popular Mind* (London: Fisher Unwin, 1897 edn), 158. Paradoxically George Rudé in his leading text *The Crowd in History 1730–1848* (London: Wiley, 1964) excludes the execution crowd from his analysis; see 4. See in general also the discussion in John Stevenson, *Popular Disturbances in England 1700–1832*, 2nd edn (London: Longman, 1992), esp. 11–12.

51 A masterly analysis can be found in V.A.C. Gatrell, *The Hanging Tree: Execution and the English People 1770–1868* (Oxford: Oxford University Press, 1994), especially chapters 2 and 3. Other works include Thomas W. Laqueur, 'Crowds, Carnivals and the English State in English Executions, 1604–1868', in A.L. Beier, David Cannadine and James M. Rosenheim (eds), *The First Modern Society: Essays in Honour of Lawrence Stone* (Cambridge: Cambridge University Press, 1989), 305; Randall McGowen, 'Civilizing Punishment: The End of the Public Execution in England', *Journal of British Studies*, 33, 3 (1994), 257–82, and the same author's 'Revisiting the Hanging Tree', *British Journal of Criminology*, 40, 1 (2000) 1–13. The change in the meaning of execution to the crowd and the consequent difference in response have still, I think, not been fully explored. From a perspective over a longer period than is usually allowed I think the loss of a central religious meaning, of the sort discussed by Mitchell B. Merback, *The Thief, the Cross and the Wheel: Pain and the Spectacle of Punishment in Medieval and Renaissance Europe* (London: Reaktion, 1999), ch. 4, is important (though for the later intellectual and theological debate, see Randall McGowen, 'The Changing Face of God's Justice: The Debates over Divine and Human Punishment in Eighteenth-Century England', *Criminal Justice History*, 9 (1988), 63). My own argument, in the Introduction of *A Want of Order*, stresses the results of demographic change in undermining the message of execution. As such I am not sure that a metropolitan crowd attending a hanging at Tyburn is *the same* as a primarily local one in Carmarthen, while that brought by railway excursion to Liverpool might have a rather different complexion to both. For railway excursions to hangings, see C.R. Clinker, 'Excursions Extraordinary', *Railway and Canal Historical Society Journal*, 34 (2004), 567. I am indebted to Bill Hines for this reference.

52 Though Gatrell records one John Parker walking ten miles in 1822 to watch Thetford Assizes, taking a neighbour's daughter 'for a treat' (Gatrell, *Hanging Tree*, 90, n.3).

53 What I have in mind here, as will be seen, is the relationship of the crowd and the prison. Many would, I think, concede a link between the execution crowd and those attending the pillory, the stocks or the public whipping, all of which disappeared as public punishments in the nineteenth century.

54 See Pat Molloy, *A Shilling for Carmarthen* (Llandysul: Molloy, 1991), 146. Such interest was by no means restricted to Wales, as Berry made clear after an English hanging in 1887: 'At this stage of my career as hangman the desire of people to see me was simply overwhelming, and I was always more or less dubious as to the feelings of the people whom I was to go amongst ... We drove straight to our destination by cab, followed by a large crowd of people' (quoted in Stewart P. Evans, *Executioner: The Chronicles of James Berry, Victorian Hangman* (Stroud: Sutton, 2004), 129).

55 A crowd estimated at 10,000 had attended the hanging of Thomas Rees in Carmarthen in 1817 (see Jones, *Crime in Wales*, 74). David Evans in 1829 was the last to die before 1889. It has been suggested that executions were never popular in Wales and served as occasions for anti-English sentiment (see Roger Wells, '"Launched into Eternity": Public Hanging in Britain and Ireland in the Eighteenth and Nineteenth Centuries', in Louis A. Knafla (ed.), *Crime, Punishment and Reform in Europe* (Westport, CT: Greenwood, 2003), 170–1). Wells sees similarities between the Welsh reaction and that in Ireland.

56 *Carmarthen Journal*, 2 February 1866. Great applause followed the conviction. The newspaper report uses the term 'audience' of those at the trial.

57 *Carmarthen Journal*, 23 March 1849. Her incarceration too saw a flow of visitors to the jail (Ireland, *Want of Order*, ch. 4).

58 See, for example, the cases of Rachel Jones (*The Welshman*, 28 July 1848) and Margaret Jones (*Carmarthen Journal*, 30 April 1856). I have found no cases in Carmarthenshire of disorder occurring in court of the kind reported in a magistrates' court in Builth which led to a call for the law to be upheld against 'the lowest classes' (see *Carmarthen Journal*, 9 January 1852).

59 '[A]lthough these cases are sometimes serious the proofs are always of a simple character', at the trial of Oliver Cromwell Howells (*Carmarthen Journal*, 1 March 1867).

60 For the applause in this case, see *The Welshman*, 1 March 1851. This intervention in cases concerning behaviour within marriage extended to more serious offences. Jones notes spousal murder as an occasion for the expression of crowd hostility at public executions of convicted husbands (Jones, *Crime in Wales*, 74). Compare the attempt at applause in court 'at once repressed' on the acquittal of Ann Phillips at the same assize for attempting to poison her husband (*Carmarthen Journal*, 1 March 1867).

And note too the address made directly to the jury, in Welsh, by Evan Jones on trial for bigamy (*Carmarthen Journal*, 20 July 1866).

61 See *Carmarthen Journal*, 14 March 1851; Molloy, *Shilling for Carmarthen*, 101–2. And note the crowd intervention in the arrest of another bigamist on an omnibus two months earlier (*Carmarthen Journal*, 3 January 1851).

62 For examples, see Gatrell, *Hanging Tree*, 35–6.

63 See Ireland, *A Want of Order*, Introduction.

64 CRO Brigstocke 1. For the use of sails, see Robin Evans, *The Fabrication of Virtue: English Prison Architecture 1750–1840* (Cambridge: Cambridge University Press, 1982), 299.

65 *Carmarthen Journal*, 16 August 1833.

66 See CRO Quarter Sessions Order Book 1832–7 46. Importantly, the issue was returned to during discussion of the rebuilding of the jail following the 1865 Prison Act (see *Carmarthen Journal*, 13 April 1866), notwithstanding the extended hiatus in executions.

67 Gaoler's Journal (CRO Acc 4916) 8, 9, 10 May 1847.

68 Ibid., 19 June 1847.

69 As I have indicated before I do not wish to suggest for a moment that there is a simple, unproblematic 'cultural' model for Ireland or indeed for England. Nor is it the case that I believe that, despite the specific factors (though clearly I think they are important ones) of language, religion and tradition which have been addressed here, the issues I have considered have no resonance for other communities. Indeed I have made this clear where I have felt that this may be so. It may well be that parts of England would recognise much of what I have described in Wales. I must leave others, better qualified for the purpose of comparison than I, to pursue that question further. But I do not want to water down my proposal too far. Wales, despite the assumptions often made to the contrary, was never merely a region of England.

70 See the argument in Martin Wiener, 'The March of Penal Progress?', *Journal of British Studies*, 26, 1 (1987), 83–96. I have argued, in *Want of Order*, ch. 4, that a tendency of Welsh juries to acquit juveniles might have undermined Victorian sentencing policy in such cases had not summary jurisdiction been extended.

Further reading

The work of David J.V. Jones has contributed greatly to the understanding of crime and attitudes towards it in this period and his *Crime in Nineteenth Century Wales* (Cardiff: University of Wales Press, 1992) contains a mass of information and a stock of references. The limitations of official statistics, of which the text warns us, should be borne in mind throughout. On the Irish and Wales, Paul O'Leary's *Immigration and Integration: The Irish in Wales 1798–1922* (Cardiff: University of Wales Press, 2000) contains a chapter on crime as part of a much more comprehensive study of its general subject. For my own views on some of the areas considered here, in particular the role of the jury and its relationship to social attitudes outside the courtroom, see R.W. Ireland, 'Putting Oneself on Whose Country? Carmarthenshire Juries and Crime in the Mid-Nineteenth Century', in T.G. Watkin (ed.), *Legal Wales: Its Past, Its Future* (Cardiff: Welsh Legal History Society, 2001), 63–87 and R.W. Ireland '"Perhaps My Mother Murdered Me": Child Death and the Law in Victorian Carmarthenshire', in C.W. Brooks and Michael Lobban (eds), *Communities and Courts in Britain 1150–1900* (London: Hambledon, 1997), 229–44. A fuller discussion of Carmarthenshire crime and its punishment may be found in R.W. Ireland, *'A Want of Order and Good Discipline': Rules, Discretion and the Victorian Prison* (Cardiff: University of Wales Press, 2007). This work is anchored in a discussion of the operation of Carmarthen Gaol, but argues for a greater understanding of the role of the prison within its specific local community. The best discussion of the execution crowd, and indeed of all aspects of the process of and challenge to capital punishment in the nineteenth century, is contained in V.A.C. Gatrell's magnificent *The Hanging Tree: Execution and the English People 1770–1868* (Oxford: Oxford University Press, 1994).

The Rebecca Riots have been well considered, not least by David J.V. Jones in *Rebecca's Children* (Oxford: Clarendon, 1989). R.A.N. Jones's 'Popular Culture, Policing and the Disappearance of the *Ceffyl Pren* in Cardiganshire *c.*1837–1850', *Ceredigion*, 11, 1 (1988–9), 19–39 is a very important article. *The Report of the Commissioners on the State of Education in Wales* (1847) remains a hugely significant text. For readers requiring a general history of Wales, John Davies's *A History of Wales* rev. edn (London: Penguin Books, 2007) is recommended.

Other references will be found in the notes which accompany the present article.

Index

Added to a page number 'f' denotes a figure and 't' denotes a table.

Abraham, Joseph 152
Abrahams, Judith 198
accomplices *see* approvers
accusation trials, German-speaking countries 64
accused
  Irish homicide prosecutions
    admission of action 160
    dying declarations 147, 159
    identification of 154–8
    statements of 153–4
administrative system, Isle of Man 122–32
Admiralty Court (Isle of Man) 122, 124
alcohol
  domestic homicide, late Victorian Scotland 220, 227–8, 234–5
  as mitigating factor in violence 40, 196–7
Aldihuela del Codonal 82–3
Anderson, Margaret 222
Andersson Hiul, Anders 111
anthropology *see* legal anthropology
Antón, Miguel de 87
approvers, Irish homicide

prosecutions 145–7, 165, 166
Aranda de Duero 84
arbitrary violence, non toleration of 58
arbitration
  19th century Wales 246
  Manx courts 127–8
arbitrators, 18th century France 45, 46
argolla 82
Armagh, homicide prosecutions
  counsel statement of case regarding an unusual aspect 143
  hearsay evidence 147, 148
  newspaper reports 140
  tendering of evidence
    identification of the accused 154, 155, 156, 157
    relating to events after the homicide 159, 160, 161
    relating to events before the homicide 154
  witnesses 150, 151–2
    reprisals and intimidation of 161–2, 167, 168
Armstrong, John 148
artisans (German-speaking), absence from criminal records 67

assaults
    in English society 194–7
        punishment 202t, 205, 206–7
        recognizances to keep the
            peace 205–6
    Isle of Man 126
    Old Regime, France 33–4, 41
assizes
    participation of counsel, Ireland
        141–4
    see also Armagh; Fermanagh;
        Kilkenny; Queen's Co.
atonement, domestic homicide, late
    Victorian Scotland 220, 231
attitudes
    19th century Wales, towards
        criminality 246–7
    English society
        towards homicide 192–3
        towards violence 191, 198,
            199–200, 207
    German-speaking craftsmen,
        towards violence 61
    to the Welsh 239
Attorney-General, Ireland 142
audiences, trials and punishment,
    19th century Wales 247–53
Augsburg 57
Ausfordern aus dem Haus
    (challenging out of the house)
    59–61, 63
Aviñante 82
Axelsson, Melchior 102

Bailliage of Mamers 44
Baker, J.H. 139–40
Bakhtin, Mikhail 77
Baldwin, David 158
Ballaugh 128
Barons' Court (Isle of Man) 124
Bazas tribunal 33, 34, 37
Beattie, John 2, 191, 193, 206
Beccaria, Cesare 53
Becker, Anders 105
beggars, exclusion from German
    courts 65
Belfast Newsletter 147
Bentley, D. 145, 148, 149

Bergin, Catherine 152, 161
Bergin, Eleanor 161
Bergin, Martin 155
Berlin 58
Berzosa de Bureba 78
bigamy cases, audiences, 19th
    century Wales 249–50
Bildungsbürgertum 68
black books 59
Black, Mary 198
Blackstone, William 202, 203, 205
Blasius, Dirk 53
blood feuds 57, 62
bloodwipes 123, 131, 132
Blundell, William 121, 122, 125
bodily insults, Spain 78
Bolaño Rivadeneira, Don Benito
    Francisco of 85, 86
Bond, Thomas 198
Bonneau, Jean 32, 35–6, 40, 45
Bound, Robert 201
Boyd, Mary 226
Brady y Llyfrau Gleison (Treachery
    of the Blue Books) 243
Branne cabaret altercation 32–9
Brennan, James 164, 168
Bromley, Ann 195
Brooks, C.W. 121
Brown, Helen 223–4
Browrigg, H.J. 166
bull races, Castile 82
Burghartz, Susanna 57
burgher prison, demand for 63
Burgos 78
Bushe, Judge 146–7

Callis, Mary 250, 251
Calvinism 220
Cannon, Thomas 163
Captain of the Parish (Isle of Man)
    123
Carberry, Patrick 148
card games, and violence 81
Carpzov, Benedict 53
Carroll, Michael 160
Carson, James 158
Carter, William 146
Castan, Nicole 3

Castile, 16th and 17th century 74–89
cavalry 89
fear and hatred of the other 83–8
insult and honour 77–81
royal pardons 77
violence
acceptance of 88, 89
games and 81–3
sources of lethal 76–7
Cathcart, Margaret 165
Cathcart, Robert 165
Catholicism 89
ceffyl pren (wooden horse) 241, 242, 246
The Celt of Wales and the Celt of Ireland 242
Central European cities, containment of violence (1500–1800) 52–68
'challenging out of the house' (Ausfordern aus dem Haus) 59–61, 63
Chancery Court (Isle of Man) 122
Chapel, as arbitrator, 19th century Wales 246
character rule, Irish homicide prosecutions 145
Chaulet, Rudy 4, 11–12, 18, 20
children, parental killing, late Victorian Scotland 223–6
cities *see* Central European Cities
citizens, and the courts, German-speaking countries 62–8
civil courts, reputation of members, Ireland 142
civil litigation
Isle of Man 125–8
significance, early modern England 120–1
civilising process 54, 60, 75–6
clannish society, Old Regime, France 35
Cleary, John 152
Cleary, Patrick 163–4
Cobbe, Frances Power 199
Cockburn, J.S. 2
Cockburn, Lord Chief Justice 208
Cole, John 164
Cologne 64, 67

Comish, Anne 128
Commentaries 203
common law, Manx 130
see also Sheading Courts
communal justice, Scandinavia 97–8
community judgment, 19th century Wales 246
community law, transition to state law 130–1
concealment of birth 221
confessions
false 109–10
Irish homicide prosecutions 145
admission of 147–9
tendering evidence of, after an alleged event 159–60
Conley, Carolyn A. 3, 14–15, 19, 139, 196
Connor, Eliza 158
Connor, John 149
Connor, Richard 155
Conrahy, Thomas 159
Constance 57, 58
control
of violence, ritual and 59–61
see also social control
Convere, Henry 156
coroners
Isle of Man 123, 132
as witnesses, Irish homicide prosecutions 150
Corrigan, Jane 233
Corrigan, John 156, 159
corroboration, Irish homicide prosecutions 145, 146–7
Cosnahan, John 128
Costello, Patrick 163
costs, court proceedings, Old Regime, France 42
Council of Castile 77
counsel, Irish homicide prosecutions 141–4
Court of General Gaol Delivery (Isle of Man) 122, 124, 131
Court of Great Sessions 241
courts
German-speaking countries 55–6, 57–8, 62–8

Isle of Man 122–3, 124, 125, 128–9
reputation of members, Ireland
142
studies, of interplay between
people, law and 4–5, 6–8
Courts of Appeal confession trials
110
Cowley, William 125
Cox, Owen 162
craftsmen, attitude towards violence
61
craftsmen's guilds, regulation of
social conduct 58–9, 61
Crane of Marown, Finlo 128–9
Crawford, Andrew 162
Crawford, William 162
Crespo, María 81, 82
crime
historiography of, German-
speaking countries 4, 53–5
studies, gender and, Scotland 3
see also sexual crimes; violent
crime
criminal justice
bureaucratisation, Scandinavia
108
change in, Europe (1500–1900) 97
history, study of 1–9
criminal procedures
17th and 18th century France
41–3
Scotland 219–20
criminal trials
accusation 64
gendered nature of violence,
England 191
inquisitorial 42, 64
punishment and audiences, 19th
century Wales 247–53
rules of evidence, Ireland 145–9
studies of criminal justice and 3
Cross, Sir Richard Assheton 208
culpable homicide, infanticide 221–2
Curran, John 232–3

Daly, Mary 165
Daniel, Thomas 196
Darcy, John 159, 163, 165

Davies, Margaret 247
Davis, John 5
Dawson, Catherine 196
Deas, Lord 224, 226, 228
deaths, from violent accidents, 19th
century England 190
debt disputes
16th and 17th century England
125–6
17th and 18th century Stockholm
100t, 101–2, 104t
Isle of Man 128
deemsters 122
defamation see slander
defence, distinction between
retaliation, Scotland 232–3
Delany, Alice 153
Delany, Daniel 153
Derby, earls of 120, 121
diminished responsibility, spousal
homicide, Scotland 228
Dinges, Martin 7, 65
Dingwall, Alexander 228
Discipline and Punish 4
discretionary power, magistrates,
English society 201–3
dispute resolution
challenging out of the house
59–61
Nordic countries 96, 97–8
Old Regime, France 43–5
violence as means of, Isle of Man
131
District Courts, Stockholm 98,
99–111
Division of Labour in Society 131
Docherty, Jane 220
doctors, Irish homicide prosecutions
152, 158–9
Doherty, Judge 149
domestic homicide, late Victorian
Scotland 219–35
children 223–6
husbands 231–3
infanticide 221–3
other relatives 233–5
wives 226–31
domestic violence

in English society 197–200
German-speaking countries 65
Donnelly, Hugh 162
Donnelly Jr, J.S. 139
Doolan, Eliza 154
Dooley, Jeremiah 152
Dooley, Terence 3
Dowling, Eliza 163
Dowling, Margaret 155
Dowling, Peter 152
Dowling, William 163
Drum, Owen 156
Duffy, Philip 156
Duncan, Elspet 225
Dunphy, John 155
'duty of restraint', Ireland 143
dying declarations, Irish homicide
    prosecutions 147, 159

ecclesiastical courts (Isle of Man)
    124
Eggert, Anders 100
Eibach, Joachim 4, 11, 15, 18
Eisner, Manuel 194
El Espinar 79
Elias, Norbert 6, 54, 75, 79
Elliot, William 163
emotional blackmail, Irish homicide
    prosecutions 165
employees of the accused, Irish
    homicide prosecutions 152
employers of the accused, Irish
    homicide prosecutions 156
England
    concealment of birth 221
    study of criminal justice 1–3
    violent crime (1700–1900) 190–210
Europe, history of criminal justice 1–9
Evans, Peter 153
evidence
    communal failure to provide,
        19th century Wales 245
    Irish homicide prosecutions 145–9
    admission of
        confessions 147–9
        from accomplices 145
        garnered during police
            questioning 149

corroborating, required for
    conviction 146–7
difficulty in securing, in cases
    of premeditation 157
identification of the accused
    154–8
inadmissibility of hearsay 147
relating to events
    after the homicide 158–61
    before the homicide 153–4
restrictions placed on 169
tendering
    rewards for 164, 166–7
    to avoid prosecution 165
    under pressure from
        authorities 164–5, 170
see also witnesses
Exchequer Court (Isle of Man) 122
execution crowds 247–8
executions
    Scandinavia 110
    spousal homicides, late Victorian
        Scotland 229
Express 160
extra-legal settlements, Isle of Man
    131
Eyquart of Branne 32, 34, 35, 38, 45

false confessions 109–10
Fannan, Patrick 151
fathers, convictions, child homicide
    cases 225
felony cases, 'duty of restraint',
    Ireland 143
female honour 35, 101, 103
Fermanagh, homicide prosecutions
    counsel statement of case
        circumstantial evidence 143
        neutral position of 143–4
    newspaper reports 140
    tendering of evidence
        identification of the accused
            154, 156, 157
        relating to events after the
            homicide 158
        rewards for 164
        role of approvers 145–6, 166
    witnesses 150, 151, 152

reprisals against 162, 167
requests for assistance to emigrate 163–4
Fernández, Marcos 80
Fernández, Mateo 84
Fettmilch uprising 63
fines
    for assault, England (1748–1835) 202t
    Sheading Courts 128–9
Finland, history of criminal justice 5
Finnane, Mark 3
Fitzpatrick, Michael 165
Fitzpatrick, Philip 158
Flanagan, Denis 155
flogging 199, 208
Florence 119–20
Foote, Lundy 161
fornication, 17th century Stockholm 103
Foucault, M. 4, 6, 110
France
    history of criminal justice 3–4
    violence
        prosecution, 17th and 18th century 32–46
        as a result of damaged honour 76
Frank, Stephen 5
Frankfurt 57, 61, 63, 64, 66
Fresnillo 84
functional violence, Old Regime, France 34

games, and violence, Castile 81–3
Gannon, Edward 165
Garnham, Neal 3, 142
Garotter's Act (1863) 208
Gatrell, V.A.C. 2
Gauvard, Claude 76
Geale, Piers 138
gender
    and responsibility, child homicide cases 225–6
    studies of crime and, Scotland 3
    see also men; women
German-speaking countries
    citizen participation in courts 62–8

court system 55–6
history of criminal justice 4, 53–5
violence and its control 56–62
Gibbs, Elizabeth 246
Gillespie, Henry 161
Gillespie, Richard 161
Gillies, Elizabeth 225
Ginzburg, Carlo 75
Girard, René 86
González, Ignacio 79
Gorman, Edward 167
Gormley, Thomas and Rose 156
Graham, Francis 151, 152
Graham, James 242
Graham, John 159
Grant, Isabella 231–2
Great Enquests (Isle of Man) 124
Great Litigation Decline 126
Green, Mary 203
Greer, D.S. 142
Griffin, Brian 166
guild statutes, evidence of use of violence 58
guilds, regulation of social conduct 58–9, 61
Gurr, Ted R. 54
Guyot, Joseph-Nicholas 45

Hagan, James 159
Hamilton, Maxwell 139
Hansdaugher, Mrs 100
Harley, Nicholas (Harloe of Castletown) 127
harmony model, conflict resolution 96
Hay, Douglas 2, 53
Hayes, Thomas 159
head, as symbolic nexus of male honour 36
hearsay, Irish homicide prosecutions 145, 147
Herborn 61
Herrero, Martín 79
Herrup, Cynthia 2
Hogan, Mathew 160
Hoggart, Richard 74
Höier, Mr 101
Holland, Ann 203

homicide
  17th and 18th century Stockholm
    100, 104t, 105
  civilising process and study of 76
  in English society 192–4
  prosecution cases, Ireland 138–70
  studies on long-term trends,
    Netherlands 5
  see also domestic homicide;
    suicidal murders
honour
  Castile, 16th and 17th century
    77–81
  France, 17th and 18th century
    34–5, 36
  German-speaking countries
    guild conflict regulations 61
    study of violence 54–5
    toleration of manslaughter in
      defence of 57
  as primary cause of homicide 76
  Sweden, 17th and 18th century
    101, 103
  violence as defence of, Middle
    Ages 56
Horsefield, Joseph 164
housewifely standards, mitigation of
  spousal violence 230–1
Howard, Sharon 2
Howell, James 164
Howells, Mr 247
Hughes, Mary 251
Huizinga, Johan 79, 81
husbands, spousal homicide, late
  Victorian Scotland 231–3
Hwyel Dda, law of 241

Iglesias, Diego 80–1
illegitimacy, child homicide cases
  223–4
imprisonment
  for assault, English society 202t,
    205
  and crowds, 19th century Wales
    250–1
improper conduct, of victims,
  spousal homicide cases 229–30
indictments, 18th century Frankfurt
  64

inducements, admissibility of
  confessions, Ireland 148–9
infanticide
  17th and 18th century Stockholm
    100t, 104t, 107–8
  late Victorian Scotland 221–3
inferior officers (Isle of Man) 123
infrajudicial dispute resolution, Old
  Regime France 43–4, 46
Ingram, William 157
inquisition trials 42, 64
insanity, domestic homicide 223–4,
  228
insults
  16th and 17th century Castile
    77–81
  17th and 18th century France
    33–4, 38, 41
interpersonal violence
  common assaults as an index of
    195
  English society
    attitudes to 207
    formal codification of 207–8
    gendered aspect of 191
    growing interest of state in
      204, 208
    official responses 210
    punishment 201, 202–3, 210
    social conditions 196
    strategies open to victims
      200–1
    see also assaults; domestic
      violence
  German-speaking countries
    extra-judicial settlements 65
    settlement through
      compensation 67
    studies 4, 54
intimidation, of witnesses, Ireland
  138–9
Ireland
  history of criminal justice 3
  homicide prosecutions 138–70
    consequences (for witnesses)
      of participation 161–4, 167
    evidence relating to events
      after the homicide 158–61
      before the homicide 153–4

identification of the accused
154–8
participation of counsel 141–4
rules of evidence 145–9
witnesses 150–3
see also Irish
Ireland, Richard 2, 15, 19, 20
Irish
comparison with Welsh 242–3
vagrancy problem, Wales 243–4
Isle of Man, legal anthropology
118–32
Ives, E.W. 132

Jacobsdaughter, Christina 107
Jacoleto, Luis 79–80
Jansson 111
Jarrick, A. 102–3, 111
Jeremy, Mr 247
Johnston, Mr 144
Jones, David 2, 240, 244
Jones, Elizabeth Reid 225
Jones, James 246
Jones, Rosemary 246
Jones, Ruth 245
Jöransson, Eric 102
journeymen, as troublesome group,
18th century 61
Joy 148
Judge, Samuel 165
judicial discretion
English society 201–3
exclusion of confessions, Ireland
148–9
judicial hostility, towards police
questioning, Ireland 149
judicial responses, to complaints,
Old Regime, France 42
judicial revolution, Scandinavia
98–9, 103, 104, 108, 112
juries
homicide prosecutions, Ireland
145–6
Isle of Man 123–4
late Victorian Scotland 219–20
rural, 19th century Wales 246–7
jurisprudence 118
Justice of the Peace and Parish Officer
202

justices of the peace, new regime,
France 46

Kaspersson, Maria 12, 16
Keating, J. 249
Keating, Justice H.S. 197, 208
Keating, Mary 162
Keefe, Judith 163
Keefe, Lucy 143, 151, 157
Keenan, Sarah 151
Kelly, Bridget 151
Kelly, Charles 156
Kelly, James 3
Kennedy, Patrick 156
Kerr, Thomas 165
Keys, John 153
Kilday, Anne-Marie 3
Kilkenny, homicide prosecutions
high rates of 140–1
newspaper reports 140
spring assizes 152
killings
distinction between honourable
and dishonourable 57
see also homicide
kindly arbitrators 45, 46
King, Peter 2, 206
Kingsworth, Sarah 198–9
Knox, Alex 208
Kramer, Karl-Sigismund 59, 60, 61
Krogh, T. 111
Küther, Carsten 53

labour disputes, Isle of Man 126
Lalor, William 165
land disputes, Isle of Man 125
Landau, Norma 2, 201, 203
Langbein, John 2, 145
Langford, Paul 190
Larkin, John 152
Lartley, William 165
Latimer, George 161
law codes, Nordic countries 96, 97
Lawlor, Dr 159
lawyers, study of legal systems 139,
140
Le Bon, G. 247
legal anthropology, Isle of Man 118–32
legal officials, Irish homicide

prosecutions 150, 154–5
legal scholars, dispute resolution,
    Old Regime, France 45
legal systems
    approaches to study of 139–40
    German-speaking countries 63
    Isle of Man 121–32
    Scandinavian countries 96–7
legitimacy, child homicide cases 223
Leinster Express 166
Lenman, Bruce 6, 15, 16, 97, 112
letters of supplication 66–7
Levi, Reba 198
Lévy, René 21
liar, prominent among insults,
    Castile 78
Libourne tribunal 32, 33, 34, 37, 41,
    44
Lieutenant Generalcy of Police,
    dispute resolution, Paris 43
lifestyle divergence, of upper and
    lower classes, German-speaking
    countries 67–8
Liliequist, J. 110, 111
Linebaugh, Peter 2
local communities, interplay
    between courts, law and 4–5, 6–8
López-Lázaro, Fabio 4
Lorain, Elizabeth 195
Lord's Council, Isle of Man 122
Lords of Man 121, 122, 129
Lorenzo, Pedro 87, 88
Lundrigan, John 162
Lutheran Church, secular power,
    Nordic countries 97

McCabe, Desmond 3
McClure, Elizabeth 222
McCormack, John 165, 168
McCreery, William 144
McCresh, Brian 154
McCresh, Michael 154
McEldowney, John 139
McFayden, Dennis 232
McGill, Edward 163
McMahon, Ellen 154
McMahon, James 168
Mc Mahon, Richard 13

McNiece, Henry 155
Magee, Owen 159
Magee, William 161
Magill, Peter 143
magistrates
    discretionary power, English
        society 201–3
    as witnesses, Irish prosecution
        witnesses 150
Maguire, John 155
Mahon, John 148–9, 151, 154
Mahoney, Daniel 162
Maine, Sir Henry 131
Major, James 139
male honour 34–5, 36, 57, 101
Maler, Ekart 58, 66
Malicious Shooting or Stabbing Act
    (1803) 203
Malone, Dick 167
Malone, Hanna 158
Malone, John 152
Malone, Richard 167
Manrique, Blas 84, 85
manslaughter, toleration in defence
    of honour 57
Mantecón, Tomas A. 4
marriage (broken promises), 17th
    and 18th century Stockholm 103,
    107
Martínez, Mateo 85
matricide 234–5
Matrimonial Causes Act (1878) 199
Matthews, Anne 249
Maxwell, Robert 157
Mayorga, Catalina de 81–2
Mazzacone, Aldo 118, 119
Meagher, Patrick 158, 159
Mealy, Robert 153
mediators, dispute resolution, Old
    Regime, France 44–5
Medina de Campo 80
Meiers, Mrs 101
men
    conditioned to violence, English
        society 191
    Victorian criminalization of 200
    see also fathers; husbands; male
        honour

Mercer, William 127
merchants (German-speaking),
    absence from criminal records 67
Meredith, Michael 164
Middle Ages, violence in 52
Miguélez, Juan 86
militarism 88–9, 190
moars (Isle of Man) 123, 132
Moley, Bernard 147
Moley, Patrick 147
Mooney, John 160
Moor, Elizabeth 128
Moore, Catherine 159–60
Moore, Walter 155–6
moral panic, over street crime 208
More, John 128
Morton, Mary 152
Mosaic Law 97
Muchembled, Robert 75, 83
Murphy, James 161

Napier, Joseph 141–2
National Assembly Law (16–24
    August 1790) 46
Naval, Manuel 79
Neames, Lord 223
negotiation
    communal justice, Scandinavia 97
    dispute resolution, France 44–5
neighbours, Irish homicide
    prosecutions 151, 156
Neisideller, Chunrat 57
Nellis, Patrick 157
Netherlands, history of criminal
    justice 5
newspapers, Irish homicide
    prosecutions 140–1
Nilsson, Mr 100
Nolan, Michael 152
Noon, Dominick 162
Nordic countries
    harmony model, dispute
        resolution 96
    legal system 96–7
    see also Finland; Sweden
Nördlingen 59
Norris, John 127
Norrström 108

not proven verdict, late Victorian
    Scotland 219–20
nourishment, right of, in
    supplication letters 66
Nublichin, Mr 101
Nuremberg 58

Old Regime France, popular
    violence 33–46
O'Leary, Paul 243
Oliver, Revd Silver 160
Olpherts, Mr 159
Olsson 101
Örn, Anna 107
Ortiz, Domínguez 83
Österberg, Eva 5, 96, 97, 112
the other, violence and fear and
    hatred of 83–8
Ottoway, James 201
out-of-court settlements 65
outdoor games, and violence,
    Castile 82

Pablos, Felipe de 78
Palacín, Lázaro de 78
Pancorbo, Pedro de 78
Parker, Geoffrey 6, 15, 16, 97, 112
Parry-Jones, D. 245
Parsen, Thomas 196
patricians (German-speaking),
    absence from criminal records 67
Payne, William 203
penal revolution 240
People Meet the Law 5
Pérez, Francisco 79–80
Pérez, Gonzalez 87–8
personal space 195
Phelan, Edward 155
Philips, David 2
physical violence, as means of
    correction 197
police
    Irish homicide prosecutions 149,
        150, 158, 163, 164–5
    studies, France 3
    violent offences known to,
        England (1857–1900) 194f
Poliso, Alonso 79–80

Poole, Mrs 248–9
popular culture
    anthropology, law and 119–20
    Castile
        acceptance of violence 88, 89
        fear and hatred of the other
            83–8
        games and violence 81–3
        insult and honour 77–81
    crime and, 19th century Wales
        239–53
    difficulties regarding concept of
        9, 75–6
    elite interference, Middle Ages 75
    linguistic eloquence and violence
        77–8
    study of criminal justice 7–8
    and violence, English society 191,
        209
popular violence, 17th and 18th
    century France 32–46
    Branne cabaret altercation 32–9
    functional aspect 34
    honour 34–5, 36
    prosecution 39–46
    suddenness and limited intensity
        of 36–7
    witnesses 37
Pospisil, Leopold 132
poverty, child homicide cases 224–5
Power, Martin 161
Power, Richard 161
Price, Patrick 148, 149, 151, 154
Prisoner's Counsel Act (1836) 144
private dispute resolution, Old
    Regime France 44
privileged classes, violence leading
    to homicide 77
property offences, English society
    193, 201
prosecutions
    homicide see Ireland, homicide
        prosecutions
    and public participation, Sweden
        98–112
        17th century 99–103
        18th century 103–9
        anomalies 109–11

change in character 111–12
    studies of violent crime and 7–8
violence
    17th and 18th century France
        39–46
    Central Europe (1500–1800) 52,
        62, 64
prostitution, 17th century Stockholm
    102
Protestant consistories, dispute
    resolution, France 43
Protestantism 97, 220
provocation 196, 229–30
public participation
    German-speaking courts 62–8
    Manx legal system 127
    Stockholm District Courts 98–111
punishment
    19th century Wales
        audiences 247–8, 251
        ceffyl pren tradition 241, 242,
            246
    interpersonal violence, English
        society (1748–1835) 202–3,
        206–7, 210
    modern orthodoxy 250
    studies on nature and changing
        role of 4
    see also sanctions
punitive justice 97
Purcell 144, 145, 148

Quatrefages, René 88
Queen's Co., homicide prosecutions
    approvers 165, 166
    high rates of 140–1
    newspaper reports 140
    tendering of evidence
        identification of the accused
            154, 155, 156, 157
        judicial discretion regarding
            confessions 148–9
        relating to events after the
            homicide 158, 159, 160
        relating to events before the
            homicide 153, 154
        rewards 164, 167
        under pressure from

authorities 164, 165
    witnesses 150, 151, 152
        reprisals against 161, 162, 167
        requests for assistance to
            emigrate 163, 168
Queen's Counsel, Ireland 142
Quintana, Manuel de 78

R v. Aylmer, Aylmer and Behan 146
R. v. Glennon, Toole and Magrath 149
R v. Sheehan 146
reasonable violence, and social
    control 197
Rebecca Riots 242, 243
recognizances, to keep the peace
    205–6
reconciliation, German courts 58, 65
Reconquista 88, 89
Reformation 97
Reinhardt, Steven 3
relatives of the accused, Irish
    homicide prosecutions 156
relatives of the deceased, Irish
    homicide prosecutions 150–1, 155–6
religion *see* Catholicism;
    Protestantism
Report of the Education Commissioners
    (1847) 243
reprisals
    against witnesses, Ireland 161–4,
        167–8
    for interpersonal violence,
        English society 200
res gestae 147
restraint, duty of, Ireland 143
Revel, Jacques 75
rewards, for tendering evidence,
    Ireland 164, 166–7
Reynolds, Rachel 200
Ribbon Society 138
rituals
    German-speaking countries
        control of violence 59–61
        study of violence 54–5
    shaming, England 191
Robert, Mathieu 32, 34, 35, 36, 37–8,
    45
Roberts, Simon 129

Robertson, David 126
Robinson, Sarah 151
Robinson, Thomas 128
Rodgers, Hessy 158, 165
Rooney, Dennis 154
Rottam, Sarah 198
Rottam, Thomas 198
Rouen 39
Rouland, Norbert 130, 132
Rowan, Hill Wilson 138–9, 167
royal justice, Old Regime, France 43
royal pardons, Castile 77
Rubio, Bartolomé 83
Ruff, Julius 3–4, 9–11, 16–17, 18
rules of evidence *see* evidence
Runbom, Elisabet 110–11
Ryan, Joseph 160

Sacheverell, William 124
Salinas, Hernando de 82
Salmon, Patrick 155
sanctions
    imposed by craftsmen's guilds 59
    see also punishment
Sandilands, James 234
Sandmo, Erling 96, 97
Santa Hermandad 88
satisfaction, violent conflict, German
    courts 65–6
Scarlet, Edward 153
Schoales, John 143–4
Schwerhoff, Gerd 4, 55, 56, 64
scolds 230
Scotland
    atonement and domestic
        homicide in late Victorian
        219–35
    history of criminal justice 3
The Scotsman 227, 229, 230, 231
seigneurial courts, dispute
    resolution, Burgundy 43
setting quests (Isle of Man) 124
sexual crimes, 17th and 18th
    century Stockholm 100t, 102–3,
    104t, 106–7
shaming rituals 191
Sharpe, James 2, 12–13, 15, 54
Sheading Courts (Isle of Man)
    122–3, 124, 125, 128–9

Shoemaker, Robert 2, 14, 54
Showers, John 200
Simancas 81
Simpson, Samuel 198
Sjöberg, Taussi 98, 111, 112
skittles, and violence, Castile 82
slander
    17th and 18th century Stockholm
        100t, 101, 104t, 105
    Isle of Man 126
Smith, Agnes 234
Smith, Alice 165
Smith, Greg T. 13–14, 17
Smith, Llinos Beverly 245
Smith, Michael 159, 168
Smith, Samuel 151
Smith, Sarah 151
Smyth, Alexander 151
social classes
    lifestyle divergence, German-
        speaking classes 67–8
    and violence, English society 209
    see also privileged classes; social
        elites; working classes
social control
    imposed by guilds 58–9, 61
    informal 65
    studies of criminal justice and 7
    violence as means of 191, 197
social elites, decline in violent
    activity 17, 67
Society for Prevention of Cruelty to
    Children (Scotland) 223, 224
socio-cultural meaning of violence,
    German studies 4, 54
sociologists, study of legal systems
    139
Söderberg, J. 102–3
Sogner, S. 96, 112
South America, history of criminal
    justice 5
Southern District Court, Stockholm
    106
Spain
    history of criminal justice 4–5
    militarism and Catholicism 88–9
    see also Castile
Sparfeldt, Mr 108

specialist juries (Isle of Man) 124
Spencer, James 160
Spierenburg, Pieter 5, 55, 75
spousal homicide 226–33
Stanleys (Isle of Man) 120, 121, 129
Staples, Sir Thomas 143
state law, transition from common
    law to 130–1
statements of the accused, Irish
    homicide trials 153–4
The State, the Community and the
    Criminal Law in Early Modern
    Europe 6–7
Stein, Peter 130
stereotyping, historical 239, 241
Stockholm, prosecution and public
    participation 98–111
Stone, Lawrence 54
Stones, Daniel 164
street crime, moral panic over 208
Stretton, Tim 121
suicidal murders, Sweden 110–11
summary courts, expanding role,
    England 207
surgeons, Irish prosecution
    witnesses 152
Sweden
    history of criminal justice 5
    prosecutions and public
        participation 98–112
        17th century 99–103
        18th century 103–9
        anomalies 109–11
        change in character 111–12
sword-carrying, Spain 88
Symonds, Jelinger 241

tax evasion, 17th century Stockholm
    102
temporal inducements, admissibility
    of confessions 148, 149
theft, 17th and 18th century
    Stockholm 100–1, 104t
Thiman, Maria Elisabeth 105
third party dispute resolution
    English society 200
    Old Regime, France 44–5
Thomas, Amelia 247

Thompson, E.P. 2, 53, 191
threat, definition of, Ireland 148
Tickell, Mr 146
Todd, Thomas 161
tolerance of violence 40, 190, 197, 210
town councils, German-speaking countries 55, 61, 62
Treaty of Union (1707) 219
Tuck, William 164
Tweedy, Alexander 159
Twomey, James and Jeremiah 168
Tywnwald Court 122

vagrants, exclusion from German courts 65
Val de San Lorenzo de Arriba 85–6
Valladolid 78–9, 81, 87
Vandeleur, Judge 148
Vargas, Francisco de 80, 81
verbal abuse see insults; slander
verdicts, late Victorian Scotland 219–20
victims
    English society, interpersonal violence 200
    improper conduct, spousal homicide cases 229–30
    Old Regime, France, legal redress 40–1
Villares, Pedro de 80
vilorto dispute 82–3
violence
    Castile, 16th and 17th century
        acceptance of 88, 89
        fear and hatred of the other 83–8
        games, culture and 81–3
        militarism and Catholicism 88–9
    control, German-speaking countries 56–62
    dispute resolution see dispute resolution
    English society
        popular culture 191, 209
        of sport and entertainment 190–1
    tolerance of 190, 197, 210
    historiography of, early modern and modern Europe 75
    homicide as an index for 193
    Middle Ages 52, 56
    non-lethal, District Courts, Stockholm
        17th century 100t
        18th century 104t
    role of courts in dealing with 7–8
    see also domestic violence;
        interpersonal violence; popular violence; reasonable violence
violent crime
    England (1700–1900) 190–210
        common assault 194–7
        domestic violence 197–200
        homicide 192–4
        responses to 200–8
        studies of criminal justice and 7–8
violent offenders, social composition, German-speaking countries 67–8
voluntary confessions, Sweden 109–10

Waldron, George 124, 126, 131
Wales
    crime and popular culture in 19th century 239–53
        attitudes towards criminality 246–7
        church discipline 246
        communal failure to provide evidence 245
        community judgment 246
        conciliation and compromise 245
        cultural distinction 241–3
        Irish and the vagrancy problem 243–4
        jurisdictional status 241
        rhetoric and reality 244–7
        trials, punishment and audiences 247–53
    see also Welsh
    study of criminal justice 2
Wallace, Andrew 225

Warburton, George 138
Ward, Patrick 156
Weiner, Martin 14, 197, 200
Welsh
    comparison with Irish 242–3
    stereotyping of 241
Westlake, Henry 251
Wetherall, Thomas 201
Whelan, Judith 161
Whelan, Maria 161
Whelan, Patrick 152, 161
White, John 156
White, William 164
Wife Torture in England 199
Williams, Nicholas 127
Wilson, Stephen 4
Wilson, Thomas 165
Wissell, Rudolf 59
witnesses
    English society, intervention in
        violent disputes 200
    inquisitorial trials, German-
        speaking countries 64
    Irish homicide prosecutions
        150–3
        consequences of participation
            161–4
        exaggeration of threats from

    the community 168
    examination of 144–5
    expenses for attending assizes
        167
    intimidation of 138–9
    rules for protection of 145–9
    tendering evidence see
        evidence
    role, popular violence, France 37
wives, spousal homicides 226–31
women
    domestic violence 198–9
    see also female honour; matricide;
        wives
Wood, Ann 200
working classes
    domestic violence as an issue of
        199
    spousal homicide, Scotland 227

xenophobia 83–8

Ylikangas, Heikki 5, 112
Young, John 230–1

Zamorano, Andrés 80
Zárate, Pedro de 84–5
Zurich 56–8, 63